*The Privileged Playgoers*
*of Shakespeare's London, 1576-1642*

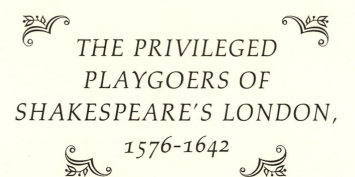

# THE PRIVILEGED PLAYGOERS OF SHAKESPEARE'S LONDON, 1576-1642

ANN JENNALIE COOK

Princeton University Press
Princeton, New Jersey

*For the Emperor*

# Contents

# Preface

In *The Privileged Playgoers*, I have used the work of social historians to shed new light on Renaissance drama. I make no claim myself to being a social historian, and for scholars in that field, the material in the first chapters will seem but a brief summary of what is well known to them. Yet the insights of the historians are, by and large, not well known to those working in Renaissance drama. Moreover, modern researchers often miss obvious levels of meaning because they are insufficiently aware of the society that so closely interpenetrated the stage in Shakespeare's day. Nowhere, of course, was such interpenetration more obvious than in the audience, where throngs of real people from the real world came year after year to see the imaginative worlds created onstage. Thus it has seemed essential to turn to history, sociology, economics, and demography in order to understand the playgoers. I have tried to consult such sources fairly, realizing from the outset that my own work was not a foray into alien disciplines, even though I made use of the findings in those disciplines.

Of necessity, the material in Chapters II and III and to some extent in Chapter VI is a radically compressed summary. With massive work like Lawrence Stone's available, it would be folly for the reader to assume anything else about these portions of the book. The notes indicate where to go for fuller treatments of the issues. The quotations from contemporary sources in these chapters represent a judicious selection from a much larger body of evidence: they were chosen for their value in illustrating points at hand and should not be considered at all comprehensive. It should be noted, however, that I have taken special care to make choices that are representative of the total evidence rather than simply supportive of my own point of view. In the chapters on playgoing itself, I have tried to be comprehensive rather than selective. There are doubtless some fugitive references not included, and certainly it is impossible to cite every address to the audience in every prologue or epilogue. Yet the direct evidence on the playgoers comes close to being a complete analysis of the extant data, drawing together far more material than any previous treatment.

In my use of evidence, I have intentionally allowed the contemporary references to speak for themselves wherever possible. The peculiarities of spelling, punctuation, capitalization, and expression, which I have elected to preserve rather than modernize, seem to me to convey more accurately the sensibilities of a world long since vanished. I hope the reader will forgive the difficulty of getting through the testimony and make an effort to enter the world from which the testimony comes. At the same time, the reader must recognize that we can only partially apprehend past reality. It is impossible to recreate perfectly or to report fully across the barrier of time, no matter how eloquent the witness that has been preserved.

In writing *The Privileged Playgoers*, I have been assisted by a summer grant from the Folger Shakespeare Library and by a grant from the Donelson Foundation. I have also received very kind cooperation from the Vanderbilt University Library. At various stages of completion, friends and colleagues read my manuscript. For this assistance, together with their advice and encouragement, I am particularly grateful to J. Leeds Barroll III, Robert G. Hunter, R. Chris Hassel, Bruce Tucker, Bernard Beckerman, Sanford Sternlicht, David Bevington, and Norman Rabkin. Whatever faults or errors of judgment remain in the book despite their sound suggestions are of course my own responsibility.

Finally, I owe the most to my husband, John Whalley, and my daughters, Lee Ann and Amy Harrod, for their patience, their support, and their love throughout the long process of research and writing. They have kept me sane and happy.

*The Privileged Playgoers*
*of Shakespeare's London, 1576-1642*

# · I ·
## A Prologue on Playgoers

Until someone perfects a time machine that can whisk a man back four centuries to enjoy an afternoon at a London theater, no one can be certain what kind of people patronized the astounding dramatic activity of the English Renaissance. Who were the people for whom Shakespeare, Marlowe, Jonson, Webster, and their fellow dramatists wrote plays? Virtually everyone in London for sixty or seventy years must have known the answer to this question, but it is one of history's continuing ironies that what everyone knows rarely seems worth recording and so must be guessed at in later centuries.

And there are difficulties with any guess, however well informed. Speculation concerning those long-dead theatergoers must rest precariously upon such fragmentary data as remain undestroyed by the harsh effects of time. A wide assortment of sermons, official complaints, regulatory documents, diaries, letters, and foreign travelers' accounts, as well as passages from plays and other works of literature, all refer to the audiences. For in his own day, the Renaissance playgoer occasioned criticism, controversy, contempt, and curiosity. Reports of his nature varied widely. Was he ignorant or intelligent, riotous or refined, libertine or law abiding, plebeian or privileged? The answers depended always upon the nature of the report and the reporter. And so they still do. Modern accounts of the audience suffer from the bias of the writer fully as much as did the contemporary accounts.

As often as not, an interpretation reveals more about the interpreter's mind than it does about the mysteries of the past. Thus in 1907, Robert Bridges expressed his Victorian bias in a now ludicrous denunciation, blaming the "vulgar" Elizabethan

4 · A Prologue on Playgoers

playgoers for the "grossness" in Shakespeare "which we must swallow." Bridges sternly warned against "degrading ourselves to the level of his audience, and learning contamination from those wretched beings who can never be forgiven their share in preventing the greatest poet and dramatist of the world from being the best artist."[1]

Some thirty-five years later, when Alfred Harbage published *Shakespeare's Audience*, "those wretched beings" seemed utterly transformed:

> We may say in the present case, quite apart from Beaumont's satirical use of them as the spectators in *The Knight of the Burning Pestle*, that a grocer, his wife, and their young apprentice form as acceptable an epitome of Shakespeare's audience as any the facts will warrant us to choose. If Shakespeare did not write to please such a little cockney family as this, he did not write to please his audience. But if he did so write, then there must be some correspondence in quality between the plays and our sample three—the grocer, his wife, and their young apprentice.[2]

Victorian prudery had been replaced by a sentimental faith in the common man.

Along with many other intellectuals of the 1920s and 1930s, Harbage felt an unshakable confidence in the common sense and intuitive good taste of the masses. He described an audience at the public theaters that was heterogeneous but chiefly peopled by London's ordinary artisans and craftsmen. Writing to appeal to such folk, Shakespeare produced his masterpieces. The transfer of allegiance to a coterie audience at the private theaters, represented by the King's Men's move to Blackfriars, signaled the demise of great drama because henceforth the plays had to appeal to decadent elitist tastes. In both *As They Liked It* and *Shakespeare and the Rival Traditions*, Harbage delineated what

[1] Robert Bridges, "The Influence of the Audience on Shakespeare's Drama," in *Collected Essays* (London: Oxford University Press, 1927), I, 19, 29.

[2] Alfred Harbage, *Shakespeare's Audience* (New York: Columbia University Press, 1941), p. 155.

he saw as a cleavage between the morality and the aesthetic worth of private and public drama, with the audience determining the nature of the plays in both cases. His lament that "the private theatres begat no second Shakespeare"[3] assumed that the Theater and the Globe did beget the first Shakespeare.

Like most subsequent scholars, G. E. Bentley followed Harbage's lead. His massive and masterful *Jacobean and Caroline Stage* is filled with references to the aristocratic audiences at Blackfriars or the Phoenix and the vulgar audiences at the Fortune or Red Bull.[4] With such a model in mind, Bentley doubted that the Venetian embassy could possibly have visited the Fortune in 1617. The well-dressed, well-behaved audience described by the Venetians sounded more like the Blackfriars. Could the translator have made a mistake? Bentley's assumptions also led him to question whether a troupe of French actors could really have been "hissed, hooted, and pippin-pelted from the stage" at Blackfriars in 1629:

> I suspect an error in the accounts. In 1629 the French had played at the Red Bull and the Fortune as well as at the Blackfriars theatre; violence among the spectators was much more characteristic of Red Bull and Fortune audiences than of those at Blackfriars and the Phoenix. If the letter erroneously attributed conduct which took place at the Red Bull or the Fortune to the Blackfriars, then the various records would accord much better with Herbert's accounts of the 1629 visit, and with our knowledge of the differences between private-theatre audiences and public-theatre audiences in the reign of King Charles I.[5]

Bentley was similarly amazed that the lowly Red Bull company could enjoy special courtly favor in 1634.[6]

[3] Ibid., p. 65.

[4] Gerald Eades Bentley, *The Jacobean and Caroline Stage* (Oxford: Clarendon Press, 1941-1968). See, e.g., VI, 12, 33, 49, 69-70, 192, 195, 199.

[5] Ibid., VI, 66. See also Bentley's *Shakespeare and His Theatre* (Lincoln: University of Nebraska Press, 1964), pp. 101-128.

[6] Bentley, *Jacobean and Caroline Stage*, I, 310-311.

By contrast, connections between the Court and the players have posed no problem for a scholar like Glynne Wickham. In his view, the Court audience and setting always represented both the norm and the aim for the acting companies, "notwithstanding notable and extensive sallies into less sophisticated places of public recreation." He too contrasted the "small, private playhouse for an aristocratic audience" with the "vulgar public gamehouse" but, unlike Harbage, did not see any pernicious effects.[7]

All the prevailing ideas about the audience appeared in a curious series of letters published in the *Times Literary Supplement* of 1974, hotly debating whether the Globe was indeed "the playhouse for which Shakespeare composed most of his mature plays." Most of the plays were originally commissioned for the Court, not for "ordinary people," said one writer, and thus should be freed from "the Globe stigma." Not so, replied an objector, for the supposedly "'gawkish groundlings' were more experienced playgoers than their counterparts today, and their interest in Shakespeare, Marlowe, and Jonson should hardly reduce these authors in our estimation." Astonished at such a claim for the groundlings, yet another writer quoted from the Lord Mayor and from Shakespeare himself to prove that "the shouting varletry" were rowdy illiterates, incapable of understanding the Bard's divine language. On the contrary, came the next reply in the debate, Shakespearean drama was originally "a popular art," whose "style is not so dauntingly elevated as to have bewildered the groundlings or prevented their trustworthy appreciation of Shakespeare."[8]

Several confusions are operating simultaneously in these current visions of the audience, and amid the confusions, the real

[7] Glynne Wickham, *Early English Stages, 1300 to 1660* (New York: Columbia University Press, 1972), II, 2: 150, 130.

[8] "The Globe Mark Two," review of C. Walter Hodges' *Shakespeare's Second Globe, Times Literary Supplement,* 4 January 1974, p. 14; Richard Levin, " 'Shakespeare's Second Globe,' " 25 January 1974, p. 81; Charles W. Hieatt, " 'Shakespeare's Second Globe,' " 1 March 1974, p. 212; Roderick L. Eagle, " 'Shakespeare's Second Globe,' " 22 March 1974, p. 295; Hieatt, " 'Shakespeare's Second Globe,' " 5 April 1974, p. 369.

issues get lost. First, there is the equation of superiority with
social rank. The snobbery that presumes courtiers more worthy
of Shakespeare is paralleled by the reverse snobbery that presumes commoners more worthy of him. The primary concern,
of course, should be to find out as exactly as possible just who
did come to see the plays, not who was worthy or unworthy
of seeing them.

A second confusion results from the use of the playgoers as
an explanation for the plays. Heterogeneous spectators—or
aristocratic spectators, depending upon the point of view—produce great drama, while the opposite sort of audience produces
lascivious decadence or drum-and-trumpet trash—again, depending upon the point of view. Here it is essential to distinguish
between approving a play and authoring a play. In a competitive
business, every dramatist hoped for success, but public taste did
not dictate his poetry nor even the true merit of his creation,
as Jonson and Webster testified when their work went unap-
preciated.

Finally, there is a myopic preoccupation with plays and playgoers that divorces the spectators from the wider social milieu
of their day and turns them into stereotypes. Thus the groundling becomes either an illiterate boor or a sensible artisan, while
the patrician becomes either a discerning connoisseur or a jaded
profligate. To arrive at any reliable assessment of the theater's
patrons, however partial, one must sift through the inevitable
distortions of bias and distance, seeking to relate each scrap of
information about the playgoers to the wider context of the
dramatic enterprise, the city of London, and the society of Renaissance England. Only then does it become possible to exchange
the strictures of stereotype for valid generalizations. It also
becomes possible to separate the confusion between attendance
and authorship and to set aside arguments over superiority and
inferiority.

Admittedly, it is impossible to achieve a full understanding
of the many thousands who attended plays between 1576, when
the first playhouse was built in Finsbury Fields, and 1642, when
the Puritans closed all the theaters. The direct evidence is

oblique, incomplete, and highly colored by the writers' varying intents. The indirect evidence, taken from demography, sociology, economics, literature, history, and a vast assortment of contemporary documents, is correspondingly difficult to interpret with certainty. Nevertheless, when all the testimony is considered, it clearly indicates the dominance of one sort of playgoer over all the others: he was the privileged playgoer.

The claim that the privileged playgoer dominated theater audiences does not mean that playhouses were filled exclusively with the privileged. Such was certainly not the case. Anyone with the price of admission could spend an afternoon seeing a play. At various times, especially on holidays, many among the masses enjoyed dramatic entertainment, and on any given day ordinary people made their way into the theaters. The real issue posed is whether or not acting companies relied principally upon the support of common folk. Were the theaters truly "dependent on large plebeian audiences,"[9] as one recent critic has claimed? And were the dramatists self-consciously "addressing a cross-section of society,"[10] especially at the large public playhouses? This present study, while not denying the presence of plebeians among the audiences, indicates that they probably attended in smaller numbers and with less frequency than has been supposed. Moreover, far from reflecting a cross-section of society, the spectators came chiefly from the upper levels of the social order.

That social order poses a special problem for a twentieth-century person. Inevitably, he imposes his concepts of a class structure upon a Renaissance world that was structured in a rather different way. The very term "privileged" is a deliberate attempt to avoid the narrow connotations of a term like "upper class." By comparison with the rest of society, the privileged were a minority—even in some senses an elite. But within their

[9] Robert Weimann, *Shakespeare and the Popular Tradition in the Theater*, ed. Robert Schwartz (Baltimore: Johns Hopkins University Press, 1978), p. 171.
[10] Harry Levin, "Dramatic Auspices: The Playwright and His Audience," in *Shakespeare and the Revolution of the Times* (New York: Oxford University Press, 1976), p. 293.

ranks, they exhibited a tremendous variety in wealth, power, status, and accomplishment, far more even than the present-day upper class. Many who would now be assigned to the middle class then proudly claimed to be gentlemen, a distinction that set them off quite firmly from the commonality. Thus the group called the privileged, though limited in size, was not at all limited in degree, for it ranged from the threadbare scholar or the prospering landholder, newly risen from the yeomanry, all the way up to nobility and royalty itself.

Thanks to wealth or birth, to education or achievement, privileged Englishmen followed a life considerably different from the rest of their countrymen. The circumstances of that life and in particular the necessity for disproportionately large numbers of the privileged to be in London, supplied the dramatic companies with a loyal, lucrative audience. It was, moreover, an audience that did not have to be lured into playgoing. The privileged had long fostered the drama as schoolboys, as patrons, and even as playwrights themselves. They enjoyed exclusive performances at Court and in their own mansions. Always regarded as the chief clientele of the small private theaters, the privileged probably dominated the huge public theater audiences as well. Others also came, but only when they had money and leisure—rare luxuries for most Londoners but commonplace commodities for the privileged. The entertainment on the stage, the peripheral pleasures available in a large gathering of one's peers and near-peers, and the entrenchment of playgoing as an habitual element of existence guaranteed largely privileged audiences in the theaters.

What follows is an analysis of the privileged life, of the forces that concentrated so many of the privileged in London, of their playgoing while there, of the profits derived from their attendance, and of their plebeian counterparts. Admittedly, the analysis reverses the process used to arrive at the conclusion that the privileged were the chief patrons of the playhouses. The research itself actually began with a consideration of the commoners, those sensible citizens whom Harbage had always seen as the mainstay of Shakespeare's audience. When it became impossible to square either the life style of such folk or the direct evidence with Harbage's conclusions, a fresh look at all the specific references to the playgoers seemed justified.[11] These references alone pointed overwhelmingly to the privileged as the principal theatergoers. But questions still remained unanswered. Was it possible that London sheltered sufficient numbers of the privileged for them to have predominated even in huge playhouses like the Globe? Was the privileged style of life compatible with intensive playgoing? Such questions necessitated extensive research into social, demographic, and economic history. The result has been a much wider way of looking at the audience, for their presence in the theater stemmed directly from their presence in London and indirectly from their special position in the social structure.

Thus for the first time, the playgoer can be seen not merely as a disembodied figure important only when he appears in a theater but rather as part of a total milieu existing in both England as a whole and, more significantly, in the unique society of London. The rise of a commercially profitable theater and the patrons who fostered that rise cannot, finally, be separated from the social setting. Both the theaters and the theatergoers were phenomena of their own time. It is to be hoped that a detailed analysis of the life of the affluent patrons will shed considerable light upon all playgoers, upon various customs associated with playgoing, and upon the plays as well. It is also to be hoped that this analysis does not simply transform an audience once seen as louts or sturdy artisans into an audience of fine gentlemen, in a kind of upward mobility of misperception. Instead, when all factors are carefully considered, it should become reasonably clear that the privileged were indeed the chief patrons of the performances. In that world now vanished it could not have been otherwise.

[11] The Harbage analysis appears in Ann Jennalie Cook's "The Audience of Shakespeare's Plays: A Reconsideration," *Shakespeare Studies* 7 (1974): 283-305, with subsequent work in "The London Theater Audience, 1576-1642," Ph.D. diss., Vanderbilt University, 1972.

# · II ·
# *The Privileged*

A privileged man was a fortunate man in Renaissance England. Elevated to the upper levels of society, he enjoyed the rewards derived from his gentle blood, his fine education, his wealth, his titles, or his personal achievement. Theology might declare all men equal in the eyes of God, but custom decreed the privileged superior in the eyes of man. Silks, jewels, preferment, estates, learning, power—all belonged to the favored few. Their voices murmured of poetry or politics, travel or trivia. Their bearing bespoke their breeding quite as clearly as their clothes or their coaches. They commanded the armies, made the laws, controlled the markets, preserved the universities. In all their prerogatives and pleasures—including the theater—the privileged Englishman clearly stood apart from his fellow Englishmen, no matter how much they shared in a common humanity.

## THE SHAPE OF SOCIETY

Thanks to the recent flow of research in social, political, and economic history, a huge accumulation of information concerning the upper levels of Tudor and Stuart society is now readily available.[1] Yet in order to interpret such information

[1] Arguments still rage over such issues as the rise of a middle class or the rise of the gentry or the decline of the aristocracy or the tug of Court against country or the relative profits of land and office or the causes of the Civil War. (See, e.g., the work of R. H. Tawney, Louis B. Wright, H. R. Trevor-Roper, Lawrence Stone, Jack H. Hexter, Valerie Pearl, Perez Zagorin, Paul Christianson, and Christopher Hill.) These issues may never be settled, and they certainly cannot be settled by researchers in other fields, such as theater history. But the treasure of data built up in the course of the debates stands ready to be plundered by those who would use it for different purposes.

properly, one must first perceive the relationship of the privileged minority at the top of the social scale to the vast majority beneath. The customary image of the English social structure as a pyramid, descending from monarch to pauper, is somewhat misleading. To twentieth-century minds, the pyramid suggests a gradual, even sloping in the ranks of society, including a substantial middle level. Recent efforts to describe Renaissance England as a narrow skyscraper set upon an immense base, or as a series of towers built atop a great, low hill, perhaps more accurately portray the reality of the past.[2] The vast majority of people lived at the lower levels, within quite narrow ranges of social mobility. A small minority, some 5 to 10 percent, occupied the upper levels of society, where the range of mobility was enormous. So too was the diversity of life style. It would be a mistake to assume that the privileged were a uniform or homogeneous group. In actuality, they displayed a far greater variety of income, occupation, education, and outward appearance than did the rest of society, as the skyscraper image clearly suggests. The possibilities for the masses were severely limited; the possibilities for the privileged, virtually unlimited. Thus it is essential from the outset to understand that the upper echelons of society, though relatively small, embraced a tremendously varied set of people.

At all social levels, hierarchical arrangements prevailed, further subdividing both the minority and the majority. Indeed it has been suggested that England presented a mosaic of complex hierarchies. The graded levels of society were obvious to that astute contemporary observer, William Harrison, who noted, "We in England divide our people commonly into four sorts, as gentlemen, citizens or burgesses, yeomen, and artificers or laborers." Within each division were further hierarchies: "Of gentlemen the first and chief (next the King) be the prince,

[2] Lawrence Stone, "Social Mobility in England, 1500-1700," *Past and Present* 33 (April 1966): 16-22, proposes the skyscraper and tower models. For an analysis of Stone's and other views, see David Cressy, "Describing the Social Order of Elizabethan and Stuart England," *Literature and History* 3 (1976): 29-44.

dukes, marquises, earls, viscounts, and barons, and these are called gentlemen of the greater sort, or . . . lords and noblemen; and next unto them be knights, esquires, and, last of all, they that are simply called gentlemen; so that in effect our gentlemen are divided into their conditions." As with the gentlemen, so with the other social levels. Among the citizens of London, for example, the Lord Mayor presided over the aldermen, and they in turn over the rest of the citizenry. Such officials invariably came from the membership of the twelve great livery companies rather than the lesser ones. Within the companies, the ranks descended from master to bachelor to freeman to journeyman to apprentice. As for the yeomen, they ranged from those who "commonly live wealthily, keep good houses, and travail to get riches" on down to the simple farmer. Although they comprised a majority of the population, Harrison found it sufficient merely to list the groups at the bottom of society: "The fourth and last sort of people in England are day laborers, poor husbandmen, and some retailers (which have no free land), copyholders, and all artificers, as tailors, shoemakers, carpenters, brickmakers, masons, etc." He also included "our great swarms of idle serv-ingmen."[3]

With this last phrase, Harrison touched upon two aspects of English life that are particularly important for understanding the difference between his time and the present. One is the concept of service to the master of a household, the household being the primary unit of organization for the entire society. As its head, the master exercised authority over his family and his servants, assuming a paternal responsibility for them. This was as true for the great nobleman, with dozens of manors and complicated retinues of retainers, as it was for the humble cot-tager, who postponed marriage until the vacancy of a piece of land and a house permitted him to take a wife, sire children, and send into service all the offspring he could not provide for

[3] William Harrison, *The Description of England*, ed. Georges Edelen (Ithaca, N.Y.: Cornell University Press, 1968), pp. 94, 117, 118, 119. For a modern analysis of the social stratification, see Anthony Richard Wagner, *English Genealogy* (Oxford: Clarendon Press, 1960).

by himself.[4] Harrison's reference to "idle servingmen" and the cost of their maintenance thus presupposed that everyone was responsible to some master or other.

At the same time, his concern over their numbers revealed a second important social reality: many people simply could not be adequately supported by the prevailing system. As Harrison advised:

> It were very good therefore that the superfluous heaps of them [the idle servingmen] were in part diminished. And sith necessity enforceth to have some, yet let wisdom moderate their numbers; so shall their masters be rid of unnecessary charge and the commonwealth of many thieves. No nation cherisheth such store of them as we do here in England.[5]

The pressures of an inflation so rampant that prices rose three times faster than wages combined all too effectively with the viciously recurring cycle of surplus population, famine, and plague to impoverish the "fourth and last sort of people." Their lives fluctuated from bare subsistence to outright starvation, according to the harvests. The poor have been variously estimated at a third to more than one-half of the total population.[6]

An accurate picture of Renaissance England must therefore incorporate two basic elements: first, an immense mass of the poor surmounted by the rest of the people; and, second, house-

---

[4] For further discussion of the household structure and its significance, see Peter Laslett, *The World We Have Lost* (London: Methuen, 1965). According to Laslett, 10 to 15 percent of the entire population were in service (p. 20). His conclusions are supported by K. J. Allison's findings in "An Elizabethan Village 'Census,' " *Bulletin of the Institute of Historical Research* 36 (1963): 91-103, that 60 percent of those between the ages of fifteen and nineteen were in service in 1599 in the village of Ealing in Middlesex. The fullest discussion of the family structure per se is Lawrence Stone's *The Family, Sex and Marriage in England, 1500-1800* (New York: Harper and Row, 1977).

[5] Harrison, *Description of England*, p. 119.

[6] Charles Wilson, *England's Apprenticeship, 1603-1763* (London: Longmans, 1965), p. xiv; Sir Thomas Wilson, "The State of England (1600)," ed. F. J. Fisher, *Camden Miscellany*, 3d ser. 52 (1936): 16-17.

hold units organized according to overlapping sets of hierarchies. Such a social arrangement meant that subservient persons—including wives, children, and unmarried servants, together with the lowest social orders—had no independent identity or power whatsoever. Though he took pride in the fact that England had no slaves, Harrison had no qualms about the dependent status of the largest group of his countrymen: "This fourth and last sort of people . . . have neither voice nor authority in the commonwealth, but are to be ruled and not to rule other[s]."[7] The equally subservient condition of women and children was so unquestioned as to require no notice. Thus, what is usually meant now by the English people of the period was not the entire population but only a small minority consisting principally of the heads of households, while the majority for whom they assumed responsibility remained largely invisible.

As many historians have pointed out, modern concepts of a class structure are inappropriate for Renaissance England, particularly when such concepts denote homogeneous groups of people with common values and interests that conflict with the values and interests of other groups in the same society.[8] The Elizabethan or Jacobean man was far more likely to define himself vertically rather than horizontally—according to those in authority above him and those in obedience below rather than according to his equals. Terms such as "working class" or "middle class" or "upper class" tend to mislead because they suggest twentieth-century realities not truly consistent with past realities. Terms such as "artisans," "yeomen," and "gentlemen" convey Renaissance life far more accurately. In this regard, then, it is essential to define the term "privileged" with particular care. Within the social framework just outlined, who were the privileged? And what did it mean to be one of the privileged?

[7] Harrison, *Description of England*, p. 118.
[8] See, e.g., Laslett, *World We Have Lost*, pp. 23, 37, 28, respectively; and Jack H. Hexter, *Reappraisals in History* (London: Longmans, 1961), pp. 71-116.

PRIVILEGE DEFINED

Contemporaries entertained no doubts about the significant difference between the few at the top and the many at the bottom. As Richard Mulcaster put it, "All the people which be in our country be either gentlemen or of the commonality."[9] Another observer was even more sweeping in his separation: "All sortes of people created from the beginninge are devided into 2: Noble and Ignoble."[10] When it came to specifying those regarded as "gentlemen" or "noble," there was remarkable consensus. The nobility, the gentry, the wealthier merchants, and the professionals (advocates, clerics, teachers, military officers, and an occasional physician), together with their wives and children, were generally accepted as members of the privileged minority, though each commentator explained the group's composition a bit differently. After discussing the barons, viscounts, bishops, and deans, Thomas Wilson listed "the meaner nobility, which are . . . knights, esquyers, gentlmen, laweyers, professors and ministers, archdecons, prebends, and vicars."[11] Barnaby Rich included "vnder the title of Gentry, all Ecclesiastical persons professing religion, all Martial men that haue borne office, and haue had commaund in the field; all Students of Artes and Sciences, and by our English custome, all Innes of Court men, professors of the Law."[12] Thomas Churchyard failed to mention the clergy and the intellectuals but did add the great merchants:

> For there is but fower sortes of true Nobilitie, or Gentlemenne. The firste is Gouernours, by whom all states and Kyngdomes are guided, brought to knowe order, and made [to] possess in quietnesse the gooddes that either good Fortune, or sweate of browes hath gotten.
> The seconde are Soldiours, whose venter and valliance hath been greate, service and labour not little, and daiely defended

[9] Richard Mulcaster, *Positions* (London, 1581), p. 198.
[10] Inner Temple MSS 538.44, fol. 13; as cited by Lawrence Stone, *The Crisis of the Aristocracy* (Oxford: Clarendon Press, 1965), p. 49.
[11] T. Wilson, "State of England," p. 23.
[12] Barnaby Rich, *Roome for a Gentleman* (London, 1609), p. 13.

with the hazarde of their liues, the libertie of their Countrey.

The thirde are upright and learned Lawyers, that looketh more to the matter thei haue in hande, then th[e] money thei receiue. And are neuer idell in dooyng their duetie, and studiyng for the quietness of matters in controuersie.

The fowerth are Marchauntes that sailes forrain countreys, and brynges home commodities: and after greate hazardes abroad, doe vtter their ware with regard of consciĕce and profite to the publike estate.[13]

The term "privileged," then, embraces all the foregoing classifications and subclassifications so typical of the Renaissance analysts. The closest equivalent contemporary term would be "gentleman," but the ranks of the privileged include some, like the great aristocracy, who would scorn to be considered mere gentlemen and others, like the merchants, who were not always regarded as true gentlemen.

Besides formal classification, the period also had more succinct ways of defining privilege, or gentility. Sir Thomas Smith simply concluded that a gentleman is whoever "can liue idlely, and without manuall labour, and will beare the Port, charge and countenance of a Gentleman."[14] And in reality, the privileged were distinguished not only by rank or profession but also by a certain style of life—a "Port, charge, and countenance"—that set them firmly apart from the rest of society. Wide disparities prevailed among the privileged, but they nevertheless shared tastes, customs, values, ideas, rights, and obligations that made them different from the commonality.

BIRTH, EDUCATION, WEALTH, LAND

Inclusion among the privileged came to most by birth. Though only the surviving eldest son of a titled father could automat-

---

[13] Thomas Churchyard, *A Generall Rehearsall of Warres* (London, 1579), M₄ᵛ.

[14] Sir Thomas Smith, *The Commonwealth of England* (London, 1635), p. 28, referring to the reign of Elizabeth.

ically expect to be called "Sir" or "My Lord," the lowliest younger son could style himself "Master" and regard himself a gentleman because he was "extracted from ancient and worshipfull parentage."[15] According to Henry Peacham, even bastards inherited their parents' gentle blood, if not their titles.[16] Besides, while all the titled were privileged, not all the privileged were titled. For example, the Whalleys were never knighted and never titled, though they could boast generations of notable figures—a fiercely loyal follower of Somerset under Edward VI, a sheriff of Nottingham and a member of Parliament under Elizabeth, a judge at the trial of Charles I. Certainly all twenty-five children of Richard Whalley could assume privileged status as rightfully theirs by birth.[17] So could thousands of others whose fathers were gentlemen.

Besides all the wellborn, both titled and untitled, the privileged also included all the well educated in England. Much has been made of the scope of education under Elizabeth and the first Stuarts, but there was a significant distinction between rudimentary petty school training and study at Oxford and Cambridge or the Inns of Court and Chancery. The vast majority had no need or opportunity for education,[18] and even illiteracy was no great handicap: "Now if we cannot write, we

[15] Thomas Fuller, *The Holy State and The Profane State*, ed. Maximilian Graff Walten (New York: Columbia University Press, 1938), II, 149.

[16] Henry Peacham, *The Compleat Gentleman*, ed. G. S. Gordon (Oxford: Clarendon Press, 1906), p. 9. A woman assumed her husband's rank rather than the rank to which she was born, though her sons could inherit some part of their mother's nobility. See Ruth Kelso, *Doctrine for the Lady of the Renaissance* (1956; reprint ed., Urbana: University of Illinois Press, 1978), pp. 34-35.

[17] A. S. Turberville, *A History of Welbeck Abbey and its Owners*, Vol. I: 1539-1755 (London: Faber and Faber, 1938), p. 11. Whalley died in 1583, having outlived two of his three wives.

[18] According to Laslett, two-thirds of the males over eighteen years of age had to make marks to sign the protestation of support for Parliament in 1642 (*World We Have Lost*, p. 196). There is no way of knowing how many could merely sign their names. For women, education was rare or nonexistent below the upper levels of society. A Monroe Stowe's *English Grammar Schools in the Reign of Queen Elizabeth* (New York: Columbia University Teachers College, 1908), pp. 11, 157-170, lists only 343 schools in all of England, some of

haue the Clerke of the church, or the Schoolemaster of the towne to helpe vs, who for our plaine matters will serue our turnes wel enough."[19] Quite clearly, training in Latin and rhetoric at a grammar school or under a private tutor, followed by advanced study of theology or the law, was reserved for those with sophisticated requirements. Exposure to the upper ranges of learning placed a man firmly in the upper ranges of society.

A university or Inns of Court education did not necessarily guarantee wealth or status, as the frustrated spirit behind the Parnassus plays indicates and as many an overeducated vicar or schoolmaster could testify. But it did guarantee an exclusive association with the privileged minority during the term of study, together with an expectation that such an association should continue for one's offspring. There is a difference in means but certainly not in intent between the wills of John Barlow, who was merely the Rector of Warmington, and Sir John Radcliffe, whose family enjoyed important Court connections. The clergyman's second son, Randull, was already at Cambridge in 1591, and his fourth son, Richard, was to have "five pownde . . . towarde the maynteyninge of him a whyle in the universytye of Cambridge."[20] Similarly, in 1590, Sir John directed that his sons "after they shall accomplishe the age of xiiij[th] years I would have them to Oxford o[r] Cambridge there to continue till on[e] of them bee able to goe to the inns of Courte if it bee his pleasure o[r] to tarrye and pceede in y[e] Univ[r]sity . . . or when hee shall bee of ability to travell then for to goe beehind the seas for his bett[r] furtherance in learning."[21]

---

which are doubtful. David Cressy also points out that tuition, fees for admission, and other charges even in "free" grammar schools made costs prohibitive to most people. In combination with the cost, discrimination in admissions to grammar schools also acted to reserve education largely for the privileged, as was the case with higher education. See "Educational Opportunity in Tudor and Stuart England," *History of Education Quarterly* 16 (1976): 307-313.

[19] Nicholas Breton, *The Court and Country*, in *Inedited Tracts*, ed. William Carew Hazlitt (London: Roxburghe Library, 1868), p. 198.

[20] 1 May 1591, *Lancashire and Cheshire Wills and Inventories*, Chetham Society, Remains, Historical and Literary, vol. 54 (1861), pp. 87-88.

[21] Ibid., p. 70. Tragically and ironically, four of Sir John's sons were killed

English education did not ensure an educated Englishman. Fully half those enrolled at the universities never took degrees, and a majority of those at the Inns of Court were never admitted as barristers.[22] After all, a superficial acquaintance with learning or the law sufficed for the young man who did not intend to pursue a career but merely wanted some intellectual polish or enough legal knowledge to manage his estates and preside as a local justice. According to Peacham, at the university "these young things, of twelve, thirteene, or foureteene . . . have no more care than to expect the next Carrier, and where to sup on Fridayes and Fasting nights: no further thought of study, than to trimme up their studies with Pictures, and place the fairest Bookes in openest view, which, poore Lads, they scarce ever opened, or understand not."[23] As for a legal education, "Knights and Barons . . . and Noblemen of the Realme, place their Children in these Innes, though they desire not to have them learned in the Lawes, nor to live by the practice thereof but only upon their Fathers allowance."[24] Plenty of intelligent, obviously well-educated gentlemen never enrolled their names on the university or Inns of Court registers: a continental tour offered a fashionable alternative to conventional education, and books were readily available. No formal record remains of the education of Rowland Whyte, who was the Sidney family's remarkable correspondent and agent at Court.[25] Similarly, of the eighty-four gentlemen who served as chief officers to Cecil,

---

"behind the seas"—the two eldest, Sir Alexander and Sir William in Ireland in 1598 and 1599, and the fourth and fifth sons, Edmund and Thomas, in Flanders in 1599. Their sister Margaret, a favorite maid to Elizabeth, died on 10 November 1599, apparently of grief (p. 68).

[22] Wilfrid R. Prest, *The Inns of Court under Elizabeth I and the Early Stuarts, 1590-1640* (London: Longmans, 1972), pp. 52-53.

[23] Peacham, *Compleat Gentleman*, p. 33.

[24] William Bird, *The Magazine of Honour, or a Treatise of the Severall Degrees of the Nobility of this Kingdom*, enlarged by Sir John Doderidge (London, 1642), p. 154.

[25] Lisle C. John, "Roland Whyte, Elizabethan Letter-Writer," *Studies in the Renaissance* 8 (1961): 218.

only thirty-two are known to have attended a university or an Inn of Court.[26] Thus, although formal institutions were not the only means of educating the privileged minority, "Whosoever studieth the laws of the realm, [and] whoso abideth in the university giving his mind to his book"[27] was definitely considered a gentleman rather than a commoner.

Besides birth and learning, wealth also distinguished the majority of the privileged. In fact, when Thomas Wilson set out to describe the state of England in 1600, he placed a money equivalent upon each rank, from the £5,000 yearly income of an earl down to the £500 to £1,000 of a mere esquire.[28] Harrison said a knight was anyone "who may dispend £40 by the year of free land."[29] As he himself indicated, there was immense variation in wealth, ranging from the princely fortunes of Lord Buckhurst in Elizabeth's day or Buckingham in James's reign to the outright poverty of Lord Vaux. Few were so miserable as Sir George Peckham, who was ejected from one friend's manor after another when his lands were lost because of debts in 1583. By 1587, he could not even buy food for himself, his wife, and his child, while his clothes looked "more like the ragges of some Roge than the garments of a gentleman."[30]

Yet many of the privileged were far from rich. Thomas Nashe sneered at the schoolmaster's "twopence a week" with considerable hyperbole, but the masters at the prestigious Merchant Taylors' School, for all their superior education, received a mere £10 per year.[31] Teachers and clerks in humbler positions fared

---

[26] Richard C. Barnett, *Place, Profit, and Power: A Study of the Servants of William Cecil, Elizabethan Statesman*, The James Sprunt Studies in History and Political Science, vol. 51 (Chapel Hill: University of North Carolina Press, 1969), p. 12.

[27] Harrison, *Description of England*, pp. 113-114. Mark H. Curtis, *Oxford and Cambridge in Transition* (Oxford: Clarendon Press, 1959), affirms the university as a means of maintaining civility or promoting social mobility.

[28] T. Wilson, "State of England," p. 22-23.

[29] Harrison, *Description of England*, p. 102.

[30] B. M. Lansdowne MSS 61/80; as cited by Lawrence Stone, "The Anatomy of the Elizabethan Aristocracy," *Economic History Review*, 18 (1948): 25.

[31] Thomas Nashe, *Last Will and Testament*, in *The Complete Works*, ed.

even worse. The income "of these small livings is of so little value that it is not able to maintain a mean scholar, much less a learned man, as not being above £10, £12, £16, £17, £20, or £30."[32] Even a wellborn tutor-companion to a rich young nobleman might consider himself lucky to get £20 a year.[33] As for younger sons and heirs awaiting inheritance, their income depended entirely upon the inclination and generosity of their parents. Some received lands and fortunes, but others had to manage on a modest allowance like the £40 Sir William Fitzwilliam III doled out to his eldest son and the £33. 6s. 8d. to his two grandsons in 1590. Sir William IV was more liberal, providing a £100 yearly pension for his younger son, John, with an increase to £200 at his death in 1618.[34] In a society where thousands begged and starved and a farm laborer received 3d. when a day's work was available, all the privileged were comparatively rich. However, judged by the standards of their social equals, many had modest resources indeed.

Despite the attention focused upon it in the twentieth century, land ownership was not necessarily the hallmark of the privileged. True, the aristocracy had immense holdings and, together with the gentry, claimed title to most of the land in England. A country estate was certainly essential for establishing a family line with an indisputable claim to gentility. Yet, though the yeomanry owned lands, they were firmly ranked below all

---

R. B. McKerrow (London: Sidgwick and Jackson, 1910), III, 279-280; F.W.M. Draper, *Four Centuries of Merchant Taylors' School, 1561-1961* (London: Oxford University Press, 1962), p. 251.

[32] Harrison, *Description of England*, p. 28. See also Kenneth Charlton, *Education in Renaissance England* (London: Routledge and Kegan Paul, 1965), pp. 161-162.

[33] Writing to his son Robert on the Continent, Sir Henry Sidney said of the young man's companion, Harry Whyte: "He shall have his *l.*20 yearly, and you your 100 *l.* and so be as mery as you may." See John, "Rowland Whyte," p. 219.

[34] M. E. Finch, *The Wealth of Five Northamptonshire Families, 1540-1640*, Publications of the Northamptonshire Record Society, vol. 19 (1954-1955), pp. 121, 127.

gentlemen. Conversely, as a consequence of entail, many a gentleman of good birth and superior education never held title to land—a fact that clearly rankled Thomas Wilson:

> I cannot speak of the [number] of yonger brothers, albeit I be one of the number myselfe, but for their estate there is no man hath better cause to knowe it, nor less cause to praise it; their state is of all stations for gentlemen most miserable, for if our fathers possess 1,000 or 2,000ᴵ yearly at his death he cannot give a foot of land to his yonger children in inheritance, unlesse it be . . . purchased by himselfe and not descended. Then he may demise as much as he thinkes good to his yonger children, but such a fever hectick hath custome brought in and inured amongst fathers, and such fond desire they have to leave a great shewe of the stock of their house, though the branches be withered, that they will not doe it, but my elder brother forsooth must be my master. He must have all, and all the rest that which the catt left on the malt heape, perhaps some smale annuytye during his life or what please our elder brother's worship to bestowe upon us if wee please him, and my mistress his wife.[35]

In practice, fathers often went to considerable lengths to provide in some way for all their children, but land ownership was simply not possible for all who were privileged.

## ADVANTAGES AND OBLIGATIONS

What did it mean to have the advantages of gentle blood, superior education, wealth, land? What did it mean to be privileged? Fundamentally, it meant a life quite different from that lived by all the rest of the people, different in substance as well as in accident, different by law as well as by custom, different in kind as well as in degree. Everything was different for the

---

[35] T. Wilson, "State of England," p. 24. For the harsh judgment on primogeniture by foreign travelers, see Joan Thirsk, "The European Debate on Customs of Inheritance, 1500-1700," in *Family and Inheritance*, ed. Jack Goody et al. (Cambridge: Cambridge University Press, 1976), p. 185.

privileged—the food they ate, the clothes they wore, the houses they occupied, the power they wielded, the rights they enjoyed, the obligations they assumed, the pleasures they pursued, the servants they commanded, even the funerals they required.

On a purely biological level, the privileged had a lower rate of infant mortality, married a bit younger, bore a few more children, and lived a little longer than the rest of the people. The reasons were fairly obvious. Never subject to want or to the "hard and pinching diet"[36] of the common sort, the better-nourished mothers of this select group produced healthier babies. With the advantages of superior housing, warm clothing, constant care, a guaranteed milk supply, and plenty of other food, the children of the privileged were more likely to survive the hazards of infancy and childhood. Though men and women at all social levels married much later than is generally supposed—brides were about twenty-four, bridegrooms almost twenty-seven—those in the upper levels married a bit younger—brides at twenty or twenty-one, bridegrooms at twenty-five or twenty-six.[37] This gave the privileged brides a few extra years of fertility, while the custom of wet nursing permitted them to become pregnant more often. Excellent housing, clothing, and diet protected families against the diseases that struck the chronically ill-housed, ill-clothed, and ill-fed, so that the privileged could expect a longer life. In times of plague, they could move, and in times of other illness, they could summon a physician.

More important than the biological advantages were the psychological advantages that accrued to the privileged minority. Chief among these was acceptance of the fact that no gentleman ever worked with his hands. In a society dependent upon the dawn-to-dusk toil of farmer and artisan, freedom from manual labor perhaps marked the most significant difference between the few at the top and the many below. Not that the privileged necessarily sat idle. They conducted affairs of state, commanded

[36] Harrison, *Description of England*, p. 132.
[37] Laslett, *World We Have Lost*, pp. 82-83.

armies, passed laws, handled all legal proceedings, directed mercantile ventures, controlled the kingdom's finances, managed
estates, preached sermons, educated the young, and wrote
books. But they never worked with their hands. And the work
they did perform gave them control over the entire political,
economic, and cultural life of England. Of equal psychological
significance was the fact that a gentleman need not perform any
tasks at all. If he could afford it and were so inclined, he could
devote his entire life to the pursuit of pleasure without incurring
the slightest social stigma. Peacham probably reported the truth
when he claimed that "to be drunke, sweare, wench, follow the
fashion, and to do just nothing, are the attributes of a great part
of our Gentry."[38]

The differences between the privileged few and the rest of
the populace received clear political expression. Not only were
offices and titles and access to land controlled by the government, but certain rights and obligations were codified so as to
set the upper ranks apart. The Satute of Artificers, for example,
specified that a gentleman born could not be compelled to serve
in husbandry.[39] The muster of 1588 listing all men between the
ages of sixteen and sixty who were fit to bear arms did not
include "noblemen, gentlemen, clergymen, scholers and laweyers, officers and such as had publicq charges."[40] Similarly,
"Gentlemen, or others of good Value or Conversation" were
exempted from the 9:00 P.M. curfew the Queen imposed following the apprentice riot in 1595.[41] And in 1605, when the
Dowager Countess of Rutland was arrested in her coach near
Aldgate on a suit instituted by a goldsmith, as if she were some
common debtor, the arresting sergeant and the goldsmith were

[38] Peacham, *Compleat Gentleman*, p. 10.

[39] 5 Eliz. cap. 4.

[40] T. Wilson, "State of England," p. 16.

[41] John Stow, *A Survey of the Cities of London and Westminster and the
Borough of Southwark*, Corrected, Improved, and very much Enlarged . . . by
John Strype (London: W. Imrys, J. Richardson et al., 1754-1755), II, 547. I use
this edition whenever possible because it incorporates more material than the
earlier versions. Subsequent references are to this edition unless otherwise
stated.

punished in Star Chamber proceedings.[42] The reply of Middleton's pimp, Primero, "Whipping? you find not that in the statute to whip satin,"[43] is a reminder both of the gentleman's exemption from such demeaning forms of punishment and of his exclusive right to wear expensive fabrics like silks, satins, and velvets, a right reserved to him by law.

Besides special rights, the law also conferred certain obligations upon the privileged. In taxes, fines, and assessments, "nay in every payment to the King, the Gentleman is more charged, which he beareth the more gladlier, and dare not gainesay, to save and keepe his honour and reputation . . . he must open his purse wider, and augment his proportion above others, or else he doth diminish his honour, and reputation."[44] For example, a royal order of 1586 commanding the repair and building of beacons in Northampton charged a lord 10s., a knight 6s. 8d., an esquire 5s., a "gentellman" 3s. 4d., and "other substantiall yeoman" 2s.[45] Other rates were similarly graded.

Then, too, it was the obligation of the truly affluent to accept such ruinous financial burdens as ambassadorships, entertainment of the sovereign on royal progresses, and costly offices. Refusal to serve was either impossible or expensive. Any man elected Sheriff of London had to discharge his duty, posting a £1,000 bond for the honor, unless he could prove he was worth less than £10,000. Failure to serve or give bond meant a £400

---

[42] William Paley Baildon, ed., *Les Reportes del Cases in Camera Stellata, 1593 to 1609* (privately printed, 1894), pp. 237-241. See also the royal proclamation of 8 April 1621 for the suppression of abuses "by base people against persons of qualitie," in James F. Larkin and Paul L. Hughes, eds., *Stuart Royal Proclamations* (Oxford: Clarendon Press, 1973), I, 508-511.

[43] Thomas Middleton, *Your Five Gallants*, in *The Works*, ed. A. H. Bullen (1885; reprint ed., New York: AMS Press, 1964), III, 244.

[44] Bird, *Magazine of Honour*, p. 148.

[45] Mildred Campbell, *The English Yeoman under Elizabeth and the Early Stuarts* (New Haven: Yale University Press, 1942), p. 54; see also pp. 358-359 for further examples. As a later instance, the act of 12 Car. II cap. 9 charges an ordinary man only 6d. a year as a poll tax, while charges for the elite range from £5 for a mere gentleman to £100 for a duke (Laslett, *World We Have Lost*, p. 35).

fine, while failure to serve as alderman meant a fine of 600 marks.[46] The prevalent attitude toward such obligations was clear enough:

> Yet, when able Men have thus declined this Honourable Service of the City, the Freemen have not taken it well at their Hands, and withal have refused to grant their Request. Such an Instance happened in Queen *Elisabeth*'s Days. One *Branch*, who notwithstanding afterwards served Sheriff and Mayor, sued to be discharged of the Office of Sheriff and Alderman, thereby also to be discharged of the Office of Mayor, when that should come to his Turn. But the Commons, upon this, expostulated the Case in some Displeasure; and shewed, first, his Abilities as he was of great Wealth in Lands and Goods, and without Issue; and moreover had married with one Mrs. *Minors*, an ancient Woman, without Issue, and in all Account past Childbearing; the Widow of Mr. *Minors*, who also was rich, and died without Issue, and left his Substance to his Wife. It was urged also, that his Father and Grandfather were also Citizens of *London*. So that, in all Men's Opinions, they said there was not a Man in *London*, whose Suit in this Matter could be more unreasonable. That the example was perillous to the City, considering the great Charge that was to be borne in these Offices, and the Unwillingness of miserable rich Men to take Charge upon them. For, one Precedent being had, they by this and like Ways would always endeavor to be discharged; and good Men, weaker in Wealth, should for Love to the City be driven to undo themselves, by taking such Offices upon them; and finally the City unserved.[47]

Yet even if the privileged had not been marked as different by their biological, psychological, and political advantages, a thousand details of their existence would have set them apart

---

[46] Stow, *Survey*, II, 204-205. On the costs of London offices, see also Frank Freeman Foster, *The Politics of Stability: A Portrait of the Rulers in Elizabethan London* (London: Royal Historical Society, 1977), p. 84.

[47] Stow, *Survey*, II, 239.

from the rest of society: "a Gentleman, if he will be accounted, he must goe like a Gentleman."[48] And so they did. They dressed in the silks, satins, velvets, furs, cloth of gold and silver, embroidery, and lace legally denied to ordinary men "and thereunto bestow most cost upon our arses."[49] They exercised their exclusive right to carry swords and daggers.[50] They indulged in the recreations and amusements prescribed for gentlemen— fencing, dancing, music, poetry, cards, dice, chess, travel, hunting, hawking, horsemanship—even as they deplored the decline of archery among the commonality. They eschewed the simple meals of dark bread and "white meats" (cheese, butter, milk) eaten by "the inferior sort" in favor of daily banquets of white bread, flesh, fish, game, and exotic delicacies either imported or cultivated in their private gardens.[51] They practiced the noble virtue of liberality, entertaining their equals, honoring their superiors, sustaining their inferiors, so that they would not be thought to live "like a hog," as one who "keeps no house nor spends a penny."[52] The privileged had to display "higher stomacke, and bountifuller liberality than others, and keepe about him idle servants, who shall doe nothing but waite upon him."[53] A mere gentleman might have no more than "a poor Page or Lackey, or . . . a pild fellow or two in Liverie" to attend him. But Henry Lord Berkeley had "his one hundred and fifty serv-

[48] Bird, *Magazine of Honour*, p. 148.

[49] Harrison, *Description of England*, p. 147. See Stone, "Anatomy of Elizabethan Aristocracy," pp. 4ff.

[50] 6 May 1562, 15 June 1574, 12 February 1580; Paul L. Hughes and James F. Larkin, eds., *Tudor Royal Proclamations* (New Haven: Yale University Press, 1969), II, 190, 384, 458, respectively.

[51] Harrison, *Description of England*, pp. 126, 133, 264-265, 269. See also Stone, *Crisis*, pp. 557-562.

[52] Said contemptuously of Lord Deincourt and Sir Francis Popham, as reported by John Aubrey in *Brief Lives*, ed. Oliver Lawson Dick (Ann Arbor: University of Michigan Press, 1957), p. 246; and a complaint leveled against Sir Roger Wilbraham as Solicitor General of Ireland in "The Journal of Sir Roger Wilbraham," *Camden Miscellany*, 3d ser. 4 (1902): ix. See Stone, "Anatomy of Elizabethan Aristocracy," pp. 6-7, for the extremes to which hospitality could run.

[53] Bird, *Magazine of Honour*, p. 149.

ants in livery that daily attended him in their Tawny coates,"
while Lord Buckhurst, first Earl of Dorset, kept at least 220
servants for a span of twenty years.[54] Even in death the privileged were different, buried in state, with funerals that could
cost thousands of pounds.[55] From the moment of his fortunate
birth to his final rest beneath a stone monument, the privileged
were set above and apart from their fellow Englishmen.

INCREASE OF THE PRIVILEGED

Quite obviously, money was more essential to the maintenance
of a privileged life than any other single factor. Money could
purchase education, land, and even gentle blood—a coat of arms
under Elizabeth, a title under James. Money could secure biological superiority, the psychological advantages of freedom
from manual labor, and the political rights and obligations of
the upper echelons of society. Money could sustain all the external trappings of privilege—clothing, jewels, houses, horses,
servants, travel, tombs. But money was not a stable element
in Renaissance England. There were certain forces at work that
placed new wealth in the hands of new people, giving ever larger
numbers the means to finance a privileged life. The appropri-
ation of church lands to the crown by Henry VIII created a
tremendous source of landed wealth for redistribution. The increase in international trade created unprecedented mercantile
wealth. Changes in methods of agrarian production and mar-
keting created fat new profits from shrewd land management.
Moreover, prices spiraled upward at treble the rate of wages,
enriching those with products to sell at the expense of those

[54] Rich, *Roome for a Gentleman*, p. 29; Stone, "Anatomy of Elizabethan
Aristocracy," p. 10 (Berkeley's financial losses later reduced the number of his
retinue to a mere seventy); Arthur Collins, *The Peerage of England* (London,
1779), II, 171. For other examples, see G. R. Batho, ed., *The Household Papers
of Henry Percy, Ninth Earl of Northumberland (1564-1632)*, Camden Society
Publications, 3d ser. 93 (1962): xxii-xxiii; and John Stow, *Annales, or a General
Chronicle of England*, continued and augmented . . . by Edmund Howes, Gent.
(London, 1631), p. 690.

[55] Stone, "Anatomy of Elizabethan Aristocracy," pp. 12-13.

with nothing but their labor to sell. The consequence: unprecedented riches and unprecedented additions to the ranks of the privileged.

What occurred was not a denial of rank or even a blurring of rank within the hierarchies; rather, it was an enlargement of the privileged levels at the top of the social order. What occurred was not the rise or the decline of any group en masse;[56] rather, it was the emergence of a great many more individuals who could "bear the Port, charge, and countenance of a Gentleman."[57] For the most part, the nouveaux riches consisted of yeomen whose land had made them wealthy or merchants whose business had made them wealthy.[58] But it would be misleading to suppose that there was a wholesale destruction or dilution of the upper ranks by its new members. The prosperous and ambitious yeomen and merchants became true gentlemen, quite abandoning their former stations, if not in the first generation, then certainly in the second. The fundamental structure of degree, priority, and place remained unchanged, even though the higher degrees were swollen somewhat larger than before. Moreover, this social change was defended by a good many theoreticians:

> Vngentle Gentle is hee whych is borne of a lowe degree, of a poore stocke, or (as the frenche phrase calleth it) *De basse*

[56] That may explain why arguments in the recent debate on the rise of the middle class or the gentry and the decline of the aristocracy or the country faction have been so easy to establish and so easy to disprove. For further discussion of the phenomenon of an enlargement in the ranks of the privileged, see Hexter, *Reappraisals*, pp. 71-116; Paul Christianson, "The Causes of the English Revolution: A Reappraisal," *Journal of British Studies* 15 (1976): 40-75; Stone's classic article on "Social Mobility" and the relevant sections in *Crisis*, esp. pp. 129-198.

[57] Harrison, *Description of England*, p. 114.

[58] Of 102 Yorkshiremen who purchased entry into the gentry ranks between the years 1558 and 1642, half were yeomen, half merchants or lawyers. See Alan Simpson, *The Wealth of the Gentry, 1540-1660*, East Anglian Studies (Chicago: University of Chicago Press, 1961), p. 29; J. T. Cliffe, *The Yorkshire Gentry, From the Reformation to the Civil War* (London: Athlone Press, 1969), p. 190; Hugh Kearney, *Scholars and Gentlemen: Universities and Society in Pre-Industrial Britain, 1500-1700* (London: Faber and Faber, 1970), p. 27.

*maison,* or a lowe house, whych man takinge hys begynning of a poore kindered, by his vertue, wyt, pollicie, industry, knowledge in lawes, valiency in armes, or such lyke honeste meanes becometh a welbeloved & hygh estemed mã, preferred then to great office, put in great charg and credict, euen somuch as he becommeth a post or stay of the commune wealthe, and so growynge rych doth thereby auance and set vp the rest of his poore line or kindred: then are the children of such one commonlye called gentlemen, of whych sort of gentlemẽ we haue now in Englãd very many, wherby it should appeare that vertue florisheth among vs. These gentilmen are now called vpstartes, a terme latelye inuented by such as pondred not the grounds of honest menes of rising or coming to promocion. . . . those mẽ may worthely be called honourable whom vertue hath auanced and reysed them to dignitie. I speake not this in defence of all new rysen men, but onely of such as worthines hath brought vnto honor: for if worthy men might not be auaunced, yᵉ worlde should seme to do them much wrong.[59]

Ben Jonson, himself the stepson of a bricklayer, claimed that all true greatness "came out of poore cradles."[60]

YEOMAN AND MERCHANT ASPIRANTS

Successful yeomen found it particularly easy to rise into the gentle ranks. If they could prosper, add to their lands, stay out of debt, and educate their sons well, then their heirs were almost certain to become gentlemen in time.

This sort of people have a certain pre-eminence and . . . commonly live wealthily, keep good houses, and travail to get riches. . . . And with grazing, frequenting of markets, and keeping of servants (not idle servants as the gentlemen do, but such as get both their own and part of their master's

[59] *The Institucion of A Gentleman* (London, 1568), B₃-B₅.
[60] Ben Jonson, *Discoveries, 1641,* and *Conversations with William Drummond of Hawthornden, 1619,* ed. G. B. Harrison (1923; reprint ed., New York: Barnes and Noble, 1966), p. 54.

living) do come to great wealth, insomuch that many of them are able and do buy the lands of unthrifty gentlemen, and often, setting their sons to the schools, to the universities, and to the Inns of the Court, or otherwise leaving them sufficient lands whereupon they may live without labor, do make them by those means to become gentlemen.[61]

The yeomanry under Elizabeth numbered at least 70,000 and perhaps as many as 200,000. Their holdings varied from 25 to 200 acres in arable lands on up to 600 acres in grazing lands, and their incomes ranged from £40 to £500 or more per year.[62] Thomas Taylor, the elder, of Witney had goods valued at £408. 2d., a house of twenty-five rooms, and money out on loan— this in addition to the value of his land holdings.[63] Though officially classed as a yeoman, he was obviously wealthier than many a gentleman. No doubt he was one of those "sundry yeomen (although otherwise for wealth comparable with many of the gentle sort) that will not yet for all that change their condition, nor desire to be apparailed with the titles of gentrie."[64]

More commonly, with this kind of prosperity, family after family moved in status from yeomen to gentlemen. Few ascended from sheep grazer to knight to baron to earl, as the Spencers did between 1500 and 1643.[65] Far more typical was the case of the Fetherstons of Packwood. William, who died in 1599, and his son John were both mere yeomen, though they acquired a house costing £340, accumulated at least 446 acres in land, paid the £12 fine of knighthood in 1630 (due from all with estates in excess of £40 yearly), and owned goods that included the horseman's gear used solely by the gentry for the militia. The elder John provided both his heir, John, and a younger son, William, with training at the Inns of Court. The eldest called

---

[61] Harrison, *Description of England*, pp. 117-118.

[62] Campbell, *English Yeoman*, pp. 102, 215-219.

[63] M. A. Havinden, ed., *Household and Farm Inventories in Oxfordshire, 1550-1590* (London: Stationery Office, 1965), pp. 10-11, 150-161.

[64] William Lambarde, *A Perambulation of Kent* (London: Baldwin, Cradock, and Joy, 1826), pp. 7-8.

[65] Finch, *Wealth of Five Northamptonshire Families*, pp. 38-65.

himself "esquire," commissioned a pedigree, and began to use a family seal by 1637, while his three younger brothers all called themselves "gentlemen." Contrary to their father's own usage, they even termed him a "gentleman" in the inventory of his goods.[66] Their story is repeated in every English county. John Baker of Uckfield in Sussex died a yeoman in 1597, but his son Michael was already considered a gentleman by 1595. In 1593, John Bull of Norfolk was a yeoman and in 1597 a gentleman.[67] Inevitably, there were sneers at "my yonge masters the sonnes of such, not contented with their states of their fathers to be counted yeomen and called John or Robert (such an one), but must skipp into his velvett breches and silken dublett and, getting to be admitted into some Inn of Court or Chancery, must ever after thinke skorne to be called any other then gentleman."[68] Yet Bishop Latimer, Sir Isaac Newton, and George Chapman all sprang from the yeomanry, as did many another successful gentleman.

Successful merchants made an equally easy transition into the gentle ranks. While it is difficult to make distinctions among merchants, retailers, craftsmen, tradesmen, shopkeepers, wholesalers, and the like because of the tremendous degree of overlapping and the wide variation in wealth, it was obvious to contemporaries that many in business were immensely rich. "I have knowne in my time 24 aldermen which were esteemed to be worth 20,000$^l$ a peece, some much more, and the better sort of Cittizens the halfe; . . . it is well knowne that att this time there are in London some merchants worth more than 100,000$^l$ and he is not accounted rich that cannot reach to 50,000 or neer itt."[69] According to Harrison, "the gentlemen and merchants keep much about one rate" at their tables, and when merchants gave great company feasts, "they are often comparable herein to the nobility of the land."[70]

---

[66] M. W. Farr, *The Fetherstons of Packwood in the Seventeenth Century*, Dugdale Society Occasional Papers, no. 18 (1968), pp. 4-8, 18.

[67] See Campbell, *English Yeoman*, pp. 38-41, for other examples.

[68] T. Wilson, "State of England," p. 19.

[69] Ibid., pp. 20-21.

[70] Harrison, *Description of England*, pp. 128-129.

Moreover, the parade of "Sirs" who year after year held the office of Lord Mayor and generally the posts of aldermen as well, testified to the firm entrenchment of the top ranks of business in the top ranks of society. Tax rates equated a company master with an esquire and a liveryman with a gentleman.[71] Gentlemen were often made free of the companies, great noblemen were regularly included at company feasts, and royalty itself did not disdain honorary membership.[72] Even the most

[71] Poll tax of 1660, 1 Car. II cap. 9; see Laslett, *World We Have Lost*, p. 248n.

[72] Stow, *Survey*, II, 258. At the Merchant Taylors feast in 1607, James II was presented

A Roll, wherein were entered the Names of such Kings and Nobles, and other great Persons, that had been free of their Company, *viz.* seven Kings, one Queen, seventeen Princes and Dukes, two Dutchesses, one Archbishop, one and thirty Earls, five Countesses, one Viscount, twenty-four Bishops, sixty-six Barons and Lords, two Ladies, seven Abbots, seven Priors, and one Sub-Prior, omitting a Number of Knights, Esquires, &c. The King then said, that he was free of another Company, yet he would so much grace the Company of Merchant-Taylors, that his eldest Son the Prince should be free thereof; and that he would see and be a Witness, when the Garland should be put upon his Head; and then they resorted unto the Prince, who dined in the great Hall; and the Company presented him with another Purse full of Gold; and the Clerk delivered his Highness another like Roll; and his Highness said, that not only himself would be free of the Company, but many other of his Lords; and commanded one of his Gentlemen and the Clerk of the Company, to go to all the Lords present, and to require them that loved him, and were not free of other Companies, to be free of his Company. And so were accordingly made free two and twenty Earls and Lords, and a great many other Knights and Esquires; and, of the Clergy, Dr. *Montague*, dean of the Chapel, and *Adam Newton*, Dean *Durham*, and the Prince's Tutor, and three Noblemen of the *Low-Countries*, Ambassadors to the King. . . . The Names of some of the *English* Nobles, that had their Freedoms of this Company granted them at this Time, were, the Duke of *Lenox*, the Earl of *Nottingham*, Lord Admiral; the Earl of *Suffolk*, Lord Chamberlain; the Earl of *Salisbury*, principal Secretary to the King; and several other Knights and Gentlemen, *Scotch* and *English*. (II, 277)

King *James* I, *June* 12, 1607, dined with the Lord-Mayor, Sir *John Watts*, Clothworker; and after went into the *Clothworkers-Hall*; and there was made free of that Company, with Sir *Patrick Murrey*, Gentleman of his Bed-Chamber, Sir *Arthur Arston* and Sir *Hugh Carmichel*, Knights, and *James Medow*, D. D. the King's Chaplain.

The Earls of Shrewsbury and Cumberland already were members (II, 286).

casual perusal of the records of these companies bears out the impression of status and wealth. Among the goldsmiths, for instance, fees and fines ranged from £10 for admission of bachelors into the livery, to £100 for a fraudently obtained freedom, to a £400 share of "Sir Walter Rawlye's ship adventure money," to a £1,600 loan to the Queen, gratis of interest.[73] Comments on the increasing numbers of members testified to the obvious attractions of the trade, while references to velvet, plush, satin, damask, fur, and gold chains in the goldsmiths' attire also testified to their wealth.[74] The requirement that apprentices had to be able to read and write revealed the upward social orientation of the goldsmiths, while the growing practice of purchasing a son's membership by patrimony instead of his earning it by apprenticeship revealed the increasing dissociation between the profits derived from the sale of gold and jewels and the manual labor required to produce such goods.[75] But the goldsmiths had no monopoly on mercantile wealth. The records of major indebtedness alone show the sums these merchant magnates were able to dispend—literally thousands and thousands of pounds.[76]

Certainly the merchants had money enough to acquire lands, houses, titles, and firm entrenchment in the ranks of the privileged. Nicholas Mosley, for example, began as the London representative of his family's Manchester cloth trade, was knighted, and served as Lord Mayor in 1599. "From a small and low estate God raised him up to riches and honour. He bought the Lordships manor of Manchester and of the Hough and built a house called the Hough-end in the place where his father's tenement stood."[77] Lionel Cranfield parlayed his fortune from trade into marriage with a Villiers, the title of Earl of

[73] Sir Walter Sherburne Prideaux, *Memorials of the Goldsmiths' Company* (London: Eyre and Spottiswoode, 1896), I, 110, 95, 89, 91, respectively.

[74] By 1595 the yeomanry were so increased that there was not room for all of them in the hall (ibid., p. 89). For references to rich attire see, e.g., ibid., pp. 80-81, 101, 116-118, 199.

[75] Ibid., pp. 26, 27, xv-xvi, 94, respectively.

[76] See H. R. Trevor-Roper, *The Gentry, 1540-1640, Economic History Review*, supplement 1 (1953), pp. 14-15; and Stone, *Crisis*, pp. 532-538.

[77] Wagner, *English Genealogy*, pp. 165-166.

Middlesex, and the post of Lord Treasurer.[78] And the fabulously wealthy William Cokayne, in the process of establishing his own dynasty, had no difficulty in obtaining Rushton Hall, the family seat of the Treshams.[79] Not every merchant was so successful, but it is certainly understandable that the legend of Dick Whittington dates from 1605.[80]

SIGNS OF SOCIAL MOBILITY

The infusion of new blood into society's upper ranks manifested itself in several ways. For one thing, either by lease or by sale, land changed hands at an unprecedented rate[81] as merchants acquired the respectability of country estates, yeomen consolidated or enlarged their holdings, and the established gentry and aristocracy either sold off manors to pay debts or bought new ones to increase their status or provide for younger children. It has been estimated that the lesser gentry (including the accretion of new arrivals) increased their holdings from 30 or 40 percent in 1500 to about 50 percent by 1688.[82] The increases sometimes came at the expense of the older families. "A prodigall who had spent his estate was pleased to jeer himself, boasting that he had cosened those who had bought his means; They gave me (said he) good new money, and I sold them my Great-great-grandfathers old land."[83] Since the law placed no social restrictions on the right to acquire land, the pressure of escalating prices and ready money eroded the more conservative

[78] Stone, *Crisis*, pp. 105-106, 123, 190, 421.

[79] Finch, *Wealth of Five Northamptonshire Families*, p. 96.

[80] C. Wilson, *England's Apprenticeship*, p. 11.

[81] Campbell, *English Yeoman*, pp. 7-79; Stone, "Anatomy of Elizabethan Aristocracy," p. 311 and Appendix A; Stone, *Crisis*, pp. 129-198; R. H. Tawney, "The Rise of the Gentry, 1558-1640," in *Essays in Economic History*, ed. E. M. Carus-Wilson (London: Edward Arnold, 1954), I, 189-201.

[82] F.M.L. Thompson, "The Social Distribution of Landed Property in England since the Sixteenth Century," *Economic History Review*, 2d ser. 19 (1966): 511. For purposes of the present discussion, it is irrelevant whether aristocratic holdings rose or declined, though this has been a pressing question for recent historians.

[83] Fuller, *Holy State*, p. 54.

tendencies to hold onto property and released it into new hands. As early as 1559, a ceiling on the amount of property that vulgar, untitled persons could buy had been proposed.[84] Nothing came of the proposal, but the legal safeguards preventing fraudulent land transfer were tightened considerably under an act of 1585[85]—an act that further enriched the lawyers but did nothing to break the feverish land sales of the 1580s and 1590s.

Another sign of a rapidly growing privileged class was the notable rise in enrollments at both the universities and the Inns of Court and Chancery. Though precise estimates vary, Oxford and Cambridge admitted anywhere from 500 to 1,000 each year between 1575 and 1642, as compared with the 150 to 300 per year in 1500,[86] an increase that far exceeded the normal growth rate for the privileged or for the population as a whole. A university education cost some £20 per year by 1600 and £30 by 1660.[87] Despite the existence of scholarships and the possibility of service to wealthier students, complaints that "poor men's children are commonly shut out and the richer sort received"[88] seemed justified by the facts. Cecil proposed that Elizabeth's first Parliament should reserve a third of all university

[84] "Considerations delivered to the Parliament, 1559," *Historical MSS Commission, MSS of the Marquis of Salisbury,* I, 162-163; as cited by Tawney, "Rise of Gentry," p. 188.

[85] 27 Eliz. cap. 4.

[86] Kearney, *Scholars and Gentlemen,* pp. 22, 40; Lawrence Stone, "The Educational Revolution in England, 1560-1640," *Past and Present* 28 (July 1964): 51, 53; Lawrence Stone, ed., *The University in Society* (Princeton: Princeton University Press, 1974), I, 6, 21-22, 91.

[87] Stone, "Educational Revolution," p. 71.

[88] Harrison, *Description of England,* p. 71. Harrison charged:
The richer sort [were] received (who in time past thought it dishonor to live, as it were, upon alms), and getting placed, most of them study little other than histories [tales, romances], tables, dice, and trifles, as men that make not the living by their study the end of their purposes, which is a lamentable hearing. Besides this, being for the most part either gentlemen or rich men's sons, they oft bring the universities into much slander. For, standing upon their reputation and liberty, they ruffle and roist it out, exceeding in apparel and haunting riotous company (which draweth them from their books unto another trade). And for excuse, when they are charged with breach of all good order, think it sufficient to say that they be gentlemen.

scholarships for gentlemen's children, and Sir Humphrey Gilbert defended his proposal for a gentlemen's academy on the grounds that "now the youth of nobility and gentlemen, taking vp their schollarshippes *and* fellowshippes, do disapoincte the poore of their livinges and avauncemente*s*."[89] Though some 41 percent of the entrants may have been of plebeian origins (50 percent gentry sons, 9 percent clergy sons), apparently none came from the very lowest levels of society, and the proportion of plebeian entrants seemed to vary according to shifts in the land market, which most directly affected the affluence of the aspiring groups.[90]

The Inns of Court showed no such dependence upon economic fluctuations. With no scholarships and no opportunities for service, anyone who entered the Inns, either directly or following a university stint, simply had to have money. These "seminaries and nurseries wherein the gentrie of this kingdome are bredd and trayned upp" cost a minimum of £40 or £50 a year, though occasionally there was a younger brother like Thomas Holles, scrimping by on the "scant allowance" of £30 that his thrifty elder brother John provided him between 1599 and 1605.[91] As prices rose still higher, even £40 meant "continual want, or short stipend."[92] Despite the expense, however, admissions to the Inns quadrupled between 1500 and 1600 and then slacked off a bit.[93] A stay at the Inns of Court not only

[89] F. J. Furnivall, ed., *Queene Elizabethes Achademy, A Booke of Precedence, etc.*, Early English Text Society, extra ser., no. 8 (1869), p. 10.

[90] Stone, "Educational Revolution," pp. 54, 60-61, 71. There is considerable debate about the social origins of university men and the question of social mobility. Mark Curtis, *Oxford and Cambridge in Transition*, insists that universities offered a means of social mobility, but Kenneth Charlton, *Education in Renaissance England*, insists that schools maintained the status quo. James McConica, "Scholars and Commoners in Renaissance Oxford," *University in Society*, ed. Stone, disputes the charges of Harrison and Gilbert that the rich were usurping the poor, claiming that the humble were not entirely shut out (p. 175).

[91] Prest, *Inns of Court*, pp. 24, 27-28.

[92] Sir Simonds D'Ewes, *The Autobiography and Correspondence*, ed. James O. Halliwell (London: Richard Bentley, 1845), I, 232.

[93] Prest, *Inns of Court*, pp. 6-7.

led to the most lucrative of all the professions but also carried such immense social prestige that it became the natural choice for those who could afford to educate their sons alongside no-bles' and gentlemen's sons. The number of such rich aspirants was small—certainly no more than a quarter and perhaps fewer than a tenth of the total membership.[94] But there were enough parvenus to occasion a complaint in 1586: "For by that free access, now permitted to yeomanrye and Merchauntes, to set their broode, to the study of common law, . . . places of high regarde . . . are now preoccupated, and vsurped."[95] By 1601, the Inner Temple restricted future members to those "of good parentage and of no evil behaviour," and James specifically de-creed "that non be from henceforth admitted into the socyete of any house of court that is not a gentleman by discent."[96] But there was no sign that his rule was ever enforced. Wealthy and ambitious families continued to send their share of sons to the legal fraternities as a means of ensuring privilege for them.

Besides acquiring land and advanced education, aspiring merchants and yeomen also acquired coats of arms and titles to announce their arrival into the privileged ranks. Between 1560 and 1589, there were 2,320 grants of new arms, and be-tween 1590 and 1639, there were 1,760—scarcely the estimated 7,000 that were said to have been issued by 1615 but certainly enough to testify to the growing numbers who desired full membership in the upper ranks of society.[97] Of course, some of these grants were acquired illegally. A bogus herald took money for tracing coats of arms for ninety families in Cheshire in 1579 before he was exposed.[98] Among the charges leveled at Sir William Dethick, who was removed as Garter King of Arms in 1605, was his granting of arms to unfit persons: "Tay, a

[94] Ibid., pp. 30-31.

[95] John Ferne, The Blazon of Gentrie (London, 1586), p. 93.

[96] F. A. Inderwick, ed., A Calendar of the Inner Temple Records (London: H. Sotheran, 1896), I, 439; The Black Books, Records of the Honorable Society of Lincoln's Inn (London: Lincoln's Inn, 1897-1898), II, 81.

[97] Stone, Crisis, pp. 67, 69.

[98] Ibid., pp. 66-67.

hosier living in Fish Street; Dungayn the plasterer, Parr the embroiderer, the son of a pedlar (to whom Garter King had sold for £10 the arms of Parr, the last Marquess of Northampton); Robert Young, a soapmaker; William Sanderson, a fishmonger; and 'Shakespear ye Player.' ''[99] Many expressed outrage at the newly armigerous man, charging, ''if need be, a King of Heralds shall give him for money armes newly made, and invented with the Creast and all: the title whereof shall pretend to have him found by the said Herault, in the perusing and viewing of old Registers, where his ancestors in the time past had been recorded to beare the same.''[100] The number of families with corrupt arms may not have been ''very neere the one half of the gentlemen of England at this day,''[101] but the number was substantial.

With James's accession, arms gave way to titles, often obtained by outright purchase. Elizabeth had been stingy with her honors—only 18 peerages and 878 knighthoods during her reign, including Essex's military elevations. By contrast, James dubbed 906 knights in the first four months of his reign, and by 1642 there were 3,281 new knights, 364 baronets, and 103 peers, exclusive of the Irish and Scots creations.[102] To many it must have seemed only slight exaggeration to say a man was ''Eyther a Knight or a knitter of Caps: for wee are now so full of Knights, that Gentlemen are had in little request.''[103]

The forthright resentment of social conservatives emerged in the declaration that ''no man can be made a Gentleman but by his father. And be it spoken (with all reuerent reseruation of Duty) the King (who hath power to make Esquires, Knights, Baronets, Barons, Viscounts, Earls, Marquesses, and Dukes) cannot make a Gentleman, for Gentilitie is a matter of race, and of blood, and of discent, from Gentile and Noble parents, and

[99] Folger Shakespeare Library MS X.d. 313.

[100] Bird, *Magazine of Honour*, pp. 147-148.

[101] This statement was made about 1590. See Lansdowne fol. 11ʳ; as cited by Elizabeth K. Berry, *Henry Ferrers, an Early Warwickshire Antiquary*, Dugdale Society Occasional Papers, no. 16 (1965), p. 22.

[102] Stone, *Crisis*, pp. 21-128; Appendices 2 and 3, pp. 754, 755.

[103] Rich, *Roome for a Gentleman*, p. 29.

auncestors, which no kings can giue to any, but to such as they beget."[104] By 1620, Sir Robert Knollys calculated "that there are in England and Wales att least 40 or 50,000 who doe wrongfully take to them selves that tytle" of esquire.[105] Of course, Sir Robert proposed a modest fee of £20 to confirm the right to the esquire's title and, consequently, to swell the royal coffers (and his own), so his estimates may be discounted. But the conclusion of historian Lawrence Stone is no doubt correct:

> Though clumsy in operation, the inflation was in principle no more than recognition of an established socio-economic fact, that the class pyramid in its upper ranges had become much broader at the base and rather lower at the top than it had been at the accession of Elizabeth. The huge expansion in the numbers of men calling themselves gentleman, esquire, knight, baronet, baron, viscount, and earl is not merely the result of the greed and folly of heralds, courtiers, and kings. Even if the heralds had been sea-green incorruptibles, Buckingham and the courtiers men of austere and blameless lives, and King James a man of iron will and an overflowing treasury, a substantial increase in titles must still have taken place.[106]

## SUBTLE DISTINCTIONS

With the new creations, inevitable quarrels over precedence arose. In London, for example, aldermen disagreed as to whether order should go according to rank and status or the date of knighthood.

> The Aldermen that were Knights tho' knighted after them, nay, tho' they were not Knights at all, stood for Precedency as Aldermen, before all Commoners Knights; one of the chief Knights Commoners at this Time was Sir *Baptist Hickes*, a

---

[104] Stow, *Annales* (1631), p. 1,068.
[105] Inner Temple MSS 538.44, fol. 264; BM Harl. MSS 1323, fol. 278; as cited by Stone, *Crisis*, p. 70.
[106] Ibid., pp. 127-128.

Mercer in *Cheapside*; who had often been burstling, he and his Wife, about this Ceremony, the Aldermen Knights, and their Wives, striving for Precedency; and Sir *Baptist* and his Lady sometimes, for Peace Sake, granting it. Sir *Baptist* kept his Shop, after he was knighted; which was looked upon as some Disparagement to him; it not being usual, as it seems, in those Times, after Knighthood, to keep their Trade going. [107]

It was finally decided that knighted aldermen took precedence in public but not in the more exclusive meetings of the great companies. "Such Respect is given to the Masters and Wardens of said Companies, that, when they meet at their several Halls, either sitting upon Business, or feasting, they take the Precedency, at their tables, of all the rest of the Society, tho' they be Batchelor Knights, or Baronets." [108]

An even greater difficulty arose in the attempts to enforce the Statutes of Apparel. Over and over again Elizabeth tried to curb excessive expense in dress, complaining against "the wasting and undoing of a great number of young gentlemen . . . and others seeking by vain show of apparel to be esteemed as gentlemen," against "the great excess of apparel in all states and degrees, but specially in the inferior sort," against "the confusion of degrees of all estates, amongst whom diversity of apparel hath always been a special and laudable mark," and against "this increasing evil . . . principally occasioned by the immeasurable charges and expenses which they are put to in superfluous appareling their wives, children, and families; the confusion also of degrees in all places being great where the meanest are as richly appareled as their betters." [109] Not surprisingly, there were efforts to get the statutes relaxed. In April of 1588, Sir George Bond, Mayor of London, presented the Lords of the Council with an alternative "Limitation and Order for Apparel of Citizens and Officers of the City in their several

---

[107] Stow, *Survey*, II, 486.
[108] Ibid., p. 257.
[109] 15 June 1574, 12 February 1580, 13 February 1588, 6 July 1597; Hughes and Larkin, eds., *Tudor Royal Proclamations*, II, 301, 454; III, 3, 175.

Degrees and Callings, and of their Wives."[110] With so much wealth in circulation outside the aristocratic ranks, effective enforcement of the sumptuary laws was impossible: a mercer could dress as well as an earl if he wished. In 1603, Parliament finally repealed the act, establishing the victory of new money over ancient custom.

Yet fine clothes, manor houses, learning, even a title or a coat of arms did not always provide the subtle social nuances some expected of a gentleman. The Earl of Carlisle dropped a man because the fellow pulled a knife out of his pocket to cut meat at the table, "the cognisance of a clown."[111] As one theorist put it, "The stock and linage maketh not a man noble or ignoble, but vse, education, instruction, and bringing vp maketh him so; for . . . if he be euilly instructed in his yong yeares, he will haue as long as he liueth such manners as are barbarous, strange, and full of all villany."[112] To prevent any sign of villeiny in the parvenus, as well as to reassure the established, manuals on every aspect of the gentle life poured off the English presses. Among the aspirants and the established alike, there was a ready market for books that declared "who is gentle, and who is vngentle: what offices, condicions, qualities and maners oughte to bee in a gentleman, & how he should differ from other sortes of mē."[113] The genre was even satirized in such works as Dekker's *Gull's Hornbook*.

In general, however, it was not satire but rather a notable defensiveness that characterized some of the manuals, a defensiveness occasioned by a widespread resentment of the newly privileged. Stephen Gosson, no writer of handbooks for gentlemen, thundered, "We are all commaunded by God to abide in the same calling wheirein we were called, which is our ordinary

---

[110] Stow, *Survey*, II, 545.

[111] BM Harleian MSS 6395/55; as cited by Stone, *Crisis*, p. 51.

[112] Guillaume de La Perrière, *The Mirrour of Policie* (London, 1598), Hh₃.

[113] "Prologue," *Institucion of A Gentleman*. The most complete modern bibliography of these treatises is Ruth Kelso's *The Doctrine of the English Gentleman in the Sixteenth Century*, University of Illinois Studies in Language and Literature, no. 14 (1929).

vocation in a commonweale. . . . So in a commonweale, if priuat men be suffered to forsake theire calling because they desire to walke gentleman like in sattine & veluet, w^th a buckler at theire heeles, proportion is so broken, vnitie dissolued, harmony confoūded, y^t the whole body must be dismembred."[114] Social ascent seemed a vice to many, like Aegremont Ratcliffe, who dedicated his translation of a French treatise on fixed vocations with these words:

> For, who euer sawe so many discontented persons: so many yrked with their owne degrees: so fewe contented with their owne calling: and such a number desirous, & greedie of change, & nouelties? Who euer heard tel of so many reformers, or rather deformers of estates and Common weales. . . . Likewise, the Plough man, doth he not thinke the Merchant happier then himselfe? The Merchant, doth he not tickle at the title of a Gentleman? The Gentleman, doth he not shoot at the marke of Nobilitie? And y^e Noble man, hath he not his eye fixed vppon the glorie and greatnesse of a Prince? What Prince could not be contented to be Monarche of the whole world? What should I say? Would not the Lawyer (thinke ye) agreeably accept the title of a Lord?[115]

Thus the writers of gentlemanly handbooks echoed popular opinion, as well as their own sentiments, when they scorned those who "haue wrongfully intruded into Gentry, & thruste them selues therein: as Batard the cart Jade might leape into the stable of Bucephalus and thrust hys hed into y^e manger with that worthy courser. . . . And althoughe they shadowe them-selues wythe the name of Gentrye, yet coppered chaynes gylded are noo pure golde."[116] Another detractor continued, "I call them counterfeit, that do vsurpe the name & title of gentlemen, that are lately crept out of a thacht house, or from the dunghil,

---

[114] Stephen Gosson, *Playes Confuted in Fiue Actions*, in *The English Drama and Stage*, ed. William C. Hazlitt (1869; reprint ed., New York: Burt Franklin, n.d.), p. 216.

[115] Aegremont Radcliffe, trans., *Politique Discourses* (London, 1578), A₃^v.

[116] *Institucion of A Gentleman*, B₈.

by scraping together a little pelfe, that haue neither pedigree, vertue, nor honesty, whereby to make claime, and yet will intrude themselues and take more vpon them then becommeth basenes."[117] Nevertheless, "base" yeomen and merchants continued to join the ranks of the privileged.

Understandably, resentment grew keenest among the old gentry of modest means, particularly among younger sons, for they experienced the most direct competition from the newcomers for place, status, and advancement. Some, like the three younger sons of John Spencer II, received good educations and went on to offices, titles, profitable marriages, and prosperity.[118] By contrast, Richard Bruen of Stapleford, a sixth son, never married and humbly begged in his will that his body might be allowed to lie in the chapel of his nephew John.[119] Sir John Ferne wistfully noted, "Of old times, colleges were built and liuinges giuen, for the maintenance of poore mens children. . . . But now, I would wish some to build colleges, for the maintenance of poore younger brethren gentlemen, destitute of succour and support."[120] The opportunities open to a younger son included warfare, learning, trade, service to the Court or the nobility, or a wealthy match.[121] Ironically, these very routes fostered a close association between the indisputable gentlemen of limited resources and the families with fortunes and dynasties still being established, either by marriage, by occupation, or by pursuit of preferment.

SHORTCUTS TO STATUS: TRADE, PREFERMENT, MARRIAGE

There was special concern over the question of apprenticeship. Quite obviously an apprenticeship in a lucrative trade offered the prospect of substantial wealth. But did such a period of

[117] Rich, *Roome for a Gentleman*, A$_2$.
[118] Finch, *Wealth of Five Northamptonshire Families*, Appendix 3, pp. 174-175.
[119] *Lancashire and Cheshire Wills*, 51:119.
[120] Ferne, *Blazon of Gentrie*, p. 95.
[121] Fuller, *Holy State*, pp. 47-50.

service forever erase or debar a claim to gentle blood? Conservatives argued that "by continuance of bying and sellynge they are not esteamed as gentlemenne but marchantes, ouerthrowing in proces of time their worshipful houses themselues, and their posteritie foreuer."[122] This point of view easily explained John Stow's report concerning certain country gentry: "Hence, also it comes to pass, that many Gentlemen in the Country utterly refuse to send up their younger Children to learn honest Trades to get Wealth, and improve their Fortunes by Merchandise, or other Traffic; chusing rather to keep them always in the Country, to live idly, and to depend sometimes on their elder Brother, or on some small Annuity; whereby not seldom they take naughty Courses for a Subsistence."[123]

Yet the conservative position could not ultimately prevail. The potential profits of trade proved too attractive for lesser families and created too many who eventually assumed the cloak of privilege. Harrison just reported the obvious, that merchants "often change estate with gentlemen, as gentlemen do with them, by a mutual conversion of the one into the other."[124] But others, like Edmund Bolton, provided a full theoretical defense for apprenticeship, and with good reason: "For, in the City of London there are at this present many hundreds of Gentlemens children Apprentises, infinite others have beene, and infinite will be; and all the parts of England are full of families, either originally raised to the dignity of Gentlemen out of this one most famous place: or so restored, and enriched as may well seeme to amount to an original raising. . . . I am very confident, that by having once beene an Apprentise in London, I have not lost to be a Gentleman of birth, nor my sonne." Many a merchant, too, had "beene at no small charge, and some care, to breed my sonne up in Gentleman like qualities."[125] They all

[122] *Institucion of A Gentleman*, $c_1$.

[123] Stow, *Survey*, II, 434.

[124] Harrison, *Description of England*, p. 115.

[125] Edmund Bolton, *The Cities Aduocate* (London, 1629), and his letter of 26 March 1631, printed in *Gentleman's Magazine* (1832), pp. 499-501; both as cited by Kelso, *Doctrine of the English Gentleman*, p. 63.

required at least the assurance that "Gentry therefore may be suspended perchance, & asleep during the apprentiship, but it awakens afterwards."[126] Certainly it was true for such families as the Ishams, who regularly sent younger sons into London apprenticeship to establish themselves afterwards with country estates.[127]

A less questionable, if more precarious, route upward for the ambitious lay in royal or noble preferment. According to Elizabeth, "My good lord, advancement in all worlds be obtained by mediation and remembrance of noble friends."[128] The reward might be no more than a liveried post under some aristocrat, complete with a luxurious style of living, a small income, and a chance to pocket gratuities from suitors for favors. But the Court dangled the prospect of such lucrative wardships and patents, offices and fines for the favored few that scant disapproval attached to the most blatant jockeying for attention. "Need obeys no law, and forgets blushing,"[129] was Sir Philip Sidney's view of the matter. So successful were the aspirants that the Court became known as "A pasture wherein Elder Brothers are observed to grow lean, and Younger Brothers fat," while scorn was heaped by the envious upon officeholders who

haue raked together some yearly revenues, more than all their ancestors were euer able to leaue to their heires and not attained vnto by vertuous industry, but gotten sometimes by deceiuing the Prince, otherwhiles by preiudicing the common wealth, & most times, by exacting & oppressing as many as they had to deale withal, but vnder these pretences, they would vsurpe to themselues a kind of preheminence, to throng and thrust before those that are their betters both by birth and qualitie: and this malapert sawcines maketh them to be

[126] Fuller, *Holy State*, p. 49.
[127] Finch, *Wealth of Five Northamptonshire Families*, pp. 5-29.
[128] Kearney, *Scholars and Gentlemen*, p. 25.
[129] Sir Nicholas Harris Nicolas, *Memoirs of the Life and Times of Sir Christopher Hatton* (London: Richard Bentley, 1847), p. 211.

the more hateful to as many as know from whence they are descended.[130]

For all the complaints, the rewards of preferment continued to be so substantial that the supply of offices eventually ran far behind the growing ranks of privileged office seekers.[131]

Not so the supply of brides. Despite the problems involved, plenty of daughters of wealthy yeomen or merchants agreed "to be maried after with 10,000$^l$ to some Covetouse Mongrell."[132] And if their plebeian marriage portions shored up the weak prospects of their gentlemen husbands, plenty of brides had gentle blood that constituted the principal dowry they brought to their prosperous yeoman or merchant husbands. "Nathelesse some hungry Squire for hope of good / Matches the churles Sonne into gentle blood."[133] John Shakespeare supported his application for a coat of arms with his marriage to Nancy Arden, daughter of Robert Arden of Wilmcote, gentleman.[134] In 1591, Lord Stafford asked Burghley to pressure "a riche citizen for his only dowghter and heire to be maryed unto my sonne."[135] Though Burghley would never have approved such a match, and though they were not customary among the peerage, these alliances were common enough at the fringes of privilege to occasion contemporary notice. Marston quipped:

> No soner is the wealthy Marchant dead,
> His wife left great in faire possessions
> But giddie rumor graspes it twixt his teeth

---

[130] Fuller, *Holy State*, p. 49; Rich, *Roome for a Gentleman*, p. 3.

[131] See Mark H. Curtis, "The Alienated Intellectuals of Early Stuart England," *Past and Present* 23 (November 1962): 25-43; Trevor-Roper, *Gentry*, p. 21; Gerald Edward Aylmer, *The King's Servants: The Civil Service of Charles I, 1625-1642* (London: Routledge and Kegan Paul, 1961), pp. 69-252; Stone, *Crisis*, pp. 466-468. Stone sets the ratio of aspirants to jobs at 5 to 1 for the 500 leading county families, 30 to 1 for the remaining gentry; he does not include those still seeking to establish themselves.

[132] T. Wilson, "State of England," p. 191.

[133] Joseph Hall, *Virgidemiarum* (London, 1597), $C_3$.

[134] For other examples, see Campbell, *English Yeoman*, p. 56.

[135] Stone, *Crisis*, pp. 629-630. In reporting the match to Sir Robert Sydney,

And shakes it bout our eares. Then thether flock
A rout of crased fortunes, whose crakt states
Gape to be sodderd up by the right masse
Of the deceased's labores. . . .[136]

Conservatives showed less charity toward these marriages, but the unions continued nonetheless, cementing the new wealth firmly into the established structure of privilege.

NUMBERS OF THE PRIVILEGED

Reasonable estimates of the number of privileged persons in England are difficult to determine, both because reliable demographic data is lacking and because this particular group was rapidly enlarging. So was the population as a whole, as everyone noted. "That the number of our people is multiplied, it is both demonstrable to the eye and evident in reason, considering on the one side that nowadays not only young folks of all sorts but churchmen also of each degree do marry and multiply at liberty, which was wont not to be, and on the other side that we have not, God be thanked, been touched with any extreme mortality, either by sword or sickness, that might abate the overgrown number of us."[137] Modern research supports Lambarde's observations, postulating a rise from some 3,800,000 in 1576 to about 4,000,000 in 1600 and about 5,000,000 by 1642.[138]

---

Whyte said, "My Lord *Staffordes* Sonne is basely married to his Mothers Chambermaid." See Arthur Collins, ed., *Letters and Memorials of State* (London, 1746), I, 363.

[136] John Marston, *What You Will*, in *Plays*, ed. H. Harvey Wood (London: Oliver and Boyd, 1934), II, 242.

[137] Conyers Read, ed., *William Lambarde and Local Government* (Ithaca, N.Y.: Cornell University Press, 1962), p. 182.

[138] See G.S.L. Tucker, "English Pre-Industrial Population Trends," *Economic History Review*, 2d ser. 16 (1963): 209, 211-212; Josiah Cox Russell, *British Medieval Population* (Albuquerque: University of New Mexico Press, 1948), pp. 271-272; Julian Cornwall, "English Population in the Early Sixteenth Century," *Economic History Review*, 2d ser. 23 (1970): 43-44; F. V. Emery, "England *circa* 1600," and H. C. Darby, "The Age of the Improver: 1600-1800,"

Over a one-hundred-year period, from 1542 to 1642, the population of England as a whole doubled, but the size of the privileged groups trebled.[139] The reasons for their disproportionate increase are to be found in a higher birth rate and in the upward movement of new families into the top levels of society.

But what of specific estimates of the numbers of the privileged? Out of the total population, Sir Thomas Wilson determined that in 1601 there were some 60 peers, 500 knights, and 16,000 of the lesser gentry. However, he gave no figures for the clergy, and he specifically excluded 10,000 "yeomen of the richest sort" and all merchants.[140] Thus to what extent his figures reflected the newly privileged is not clear. Some of the 2,320 families granted new coats of arms by 1600 or the 3,823 elevations to knighthoods and baronetcies may have been included but certainly not all of them. Besides, Wilson was referring to families rather than to individuals. With the average number of children from first marriages set at 4.11 (allowing for infant deaths),[141] not to mention the children of second and third marriages, the size of the privileged minority was obviously substantial—far in excess of 100,000. A figure in excess of 100,000 accords with even the most conservative of all modern estimates,[142] but the actual number was probably much higher. By the 1630s, 2.5 percent of the male population were being educated in an institution of higher learning,[143] though university entrants do not begin to account for all the privileged.

---

in *A New Historical Geography of England*, ed. H. C. Darby (Cambridge: Cambridge University Press, 1973), pp. 231, 304, respectively.

[139] Stone, "Social Mobility," pp. 23-24. He sets the fertility rate for peers at a replacement of 1.5 between 1550 and 1600.

[140] T. Wilson, "State of England," pp. 22-24, 19, respectively.

[141] Stone, *Crisis*, pp. 166-174, and Appendix 13, p. 768.

[142] Ibid., p. 51. Stone sets the number at 2 percent of the population, but he restricts himself to the bona fide gentry and focuses upon the aristocracy. In his article on "Social Mobility," he variously sets the privileged sector at 5 percent and 10 percent (pp. 16, 20).

[143] Stone, "Educational Revolution," p. 57. The percentage was probably higher, since Stone has set his figures for university entrants at a minimum.

Probably a more just estimate is Peter Laslett's figure of 4 to 5 percent of the population.[144]

When adjusted to reflect a trebling in size over the course of a century, the suggested percentages for numbers of the privileged yield the following possibilities:

| Year | Total Population | Numbers of the Privileged | | |
|------|------------------|---------------------------|---|---|
| 1542 | 2,500,000 | 75,000 (3%) | 100,000 (4%) | 125,000 (5%) |
| 1576 | 3,800,000 | 133,000 (3.5%) | 178,000 (4.7%) | 220,000 (5.8%) |
| 1603 | 4,000,000 | 160,000 (4%) | 213,000 (5.3%) | 264,000 (6.6%) |
| 1642 | 5,000,000 | 225,000 (4.5%) | 300,000 (6%) | 375,000 (7.5%) |

These figures are not intended as anything like a census count but rather are designed to show the range of possibilities that emerge from a correlation between the general population and various estimates of the percentage of the privileged. The increase in size, regardless of the percentage used, of course reflects the higher birth rate and survival rate of this group, as well as the steady accretion of new members from other social strata. The fairest conclusion that can be reached regarding the total size of the privileged minority is that their numbers ranged from a bare minimum of 130,000 or so in 1576 to as many as 350,000 or more by 1642.

These, then, were the privileged, including the families of all the wellborn, well-educated, wealthy, and powerful men in England. They enjoyed a superior life, exercised rights denied to everyone else, assumed obligations not required of anyone else, expected total freedom from manual labor, pursued riches or power or pleasure. A convergence of political and economic forces swelled their ranks with prosperous and ambitious yeomen and merchants, who sought and won the external trappings of membership in the elite, despite the complaints of the conservative and the displaced. These privileged few, crowding into London, possessed ample time and means to patronize the drama.

[144] Laslett, *World We Have Lost*, p. 26. He variously refers to one in twenty (p. 42) and one in twenty-five (p. 216).

# · III ·

# *The Privileged in London*

Renaissance London was not England writ large—it was not a gigantic multiplication of life in hamlet, manor, countryside, and shire. London was quite different, and her difference stemmed partly from sheer size. By 1576, the city contained at least 150,000 residents; by 1642, perhaps 350,000. Norwich and Bristol, the next largest cities, numbered a mere 12,000-13,000,[1] and most parishes could number communicants at a few hundred or less. It is now almost impossible to imagine the shocking disparity between open countryside or small clusters of houses along a few streets and a metropolis crowded with buildings, labyrinthine with highways and passageways, and teeming with people. Nor can the exotic character of the city be overemphasized. Flemish, Dutch, Italian, Spanish, French, even Blackamoors and Indians came there, dressing strangely, observing outlandish customs, speaking their native tongues or accenting the English language in peculiar ways. Englishmen, too, displayed a fantastic spectrum of humanity. The Queen or King, attended by the royal party, might pass through the streets or move down the Thames upon barges in magnificent splendor. The Lord Mayor's pageant presented dazzling spectacle year after year. Burly soldiers and seamen elbowed the swarms of beggars, blue-capped apprentices, gentlemen in silks and velvets, sober-suited divines, cutpurses, strumpets, marketwomen. A forest of masts filled the harbor, and a fleet of watermen's boats plied the river, as carts rumbled along the streets past the occasional coach or carriage, maneuvering perilously through the throngs of people. Shops

---

[1] A. L. Rowse, *The England of Elizabeth* (London: Macmillan, 1950), p. 159; Peter Clark and Paul Slack, *Crisis and Order in English Towns, 1500-1700* (London: Routledge and Kegan Paul, 1972), pp. 30-31.

offered the luxuries of the world for sale, while great theaters, baiting rings, brothels, and taverns offered the pleasures of the world for sale. Yes, London was different. No other place in England could be remotely compared with this mushrooming city. First-time visitors from the country must have felt like travelers to some fabled land.

COURT ATTENDANCE

For the privileged, London possessed special attractions that drew them to live and visit the city in increasing numbers. Perhaps the primary attraction was the Court. John Stow observed that

> the Court, which is now a dayes much greater & more gallant then in former times, and which was wonte to bee contented to remaine with a small companie, sometimes at an Abbey or Priorie, sometimes at a Bishops house, and sometimes at some meane Mannor of the kings own, is now for the most part either abiding at London, or else so neare vnto it, that . . . the Gentlemen of all shires do flie and flock to this Citty.[2]

By 1603, eight royal residences stood along the Thames, all within easy reach of London: Windsor, Hampton Court, Oatlands, Richmond, Westminster, Whitehall, the Tower, and Greenwich. The gift of Denmark House to Queen Anne added a ninth palace. Despite royal progresses and hunting expeditions into the country, London remained the chief locus of the Court throughout the period.

As a result, all who served Queen or King, from the most eminent noble advisors to the most obscure household officers, together with all who sought favor with the monarch or served the courtiers, inevitably found themselves in London, either

[2] John Stow, *A Survey of London*, ed. Charles Lethbridge Kingsford (Oxford: Clarendon Press, 1908), II, 211-212; hereafter cited as Stow, *Survey*, ed. Kingsford, to avoid confusion with the 1754-1755 edition. For a good general description, see T. F. Reddaway, "London and the Court," *Shakespeare Survey* 17 (1964): 3-12.

temporarily or permanently. Queen Elizabeth early on considered herself pestered with the parasites who attached themselves to members of her Court. She issued commands "that all vagabonds and other idle persons which have used to follow the court, [are] to depart thence within 24 hours" and "that no person or persons, of what estate or degree soever he or they be of, do from henceforth keep any more number of persons or servants retaining unto them within the court than doth appertain unto them to do; nor that any of them shall keep any pages or boys to be attendant upon any of them within the said court."[3]

However, such commands against parasites proved futile. As Giovanni Botero noted, the locale of the monarch invariably attracted people:

> it doth infinitely avail to the magnifyinge and making cities greate and populous [to have] the residency of the prince therein, . . . for where the prince is resident there also the parliaments are held and the supreme place of justice is there kept. All matters of importance have recourse to that place, all princes and all persons of account, ambassadores of princes and of commonwealths . . . make their repair thither; . . . all such as aspire and thirst after offices and honours run thither amain with emulation and disdain at others. Thither are the revenues brought that pertain unto the state, and there are they disposed out again.[4]

PREFERMENT

Quite obviously, Court attendance might have been a duty for some and a pleasure for others, but for a great many it was also a necessity. There was simply no other way to obtain the offices

---

[3] 2 September 1561; Paul L. Hughes and James F. Larkin, eds., *Tudor Royal Proclamations* (New Haven: Yale University Press, 1969), II, 173.

[4] Giovanni Botero, *A Treatise Concerning the Causes of the Magnificencie and Greatness of Cities*, trans. Robert Pearson, and *The Reason of State*, trans. P. J. and D. P. Waley (New Haven: Yale University Press, 1956), p. 261.

and favors that lay within royal control or were dispensed by the circle of royal favorites. Burghley was blunt about it: "As fishees are gotten with baytes, so ar offices caught with sekyng," so that a man without a friend at Court was "like a hop without a pole."[5] The Earl of Essex profited to the tune of £300,000 when he enjoyed the Queen's favor, and if few aspired to such munificent rewards, everyone hoped for some share in the bonanza:[6] a post in the royal household, perhaps, or the wardship of a rich orphan, a license or a stewardship, some land or a profitable lease, a title or the spoils of confiscation—the list of favors was endless. Even so notorious a character as the cutpurse Margaret Harding managed to stave off her execution until 1582 through her Court connections: "And there was now a Gentleman at the Court, that had an hundred Marks of her. The Woman had before the Benefit of sundry other Pardons, as well general as special: Such Prevalency had her Bribes at Court, or so dexterous were her Cheats, that they procured her many Friends to intercede for her."[7] With some justification, Thomas Wilson complained: "Of the Confiscations of Capitall offenders of late there comes no greate profett to the Queen, for as they happen nowe a daies seldom soe when they hapen (yea and before many times) one impudent cortier or other, for his greate service done in standing an houre or 2 in a day barheaded in the presence chamber, is ready to begge them, soe they seldome

[5] *Calendar of State Papers, Domestic, of the Reigns of Edward VI, Mary, Elizabeth, and James* (Great Britain: Public Record Office, 1856-1872), I, 309.

[6] Ibid., I, 554, 583; Lawrence Stone, "The Anatomy of the Elizabethan Aristocracy," *Economic History Review*, 18 (1948): 28. See also the work of H. R. Trevor-Roper, *The Gentry, 1540-1640, Economic History Review*, supplement 1 (1953), pp. 10-11, 17, *passim*, and "The Elizabethan Aristocracy: An Anatomy Anatomized," *Economic History Review*, 2d ser. 3 (1950-1951): 279-298; Wallace T. MacCaffrey, "Place and Patronage in Elizabethan Politics," in *Elizabethan Government and Society*, ed. S. T. Bindoff, Joel Hurstfield, C. H. Williams (London: Athlone Press, 1961), pp. 95-126.

[7] John Stow, *A Survey of the Cities of London and Westminster and the Borough of Southwark*, Corrected, Improved and very much Enlarged . . . by John Strype (London: W. Imrys, J. Richardson et al., 1754-1755), II, 541. See Chapter II, note 41.

or never come into the exchequer."[8] Whatever the prize, it required attendance at Court, the ear of a patron, and gifts to ensure the desired reward.

Of course the Court was not the only place in London where preferment obtained. Like so many satellite princes, the nobility also dispensed benefits. And the steady stream of friends and favor-seekers who applied to the nobility helped to swell still further the numbers of the privileged who came crowding into London. Again, Botero was astute in his judgment on this matter:

> experience teacheth [that] the residence of noblemen in cities makes them to be more glorious and more populous not only because they bring their people and their families unto it, but also more because a nobleman dispendeth much more largely, through the access of friends unto him and through the emulation of others in a city where he is abiding and visited continually by honourable personages.[9]

Usually the "honourable personages" merely wanted a favor, perhaps a recommendation or a timely word to the crown. Often they asked the nobleman to provide a sophisticated rearing for their offspring or for the sons of friends or kin. Francis Cottington, for example, was trained in the London household of Sir Edward Stafford from the age of eleven until his patron's death in 1605. Francis then obtained a place in the service of Sir Charles Cornwallis, newly appointed ambassador to the Spanish Court of King Philip II.[10] Such places of service were particularly in demand, for a position in the household of a powerful lord offered the promise of advancement, security, and a luxurious life to talented, ambitious gentlemen.[11] Each of the

---

[8] Sir Thomas Wilson, "The State of England (1600)," ed. F. J. Fisher, *Camden Miscellany*, 3d ser. 52 (1936): 28.

[9] Botero, *Treatise*, p. 260.

[10] Martin J. Havran, *Caroline Courtier: The Life of Lord Cottington* (Columbia: University of South Carolina Press, 1973), pp. 3-5.

[11] Lawrence Stone, *The Crisis of the Aristocracy* (Oxford: Clarendon Press, 1965), pp. 289-294.

London houses of the nobility had its clutch of privileged retainers entrusted with the management of their master's affairs
as cofferer, comptroller, steward, secretary, or solicitor. Their
household accounts regularly identified them as "gentleman"
or "esquire," clearly indicating their social standing.[12] According
to Brathwaite, "I have known, not only gentlemen of great
livings, but also many Knights, yea Barons' sons, and some
Earls' sons, to serve Earls in places of office."[13]

Gentlemen retainers who did not live permanently in London
could expect to be sent there frequently on their lord's business.
The private correspondence of Rowland Whyte to the Sidney
family and his newsletters to the Earl of Shrewsbury testified
to constant missions to London. In 1595, Sir Robert Sidney sent
Whyte to "sollicit his Affairs at the Court and to relate to him
what passed there," and for five years the correspondent sent
back a series of letters written from "London" or "the Strand"
or "the Black Boy in the Strand" or a "Scriveners ship [shop]
by the Exchange" or "Capt. Berries Chamber in Fleetstreat."[14]
In fact, Whyte's last letter, written 27 July 1626, came from
Baynard's Castle in London, saying, "I stay here 3 or 4 Dayes
longer, to see whither the King will bestow these Places spoken
of."[15] Like Whyte, agents, correspondents, attorneys, and stew-
ards moved in and out of London throughout their careers,
conducting the complicated affairs of the noblemen they served
and garnering for themselves whatever offices, gratuities, and
opportunities came their way.

Besides the Court and the nobility, the power structure of

[12] G. R. Batho, ed., *The Household Papers of Henry Percy, Ninth Earl of
Northumberland (1564-1632)*, Camden Society Publications, 3d ser. 93 (1962):
29, 43, 44, 66, 77, 85.

[13] Richard Braithwaite, *The English Gentleman and The English Gentle-
woman*, 3d ed. (London, 1641), p. 15. For further examples of gentlemen
serving in noble households, see Stone, *Crisis*, pp. 207-209, 288-293.

[14] Algernon Sidney, Lord de l'Isle and Dudley, *Report on the Manuscripts
of Lord de l'Isle and Dudley* (Great Britain: Historical Manuscripts Commission,
1925-1966), II, 176, 477, 242, 245, respectively.

[15] Arthur Collins, ed., *Letters and Memorials of State* (London, 1746), II,
369-370.

the City of London itself had favors to dispense. The records were filled with almost daily requests. In 1580, the Lord Mayor and aldermen received a letter from Lord Burghley, the Earl of Leicester, and Sir Francis Walsingham asking the place of attorney in the Guildhall for Valentine Penson; in 1611 came a letter from Sir Julius Caesar asking offices for a poor kinsman, Rowland Hinton; in 1624, Sir William Jones received an epistle asking the appointment of Mr. Edward Bushopp as one of the City's counsel.[16] These solicitations typified not only the hundreds of petitions for particular appointments but also the interlocking system of preferment among the powerful and the privileged in Court and City.

The periodic sessions of Parliament also brought the privileged to London and also represented another center of patronage and favor. Hosts of petitioners accompanied the members of Parliament to the city. Some were humble, like the messenger sent by the little village of Staveley in 1621.[17] More, however, were sophisticated manipulators of the system of gifts and rewards, simply applying to Parliament the methods that worked so successfully everywhere else. Indeed, since it was customary for seats in the House of Commons to be passed out to favored retainers,[18] it is not surprising that Parliament indulged in preferment too.

LEGAL MATTERS

Besides advancement at the hands of the powerful, the privileged from all over England sought advancement through the London legal system. Although speaking of the growth of cities in gen-

[16] *Analytical Index, to the Series of Records Known as the Remembrancia, 1579-1664* (London: E. J. Francis, 1878), pp. 271, 233, 303, respectively. Hereafter cited as *Remembrancia*. For further examples of grants, loans, offices, and reciprocal favors with the Court, see Frank Freeman Foster, *The Politics of Stability: A Portrait of the Rulers in Elizabethan London* (London: Royal Historical Society, 1977), pp. 138, 149-151.

[17] Mildred Campbell, *The English Yeoman under Elizabeth and the Early Stuarts* (New Haven: Yale University Press, 1942), p. 151.

[18] Stone, *Crisis*, p. 291.

eral, Botero correctly assessed the effect of Westminster as the seat of justice:

> cities that have . . . courts of justice must needs be much frequented, as well for concourse of people that have cause of suit unto it, as also for the execution of justice. For it cannot be ministered without the help of . . . advocates, proctors, solicitors, notaries, and such like. Nay, more than that (which it grieves me to think on) expedition of justice cannot be made these our days without ready money.[19]

In an era when litigation was replacing violence as a means of settling disputes, the courts coped haphazardly with an explosion of suits, and lawyers enjoyed the fallout of enormous profits. Between 1550 and 1625, the number of plea rolls increased 600 percent in Common Pleas, 100 percent for the King's Bench. The Courts of Request and the Star Chamber witnessed a 1,000 percent increase in cases, and by 1621 the Chancery courts were issuing 20,000 subpoenas each year.[20] Since a final decision required at least five years—and enforcement even longer—the privileged shuttled back and forth between London and their country seats term after term. The Earl of Hertford spent more than thirty-two years in an action against Lord Mounteagle, while Henry Lord Berkeley's suit with the Dudleys lasted for some thirty-eight years—and that was only one of the fifty or so cases in which Berkeley was involved during his lifetime.[21] Strafford's biographer and legal officer reported that after 1614, "He spent eight Years Time, besides his Pains and Money in solliciting the Businesses . . . of his Nephews . . . going every Term to *London*, about that only." By 1622, his main household was located in London for more than six months of the year, and his greatest expenses were his trips to London.[22]

[19] Botero, *Treatise*, p. 253.

[20] Stone, *Crisis*, p. 240.

[21] Stone, "Anatomy of Elizabethan Aristocracy," pp. 14-15; see *Crisis*, pp. 240-242, for further discussion of this phenomenon.

[22] William Knowler, ed., *The Earl of Strafforde's Letters and Dispatches* (London, 1739), II, 436, 430, respectively.

Nor were the great nobles the only ones involved in litigation—even the clergy joined the parade to the law courts. Asked a contemporary: "How many . . . Divines have we, (I appeale to the Courts,) heires of their fathers, friends, and purchased advousons, whom the buckram bagge would not better beseeme than the Bible? being never out of law with their parishioners, following their Suites and Causes from Court to Court, Terme to Terme, no Atturney more."[23] Perhaps the most noted cleric to cool his heels during term was William Harrison, who spent his idle hours in London writing his *Description of England* and fulminating against the rapacity of the lawyers.

> The time hath been that our lawyers did sit in Paul's upon stools against the pillars and walls to get clients, but now some of them will not come from their chambers to the Guildhall in London under £10, or twenty nobles at the least. And one, being demanded why he made so much of his travel, answered that it was but folly for him to go so far when he was assured to get more money by sitting still at home. . . . But enough of these matters, for if I should set down how little law poor men can have for their small fees in these days and the great murmurings that are on all sides uttered against their excessive taking of money (for they can abide no small gain), I should extend this treatise into a far greater volume than is convenient for my purpose.[24]

So many jostled into the courts that by 1596 some special provisions had to be made for the privileged litigants. The Lord Keeper ordered that the empty room at the east side of the court had to "be reserved for men of good account in the country and for gentlemen 'towardes the lawe,' and shall not be plagued [*pester*] with 'base fellowes' and women or other suitors, as it

---

[23] Henry Peacham, *The Compleat Gentleman*, ed. G. S. Gordon (Oxford: Clarendon Press, 1906), pp. 34-35.

[24] William Harrison *The Description of England*, ed. Georges Edelen (Ithaca, N.Y.: Cornell University Press, 1968), p. 174. Harrison came to London for the law terms from 22 June to 11 July 1576, 9 October to 28 November 1576, and 23 January to 12 February 1577.

has been."[25] Despite the interminable delay, exorbitant cost, unavoidable inconvenience, and undeniable caprice of the final decision, people still flocked to London to press their cases. And the very economics of the judicial system ensured that most of the litigation came from the privileged ranks of society.

In addition to its hold on court cases, London exercised a near monopoly on other legal procedures for the elite, particularly land transfers and marriage settlements. With the increasingly complex regulations governing the lease or sale of land, London's attorneys developed an expertise in such matters that drew the privileged to consult them in unprecedented numbers. The recurrent availability of crown lands, added to the eagerness of London merchants to invest their wealth in land, simply increased the city's power as a center of land transfer.

No less important than land contracts were the marriage contracts negotiated by the privileged. Agreements swelled from a page or two into massive documents, as the lawyers and clerks took over the details. With marriage portions and jointures running into thousands of pounds,[26] careful fathers wanted to guard against any conceivable legal loophole, and the London conveyancers profited accordingly. In addition, the attorneys often acted as bride brokers. In 1607, when the Ishams were seeking a suitable match for their son and heir, John, they received information regarding the three Darcy sisters from a Mr. George Wrightington at the Middle Temple.[27] Then, too, the mercantile wealth centered in London made the city a target for those hoping to increase their fortunes by a wealthy match. Widows of merchants were especially sought after.

[25] William Paley Baildon, ed., *Les Reportes del Cases in Camera Stellata, 1593 to 1609* (privately printed, 1894), p. 39.

[26] Stone documents a tenfold increase in marriage portions between 1425 and 1675, with a tremendous upsurge from 1600 onwards. See "Marriage among the English Nobility in the Sixteenth and Seventeenth Centuries," *Comparative Studies in Society and History* 3 (1960-1961): 189, and *Crisis*, p. 641.

[27] M. E. Finch, *The Wealth of Five Northamptonshire Families, 1540-1640*, Publications of the Northamptonshire Record Society, vol. 19 (1954-1955), p. 28.

When all is gone, tis weaknesse to dispaire,
Are there not wealthy *Widdowes* eu'ry where.
Ambitious sick, woo'd part from all their *Good*;
To crowne their latter dayes with a *French-hood*?[28]

Thus, the great marriage mart of London drew the privileged, whether they were seeking a mate or aspiring to a secure contract for a match.

In some circumstances, London's judicial system claimed the presence of the privileged by force, since the city served as the place of imprisonment for important subjects who ran afoul of law or politics. Confinement may have been inconvenient and somewhat less than luxurious, but a gentleman could expect suitable company and tolerable comfort. Henry Ferrers, who handled legal affairs for himself and other Warwickshire gentry in the 1580s and 1590s, was put in jail for debt in 1590. Among his fellows there he listed "my acquayntance in the kings benche" and "gentlemen no prisoners."[29] The nobility fared even better. When Henry Percy, ninth Earl of Northumberland, was sentenced to the Tower, he sold Walsingham House; but until his release in 1621, he continued to rent both Essex House and a house on Tower Hill to accommodate such members of his household as his extensive Tower suite would not hold in comfort.[30] Even a recusant might receive special treatment if he were titled. After repeated and costly trips to London "to shewe himselfe to the Quenes Majestie," Sir Thomas Cornwallis was finally remanded into custody of the Bishop of London. Yet he obtained permission first to stay with a Mr. Blague at Lambeth, then at Sir Thomas Kytson's house, then at the house of Mr. Taylor, where he had liberty to go as far as Highgate, and finally "downe to his house in Brome for three monethes before the expiracion wherof he had Further favor to make his abode

[28] Henry Fitzgeffrey, *Satyres and Satyricall Epigrams: with Certaine Observations at Blacke-Fryars* (London, 1617), F₄.

[29] Lansdowne MSS fol. 95ᵛ; as cited by Elizabeth K. Berry, *Henry Ferrers, An Early Warwickshire Antiquary*, Dugdale Society Occasional Papers, no. 16 (1965), p. 14.

[30] Batho, ed., *Household Papers of Henry Percy*, p. xix.

wher he should best like, untill he should agayne be called for."[31] Though Sir Thomas suffered the interminability of the legal process, he also benefited from the preferential consideration accorded to its privileged victims.

## BUSINESS MATTERS

Along with the patronage system and the legal system, London's mercantile system exerted a powerful attraction upon the privileged throughout England. Despite the possible descent in social status, the potential rewards from a membership in one of the great companies had long persuaded gentry families to apprentice their younger sons in the city. As a result, interlocking webs of kinship developed between London and the various shires, so that a young man frequently served under a relative. The pattern emerged unmistakably in the records of the College of Heralds, where country families consistently listed their various city branches.

Despite the heavy involvement of the privileged in London trade, not everyone regarded such careers as permanent. Instead of founding bourgeois dynasties on the Dutch model, many merchants rose to affluence, bought land, and returned to the country, sometimes in a single lifetime, sometimes over the course of two or three generations. This cyclical pattern became well established. When Stow declared that London's "Marchantes and rich men, being satisfyed with gaine, doe for the most part marry theyr Children into the Countrey," he was merely repeating William Caxton's observation a full century earlier that London families "can vnnethe contynue vnto the thyrd heyr or scarcely to the second."[32] Fewer than a third of

[31] Recorded by Cornwallis's accountant; as quoted in Alan Simpson, *The Wealth of the Gentry, 1540-1660*, East Anglian Studies (Chicago: University of Chicago Press, 1961), p. 175.

[32] Stow, *Survey*, ed. Kingsford, II, 208. W.J.B. Crotch, *The Prologues and Epilogues of William Caxton*, Early English Text Society, no. 176 (1928), pp. 77-78. Sylvia Thrupp's study of the great companies also concludes that only a small percentage of merchants pursued trade for three generations or more.

London's Lords Mayor for the years 1576 to 1642 were themselves the sons of Londoners, and a mere handful were the grandsons of Londoners.[33]

The strong bonds between country and city also appeared in the wills of London's merchants. Over and over again, a will disposed of property in both London and some native county, made bequests to kin in both city and country, set up charities in an obscure village and a London parish, and almost always requested burial in the childhood parish of the deceased. For example, James Ayscoughe, though a resident of the parish of St. Lawrence in the Jewry, wanted to lie in the church "Closset" belonging to the manor of Nuthall, his body being "embalmed ceared and encoffined or any other way soe as it may be carried safely in good sorte to Nuthall aforesaid w$^{th}$out feare or danger of burstinge open or other disgrace in the way And in a Coache or otherwise as shalbe more fitt."[34] Ayscoughe may have been atypical in his detailed instructions for his body's removal but not in his assumption that Nuthall church was the proper place for his final rest. The now obscure man was just one among thousands of the privileged who came up to prosper in London trade and then returned to the country, living or dead.

---

See *The Merchant Class of Medieval London* (Chicago: University of Chicago Press, 1948), pp. 204-206.

[33] Stow, *Survey*, II, 225-231. The list also reveals a tremendous diversity among counties of family origin. Actually, the percentage of London-born mayors may have been higher than the percentage of London-born merchants as a whole. By 1690, when Gregory King at last provided some reasonably sound demographic data, only one-fifth of all apprentices enrolled were from London and only one-third from the greater London area (Middlesex and Surrey). See D. V. Glass, "Socio-Economic Status and Occupations in the City of London at the End of the Seventeenth Century," in *Studies in London History*, ed. A.E.J. Hollaender and William Kellaway (London: Hodder and Stoughton, 1969), p. 387. For a qualification of the conventional view of the London merchants' movement into the landed gentry, see R. G. Lang, "Social Origins and Social Aspirations of Jacobean Merchants," *Economic History Review*, 2d ser. 27 (1974): 28-29; and Foster, *Politics of Stability*, pp. 9-10, 93-94.

[34] 16 September 1618; *Calendar of Wills Proved and Enrolled in the Court of Husting, London, 1258-1688*, ed. Reginald R. Sharpe (London: Corporation of the City of London, 1890), II, 752.

Some wills shed specific light on the kinship-apprenticeship-mercantile system, as when John Holmes, a "weyvor," gave to "John, son of George Holme of Blackrode, citizen and grocer of London, one hundred pounds with which to set himself up, and his livery gown of 'browne blewe' faced with budge."[35] The young grocer no doubt welcomed his uncle's assistance, for an independent business cost enough money to separate the sons of the privileged quite radically from the common apprentice, who could expect no better future than a journeyman's wages. Even a really good London apprenticeship was too costly for the ordinary family. The Cullums paid £50 to £60 to place their son Thomas with a master, though the official rate was far lower.[36] In a good many cases, where the route to affluence had already been secured, apprenticeship represented merely a token service anyway. In guilds like the Goldsmiths' Company, eldest sons could succeed by patrimony, or the right of inheritance, if the father was a free master in the trade. And wellborn sons frequently paid only nominal attention to learning the business their families had chosen, as witnessed by the letter sent to Richard Archer in London from his concerned father: "I would willinglie heare that you stand in Mr. Rouse his shopp to wey out some spices wch. will best breede you in experience than only to talk of Tradinge and put nothinge in practise."[37] Countless young men like Richard came up to London seeking either to maintain their privileged status or, better yet, to enlarge their fortune through trade.

The lure of profit drew the privileged into other kinds of London enterprises as well. Men with wool or meat or grain to sell often found it best to deal directly with the London markets, as did Robert, Lord Spencer. By 1600, he was avoiding

[35] Dated 18 September 1568, recorded 1580; ibid., pp. 702-703.

[36] Simpson, *Wealth of the Gentry*, p. 116; O. Jocelyn Dunlop and Richard D. Denman, *English Apprenticeship and Child Labour* (New York: Macmillan, 1912), p. 46.

[37] Philip Styles, *Sir Simon Archer, 1581-1662*, Dugdale Society Occasional Papers, no. 6 (1946), p. 11. Richard Archer really did not have to worry about weighing out spices. By 1619 he had married the daughter and heir of Rowland Ball of Neithrop near Banbury, and by 1623 he had come into his wife's estates.

the uncertainties of local conditions through exclusive sales to one or two London butchers.[38] Stow indicated that Lord Spencer's practice was common: "For hereby it commeth to passe that the Gentlemen . . . playing the Farmours, Grasiars, Brewers or such like, more then Gentleman were wont to doe within the Countrie, Retaylers and Artificers, at the least of such thinges as pertayne to the backe or belly, do leaue the Countrie townes, where there is no vent, and do flie to London, where they be sure to finde ready and quick market."[39] The nobility also became heavily involved in land development in the City and its suburbs, while lesser men found that even modest investment in London real estate netted excellent returns. Foreign trade offered another opportunity for making money, with London acting as the center for entry into these ventures. Out of some 5,000 known investors in overseas exploits between 1575 and 1630, more than 70 percent could clearly be identified as members of the privileged levels of society. More striking, almost half of the gentry investors were also members of Parliament, their involvement generally being preceded by a trip to London to sit in Commons. For example, of the 478 gentlemen in the Virginia Company, 275 sat in Parliament, and 188 of the 275 entered Commons either before or during the same year as their investment.[40] Finally, for those among the privileged with sophisticated talents or professional skills, London stood virtually alone in offering any hope of fame or financial success. Writers, artists, architects, musicians, and physicians inevitably converged upon the city because, like the apprenticed younger son or the member of Parliament with cash to invest or the baron with meat to sell, they could not make as much money anywhere else.

The availability of mercantile capital made London the preeminent center for the moneylending business. According to the

[38] Finch, *Wealth of Five Northamptonshire Families*, pp. 44-45.
[39] Stow, *Survey*, ed. Kingsford, II, 212.
[40] Theodore K. Rabb, "Investment in English Overseas Enterprise, 1575-1630," *Economic History Review*, 2d ser. 19 (1966): 71-79; Sidney Pollard and David W. Crossley, *The Wealth of Britain, 1085-1966* (New York: Schocken Books, 1969), p. 123.

records, the privileged constantly needed more money. The aristocracy ran up debts as immense as the £121,000 owed by the Earl of Arundel.[41] While young Edward Wingfield contracted a far more modest debt, it was sufficient for him to stand in danger of prosecution before he was even of age.[42] Indebtedness became a way of life for many a gentleman, a vice gently scoffed at by the poets.

> To Borrow is a *Vertue*, when to Lend,
> Is to beget an euerlasting freind:
> And may a man haue more said in his grace,
> Then to be *Credited* in euery place?
> Hee's not a Gentleman I dare maintaine,
> Whose *Word* runnes not as Current as his *Coyne*.
> .........................................................
> His swaggering *Humor*, vowes that all he spends,
> He getteth brauely by his *Fingersends*.
> There's not a *Cheapside* Mercer (if he looke)
> That will not sweare to't deeply on his booke.
> No notedd *No[t]ary* in *Cornwell* row,
> But is subscribed *Witnesse* there too.
> *Silkmen, Haberdashers, Tradesmen* all:
> Inamor'd on him, for his *Custome* call,
> And he takes *all* of them . . .[43]

With a solid 10 percent in interest to be realized on loans and an inexhaustible demand for those loans, it was no wonder that "generally al Merchants, when they haue gotten any great wealth, leaue trading and fall to Vsury, the gaine whereof is so easie, certain, and great."[44] Henry Percy complained that when he was forced to pay his debts by selling his woods, there were "jewellers and silkmen making their nests in the branches."[45] Silkmen James Anton and Sir Baptist Hicks, draper John Lang-

[41] Stone, *Crisis*, p. 543.

[42] 28 January 1582; *Remembrancia*, pp. 490-491.

[43] Fitzgeffrey, *Satyres and Satyricall Epigrams*, F$_3$$^v$-F$_4$$^v$.

[44] Sir Thomas Culpeper, *A Tract aginst Usurie* (London, 1621), A$_2$.

[45] Henry Percy, Ninth Earl of Northumberland, *Advice to his Son*, ed. G. B. Harrison (London: Ernest Benn, 1930), p. 82.

ley, goldsmiths Sir William Herrick and Alexander Prescot, brewer Abraham Campion, mercer Sir William Stone, grocer Richard Burrell, and clothworker Sir John Spencer all profited from moneylending.[46] Such merchants, together with certain affluent lawyers and officers of the Court who had access to crown funds, floated the loans with which the highly privileged maintained themselves in luxury. By 1600, even the London scriveners, who had originally served only as agents to draw up legal documents, had themselves entered the lucrative money market, acting as brokers between lesser gentry, city widows, or smaller merchants with funds to invest and those in need of such funds. While some indebtedness was simply written on the books of tradesmen or secured by pawns of plate and jewels, lenders were shrewd enough to require enforceable documents, such as bills, bonds, statutes, or mortgages, for large loans. The negotiation of such loans, the preparation of the loan instruments, and the prosecution of defaults drew the privileged into London and poured a stream of gold into the laps of lawyers and lenders alike.[47]

EDUCATION

Still another of London's attractions for the privileged was its unique array of educational opportunities. Though Oxford and Cambridge claimed the country's great universities, London offered the Inns of Court and Chancery, St. Paul's and the Merchant Taylors' schools, plus a wealth of lectures, tutors, and specialized instruction available nowhere else in the kingdom. The Inns of Court naturally drew the most notable contingent of young gentlemen down to the city.[48] The ambitious, the conscientious, the financially insecure no doubt applied them-

[46] Stone, *Crisis*, pp. 532-534.

[47] A fuller discussion of indebtedness is presented by Stone, "Anatomy of Elizabethan Aristocracy," and *Crisis*, pp. 505-546; see also Trevor-Roper, "Elizabethan Aristocracy: An Anatomy Anatomized," and *Gentry*.

[48] Peer-esquires comprised 40.6 percent of the enrollment, gentlemen, 47.8 percent. See Wilfrid R. Prest, *The Inns of Court under Elizabeth I and the Early Stuarts, 1590-1640* (London: Longmans, 1972), p. 30.

selves seriously to the bolts and moots and readings, sitting in on court sessions, digging through law books, studying with tutors, serving out the seven years in commons before the call to the bar, spending three years as Utter Barrister before admission to full practice, and perfecting legal skills during several additional years. But these constituted a decided minority. Between 1590 and 1639, only one in six admitted to the Inns was even called to the bar.[49] Most of the "young Gentlemen, the sonnes of the best or better sort of Gentlemen of all the Shires of England"[50] came to London's Inns of Court primarily for reasons of prestige and only secondarily for a smattering of the law.

Lacking the close supervision of the universities, the Inns housed a set of several hundred wealthy and essentially idle young men. Their letters home constantly requested money, no matter what the size of their allowances. Thomas Archer begged funds for clothes, "for what I have is almost past wearinge."[51] Some notion of the sort of expense he had in mind was revealed by the £24 Edward Heath's father laid out in 1630 for a new cloak and suit, in addition to £13 for a length of green velvet.[52] Rooms cost money too. After several weeks of temporary lodging young George Radcliffe wrote, "If you can provide me 20 pounde I can buy a fair chamber therewith, together with what my good friends will lend me." A month later he reported, "I am now about a chamber: it is a faire chamber, butt will coste me much. Send me worde when I shall have money towardes it, and how much you can well provide. I have already taken uppe of my quarterage 9 pounde, and I shall neede more this quarter 3 pounde."[53] With dancing, dueling, dinners, drink-

[49] Ibid., p. 52.
[50] Sir George Buck, "The Third Universitie of England," in John Stow, *Annales, or a General Chronicle of England,* continued and augmented . . . by Edmund Howes (London, 1631), p. 1,073.
[51] Styles, *Sir Simon Archer,* p. 11.
[52] Prest, *Inns of Court,* p. 28.
[53] 17 April 1613 and 11 May 1613; T. D. Whitaker, *The Life and Original Correspondence of Sir George Radcliffe* (London: J. Nichols and Son, 1810), pp. 92, 93.

ing, dicing, and all the other delights of the city, the temptation to fall into dissipation often proved irresistible. According to Francis Lenton's rhymes:

> Now here the ruine of Youth begins,
> For when the Country cannot finde out sinnes
> To fit his humor, *London* doth inuent
> Millions of vices, that are incident
> To his aspiring minde . . .[54]

Of the Inns of Court men, Harrison complained, "the younger sort of them abroad in the streets are scarce able to be bridled by any good order at all."[55] George Whetstone probably put it most accurately: "Those that are disposed, studdie lawes; who so liketh, without checke, maye followe dalliance."[56]

If the Inns of Court occasioned the most comment, they certainly were not unique in catering to the educational requirements of the privileged in London. The Inns of Chancery—eight in all—supplied the needs of those who wished either to try the law and then transfer to an Inn of Court or else to establish a more restricted legal practice. Regular lectures in surgery and anatomy were held by the College of Physicians "for the better enabling of the Chirurgians or Surgians in and about London."[57] Sir Thomas Gresham provided revenues to establish lectures in law, rhetoric, divinity, music, physics, geometry, and astronomy, with the first Gresham professors installed at Michaelmas in 1598.[58] The Gresham lectures stood out as the most noted of the period, but ten years earlier Sir Thomas Smith (later the first Governor of the East India Company), along with other London merchants, had set up a mathematical lecture covering navigation, geometry, astronomy,

[54] Francis Lenton, *The Young Gallant's Whirligig* (London, 1629), pp. 3-4.
[55] Harrison, *Description of England*, p. 76.
[56] George Whetstone, "Dedicatory Epistle," *The English Myrror* (London, 1586).
[57] Buck, "Third Universitie," p. 1,079.
[58] Kenneth Charlton, *Education in Renaissance England* (London: Routledge and Kegan Paul, 1965), pp. 283-284.

geography, and hydrography, with Thomas Hood as the first lecturer.

A growing number of writing masters, including John Davies and the famous Peter Bales, who won the pen of gold in the 1591 "Combat of the Pen,"[59] taught the various hands of writing. Especially noteworthy to contemporaries was "the Art of *Brachygraphie*, which is an Art newly discouered, and newly recouered, and is of very good and necessary vse, being well and honestly exercised: for by the meanes and helpe thereof (they which know it) can readily take a Sermon, Oration, Play, or any long speech, as they are spoken, dictated, acted, and vttered in the instant."[60] Visiting England in 1641, Comenius was so impressed with the young men transcribing sermons that he claimed, "Almost all of them acquire this art of rapid writing, as soon as they have learnt at school to read the scriptures. It takes them about another year to learn the art of shorthand."[61]

How many of the wellborn or the well educated found such practical skills useful, it is impossible to say. Without question, however, the privileged patronized London's many foreign language tutors. Pupils could study not only the Greek and Latin familiar to them from grammar school onwards but also Hebrew, Chaldean, Syriac, Arabic, Italian, Spanish, French, Dutch, Polish, Persian, Morisco, Turkish, Muscovian, Sclavonian—"in brief diuers other Languages fit for Ambassadors and Orators, and Agents for Merchants, and for Trauailers, and necessary for all Commerce or Negotiation whatsoeuer."[62]

According to Sir George Buck, certain other arts taught in the "Third University" of London were exclusively designed for the privileged—horsemanship, the military art ("the proper occupation and profession of Princes and Gentlemen"), swimming, dancing ("commendable & fit for a Gentleman"), her-

---

[59] Stow, *Survey*, I, 128-129.

[60] Buck, "Third Universitie," p. 1,084.

[61] Robert Fitzgibbon Young, *Comenius in England* (Oxford: Oxford University Press, 1932), p. 65.

[62] Buck, "Third Universitie," p. 1,082.

aldry, and music.[63] Fencing schools proved especially popular, as dueling became the gentleman's sport, thanks to royal proclamations against teaching the art to "the multitude of the common people."[64] In 1576, Rocco Bonetti set up school in Blackfriars, and in the 1590s, Jeronimo and Vicentio Saviola set up another. By 1605, the London Masters of Defence obtained a warrant for incorporation.[65]

If a gentleman sought more esoteric learning, he could always apply to London's many *"Philosophers, Cabalists, Thomists, Scotists, Humanists, Philologers, Historians, Politicians, Astrologers, Antiquaries,"*[66] and the like. And some did. London boasted a circle of highly talented theoretical experimenters, including Raleigh's set at the Tower of London. Asorius reported that "many . . . excellinge in qualities of witte, to avoide a Courtiers life, have addicted them selves to the dimensions of Geometry, or the rules of Phisicke, or the recordes and sweet Harmony of Musicke."[67] It must not be forgotten, too, that London virtually monopolized the publication of books, which provided the age's most important form of learning—but only to people with the ability to read the books and the money to buy them. Thus London's impressive panoply of informal education, much of it extremely sophisticated, supplemented the rather limited regime of the formal school system.

Yet, in addition, London also offered the very best of formal schooling; and, not surprisingly, the privileged throughout the kingdom frequently sent their children to St. Paul's or the Merchant Taylors' School, where they were educated alongside the sons of the city's privileged. Theoretically, a certain number of places were reserved for poor men's children, but the defi-

[63] Ibid., pp. 1,082-1,086.

[64] 12 February 1566; Hughes and Larkin, eds., *Tudor Royal Proclamations*, II, 282.

[65] Stone, *Crisis*, p. 244.

[66] Buck, "Third Universitie," p. 1,087.

[67] Asorius, *Civile Nobilitie*, Bk. I, fol. 5b-6a; as cited by Ruth Kelso, *The Doctrine of the English Gentleman in the Sixteenth Century*, University of Illinois Studies in Language and Literature, no. 14 (1929), p. 125.

nition of "poor" proved fairly elastic: plenty of gentry families were eager for the secure nominations to St. John's College that awaited Merchant Taylors' boys with at least three years' seniority. When the plague struck in 1630, Headmaster Gray had "divers Gentlemens children boarding with him,"[68] while at an earlier date, Richard Mulcaster had been reproved for boarding an excessive number of scholars in his home.[69] London's less prestigious schools received some share of gentlemen's children and also produced some humbly born scholars who went on to the universities and into the ranks of the privileged. For example, the adventurer and classicist Thomas Farnaby reportedly taught more than three hundred young aristocrats and others at his school in Goldsmith's Alley.[70] Between meeting the needs of its own citizenry and supplying specialized training for the whole of England, London supported an immense educational complex, attracting the privileged for training of every sort at every level. Over half the male population were literate,[71] and a truly astonishing number were men of intellectual, cultural, or social sophistication.

## PLEASURE AND LUXURY

While education, litigation, and ambition unquestionably drew the privileged into London, the city's diversions were so unique that many people came for pleasure alone, with or without the excuse of legitimate business. To begin with, the very congregation of large numbers from the upper social strata offered the stimulating company of one's peers and superiors instead of the

[68] F.W.M. Draper, *Four Centuries of Merchant Taylors' School, 1561-1961* (London: Oxford University Press, 1962), p. 53.

[69] Richard L. DeMolen, "Richard Mulcaster: An Elizabethan Servant," *Shakespeare Studies* 8 (1975): 39n.

[70] F. J. Fisher, "The Development of London as a Centre of Conspicuous Consumption in the Sixteenth and Seventeenth Centuries," in *Essays in Economic History*, ed. E. M. Carus-Wilson (London: Edward Arnold, 1962), II, 200.

[71] Lawrence Stone, "The Educational Revolution in England, 1560-1640," *Past and Present* 28 (July 1964): 68.

restricted social life of the country. Complaints about the dullness of rural existence mounted as increasing numbers were exposed to the glitter of London, their appetites for pleasure permanently whetted during impressionable years spent in school or at the Inns of Court. From his exile at Wilton in 1601, the Earl of Pembroke voiced a common opinion: "I have not yet been a day in the country and I am as weary of it as if I had been prisoner there seven year." Even the cards were dull and out of date, for "here there is no game known but trump."[72] By contrast, the city abounded with intrigue, gossip, gambling, whoring, dueling, theaters, lavish feasts, outré fashions, and every bizarre amusement known to the period. Two live young crocodiles and a wild boar from Hispaniola were presented at Court in 1605. Captured porpoises, lions whelped at the Tower,[73] bears and bulls baited at Paris Garden, Holden's camel, and Banks's horse Morocco were wonders not to be seen save in London.

Nor could country seamstresses compete with London tailors. As early as 1549, the conservative voice protested: "And specially, no gentleman can be content to have either cap, coat, doublet, hose, or shirt made in his country, but they must have this gear come from London, and yet many things thereof are not there made but beyond the sea; whereby the artificers of our good towns are idle and the occupations in London, and specially of the towns beyond the sea, are set to work even upon our costs."[74] Excess in fashion grew progressively more fantas-

[72] *HMC Salisbury MSS* xi, p. 361; as cited by Stone, *Crisis*, p. 392.

[73] John Stow, *Annales, or a General Chronicle of England*, continued and augmented . . . by Edmund Howes, Gent. (London, 1631), pp. 871, 881, 844, 865, respectively.

[74] Mary Dewar, ed., *A Discourse of the Commonweal of this Realm of England*, attributed to Thomas Smith (Charlottesville: University Press of Virginia, 1969), p. 122. Although this work was first published in 1581, it was written much earlier during the late summer of 1549. Smith's complaints were borne out by the facts. Silk stockings, for example, were available only in London until after 1650. A pair cost at least 20s., more if embroidered in gold or silver. In 1575, Sir Henry Sidney paid up to £3 for a single pair. See Joan Thirsk, *Economic Policy and Projects: The Development of a Consumer Society in*

tic, as the portraits of the period attested. It could be claimed with some justification that

> except it were a dog in a doublet, you shall not see any so disguised as are my countrymen of England. And as these fashions are diverse, so likewise it is a world to see the costliness and the curiosity, the excess and the vanity, the pomp and the bravery, the change and the variety, and finally, the fickleness and the folly that is in all degrees, insomuch that nothing is more constant in England than inconstancy of attire.[75]

Statistics bore out the impression of fashion run rampant. London mercers grew in number from thirty to three hundred between 1550 and 1600, almost a ton of gold and silver thread and three tons of copper thread were shipped in from 1594 to 1598, silk imports doubled between 1592 and 1600, and smuggled velvets from the Stade alone totaled 97,500 yards in 1597.[76] In fact, purchases of luxury cloths from abroad increased sixfold, representing the largest single alteration in the pattern of English imports between 1560 and 1600.[77] With individual garments costing tens and hundreds of pounds, Ben Jonson could well advise, "First (to be an accomplished gentleman . . .) you must give o're house-keeping in the countrey, and liue altogether in the city amongst gallants; where at your first apparance, 'twere good you turn'd foure or fiue hundred acres of your best land into two or three trunks of apparel."[78]

Nor were clothes the only luxuries that gentlemen coming

---

*Early Modern England* (Oxford: Clarendon Press, 1978), pp. 109, 113, 120-121.

[75] Harrison, *Description of England*, p. 146.

[76] Stone, "Anatomy of Elizabethan Aristocracy," pp. 5-6.

[77] Stone, "Elizabethan Overseas Trade," *Economic History Review*, 2d ser. 2 (1949-1950): 49. The second largest increase was the doubling of wine imports, another luxury item.

[78] Ben Jonson, *Euery Man out of his Humour*, in *Ben Jonson*, ed. C. H. Herford and Percy Simpson (Oxford: Clarendon Press, 1925-1952), III, 445.

to London indulged in. The haberdashers specialized in tempt-
ing—and expensive—imported items.

> Their Shops made a very gay Shew, by the various foreign
> Commodities they were furnished with; and, by the Pur-
> chasing of them, the People of *London*, and of other Parts
> of *England*, began to spend extravagantly; whereof great
> Complaints were made among the graver Sort. There were
> but a few of these Milliners Shops in the Reign of King
> *Edward the Sixth*, not above a Dozen in all *London*; but,
> within forty Years after, about the Year 1580, from the City
> of *Westminster* along to *London*, every Street became full
> of them. Some of the Wares sold by these Shop-keepers were,
> Gloves made in *France* or *Spain*, Kersies of *Flanders* Dye,
> *French* Cloth or Frizado, Owches, Brooches, Agglets made
> in *Venice* or *Milan*, Daggers, Swords, Knives, Girdles of the
> *Spanish* Make, Spurs made at *Milan*, *French* or *Milan* Caps,
> Glasses, painted Cruses, Dials, Tables, Cards, Balls, Puppets,
> Penners, Inkhorns, Toothpicks, Silk-Bottoms and Silver-Bot-
> toms, fine earthen Pots, Pins and Points, Hawks-Bells, Salt-
> cellars, Spoons, and Dishes of Tin. Which made such a Shew
> in the Passengers Eyes, that they could not but gaze on them,
> and buy some of the Knicknacks, though to no Purpose nec-
> essary.[79]

Similarly, the goldsmiths' shops presented an unparalleled array of plate and jewels. Even as early as 1500, according to the
Venetian ambassador, "In one single street, named the Strand,
leading to St. Paul's, there are fifty-two goldsmiths' shops, so
rich and full of silver vessels great and small, that in all the
shops in Milan, Rome, Venice, and Florence put together, I do
not think that there would be found so many of the magnificence
that are to be seen in London."[80] With the establishment of the
Royal Exchange in 1614, London enjoyed the Renaissance

[79] Stow, *Survey*, II, 279.
[80] Charlotte Augusta Sneyd, ed. and trans., *A Relation, or rather A True Account, of the Island of England* . . . , Camden Society Publications, vol. 37 (1847), pp. 42-43.

equivalent of a two-story shopping mall, where the haberdashers

> solde Mouse-trappes, Bird Cages, Shooing-horns, Lan-
> thornes, and Jewes trumpes, &c. there was also at that time
> that kept shoppes in the upper pawne of the Royall Exchange,
> Armorours, that sold both olde and new Armor, Apothecaries,
> Booke-sellers, Goldsmiths, and Glassesellers, although now
> it is as plenteously stored, with all kinde of rich wares and
> fine commodities, as any particular place in Europe, vnto
> which place many forraine Princes dayly send, to be best
> serued of the best sort.[81]

And although Parliament might decry the importation of £2,800 worth of playing cards, £1,700 worth of tennis balls, and £178 worth of dolls,[82] the flow of extravagant goods and services into London continued unabated. Venetians set up glass houses, Dutchwomen specialized in the mysteries of starching ruffs and undergarments, Italians sold silks and damasks,[83] gardeners from the Low Countries transformed the outlying land with saffron, licorice, cherries, strawberries, and other delicacies for the tables of the privileged, while ships brought in spices, wines, oils, almonds, and currants.

The success of London merchants in pressing their expensive goods upon prosperous buyers was evident everywhere. Wills

---

[81] Stow, *Annales* (1631), p. 869.

[82] Stone, "Elizabethan Overseas Trade," p. 43.

[83] Stow reports this of the Italians:

For the *Italian* Merchants, whom the *English* Citizens could not well brook for their great Wealth, which they got here by their rich Silks and Damasks which they brought over; there were of them *Florentines, Luccasses, Venetians, Genoese,* &c. and they chiefly resided in *Broad-street* Ward, in St. *Bartholomew's* near the *Exchange,* and St. *Bennet-Fink.*

As for their Trades and Occupations, some of them followed the Calling of Merchants; others were Jewellers, Brokers, Weavers, Taylors, Shoe-makers, Stone-cutters, Hatband-makers, Potters, Painters, School-masters, Physicians, Surgeons, Joiners, and Butchers. And many were of no Trades at all, but lived of what they brought over with them.

See *Survey,* II, 403.

throughout the kingdom mentioned London luxuries—Sir William Booth of Dunham left his wife "the chaine of golde w$^{ch}$ I brought w$^{th}$ me last from London"; Richard Bradshaw bequeathed to his brother Thomas "all my apparell at London w$^{th}$ my rapier and dagger there"; Anthony Calveley passed on to his sister "iii of the spoones that were last made at London that have ii lr̄es at the endes for my name."[84] Letters to relatives in London were filled with requests for purchases. One year young George Radcliffe sent his sister a hat ("it cost 9s. or 11s. I forgette which"), and the following year he promised her a saddle ("about 6 pounde or 20 nobles will buy a faire one, with studdes well guilte").[85]

As a result of all of this self-indulgence, moralists issued stern warnings against indebtedness:

> Wel are the marchaunt men of London acquainted with the infirmities of suche gentlemen, and better acquaintaunce dayly groweth emong them, when as the pollitike deuices of the marchaunte ioyneth wyth the simplicitie of the gentleman, & neuer leaueth acquayntaunce nor familiaritie with hym vnto such tyme as the marchauntes moneye hath boughte the gentilmans land. Then is y$^e$ marchaunt lord of the gentlemans house, & the gentleman no neerer of acquayntance with the marchaunt man then though he had neuer sene him before. Take hede of this gentlemen, use your vocation in such sort as ye may haue no more to do with those kinde of men, then for your mony to haue their marchandies: it is a greate aduantage to haue a man subiecte to mony.[86]

At the same time, chauvinists proclaimed the glory of "your Citie filled more abundantly with all sorts of silkes, fine linnen,

[84] 25 November 1579, 3 September 1592; *Lancashire and Cheshire Wills and Inventories*, Chetham Society, Remains, Historical and Literary, vol. 51 (1860), p. 65; vol. 33 (1857), p. 139.

[85] 18 December 1613, 13 June 1614; Whitaker, *Life . . . of Sir George Radcliffe*, pp. 97, 102.

[86] *The Institucion of A Gentleman* (London, 1568), E$_2$.

oyles, wines, and spices, perfection of Arts, and all costly or-
naments, and curious workmanship, then any other Province:
so as London well deserues to beare the name of the choicest
storehouse in the world, and to keepe ranke with any royall
Citie in Europe."[87] Whether damnable or praiseworthy, London's "choicest storehouse" supplied unending delights for the
affluent in her midst.

Private pleasure on a grand scale became a way of life for
many of London's privileged, providing real substance to Viscount Conway's classic remark: "We eat and drink and rise up
to play and this is to live like a gentleman; for what is a gentleman but his pleasure?"[88] It pleasured Sir Francis Willoughby
to invite forty-eight gentlemen to dinner and forty-two to supper at Lincoln's Inn when he came to London one November
day in 1580.[89] It amused Sarah Harrington to gamble to the
extent of a £500 loss at cards in a single night. The Duchess of
Newcastle and her sisters fought boredom by going "to ride in
their coaches about the streets to see the concourse and recourse
of people and in the spring time to visit the Spring Garden,
Hyde Park, and the like places; and sometimes they would have
music and cup in barges upon the water."[90] Goldsmith John
Scacie went to prison for "having been in the habit, whilst apprenticed, of conveying himself through his master's doors at
midnight, to masks, banquets, and such like dissolute meetings
notwithstanding that he endangered thereby his master's goods,
and the safety of his person, through leaving the doors open
at night."[91] Lord Berkeley dissipated his entire fortune during
three years in London "having noe suites in lawe, nor daughters
then married away, forraign embassies, domesticke services in
Court or Country, nor any other extraordinary expense in the

[87] Buck, "Third Universitie," p. 1,090.
[88] As quoted by Maurice Ashley, *England in the Seventeenth Century* (Baltimore: Penguin Books, 1952), p. 18.
[89] Stone, "Anatomy of Elizabethan Aristocracy," pp. 7, 9.
[90] Henry B. Wheatley and Peter Cunningham, *London Past and Present*
(London: John Murray, 1891), III, 295.
[91] Sir Walter Sherburne Prideaux, *Memorials of the Goldsmiths' Company*
(London: Eyre and Spottiswoode, 1896), I, 94-95.

world."[92] Francis Tresham, extravagant, impulsive, deeply in debt, joined the Essex rebellion, escaped a charge of treason with a bribe of £1,000 and a fine of £2,000, and then was executed for his role in the Gunpowder Plot. His brother Lewis, having been expelled from his Inner Temple lodgings for brawling in 1599, was still fighting duels almost twenty years later.[93]

Curbs on one's pleasure were resented and resisted. Why should anything interfere with an aristocrat's fashionable pursuits? Lord William Howard (brother to the Earl of Surrey), when checked by "certain of the most discreet citizens of the best Companies" for violating the Queen's express commands against ruffs of excessive length, simply "reviled them with the very odious names of culines, rascals, and such like."[94] According to the sarcastic voice of one contemporary:

> What is a man if he knowe not howe to weare his apparell after the best facion? to kepe company with gentilmen and to play his cc nobles at cardes or dice, at tables, at post, Cente, glek, or suche other games: for he that cannot thus dooe is called a lout or a miser and one that knoweth no facion. But it becommeth a gentleman (saye they) to be a Royster, whych worde I doe not well vnderstand onles it signifie a ruffian. . . . and to bee instructed therein more at large, a yonge Gentilmanne shall easelye fynde in London, many cunnyng Scholemasters, whiche shall teache hym the verye perfection of that arte. Whereby althoughe at the fyrste he take some pleasure, followynge therein a delicious begynyng, yet the contynuauns therof chaungeth Gentry into vilany, and the ende bringeth vtter confusion to manye a noble personage.[95]

Similarly, it was futile to exclaim against buildings "vsed for Gameing-howses, Brothell-howses, and for secrett dennes for Theeves, Cheaters, Shyfters, and such lyke, w^ch only desire to

[92] John Smyth, *The Berkeley Manuscripts* (Gloucester: Printed by John Bellows for the Subscribers, 1883), II, 286.

[93] Finch, *Wealth of Five Northamptonshire Families*, pp. 82-83, 93, 94-95.

[94] *Remembrancia*, p. 55.

[95] *Institucion of A Gentleman*, $A_6$-$A_7$.

plante themselves in covert-places the better to praye vpon younge Heires, Marchantes, and other Novizes"[96] because the privileged Englishmen trooping into London presented too rich a market for every sort of pleasure monger. In London, as nowhere else, "to be drunke, sweare, wench, follow the fashion, and to do just nothing are the attributes of a great part of our Gentry."[97]

## TRAVEL AND LODGING

The influx of the privileged presented certain logistical problems of transportation and accommodation. In the early years of the period, men traveled by horseback, with overnight stays at inns or at the homes of friends and relatives. With horses costing at least thirty or forty shillings and ranging upwards to a hundred shillings or more,[98] exclusive of bridle, saddle, or other gear, this form of transportation was restricted to those with comfortable incomes. When coaches gradually became more common, their use was still further restricted, for they were ruinously expensive—at least £25 or £30 for the body, with another £20 or more for the harness, a minimum of £50 for velvet or damask upholstery, additional sums for gilding, and the cost of four to six horses. By the time of the Civil War, a coach, exclusive of horses, cost as much as £200.[99] Nonetheless, coaches were quickly adopted by the wealthy because they made travel to and from London so much more comfortable, particularly for women, who visited the city in increasing numbers after the introduction of this new mode of transportation. As Stow's *Annals* reported the matter:

> In the yeere 1564. Guilliam Boonen, a Dutchman, became the Queenes Coachman, and was the first that brought the

---

[96] "A brief Discoverie of the great purpesture of newe Buyldinges neere the Cittie . . . ," Lansdowne MSS 160, fol. 90; printed in *Archaeologia* 23 (1831): 125.

[97] Peacham, *Compleat Gentleman*, p. 10.

[98] Campbell, *English Yeoman*, p. 206.

[99] Stone, *Crisis*, pp. 566-567.

vse of Coaches into England. And after a while, diuers great Ladies, with as great Jealousie of the Queens displeasure, made them Coaches, and rid in them vp and downe the Countries, to the great admiration of all the beholders, but then by little and little, they grew vsuall among the Nobilitie, and others of sort, and within twentie yeeres became a great trade of Coachmaking. . . . Lastly, euen at this time, 1605. began the ordinary vse of Caroaches.[100]

His analysis was essentially correct. By 1584, Lyly's *Alexander and Campaspe* (written for performance at Court) complained that men who once rode to battle on horseback now rode about in coaches, thinking only of the pleasures of the flesh.[101] The Earl of Rutland's accounts for 1587 listed "Coach, a newe, bought in London, xxxviii *li* xiiis. ii d."; Sir John Radcliffe had a coach by 1590; and by 1601, a bill was introduced in Parliament to restrain the excessive use of coaches.[102] Conservatives lamented that "now of late yeares the vse of coatches brought out of Germanie is taken vp, and made so common, as there is neither distinction of time, nor difference of persons obserued: for the world runs on wheeles with many, whose parents were glad to goe on foote."[103] Harsher social critics sneered, "Sir *Giles* himselfe must haue his satten suite, and my good Lady his wife, must needs haue her Coach, for to see a Lady to walke the streetes without a Coatch is like my Lord Maior, when he comes from Westminster without a Pageant, or like a Shroue Tuesday without a pancake."[104] Status notwithstanding, coaches made London more readily accessible to the affluent and thus contributed significantly to the influx of the privileged from 1576 onwards.

[100] Stow, *Annales* (1631), p. 867.
[101] John Lyly, *Campaspe*, in *The Complete Works*, ed. R. Warwick Bond (Oxford: Clarendon Press, 1902), II, 347.
[102] A. Ashmore, "Household Inventories of the Lancashire Gentry, 1550-1700," *Transactions of the Historic Society of Lancashire and Cheshire* 110 (1958): 103.
[103] Stow, *Survey*, ed. Kingsford, I, 84.
[104] Barnaby Rich, *Roome for a Gentleman* (London, 1609), pp. 29-30.

Once in London, the privileged had to find lodgings, either temporary or permanent. Kinsmen frequently opened the doors of their London homes to relatives from the country. For the solitary gentleman or one with few attendants, inns were always a possibility—"Howbeit, of all in England there are no worse inns than in London."[105] Rowland Whyte usually lodged in the Strand, most often at the Black Boy, but if the quarters were not to his liking, he did not say so.[106] There was such a brisk demand for permanent chambers that they were even disposed of by will. Anthony Calveley, younger son of Sir George Calveley, decreed, "Unto my cosin Highkin Byston all my beddinge w$^{th}$ the bedde case the henginges of the chameber w$^{th}$ a cofer w$^{ch}$ standeth at London w$^{th}$in Holburne castell willinge him that Rauffe Calvely my sone maye be chameber felowe w$^{th}$ him when he cometh to the Innes of the Cowrte."[107] Inns of Court lodgings were particularly desirable, since they offered suitable company, a bountiful table in commons, and private walks and gardens as well. By 1583, two Inner Temple students "continued there by the space of foure yeres and could never as yet gett any chamber in the house by reason of the scarcitie of them."[108] Twenty years later, Lewis Bagot appealed to Sir Walter Aston, "to helpe me to a chamber, whose answer was hee knew of none that were voide." Yet Sir Walter kindly let the young man use his own chamber when he "went into the cuntrye."[109] Much lending and sharing of chambers went on, even to nonmembers. In 1634, the judges issued orders against "harbouring ill subjects and dangerous persons," demanding also the ouster from the Inns of any "knight or gentleman, foreigner or discontinuer"[110]

---

[105] Harrison, *Description of England*, p. 399.

[106] Lisle C. John, "Roland Whyte, Elizabethan Letter-Writer," *Studies in the Renaissance* 8 (1961): 222-223.

[107] 23 September 1563; *Lancashire and Cheshire Wills*, 33:142.

[108] Prest, *Inns of Court*, p. 13.

[109] Folger Shakespeare Library MS L.a. 63.

[110] F. A. Inderwick, ed., *A Calendar of the Inner Temple Records* (London: H. Sotheran, 1896-1904), II, 83-84. See also Charles Trice Martin, ed., *Minutes of Parliament of the Middle Temple* (London: Butterworth, 1904), II, 587-588;

who was not a member. The London companies faced a similar problem deriving from the demand for suitable lodgings. In 1613 the goldsmiths proclaimed:

> The chambers in Bachelors Alley were of ancient time given to the Company to the intent that the Bachelors thereof should have their habitations therein at the will of the Company, but for so long only as they should remain unmarried, at very small and easy rents, the greatest not to exceed 8s. per annum; and that they should be admitted to the same chambers by the Wardens for the time being, which custom hath had very long continuance, until of late divers persons of the society, for gain and other private reasons, by compact and confederation amongst themselves, have, without leave of the Wardens, entered and intruded into the said chambers, and thereof made sale from one to another in contempt of the government of the Company.[111]

A single chamber, however, would not accommodate larger households. Sir Richard Cholmley of Roxby in Yorkshire "never took a journey to London that he was not attended with less than thirty, sometimes forty men-servants, though he went without his lady."[112] A more modest entourage was described in George Radcliffe's letter to his wife in October of 1626: "Your aunt talkes of coming downe, and to allow you for her boarde 20 shillinges a weeke, 10 apiece for her usher and gentle-woman, and 8 shillings apiece for her other servants."[113] The great lords, of course, required even more attendants. The solution for many lay in the ownership of a large London house. The episcopal palaces, together with monastic properties, were quickly snatched up by the peerage after the Dissolution. As suitable properties became harder to find, noblemen dispersed

---

and Reginald J. Fletcher, ed., *The Pension Book of Gray's Inn* (London: Chiswick Press, 1891), I, 213.

[111] Prideaux, *Memorials of the Goldsmiths' Company*, I, 123.

[112] J. T. Cliffe, *The Yorkshire Gentry, From the Reformation to the Civil War* (London: Athlone Press, 1969), p. 112.

[113] Whitaker, *Life . . . of Sir George Radcliffe*, p. 127.

into the suburbs, with a host of the lesser gentry following their example. The vast palaces along the Thames were divided into leased apartments, and after 1600, there was a tremendous development of leasehold property north of the Strand to supply housing for the affluent.

Virtually every important aristocrat had a London residence, and some had several. Cecil had Burghley House in the Strand, where he entertained the Queen.[114] Henry Percy acquired Syon House in 1594, sold a house in St. Anne's for £1,000 in 1607, apparently kept a house at Katherine Hill, but actually lived in a succession of hired residences, including Essex House. He bought Walsingham House when he became Privy Counselor in 1603, sold it at a loss when he went to the Tower three years later, and rented yet another house on Tower Hill in addition to Essex House.[115] The story was the same for lesser figures. Sir Thomas Tresham kept two houses in London, one in Westminster and one in the suburbs at Hoxton.[116] Sir Anthony Denton of Tonbridge, Kent, had two London townhouses in 1601, as befitted a Gentleman Pensioner at Court.[117] The goldsmiths leased handsome properties to Sir Richard Martyn, Sir Henry Yelverton, Sir Hugh Myddelton, and the Earl of Manchester, at rates ranging from £240 to £500.[118] Sir William Fitzwilliam leased a house at Camberwell in 1574 for £40 per year. Apparently he was still there in 1578, though correspondence of 1576 and 1578 describes him as "dwelling over against the glasse house by the Tower." He had taken a house in St. Olave parish by April of 1584, and from 1586 to at least 1602, he had a house in St. John's Street at £14 a year. In addition, he rented a chamber at Richmond and another at Greenwich, the former at £2 a year and the latter at 4s. a week plus £2 a year for

---

[114] Richard C. Barnett, *Place, Profit, and Power: A Study of the Servants of William Cecil, Elizabethan Statesman*, The James Sprunt Studies in History and Political Science, vol. 51 (Chapel Hill: University of North Carolina Press, 1969), p. 6.

[115] Batho, ed., *Household Papers of Henry Percy*, p. xix.

[116] Finch, *Wealth of Five Northamptonshire Families*, p. 81.

[117] Ibid., p. 26.

[118] Prideaux, *Memorials of the Goldsmiths' Company*, I, 86, 121, 127, 178.

stabling.[119] Great and small, fabulously rich and relatively poor, the privileged pressed into London, filling its houses and apartments and chambers, fattening the pockets of shrewd property owners.

## SIGNS OF A SWELLING STREAM

It is impossible to say how many actually came down to London during those years, but much evidence suggests that the numbers were far greater than has been supposed. Contemporary witnesses seemed convinced that the gentry were deserting the duties of the country to pursue the follies of the city. The poet protested:

> The stately lord, which woonted was to kepe
> A court at home, is now come vp to courte,
> And leaues the country for a common prey,
> To pilling, polling, brybing, and deceit:
> (Al which his presence might haue pacified,
> Or else haue made offenders smel the smoke.)[120]

Some attributed the defection to financial necessity, explaining that "Some other [gentlemen] seeing the charges of household increase so much as by no provision they can make it can be helped, give over their households and get them chambers in London or about the Court and there spend their time; some of them with a servant or two, where he was wont to keep thirty or forty persons daily in his house."[121] However, a much harsher voice declared, "I detest that effoeminacy of the most, that burne out day and night in their beds, and by the fire side; in trifles, gaming, or courting their yellow Mistresses all the Winter in a City, appearing but as Cuckoes in the Spring, one time in the yeere to the Countrey and their tenants, leaving the care of keeping good houses at Christmas, to the honest Yeomen of the Countrey."[122]

[119] Finch, *Wealth of Five Northamptonshire Families*, p. 121n.
[120] George Gascoigne, *The Steele Glas* (London, 1576), $D_3$.
[121] Dewar, ed., *Discourse of the Commonweal*, p. 81.
[122] Peacham, *Compleat Gentleman*, p. 220.

Government records supported the social critics' complaints of wholesale defection to London by the gentry. A casual note on a 1577 muster roll from Dorset reported that "some of our welthie men and merchauntes be gone from us."[123] In 1583, the Lord Mayor objected that aldermen and other Londoners with second houses in the nearby counties were charged for musters in both city and county, "while on the other side such gentlemen as resided in the country, and had lodgings or houses in the City, to which they resorted in term or other times, had not been thus doubly charged."[124] Elizabeth issued proclamation after proclamation ordering all gentlemen home: "Firste. her Ma^{tie} speciallye requyrethe & Commaundeth, not onely all Justices of peace, but all sortes of gentlemen of what sorte or qualitye soeuer, w^{ch} haue lefte or forsaken there Country dwellinges & habitations to liue in Cityes or towne Corporates, presently to repayre to there Country dwellings, & there to make there Continuall aboade, as they will aunsweare to the Contrarye vpon there perill & her Ma^{tie's} highe displeasure." After futile exhortation, the Queen ordered: "And the Attorney-general shall make a certificate of all gentlemen who dwell in London or Westminster, and shall inform against them."[125] Apparently, even this command had little effect.

After James's accession, the proclamations continued, also without success, as this report of crowded conditions in the law courts attested:

> for in all partes the numbers are so increased that those that are the doers & beare the burden of the busynes can haue no place at the benche, nor hardelye gette into the Cowrte . . . for the number of newe & younge knightes, that Come in there braueryes & stande there lyke an Idoll to be gazed vpon, & doe nothinge, ys so greate & pressinge for place, Countenaunce & estimacyon: but they must knowe they are

---

[123] Finch, *Wealth of Five Northamptonshire Families*, pp. 259-260.

[124] 29 September 1583; *Remembrancia*, p. 473.

[125] 28 June 1599; Baildon, ed., *Reportes*, pp. 56, 106; 2 November 1587; Hughes and Larkin, eds., *Tudor Royal Proclamations*, II, 541-543, offers another example.

not . . . to be quarter Justices, as many of them are, that lye aboute this towne 3 partes of the yeare, & goe downe onelye for there pleasure in hawkinge & huntinge; but the Lo. Maior of london must now make accounte what they are that lurke aboute the towne, & the Judges retorne to his Ma^tie the names of them that abyde not in there Cuntrye dwellinges & keepe hospitalitye, w^ch now his Ma^tie by his proclamacyon inioynethe them all to doe.[126]

James fulminated against "those swarms of gentry who, through the instigation of their wives and to new-model and fashion their daughters (who, if they were unmarried, marred their reputations, and if married, lost them) did neglect their country hospitality, and cumber the city, a general nuisance to the kingdom."[127] That prolific correspondent John Chamberlain reflected the prevailing attitude toward James's repeated commandments to depart: "even upon Christmas eve came foorth another proclamation, for their wives and families and widowes to be gon likewise, and that henceforward gentlemen should remain here during termes only or other busines, without bringing their wives and families, which is *durus sermo* to the women."[128]

By 1632, Charles took firmer measures, actually prosecuting in the Star Chamber two hundred and fifty peers and gentlemen remaining in London after one of his proclamations.[129] A couple of years later Garrard reported, "We have very plausible Things done of late. . . . To encourage Gentlemen to live more willingly in the Country, all Game Fowl, as Pheasant, Partridges, Ducks, as also Hares are by Proclamation forbidden to be dressed or eaten in any Inns, and Butchers are forbidden to be Graziers."[130]

---

[126] 16 June 1608; Baildon, ed., *Reportes*, p. 367. See also James F. Larkin and Paul L. Hughes, eds., *Stuart Royal Proclamations* (Oxford: Clarendon Press 1973), I, 21, 44, 151, 323, 356, 369, 408, 434, 561, 572, 608.

[127] Fisher, "Development of London," p. 203.

[128] Norman E. McClure, ed., *The Letters of John Chamberlain* (Philadelphia: American Philosophical Society, 1939), II, 475.

[129] John Rushworth, *Historical Collections* (London, 1721), II, 288-293.

[130] Knowler, ed., *Earl of Strafforde's Letters*, I, 176.

However, as the very persistence of such efforts demonstrated, nothing could abate the flow of the privileged minority into London. The city's attractions were far too powerful.

In some ways, the city actively encouraged the affluent to come to London. Those assessed for taxes at £5 in goods or £3 in lands were exempt from the bans on "Inmates or Undersitters" in existing houses.[131] They were also exempt from the repeated bans on new buildings. It was decreed that the buildings "erected by great persons, or by providente Gentillmen of the Countrey, either to save Charge of hospitalitie, or for some other their private vse and pleasure, when they shall at any tyme have occasion to repayre vnto the Cittie; or . . . buylte by rytche Citizens in Gardens, and other conveniente places nere vnto the Cittie, . . . were erected for private and necessary vses."[132] No nonsense here about unneccessary construction. The city fathers welcomed residents with purses fat enough to pay taxes or to purchase London's luxuries.

In fact, officials were deeply concerned about the lack of suitable housing for eminent figures and about their safety in the city. The aldermen lamented that "the best houses, and such as were fit for the receipt of ambassadors or persons of the best quality, were caught up to be converted into taverns." Even the houses of a former mayor and a former alderman had been turned into taverns.[133] The taverns, in turn, were regarded as havens for papists and worse:

> Thother sorte are such as rejectinge all honeste labors, doe lyve by Theevinge, Cheatinge, Conseninge, and many other such lewde courses; and thes for the moste parte are harboured in Ale-howses, Gaming-howses, Brothell-howses, or

[131] 7 July 1580; Hughes and Larkin, eds., *Tudor Royal Proclamations*, II, 466-468.

[132] "A briefe Discoverie," p. 124.

[133] *Remembrancia*, pp. 10-15, 541, 544-545. The kind of mansion considered suitable for an ambassador was a residence like that of Sir Horatio Palavicino, which was leased to the French ambassador in 1598 and then to the Austrian ambassador in 1603. See Lawrence Stone, *An Elizabethan: Sir Horatio Palavicino* (Oxford: Clarendon Press, 1956), p. 269.

such lyke places, and there doe they spend their tyme lewdly and idely in plottinge their devises howe to lyve upon the spoyle of other men. . . . and thes badd sorte of people have m'cenarie Mydwyves, Bawdes, and Panders in paye, to entize younge gentillmen, prentizes, and other novizes to stoope to their stales, and not to leave them vntill they have intrapped them in their snares, to the vtter spoyle of them.[134]

Periodically, officials sought out "Receivers of Felons." On a single day in 1585, Recorder Fleetwood and others on the bench "got the Names of forty-five masterless Men and Cutpurses, whose practice was to rob Gentlemens Chambers."[135] Thus the city's efforts to protect the privileged from the unscrupulous and to keep them suitably housed acted in concert with London's natural attractions to guarantee that the stream of the affluent did not dwindle.

And, despite the royal proclamations, the stream did not diminish. Rents grew steeper and leases shorter, a situation that favored the rich tenant over the poor. Shops and services catering exclusively to the rich proliferated, indicating a growing clientele. The outlying orchards and gardens supplied delicacies too expensive save for the tables of the privileged. With a guaranteed London market for crops and a brisk trade in estates near the city, the adjoining counties became the wealthiest in all England, while London itself was a lodestone of wealth, far exceeding any other place in the kingdom. Parish registers and rent rolls were sprinkled liberally with "Sir" and "Lord" and "Mr." alongside the humbler, untitled names. By 1600, coach traffic grew heavy enough to require control in the narrow streets. Observers were uniformly amazed at the imports of gold, silver, pearl, spice, pepper, wine, fruit, sugar, drugs, silk, linen, and other luxuries.

the vnmeasurable, and vncomparable encrease of all which commodities, comming into this Citie, and the encrease of

---

[134] "A briefe Discoverie," pp. 124-125, 122, respectively.
[135] Stow, *Survey*, II, 543.

houses, and inhabitants within the compasse and tearme of fiftie yeeres, is such and so great, as were there not now two third parts of the people yet liuing, hauing bin eye witnesses of the premises, and the bookes of the Custome house, which remaine extant, the truth and difference of all things afore mentioned were not to be Justified, and beleeued.[136]

## NUMBERS

Although it is an undeniable fact that tremendous numbers of the privileged came to London, an attempt to arrive at precise numbers—or even reasonable estimates—for these residents and visitors is quite difficult. The Visitation of Heralds in 1568 listed 434 armigerous families in London, while the Visitation of 1633 to 1635 added another 1,160 families.[137] Yet these figures applied only to arms not previously recorded and to families considered resident in London. By far the majority regarded a country parish as their family seat and, as has already been noted, the privileged included some who were not armigerous. A look at London's merchants is equally unsatisfactory. Strype reported that "About the Year 1590, the Number of the chiefest Merchants in *London* increased greatly, I find two Hundred and eighty Names to one Petition."[138] A 1590 subsidy named 486 London merchants prosperous enough to bear assessments of £50 to £100. One survey of the estates of freemen showed that the number worth more than £500 rose from 26.51 percent in 1586 to 41.25 percent in 1693, while another survey for 1586 to 1614 claimed 42 percent left personal estates of £500 or more.[139] However, estates do not include real property, and

[136] Stow, *Annales* (1631), p. 868.

[137] *The Visitation of London in the Year 1568*, ed. Joseph Jackson Howard and George John Armytage, and *The Visitation of London, 1633, 1634, and 1635*, ed. Joseph Jackson Howard and Joseph Lemuel Chester, Harleian Society Publications, vols. 1 (1869), 15 (1880), and 17 (1883).

[138] Stow, *Survey*, II, 396.

[139] Richard Grassby, "The Personal Wealth of the Business Community in Seventeenth-Century England," *Economic History Review*, 2d ser. 23 (1970): 227, 229.

percentages of samples are not convertible into absolute numbers. More recently, an analysis of London records has identified some 273 chief rulers of the city, 500 assistants, and 800 to 1,000 lesser officials.[140] The analysis covers a period of several years and thus includes more than one generation. Then, too, the study is restricted to the City of London itself and so excludes officials in Westminster, Middlesex, and the other suburban areas. Hence, subsidies, estates, petitions, and lists of officials are equally resistant to reliable estimates.

Because of their more precise records, the Inns of Court provide a little more help. The rate of annual admissions quadrupled between 1590 and 1639. However, admission did not necessarily entail residence, except during the initial years of instruction and afterwards during law terms. The Venetian ambassador seriously underestimated when he reported in 1612 that the Inns contained "five hundred of the wealthiest gentlemen of this kingdom."[141] By 1600, the four societies probably accommodated about one thousand members during Michaelmas, Hilary, Easter, and Trinity, with a lesser number at other times.[142] But a good many members had other lodgings and thus would not be included in this figure. Then, too, the Inns of Court estimates alone offer no clue as to how large the total legal community might have been.

On the whole, specific data for various groups provide more confusion than enlightenment. Perhaps more useful is a common-sense approach correlating the kinds of privileged persons known to be in London with their numbers as a whole and with the total population of the city. Except for a few prosperous provincial merchants, most of the mercantile families that could reasonably be termed privileged lived in London. Many wealthy foreigners, including travelers, merchants, James's Scottish lords, and the ambassadorial entourages, came to London. Courtiers—some 1,500 in Elizabeth's day and a far larger number

[140] Foster, *Politics of Stability*, p. 54.
[141] *Calendar of State Papers, Venice* (Great Britain: Public Record Office, 1864-1947), XII (1610-1613), pp. 446-447.
[142] Prest, *Inns of Court*, pp. 6-7, 10-11, 244-245, 16, respectively.

during Stuart rule[143]—settled in London for varying lengths of time, bringing their families and various household attendants who were members of the privileged minority. Young sons of the country gentry lived in London as students, apprentices, and retainers. The legal fraternity, together with those having suits at law, crowded into the city, particularly at term time. Those with business to transact, property to be transferred, or marriages to arrange came to London. Except for parish priests, village schoolmasters, and university dons, nearly all the English intellectuals, scientists, artists, and professionals clustered in London. Finally, anyone with the money and freedom to pursue a life of sheer pleasure was certain to be in London much of the time. It is most likely that virtually every privileged family in the kingdom had one or more of its members in the city at any given time, and a good many families or family members lived there all the time.

Throughout England as a whole the privileged constituted about 4 to 5 percent of the population. In London, however, the percentage was certainly far larger. Even 5 percent would be an inadequate measure of the privileged who were permanent residents, and it would not include the enormous numbers who visited the city or lived there while considering themselves resident elsewhere. By any conservative estimate, London's elite minority constituted more than 10 percent of the city's permanent population; figuring in temporary dwellers, it was probably closer to 15 percent of the population. Demographers despair when confronted with the task of estimating the latter category. In 1600, it may have housed anywhere from 150,000 to 300,000, though 250,000 is the estimate usually accepted. By the 1630s, the estimates rise to 320,000, with 350,000 a reasonable figure for 1642.[144] Backward projection would indicate

---

[143] Edward Potts Cheyney, *A History of England from the Defeat of the Armada to the Death of Elizabeth* (New York: Longmans, Green, 1914), I, 18-19, 47.

[144] Peter Ramsey, *Tudor Economic Problems* (London: V. Gollancz, 1963), p. 109; Charles Wilson, *England's Apprenticeship, 1603-1763* (London: Longmans, 1965), p. 45; Valerie Pearl, *London and the Outbreak of the Puritan*

some 180,000 or so in 1576. When correlated with the total population of England and the range of possibilities for the numbers of privileged, the London residents appear as follows:

| Year | Total Population | Privileged Population | London Population | Privileged in London |
|------|------------------|-----------------------|-------------------|----------------------|
| 1576 | 3,800,000 | 133,000 (3.5%)-220,000 (5.8%) | 180,000 | 27,000 (15%) |
| 1603 | 4,000,000 | 160,000 (4%)-264,000 (6.6%) | 250,000 | 37,000 (15%) |
| 1642 | 5,000,000 | 225,000 (4.5%)-375,000 (7.5%) | 350,000 | 52,000 (15%) |

Again it must be emphasized that the foregoing figures are no more than estimates, since no reliable statistics for the period exist. The chart is simply intended to suggest some reasonable possibilities and some reasonable correlations. Thus it seems a reasonable possibility that the privileged amounted to some 15 percent of London's population when due allowance is made for their disproportionate presence both as permanent residents and as visitors to the city. But that percentage cannot be accepted as a hard fact. Similarly, it seems reasonable to suggest a range from 27,000 in 1576 to 52,500 in 1642. When correlated with the most conservative estimates for the total size of the privileged, that range would place slightly fewer than 20 percent of their numbers in London at the beginning of the period and slightly more than 20 percent toward the end of the period when more and more of the gentry seem to have swarmed into the city. Such a range also means that no more than one in five of all the privileged in England were in London, either permanently or temporarily, at any given time—a fair and certainly a conservative proportion. Indeed, if one favors a higher percentage of the privileged in the total population, then only one in eight would have been in London. The figures thus offer modest, reasonable suggestions.

Although the composition of London's privileged segment

Revolution: City Government and National Politics, 1625-43 (London: Oxford University Press, 1961), p. 14; Stone, Crisis, p. 386.

cannot be precisely determined, certain generalizations concerning it can be made. There were far more men than women, since wives and daughters of the country gentry were often left at home. (However, coach travel made their presence more likely after 1600.) There was a disproportionate number of unmarried men because marriage occurred after formal education, apprenticeship, study at the Inns of Court, and establishment in some secure position had been achieved.[145] As a result, there were comparatively few children, except for grammar school students, the offspring of resident London families, well-to-do apprentices, and youths in service to the nobility.[146] Few were native Londoners,[147] and thus few yielded the city their basic loyalty. Except for the heavily burdened minister of state, the conscientious merchant, the strictly supervised apprentice, or the cloistered grammar school pupil, the privileged in London enjoyed remarkable freedom to do as they pleased with their time. Finally, London's privileged were probably more affluent—or at least more extravagant—than their counterparts in the country, both because city expenses were higher and because the temptations to spend money were much greater.

The presence of so many wealthy, titled, ambitious, educated, sophisticated, and relatively idle people had a significant influence upon all aspects of life in London. By comparison with the glittering impact of the privileged, any other set of Londoners faded into silent obscurity. In fact, the city's complex, cosmopolitan culture principally reflected the tastes and temperament of this select group. And whereas it is possible that mere co-

[145] Also, as Stone indicates, the huge birthrates of the 1560s and 1570s produced "a great mass of young men reaching manhood in the 1590's" (*Crisis*, p. 329).

[146] T. H. Hollingsworth, *Historical Demography* (Ithaca, N.Y.: Cornell University Press, 1969), p. 83.

[147] For example, Ramsey points out that between 1480 and 1660 only 8 percent (14) of 172 mayors, only 9 percent (75) of 813 liveried merchants, only 4 percent of 389 shopkeepers and retailers, only 10 percent of the "great merchants," and only 10 percent at the Inns of Court were London born (*Tudor Economic Problems*, p. 110).

incidence accounted for the convergence of thousands of England's elite into the city concurrently with the rise of impressive theaters and the first emergence of drama as a profitable commercial enterprise, the surviving evidence seems to indicate a much closer connection between London's playhouses and London's privileged.

# · IV ·

## The Privileged as Playgoers

In a city where idleness and out-right debauchery abounded, playgoing represented only one of many pleasures available to the privileged. Yet by all accounts, the theater occupied a central, if casual, place in the daily lives of London's elite. Edward Guilpin's sketch "Of Gnatho" only slightly exaggerated the regular round of amusement that many gentlemen followed.

> My Lord most court-like lyes in bed 'till noone,
> Then, all high-stomacht riseth to his dinner,
> Falls straight to Dice, before his meate be downe,
> Or to digest, walks to some femall sinner.
> Perhaps fore-tyred he gets him to a play,
> Comes home to supper, and then falls to dice,
> There his deuotion wakes 'til it be day,
> And so to bed, where vntill noone he lies.
> > This is a Lords life, simple folke will sing.
> > A Lords life? what to trot so foule a ring?
> > Yet thus he liues, and what's the greatest griefe,
> > *Gnatho* still sweares he leads true vertues life.[1]

According to Thomas Dekker, the "Vintners, Players and Puncks" gained even more from gullible gentlemen "then Vsurers do by thirty in the hundred,"[2] and others agreed. John Earle proclaimed that a gallant's "businesse is the street: the Stage, the Court and those places where a proper man is best showne," with Paul's Walk being "the other expence of the day, after

---

[1] Edward Guilpin, "Of Gnatho," in *Skialetheia* (London, 1598), A₈.
[2] Thomas Dekker, "Dedication," *The Gvls Horne-booke*, in *The Non-Dramatic Works*, ed. Alexander B. Grosart (1884; reprint ed., New York: Russell and Russell, 1963), II, 197.

Playes, Tauerne, and a Baudy house."[3] Addressing his friends, Sir Revel asked,

> Speak gentlemen, what shall we do to-day?
> Drink some brave health upon a Dutch carouse?
> Or shall we to the Globe and see a play?
> Or visit Shoreditch for a bawdy house?
> Let's call for cards or dice and have a game,
> To sit thus idle is both sin and shame![4]

For Sir Revel, idleness might have seemed sin and shame, but others viewed his proposed diversions as far greater wickedness. Early in the period, Puritans denounced the "theaters, Curtines, Heauing houses, Rifling boothes, Bowling alleyes, and such places, where the time is so shamefully mispent" and complained that "There is no Dicing house, Bowling alley, Cock pit, or Theater that can be found empty."[5] Later, during Charles's reign, the story continued much the same, with Richard Rawlidge deploring the "Play-houses, Ale-houses, Bawdy-houses, Dising-houses, . . . All which houses, and traps for Gentlemen, and others of such Receipt," he felt, should be utterly suppressed.[6]

From a gentleman's point of view, the situation naturally looked quite different. After all, how else should a man of leisure and means spend his time? Thomas Nashe offered an entirely reasonable defense for playgoing:

> For whereas the after-noone beeing the idlest time of the day;
> wherein men that are their owne masters (as Gentlemen of

---

[3] John Earle, No. 19, "A Gallant," and No. 53, "Paules Walke," in *Microcosmographie* (London, 1628).

[4] Samuel Rowlands, Epigram 7, *The Letting of Humour's Blood in the Head-Vein* (London, 1600).

[5] John Feilde, *A Godly Exhortation, by Occasion of the Late Iudgement of God, Shewed at Parris-Garden, the Thirteenth Day of Ianuarie* (London, 1583), B₄.

[6] Richard Rawlidge, *A Monster Lately Found Out and Discovered, or the Scourging of Tipplers*; as cited by E. K. Chambers, *The Elizabethan Stage* (Oxford: Clarendon Press, 1923), II, 360.

the Court, the Innes of the Courte, and the number of Captaines and Souldiers about *London*) do wholy bestow themselues vpon pleasure, and that pleasure they deuide (howe
vertuously it skils not) either into gameing, following of harlots, drinking, or seeing a Playe: is it not then better (since
of foure extreames all the world cannot keepe them but they
will choose one) that they should betake them to the least,
which is Playes?[7]

Nashe may have been stretching a point when he contended,
"Faith, when Dice, Lust, and Drunkennesse all haue dealt vpon
him, if there be neuer a Playe for him to goe too for his pennie,
he sits melancholie in his Chamber deuising vpon felonie or
treason, and howe he may best exalt himselfe by mischiefe."[8]
However, his basic argument was repeated by others. Joseph
Wybarne conceded that "if we marke how young men spend
the latter end of the day in gaming, drinking, whoring, it were
better to tollerate Playes," while Hopton suggested that if the
theater "did nothing but in pleasing sort, / Keepe gallants from
mispending of their time, / It might suffice."[9] Obviously, the
theater did not keep idle gentlemen out of the brothels, taverns,
and gaming houses, but it did offer a continuing source of
entertainment for them.

PATRONAGE

Theatergoing was an entirely natural, perhaps even inevitable,
outgrowth of the relationship of the drama to the privileged
classes. After all, the troupes of professional actors were formally patronized by members of the nobility under Elizabeth
and by royalty itself after the accession of the Stuarts. The

[7] Thomas Nashe, *Pierce Penilesse*, in *The Complete Works*, ed. R. B.
McKerrow (London: Sidgwick and Jackson, 1910), I, 212.

[8] Ibid., p. 214.

[9] Joseph Wybarne, *The New Age of Old Names* (London, 1609), p. 53; Ar.
Hopton, Commendatory verse to Thomas Heywood, in *"An Apology for Ac-
tors"* (1612) with *"A Refutation of the Apology for Actors"* (1615), ed. Richard
H. Perkinson (New York: Scholars' Facsimiles and Reprints, 1941), p. 22.

roster of those lending the power of their position to acting groups included names such as Leicester, Oxford, Warwick, Essex, Strange, Derby, the Lord Admiral, and the Lord Chamberlain—some of the most important nobles in the kingdom. In 1598, Parliament made it illegal for anyone save a baron "or any honorable Personage of greater Degree" to keep a company of actors.[10] The Queen herself was responsible for the boys' troupes attached to her royal chapels who performed both at Court and before the public until 1590 or so. Indeed, the entire rationale for the existence of dramatic companies was that they provided essential recreation for the sovereign. As Fuller put it, "Seeing Princes cares are deeper than the cares of private men, it is fit their recreations also should be greater, that so their mirth may reach the bottom of their sadness."[11] In theory, at least, public performances merely provided an opportunity for rehearsal and perfection of plays before they were presented at Court. Thus, in 1578, the Privy Council required the Lord Mayor to allow six companies "to exercise playing within the City" because "the companies aforenamed are appointed to play this time of Christmas before her Majesty."[12]

Legally, the actors were considered servants of their patrons, entitled to his livery, his protection, and his preferment. However, by 1576, when the Theater was built in Finsbury Fields, the adult companies had become economically independent of their masters, relying on profits from performances rather than on household board and wages. This quasi-independent relationship, a deviation from the usual servant status, provoked bitter criticism in some quarters:

> since the reteining of these Caterpillers, the credite of noble men hath decaied, they are thought to be couetous, by per-

---

[10] Glynne Wickham, *Early English Stages, 1300 to 1660* (New York: Columbia University Press, 1963, 1972), II, 2:18, and II, 1:105-106, respectively.

[11] Thomas Fuller, *The Holy State and The Profane State*, ed. Maximilian Graff Walten (New York: Columbia University Press, 1938), II, 304.

[12] John Roche Dasent, ed., *Acts of the Privy Council, 1542-1604* (London: Stationery Office, 1890-1964), X, 436.

mitting their seruants, which cannot liue of them selues, and whome for neerenes they wil not maintaine, to liue at the deuotion of almes of other men, passing from countrie to countrie, from one Gentlemans house to another, offering their seruice, which is a kind of beggerie.[13]

Stubbes made the same point a bit later, criticizing actors as "ydle Persons, doing nothing but playing and loytring, hauing their lyuings of the sweat of other Mens browes, much like vnto drones deuouring the sweet honie of the poore labouring bees."[14] Another writer expressed it more succinctly: "So howsoever hee pretends to have a royall Master or Mistresse, his wages and dependance prove him to be the servant of the people."[15] Equally offensive were the occasional rich rewards lavished upon actors for their performances. Sir Christopher Hatton's letter writer, Samuel Cox, perhaps thinking of his own meager compensation, complained that "rich men give more to a player for a song which he shall sing in one hour, than to their faithful servants for serving them a whole year."[16] Another social critic termed "rewardes to plears of interludes" a form of the "vice of prodigality," as distinguished from the virtue of liberality that every true gentleman should practice.[17]

Despite the irregular financial relationship, the performer's role as servant to his noble or royal patron was more than a mere technicality. Successful troupes enhanced the prestige of their sponsors—it was surely no accident that James I chose the best company to become the King's Men. The players also offered a convenient source of entertainment. Thus, Leicester took his company with him on his expedition to the Netherlands in

---

[13] [Anthony Munday], *A Second and Third Blast of Retrait from Plaies and Theaters*, in *The English Drama and Stage*, ed. William C. Hazlitt (1869; reprint ed., New York: Burt Franklin, n.d.), pp. 133-134.

[14] Philip Stubbes, *The Anatomie of Abuses* (London, 1583), p. x.

[15] J. Cocke, "A common Player"; as cited by Chambers, *Elizabethan Stage*, IV, 256.

[16] Letter from Samuel Cox to the brother of a Mr. Lewin, 15 January 1590, in Sir Nicholas Harris Nicolas, *Memoirs of the Life and Times of Sir Christopher Hatton* (London: Richard Bentley, 1847), p. xxx.

[17] *The Institucion of A Gentleman* (London, 1568), $D_6$.

1585, Prince Charles's company attended the royal progress through the country in 1634, and the King's Men enjoyed the same favor in 1636.[18] Under Elizabeth, a Court appearance seemed important to a patron's advancement, for there was a striking correlation between the performance of a nobleman's troupe at Court and the crown's reward of offices or other favors to that nobleman.[19]

More importantly from the players' perspective, a powerful patron afforded invaluable protection. At the simplest level, his livery prevented the actors from being arrested as masterless men, a penalty they would otherwise have suffered under the Statute of 1563. A patron also stood between his troupe and hostile officials, particularly the London Council, much to the dismay of the Puritans. Munday lamented, "Alas, that priuate affection should so raigne in the Nobilitie, that to pleasure, as they thinke, their seruants, and to vphold them in their vanitie, they should restraine the Magistrates from executing their office!"[20] Leicester had no sooner secured the release of the stern John Feilde from prison in 1581 than the divine boldly reproached his benefactor for a similar intercession on behalf of the actors: "I humblie besech your honour to take heede howe you gyve your hande either in euill causes, or in the behalfe of euill men, as of late you did for players to the greate grief of all the Godly."[21] Despite pleas to "some Hercules in the Court"[22] to cleanse the Augean stable of the theater, powerful

---

[18] Chambers, *Elizabethan Stage*, I, 311; Gerald Eades Bentley, *The Jacobean and Caroline Stage* (Oxford: Clarendon Press, 1941-1968), I, 310, 49, respectively.

[19] J. Leeds Barroll, "The Social and Literary Context," in *The Revels History of Drama in English*, ed. Clifford Leech and T. W. Craik (London: Methuen, 1975), III, 4-27; Marion Jones, "The Court and the Dramatists," *Elizabethan Theatre*, Stratford-upon-Avon Studies, no. 9 (New York: St. Martin's Press, 1967), pp. 177, *passim*.

[20] See, e.g., Munday, *Second and Third Blast*, p. 133.

[21] Eleanor Rosenberg, *Leicester: Patron of Letters* (New York: Columbia University Press, 1955), p. 255.

[22] Stephen Gosson, *Playes Confuted in Fiue Actions*, in *The English Drama and Stage*, ed. William C. Hazlitt (1869; reprint ed., New York: Burt Franklin,

courtiers continued to lend their influence to the dramatic companies.

Some glimpse of the importance of a powerful patron emerged from a description of James Burbage's behavior when he was summoned by the Lord Mayor in 1584 to account for a row near the Theater. According to the Lord Mayor:

> The chiefeste of her highnes players advised me to send for the owner of the Theater [Burbage], who was a stubburne fellow, and to bynd him. I dyd so; he sent me word that he was my Lo. of Hunsdons man, and that he wold not come at me, but he wold in the mornyng ride to my lord; then I sent the vndershereff for hym and he [the undersheriff] browght hym to me; and at his commyng he stowtted me owt very hastie; and in the end I shewed hym my Lo. his mrs. hand and then he was more quiet; but to die for it he wold not be bound. And then I mynding to send hym to prison, he made sute that he might be bound to appere at the Oier & determiner, the which is to morrowe; where he said that he was suer the Court wold not bynd hym being a Counselers man.[23]

Quite obviously, Burbage did not regard Lord Hunsdon's sponsorship as a mere formality, even when challenged by the Lord Mayor himself.

After James's accession, when royalty assumed patronage of the dramatic companies, the need for special protection largely ceased. No one presumed to challenge royal patents in which the sovereign called for "Our loving subjects as you tender Our Pleasure, not onely to permitt and suffer them herein without any your Letts, Hinderances or Molestations . . . but alsoe to be aydeing and assisting to them if any Wrong be to them

---

n.d.), p. 161. Gosson addresses his Epistle to Sir Francis Walsingham — his "Hercules."

[23] William Fleetwood to Lord Burghley, 18 June 1584; *Malone Society Collections* (Oxford: Oxford University Press, 1907-1975), I, 163; Chambers, *Elizabethan Stage*, IV, 298.

offered." James also assured his subjects that "what further Favour you shall shew to these Our Servants and the rest of theire Associats for Our Sakes, Wee shall take kindly at your hands."[24] Even when Blackfriars and Whitefriars, along with the other crown liberties, were surrendered to the control of the City of London in 1608, the acting companies' old enemies on the council refrained from hindering their activities, except for some attempt at traffic regulation.[25]

Through their powerful social position, patrons could render other favors to their troupes in addition to legal protection. Lord Hunsdon personally petitioned the Lord Mayor to permit his company to resume playing in 1594, and the Countess of Derby wrote Sir Robert Cecil to ask that her husband's men not be barred from playing.[26] The Lord Admiral, Charles Howard, Earl of Nottingham, used his influence to get Edward Alleyn's new playhouse, the Fortune, approved in 1600.[27] Sometimes actual grants of money were made to tide a troupe over a particularly difficult period, as when plague payments to the King's Men were ordered in 1603, 1608, 1609, and 1610.[28] A 1631 edition of Stow's *Annals* even claimed that after the Globe burned in 1613, it was "built vp againe in the yeare 1613, at the great charge of King Iames, and many Noble men and others."[29] Although no independent corroboration of such financing exists,

---

[24] Bentley, *Jacobean and Caroline Stage*, I, 17-18.

[25] 20 September 1608; Walter de Gray Birch, *The Historical Charters and Constitutional Documents of the City of London* (London: Whiting, 1887), pp. 144-145. After 1640, two of the most rabidly Puritan areas of the City were Whitefriars and Blackfriars, a factor that surely contributed to the prompt closure of the theaters in 1642. See Valerie Pearl, *London and the Outbreak of the Puritan Revolution: City Government and National Politics, 1625-43* (London: Oxford University Press, 1961), pp. 40-42.

[26] Lord Hunsdon to Lord Mayor, 8 October 1594; *Malone Society Collections*, I, 73; Chambers, *Elizabethan Stage*, IV, 316; *Malone Society Collections*, II, 2: 147-148.

[27] Warrant of 12 January 1600; Walter W. Greg, ed., *Henslowe Papers* (London: A. H. Bullen, 1907), p. 49.

[28] Chambers, *Elizabethan Stage*, I, 218.

[29] Manuscript addition noted in ibid., II, 374.

contemporaries apparently did not question the truth of the report. In short, the entire dramatic enterprise was deeply enmeshed in the network of patronage and preferment associated with the socially privileged.

EDUCATIONAL PERFORMANCES

Factors beyond a mere formal sponsorship help to explain such an association. For one thing, plays formed an intrinsic part of a gentleman's education. Not only were the comedies of Plautus and Terence included as exercises in Latin classes but students in grammar schools and universities frequently presented plays as well. The boys at the Merchant Taylors' School in London performed publicly in the company's Common Hall until 1574, when

> by reason of the tumultuous disordered persones repayringe hither to see suche playes as by our schollers were here lately played, the Maisters of this Worshipful Companie and their deare ffrends could not have entertaynmente and convenyente place as they oughte to have had, by no provision beinge made, notwithstandinge the spoyle of this howse, the charges of this Mystery and theire juste authoritie which did reasonably require the contrary.[30]

Affronted by the disregard of their prerogatives, the masters of the guild banned further public performances.

However tumultuous that occasion, the Merchant Taylors' School was not unique in having disorder attend its dramatic performances. When scholars at Oxford presented a play before Queen Elizabeth, there was such a "great presse" up the steps to the door that a stone guardwall was broken down and three men killed.[31] Worse perhaps than damage and disorder, at least for the audience, was the sheer boredom of many academic

---

[30] Charles M. Clode, *The Early History of the Guild of Merchant Taylors* (London: Harrison and Son, 1888-1889), I, 234-235.

[31] Leslie Hotson, *Shakespeare's Wooden O* (London: Rupert Hart-Davis, 1959), p. 302.

performances. James I reportedly fell asleep when the St. John's men presented *Vertumnus* for him in 1605.[32] Holyday's *Technogamia*, "prepar'd for our Platonique King" by the undergraduates at Christ Church, Oxford, proved sufficiently tedious to inspire a derisive poem by one of the Magdalen Fellows.[33] Lovelace may have had such plays in mind when he wrote, "From learned Comedies *deliver me!*"[34]

Some felt that the universities should be delivered from plays altogether, notably the theater's Puritan enemies. Defenders of the actors, such as Thomas Heywood, declared, "Do not the Vniuersities, the fountaines and well springs of all good Arts, Learning, and Documents, admit the like in their Colledges? and they (I assure my selfe) are not ignorant of their true vse. In the time of my residence in *Cambridge*, I haue seene Tragedyes, Comedyes, Historyes, Pastorals and Shewes, publickly acted, in which the Graduates of good place and reputation, haue been specially parted."[35] But the critics held a much more severe opinion of the academic playwrights, actors, and audiences.

> the Vniuersities sometime institute *Stage-playes*: more is the pittie, that the most famous lights of learning in the world should be branded with infamie, through the meanes of some phantasticals which are in them. Wherefore admit they doe: who then most commonly doe compose their Playes? Idle branes, that affect not their better studies. Who are the Actors? Gentle-bloods, and lusty swash-bucklers, such as prefer an ounce of vaine-glorie, ostentation, and strutting on the Stage, before a pound of learning; and are sent to the Vniuersities, not so much to obtaine knowledge, as to keepe them from the common ryot of Gentlemen in these daies. . . . And

[32] F.W.M. Draper, *Four Centuries of Merchant Taylors' School, 1561-1961* (London: Oxford University Press, 1962), p. 31.

[33] Peter Heylen's poem survives in a commonplace book, now Folger Shakespeare Library MS V.a. 162, fols. 140-142.

[34] Richard Lovelace, "Prologue to *The Scholars*," in *The Poems of Richard Lovelace*, ed. C. H. Wilkinson (Oxford: Clarendon Press, 1925), II, 58.

[35] Heywood, *Apology*, C$_3$$^v$.

who are the spectators? but such like as both Poets and Actors are, euen such as reckon no more of their studies, then *spend-all* Gentlemen of their cast sutes.[36]

Like most with a university education, John Harington expressed a more level-headed view: "But, for my part, I commend not such sowere censurers, but I thinke in stage-playes may bee much good, in well-penned comedies, and specially tragedies; and I remember, in Cambridge, howsoever the presyser sort have banisht them, the wyser sort did, and still doe mayntayn them."[37] Certainly the "presyser sort" did not prevail, for plays remained part of the education of the privileged even under the Commonwealth.[38]

If a young gentleman were sent abroad to complete his education, he routinely included plays in his activities. Thus in June of 1605, the twenty-three-year-old Dudley, Lord North, attended some plays in Antwerp, besides taking in the sights and trying a little gambling.[39] Revealing a thorough familiarity with playhouse customs, Thomas Coryat visited a theater in Venice, though he paid more attention to the courtesans than to the performance:

They [the courtesans] were so graced, that they sate on high alone by themselves, in the best roome of all the Playhouse.

[36] I. G., *A Refutation of the Apology for Actors*, in Heywood, *Apology*, $C_2$. The wisdom of university plays had been argued earlier by Dr. Rainolds and William Gager. Latin correspondence on the issue between Rainolds and Alberico Gentili was published in *Th' Overthrow of Stage-Playes* (London, 1599), with two subsequent reprints. See J. W. Binns, "Women or Transvestites on the Elizabethan Stage?: An Oxford Controversy," *Sixteenth Century Journal* 5 (1974): 95-120.

[37] John Harington, "A Treatise on Play," in *Nugae Antiquae* (London: J. Wright, 1804), I, 191.

[38] In *A New Discovery of the Old Art of Teaching Schoole*, Schoolmaster Charles Hoole reported in 1660 that in London and elsewhere on the last day of school, "The higher Forms should entertain the company with some elegant Latine Comedy out of Terence or Plautus, and part of a Greek one out of Aristophanes" (Draper, *Four Centuries of Merchant Taylors' School*, p. 47).

[39] Lawrence Stone, *The Crisis of the Aristocracy* (Oxford: Clarendon Press, 1965), p. 696.

> . . . I saw some men also in the Play-house disguised in the
> same manner with double vizards, those were said to be the
> favourites of the Courtezans: they sit not here in galleries
> as we doe in London. For there is but one or two little galleries
> in the house, wherein the Courtezans only sit. But all men
> do sit beneath in the yard or court, every man upon his
> severall stoole, for which he payeth a gazet.[40]

Even aristocrats traveling on the Continent had opportunities
to see English troupes performing, either on an occasional tour
or in the employ of European nobles. Heywood reported that
"The King of *Denmarke* . . . entertained into his seruice a
company of *English Comedians*, commended unto him by the
honourable the Earle of *Leicester*: the Duke of *Brounswicke* and
the *Landgraue* of *Hessen* retaine in their Courts certaine of ours
of the same quality" and that "The Cardinall at *Bruxels* hath
at this time in pay a company of our English comedians."[41]
Consequently, any privileged young man with a taste for plays,
perhaps developed during his university days, could pursue this
particular pleasure in Europe as well as in London.

INNS OF COURT PERFORMANCES

For those seeking a privileged education at one of London's Inns
of Court, the opportunity for playgoing was even greater. The
Inns had long-entrenched associations with the drama. Two
members of the Inner Temple, Thomas North and Thomas Sack-
ville, wrote *Gorboduc*, the first English tragedy in blank verse,
for the Inn's Christmas revels in 1561, and plays continued to
be featured at the Inns of Court during festival seasons right
through to the end of the period. Drama written and performed
by members of the Inns eventually gave way to professional
presentations, with Thomas Hughes's *Misfortunes of Arthur*,
presented at Greenwich by the gentlemen at Gray's Inn in 1589,
as the last indigenous play on record. Under the Stuarts, the

---

[40] Thomas Coryat, *Coryat's Crudities* (Glasgow: James MacLehose and Sons,
1905), I, 386-387.
[41] Heywood, *Apology*, E, G₃.

vogue for masques rivaled the popularity of plays, but the actors entertained the lawyers in one fashion or another year after year.

The uproarious nature of the festivities sometimes made performance difficult, as in the famous Christmas revels at Gray's Inn in 1594.

> When the Ambassador was placed, as aforesaid, and that there was something to be performed for the Delight of the Beholders, there arose such a disordered Tumult and Crowd upon the Stage, that there was no Opportunity to effect that which was intended: There came so great a number of worshipful Personages upon the Stage, that might not be displaced; and Gentlewomen, whose Sex did privilege them from Violence, that . . . at length there was no hope of Redress for that present. The Lord Ambassador and his Train thought that they were not so kindly entertained, as was before expected, and thereupon would not stay any longer at that time, but departed, in a sort, discontented and displeased. After their Departure the Throngs and Tumults did somewhat cease, although so much of them continued, as was able to disorder and confound any good Inventions whatsoever. In regard whereof . . . it was thought good not to offer any thing of Account, saving Dancing and Revelling with Gentlewomen; and after such Sports, a Comedy of Errors (like to *Plautus* his *Menechmus*) was played by the Players.[42]

Other records of Inns of Court performances included those at the Middle Temple seen by Benjamin Rudyerd in 1597 and 1598, the presentation of *Twelfth Night* mentioned by John Manningham, and an unnamed play witnessed by Justinian Pagitt in 1633.[43] *Troilus and Cressida*, "neuer clapper-clawd with the palmes of the vulger," was very likely played for an

[42] *Gesta Grayorum* (London: Malone Society, 1914), p. 22.

[43] Sir Benjamin Rudyerd, *Memoirs*, ed. James Alexander Manning (London: T. and W. Boone, 1841), pp. 12, 13; John Manningham, *Diary*, ed. John Bruce, Camden Society Publications, vol. 99 (1868), p. 18; Harleian MSS 1026, fols. 70-70ᵛ; as cited by Wilfrid R. Prest, *The Inns of Court under Elizabeth I and the Early Stuarts, 1590-1640* (London: Longmans, 1972), p. 169.

Inns of Court audience as well.[44] The treasurer's accounts for the Inner Temple, extant from 1605, list payments ranging from £5 to £10 for a play every year at Candlemas and/or All Saints' Day. When the performances were banned in 1611, "for that great disorder and scurrility is brought into this House by lewd and lascivious plays," there was enough protest to have the custom reinstated before the year was out, after which time payments were resumed twice yearly.[45] When one of their number, William Prynne, wrote a thousand-page diatribe against the theater and actually dedicated it to the Masters of the Bench, the gentlemen of Lincoln's Inn were so outraged that they expelled Prynne from membership. Bulstrode Whitelocke claimed that James Shirley's masque, *The Triumph of Peace*, performed for Charles I and Henrietta in 1634 by Gray's and Lincoln's Inns and the Middle and Inner Temples, was intended as a repudiation of Prynne's *Histrio-Mastrix*.[46] Quite clearly, the Inns of Court not only enjoyed plays but defended them as well. Hence, no gentleman who went up to the Inns could avoid exposure to drama any more than he could in grammar school or the university. Plays formed an intrinsic part of his life and education.

PRIVATE PERFORMANCES

Predictably, the privileged regularly included the drama as entertainment for special occasions in their own homes and elsewhere, though critics like Prynne demanded to know, "Why doe men send for Stage-Players to their houses?"[47] Apparently this question did not often occur to the great lords who summoned the players whenever they needed impressive amuse-

[44] William Shakespeare, "A Neuer Writer, to an Euer Reader," *The Famous Historie of Troylus and Cresseid* (London, 1609).

[45] F. A. Inderwick, ed., *A Calendar of the Inner Temple Records* (London: H. Sotheran, 1896-1904), II, 23ff., 64, 70ff.

[46] Bulstrode Whitelock, *Memorials of the English Affairs* (Oxford: Oxford University Press, 1853), I, 53-55.

[47] William Prynne, *Histrio-Mastrix* (London, 1633), p. 47.

ment. According to a direction in William Percy's *Aphrodysial,* the performers sometimes had to cope with improvised and crowded stage arrangements: "Here went furth the whole Chorus in a shuffle as after a Play in a Lord's howse."[48] Yet despite the inconveniences, the companies performed privately for the powerful throughout the period. Recorder Hatfield saw a play at a dinner with the outgoing sheriffs in September of 1575.[49] On 9 December 1595, Sir Edward Hoby wrote to Sir Robert Cecil, inviting him to what was probably a performance of *Richard II* at his house in Canon Row, "where, as late as shall please you, a gate for your supper shall be open, and K. Richard present himself to your view."[50] Rowland Whyte, Sidney's correspondent, recorded a number of special occasions that featured plays performed before the nobility:

### 30 JANUARY 1598

My Lord *Compton,* my Lord *Cobham,* Sir *Walter Rawley,* my Lord *Southhampton,* doe severally feast Mr. Secretary before he depart, and have Plaies and Banquets. My Lady *Darby,* my Lady *Walsingham,* Mrs. Anne *Russell,* are of the Company, and my Lady *Rawley.*

### 15 FEBRUARY 1598

Sir *Gilley Meiricke* made at *Essex* House Yesternight a very great Supper. There were at yt, my Ladys *Lester, Northumberland, Bedford, Essex, Rich,* and my Lords of *Essex, Rutland, Monjoy,* and others. They had 2 Plaies, which kept them vp till 1 a Clocke after Midnight.

### 8 MARCH 1600

All this Weeke the Lords haue bene in *London,* and past away the Tyme in Feasting and Plaies; for *Vereiken* dined vpon *Wednesday,* with my Lord Treasurer, who made hym a Roiall Dinner; vpon *Thursday* my Lord Chamberlain feasted hym,

---

[48] William Percy, *Aphrodysial;* as cited by Chambers, *Elizabethan Stage,* I, 220.

[49] *Hatfield MSS,* II, 116; as cited by Chambers, *Elizabethan Stage,* I, 221.

[50] *Hatfield MSS,* V, 487; as cited in ibid., II, 194.

and made hym very great, and a delicate Dinner, and there in the After Noone his Plaiers acted, before *Vereiken*, Sir *John Old Castell*, to his Great Contentment.[51]

Other correspondents also testified to the popularity of plays among the aristocracy. Sir Dudley Carleton reported a great feast given in January 1605 by the Spanish ambassador for the Duke of Holst and the entire Court, adding, "But after Dinner he came home to us, with a Play and a Banquett."[52] The following year, John Chamberlain wrote that he attended a play at Sir Walter Cope's, where Chamberlain "had to squire his daughter about, till he was weary."[53] In 1613, when Sir John Swinnerton was Lord Mayor, he offered entertainment that included a play. According to Chamberlain, "on Tewsday, he was at the Lord Mayor's where besides all other cheere they had a play."[54] Apparently the Lords Mayor frequently summoned the players before important guests, at least under James. To celebrate the marriage of the Earl of Somerset to Lady Francis Howard, the Lord Mayor and the aldermen hosted a play at the Merchant Taylors' Hall in 1614.[55] However, such glittering occasions could give rise to behavior fully as raucous as that at the Inns of Court:

On Saterday the Knights of the Bath were entertained by the Lord Mayor at Drapers Hall with a supper and a play, where some of them were so rude and unruly and caried themselves

[51] Arthur Collins, ed., *Letters and Memorials of State* (London, 1746), II, 86, 90-91, 175. Louis Verreyken was the Flemish ambassador.

[52] Sir Ralph Winwood, *Memorials of Affairs of State in the Reigns of Q. Elizabeth and K. James I*, ed. Edmund T. Sawyer (London, 1725), II, 44. Chambers believes that this performance occurred 3 January and was given by the Queen's Revels (*Elizabethan Stage*, IV, 119).

[53] *Calendar of State Papers, Domestic, of the Reigns of Edward VI, Mary, Elizabeth, and James* (Great Britain: Public Record Office, 1856-1872), VIII (1603-1610), p. 296. Hereafter cited as *C.S.P.D.*

[54] Norman E. McClure, ed., *The Letters of John Chamberlain* (Philadelphia: American Philosophical Society, 1939), I, 457.

[55] 4 January 1614; John Stow, *Annales, or a General Chronicle of England*, continued and augmented . . . by Edmund Howes, Gent. (London, 1631), p. 1,005.

so insolently divers wayes but specially in putting citizens wives to the squeake, so far foorth that one of the sheriffes brake open a doore upon Sir Edward Sackvile, which gave such occasion of scandall, that they went away without the banket though it were redy and prepared for them.[56]

COURT PERFORMANCES

Despite the frequency of plays at the schools and universities, the Inns of Court, and the great halls of the wealthy, the Court itself held center stage when it came to dramatic performances. Year after year the records testified to the popularity of the players.[57] According to a late witness, "how well shee [Queen Elizabeth] approved of these Recreations, being (as shee termed them) *harmlesse spenders of time,* the large exhibitions which shee conferred on such as were esteemed notable in that kind may sufficiently witnesse."[58] Actually, Elizabeth was notably parsimonious about financing the costs of setting up the special scaffolds, stages, tents, and costumes required for Court performances. Thomas Wilson may have claimed:

Her pleasures cost her much, as shewes, triumphs and such like great mariages with any of her maids or Ladyes publiquely in the Court, and comedies, shewes, devises and entertainement of Ambassadors publicquely as I have seen divers vizt the Duke of Bullion who cost her every day 100[1], besides the charge of his solemne entertainment att her owne Table, likewise the Danish Ambassador and others of these. She spends ordinarely 5,000[1] yearly, and some time so much in a month, as occasion serve.[59]

[56] McClure, ed., *Letters of John Chamberlain,* II, 35.

[57] For records of the performances, see Albert Feuillerat, *Documents Relating to the Office of the Revels* (Louvain: A. Uystpruyst, 1908), pp. xiii-xvii; Chambers, *Elizabethan Stage,* IV, 75-130; Bentley, *Jacobean and Caroline Stage,* I, 94-101.

[58] Richard Brathwaite, *The English Gentleman and The English Gentlewoman,* 3d ed. (London, 1641), p. 106.

[59] Sir Thomas Wilson, "The State of England (1600)," ed. F. J. Fisher, *Camden Miscellany,* 3d ser. 52 (1936): 32.

But in reality, the Queen spent as little as she could on her pleasures, preferring to let her courtiers bear that expense whenever possible, as her Lord Chamberlain did during Christmas of 1601. Carleton reported, "The Queen dined to-day privately at my Lord Chamberlain's; I have just come from the Blackfriars, where I saw her at the play with all her *candidae auditrices.*"[60] When contemporaries noted that plays "flourisht more than ordinarie"[61] a month before her death, they probably had reference to such "gift" presentations, for the official accounts listed only two plays for March of 1603. At least in her later years, Elizabeth did not always bother to attend the performances, for Rowland Whyte found it noteworthy in 1599 that the Queen "graced the dauncing and plaies with her own presence."[62]

With the advent of the Stuarts, this niggardly attitude toward the drama underwent a radical reversal. At James's first Christmas, "It is said there shall be 30 playes,"[63] and the rumor exceeded the facts by very little:

> The first holy dayes we had every night a publicke play in the great hale, at which the king was ever present, and liked or disliked as he saw cause; but it seems he takes no extraordinary pleasure in them. The Queen and Prince were more the players frends, for on other nights they had them privately, and hath since taken them to theyr protection.[64]

James's heir and his wife indeed became the chief patrons of the acting companies, although the King was certainly present at many performances and always at those given for state occasions such as the visit of the King of Denmark in 1606 and

---

[60] 29 December 1601; C.S.P.D., VI (1601-1603), p. 136.

[61] Chambers, *Elizabethan Stage*, I, 6.

[62] Collins, ed., *Letters and Memorials of State*, II, 425.

[63] E. T. Bradley, *The Life of Lady Arabella Stuart* (London: Richard Bentley and Son, 1889), II, 195. For a full analysis of Court entertainment under the Stuarts, see Roy Strong, *Splendor at Court: Renaissance Spectacle and the Theater of Power* (London: Weidenfeld and Nicolson, 1973).

[64] Dudley Carleton to John Chamberlain, 15 January 1604; as cited by Chambers, *Elizabethan Stage*, I, 7n.

the marriage of his daughter Elizabeth in 1613. But Prince Henry and his party sometimes had "every night a play."[65] As for the Queen, hostile tongues reported that she had special reasons for enjoying the players. Beaumont, the French Ambassador, said, "Consider for pity's sake what must be the state and condition of a prince, whom the preachers publicly from the pulpit assail, whom the comedians of the metropolis bring upon the stage, whose wife attends these representations in order to enjoy the laugh against her husband."[66] Irrespective of the truth or falsity of that report, drama flourished at the Jacobean Court.

The tradition continued and even expanded under Charles I. Both the gorgeous new banqueting hall, finished just before James's death, and the new theater in the remodeled Cockpit at Whitehall provided fresh settings for the players. Upon occasion, the Queen and her party even visited the Blackfriars theater. On 13 May 1634, she saw "Messingers playe" there, and in late 1635 or early 1636, "the Quene saw Lodowick Carlile's second part of Arviragus and Felicia acted, w$^{ch}$ is hugely liked of every one." In May of 1636, she and the Prince Elector Alfonso again went to Blackfriars, where they watched one of the twenty-two plays the King's Men acted for the Court that year.[67]

In addition to the English troupes, the Queen also promoted a French troupe:

> On tuesday night the 17 of February, 1634 [1635], a Frenche company of players, being approved of by the queene at her house too nights before, and commended by her majesty to the kinge, were admitted to the Cockpitt in Whitehall, and

[65] McClure, ed., *Letters of John Chamberlain*, I, 330.

[66] 14 June 1604; Friedrich Ludwig Georg von Raumer, *History of the Sixteenth and Seventeenth Centuries, Illustrated by Original Documents* (London: J. Murray, 1835), II, 206.

[67] Joseph Quincy Adams, ed., *The Dramatic Records of Sir Henry Herbert, Master of the Revels, 1623-1673* (New Haven: Yale University Press, 1917), pp. 65, 75-76; letter from Charles, Prince of the Palatinate, to his mother, Queen of Bohemia; as cited by Bentley, *Jacobean and Caroline Stage*, I, 48.

there presented the king and queene with a Frenche Comedy called *Melise*, with good approbation: for which play the king gives them ten pounds.[68]

At another time Queen Henrietta incurred considerable trouble to see a repeat performance of a play she had enjoyed at Oxford:

the Queen sent to the Chancellor that he would procure of Christ Church the Persian attire of the Royall Slave and other apparell wherein it was acted, to the end that she might see her own Players act it over again, and whether they could do it as well as was done by the University. Whereupon the Chancellor caused the Cloaths and Perspectives of the Stage to be sent to Hampton Court in a Waggon, for which the University received from her a letter of thanks. So that all of it being fitted for use (the author thereof being then present) 'twas acted soon after, but by all mens confession, the Players came short of the University Actors.[69]

However glittering the setting or exalted the company, Court festivities could be as raucous as any others. After *The Masque of Blackness*, presented on Twelfth Night in 1605, Dudley Carleton reported:

The confusion in getting in was so great that some Ladies lie by it and complaine of the fury of the white stafes [ushers]. In the passages through the galleries they were shut up in several heapes betwixt dores and there stayed till all was ended, and in the cuming out a banquet which was prepared for the king in the great chamber was overturned table and all before it was skarce touched. It were infinit to tell you what loses there were of chaynes, Jewels, purces and such like loose ware.[70]

A few years later, the Venetian embassy's chaplain, Father Busino, told of a similar incident at the banquet following the

---

[68] Adams, ed., *Dramatic Records of Sir Henry Herbert*, p. 60.

[69] Anthony Wood, *Historia et Antiquitates Universitatis Oxoniensis*, II, Bk. I, 412-413; as cited by Bentley, *Jacobean and Caroline Stage*, I, 52.

[70] P.R.O. SP 14/12/6; as cited by G.P.V. Akrigg, *Jacobean Pageant, or The Court of King James I* (New York: Athenaeum, 1967), p. 229.

performance of *Pleasure Reconciled to Virtue:* "The repast was served upon glass plates or dishes and at the first assault they upset the table and the crash of glass platters reminded me precisely of a severe hailstorm at Midsummer smashing the window glass. The story ended at half past two in the morning and half disgusted and weary we returned home."[71] How different was the scene at the last Christmas in the Caroline Court. "On Twelfe Night, 1641 [1642], the prince had a play called *The Scornful Lady*, at the Cockpitt, but the kinge and queene were not there; and it was the only play acted at courte in the whole Christmas."[72] The plays ceased when the reign of their royal patrons ceased, but for the preceding decades, the drama had proved an especially favored pleasure for the courtly circle.

## PERSONAL ASSOCIATIONS

Though the drama became closely connected with the education and the entertainment of virtually all the privileged, some gentlemen developed unusually intimate associations with the players. A sophisticated man like Sir Philip Sidney could criticize the drama expertly in his *Defense of Poetry*, but this ability would be expected from a polished writer and courtier who had witnessed countless performances. Dedications to noble patrons and fulsome tributes from titled admirers regularly graced the pages of published plays, but this flattery also reflected no more than the accepted system of literary patronage.

Less usual, but by no means uncommon, was the aristocrat who actually wrote plays or performed in them or admitted players as his intimates. The Countess of Pembroke's circle were perhaps best known for their efforts at dramatic literature. But Lord Derby too was reported to be "busy penning comedies for the common players" in June of 1599, when he became patron of the actors at the Boar's Head.[73] Apparently Derby had always shown an unusual interest in his troupes. Some years earlier

---

[71] *Calendar of State Papers, Venice* (Great Britain: Public Record Office, 1864-1947), XV (1617-1619), p. 114. Hereafter cited as *C.S.P.Ven.*

[72] Adams, ed., *Dramatic Records of Sir Henry Herbert*, p. 58.

[73] *C.S.P.D.*, V (1598-1601), p. 227; Herbert Berry, "The Playhouse in the

his countess had petitioned Secretary Cecil that her husband's men "not be bared from ther accoustomed plaing . . . for that my Lo: taking delite in them it will kepe him from moer prodigall courses."[74] Bulstrode Whitelock was involved not with the players but with the Blackfriars musicians.

> I was so conversant with the musicians, and so willing to gain their favor, especially at this time, that I composed an air myself, with the assistance of Mr. Ives, and called it *Whitelock's Coranto*; which being cried up, was first played publicly by the Blackfriars Music, who were then esteemed the best of common musicians in London. Whenever I came to that house . . . to see a play, the musicians would presently play *Whitelocke's Coranto*, and it was so often called for that they would have played it twice or thrice in an afternoon.[75]

Besides writing commendatory verses, dramatic criticism, plays, and music, the aristocracy occasionally performed as well. Gentlemen from the Inns of Court and courtiers alike delighted to take roles in the elaborate masques presented before James and Charles. Amateur theatricals by the privileged evidently seemed so common that as early as 1602, several hundred people paid a stiff admission price to see *England's Joy*, a spectacular "to be acted only by certain gentlemen and gentlewomen of account."[76] When the production, promoted by Richard Vennor, a member of Lincoln's Inn, turned out to be a hoax, the outraged crowd that had filled the Swan reacted with considerable violence.

Close friendships developed between certain players and the privileged, although detractors objected that "it seemeth to me a thing of great inconuenience, that a noble or Sage man should

---

Boar's Head Inn, Whitechapel," in *The Elizabethan Theatre*, ed. David Galloway (Toronto: Archon Books, 1970), p. 53.

[74] *Malone Society Collections*, II, 2: 148.

[75] Charles Burney, *A General History of Music from the Earliest Ages to the Present Period*, ed. Frank Mercer (London, 1782-1789), II, 299.

[76] John Chamberlain to Dudley Carleton, 19 November 1602; McClure, ed., *Letters of John Chamberlain*, I, 172.

accept any such Iester as his friend."[77] To prevent any such unsuitable friendship, one conservative grandparent vowed, "The first thing I shall do w$^{th}$ you If I Live to send you to the Inns of Court is to inquire & find out some person w$^{th}$ whose acquaintance I dare trust you. . . . [for] it is a Lamentable sight to see how young Gentlemen w$^{n}$ they come to an university or Inns of Court loose themselves . . . w$^{th}$ Stage players Tapsters Ostlers Fidlers common Gamesters thredbare poets Servingmen & such like."[78] Nevertheless, actors and playwrights continued to find favor with their betters. While a tutor to one of the Sidneys, Ben Jonson caroused with his young charge, until the poet was "trundled . . . about the streets dead drunk in a cart for the amusement of the bystanders."[79] A friend of such other aristocrats as Edward Hyde, Jonson grew so fond of exchanging "curtezies, and complements with Gallants in the Lordes roomes" that his habit was satirized.[80] The great actor Richard Burbage commanded the respect and affection even of peers. After Burbage's death, the Earl of Pembroke wrote Lord Doncaster in Germany that "my Lord of Lenox made a great supper to the French Embassador this night here and even now all the company are at the play, which I being tender-harted,

---

[77] I.G., *Refutation of the Apology for Actors*, p. 46.

[78] British Museum Harleian MS 4009, pp. 73–74. Sir Matthew Hale, the author of these words, held firm opinions on plays and playgoing. His biographer reports that at Oxford,

> the Stage Players coming thither, he [Hale] was so much corrupted by seeing many Playes, that he almost wholly forsook his Studies. By this, he not only lost much time, but found that his Head came to be thereby filled with such vain Images of things, that they were at best Improfitable, if not hurtful to him; and being afterwards sensible of the Mischief of this, he resolved upon his coming to *London* (where he knew the opportunities of such Sights would be more frequent and Inviting) never to see a Play again, to which he constantly adhered.

See Gilbert Burnett, *The Life and Death of Sir Matthew Hale* (London, 1682), p. 4.

[79] *Ben Jonson*, ed. C. H. Herford and Percy Simpson (Oxford: Clarendon Press, 1925–1952), I, 140.

[80] Thomas Dekker, *Satiromastix*, in *The Dramatic Works*, ed. Fredson Bowers (Cambridge: Cambridge University Press, 1953–1961), I, 382.

could not endure to see so soone after the loss of my old acquaintance Burbage."[81]

Relationships more permissive than mere friendship occasionally developed. For example, this choice piece of gossip reached Lord Hay from Sir William Trumbull in Brussels in June of 1619: "I am told he [the Earl of Argyll] was privy to the payment of £15 or £16 poundes . . . for the nourseing of a childe which the world sayes is daughter to my lady [Argyll] and N[at] Feild the Player."[82] Nor was Lady Argyll the only wellborn woman with whom the actors took liberties. Though impudence rather than seduction was involved, the clown Tarleton brazenly criticized Queen Elizabeth herself before all her Court. According to Bohun:

> Tarleton, who was then the best comedian in England, had made a pleasant play, and when it was acting before the Queen, he pointed at Sir Walter Raleigh and said "See, the Knave commands the Queen", for which he was corrected by a frown from the Queen; yet he had the confidence to add that he was of too much and too intolerable a power; and going on with the same liberty, he reflected on the overgreat power and riches of the Earl of Leicester, which was so universally applauded by all that were present, that she thought best to bear these reflections with a seeming unconcernedness. But yet she was so offended, that she forbad Tarleton and all her jesters from coming near her table, being inwardly displeased with this impudent and unseasonable liberty.[83]

This particular story may have been apocryphal, but Tarleton's favored status at Court was widely reported.[84]

Once in a while the good will between the players and the privileged gave way to hostility. Twice in 1580 the Earl of Oxford's players were accused of the "committing of disorders

---

[81] May 1619; Egerton MS 2592, fol. 81; as cited by Bentley, *Jacobean and Caroline Stage*, I, 6.

[82] E.J.L. Scott, "The Elizabethan Stage," *The Athenaeum* 1 (1882): 103.

[83] Edmund Bohun, *The Character of Queen Elizabeth* (London, 1693), p. 352.

[84] See, e.g., *Tarlton's News out of Purgatory* (London, 1590), p. 42; and Heywood, *Apology*, p. E₂ᵛ.

and frayes appon the gentlemen of the Innes of Courte." The next year, following a Sunday performance, Lord Berkeley's men got into a fight with "a dysordered companye of gentlemen of the Innes of Courte & others," with both sides committed to the Counter for their behavior.[85] For the most part, however, the actors enjoyed the amity and sometimes the affection of all the socially privileged except the severe Puritans.

PLAYERS AS GENTLEMEN

Because of their close associations, some accused the players of pretending to be gentlemen themselves. Henry Peacham specifically excluded from gentility those who "have no share at all in Nobility or Gentry: as Painters, Stage-players, Tumblers, ordinary Fidlers, Inne-keepers, Fencers, Iuglers, Dancers, Mountebanckes, Bearewards, and the like."[86] In the case of the actors, he was protesting against men who spoke, dressed, and behaved like the gentlemen they entertained. Clothes, which of course marked the outward distinction between the privileged and the plebeian, developed into a particularly touchy issue. As early as 1579, Stephen Gosson complained: "Ouerlashing in apparel is so common a fault that the very hyerlings of some of our players, which stand at reuersion of vi.s by the weeke, iet vnder gentlemens noses in sutes of silke."[87] When a player could boast that "my very share in playing apparell will not be solde for two hundred pounds," it was but partly ironic for a stranger to exclaim upon meeting him, "A player . . . I tooke you rather for a Gentleman of great liuing, for if by outward habit men shuld be censured, I tell you, you would bee taken for a substantiall man."[88] Satirists delighted in the player's

---

[85] 13 April 1580, 26 May 1580, 11 July 1581; Dasent, ed., *Acts of the Privy Council*, XI, 445, and XII, 37; *Malone Society Collections*, I, 51; Chambers, *Elizabethan Stage*, IV, 280, 282.

[86] Henry Peacham, *The Compleat Gentleman*, ed. G. S. Gordon (Oxford: Clarendon Press, 1906), p. 13.

[87] Stephen Gosson, *The Schoole of Abuse*, ed. Edward Arber, English Reprints, no. 3 (London: A. Murray and Son, 1869), p. 39.

[88] Robert Greene, *Groats-worth of Witte*, ed. G. B. Harrison (New York: Barnes and Noble, 1966), p. 33.

gentlemanly pretensions: "He hath beene familiar so long with out-sides, that he professes himselfe (being unknowne) to be an apparent Gentleman. But his thinne Felt, and his silke Stockings, or his foule Linnen, and faire Dublet, doe (in him) bodily reveal the Broker."[89] Yet the gentlemen themselves fostered the confusion by making gifts of their clothing to the actors.[90]

Even though the actors who passed as counterfeit gentlemen evoked ridicule and resentment, it must be remembered that some in the dramatic enterprise were true gentlemen. While it was an exaggeration to claim that "Every Poët writes Squire now,"[91] certain playwrights and players rightfully belonged in the ranks of the privileged. William Shakespeare came of a good family, received a proper education, obtained a coat of arms, and retired to Stratford-upon-Avon to live as a prosperous gentleman in a fine house. Similarly, Shakespeare's colleagues—Burbage, Hemminges, Phillips, and Pope—all acquired coats of arms. Ben Jonson, though a bricklayer's stepson, enjoyed superior schooling at Westminster School, served as tutor and companion to the Sidneys, and presided over masques at the Stuart Court. James Shirley attended the Merchant Taylors' School, Oxford, and Cambridge and was headmaster at St. Alban's until 1625. Thomas Heywood, Robert Greene, Philip Marlowe, and Philip Massinger were all university men, while Thomas Lodge was a resident at Lincoln's Inn and John Marston at the Middle Temple. Francis Beaumont and John Fletcher were born into privilege, Beaumont the son of a knight and Fletcher the son of a bishop. Beaumont studied at both Oxford and the Inner Temple, retiring from the theater when he married into a wealthy Kent family. The financier behind the Swan and the Boar's Head, Francis Langley, was nephew to a Lord Mayor of London and always styled himself "gentleman," though he was never formally schooled. Edward Alleyn, for twenty years a

[89] Cocke, "A common Player"; as cited by Chambers, *Elizabethan Stage*, IV, 2.

[90] Adams, ed., *Dramatic Records of Sir Henry Herbert*, p. 61; William Knowler, ed., *The Earl of Strafforde's Letters and Dispatches* (London, 1739), II, 150.

[91] Jonson, *The Magnetic Lady*, in *Ben Jonson*, VI, 510.

favored actor, amassed sufficient wealth to purchase a £10,000 manor in Surrey and to establish Dulwich College. Alleyn's father-in-law, Philip Henslowe, married a rich widow, invested in theatrical enterprises, bought valuable property, and held minor Court offices under both Elizabeth and James.

Henslowe or Alleyn or even Shakespeare himself could have formed the target for Henry Crosse's attack upon the "buck-orome gentlemen" in 1603: "And as these copper-lace gentlemen growe rich, purchase lands by adulterous Playes, & not a fewe of them vsurers and extortioners, which they exhaust out of the purses of their haunters, so are they puft vp in such pride and self-loue, as they enuie their equalles, and scorne theyr inferiors."[92] Yet, however precarious and marginal their status, several members of the dramatic companies could fairly be designated as privileged by birth, education, wealth, or achievement. Slurs upon their status provoked anger, too, as this little incident of 1580 indicated: "The Duttons and theyr fellow-players forsakying the Erle of Warwycke theyr mayster, became followers of the Erle of Oxford, and wrot themselves his CO-MOEDIANS, which certayne Gentlemen altered and made CAMOELIANS. The Duttons, angry with that, compared themselves to any gentleman."[93] Contracts and other legal documents regularly identified some members of the companies as "Mr."— a gentleman's proper title.

PUBLIC PERFORMANCES

Under any circumstances, London's privileged residents might have been attracted to playhouses that could offer the writing of William Shakespeare or the acting of Edward Alleyn. But the

---

[92] Henry Crosse, *Vertues Common-wealth: Or the High-way to Honour*, in *Occasional Issues*, ed. Alexander B. Grosart (Manchester: C. E. Simms, 1878), VII, 111. For an analysis of the playwright's income, which was far superior to that of schoolmasters, curates, or other professional writers, see Gerald Eades Bentley, *The Profession of the Dramatist in Shakespeare's Time, 1590-1642* (Princeton: Princeton University Press, 1971), pp. 95-105.

[93] Thomas Wright and James O. Halliwell, *Reliquae Antiquae* (London: William Pickering, 1843), II, 122.

attraction of the theater was decidedly strengthened because gentlemen customarily saw plays at school, at the Inns of Court, in their own homes, and at Court. Since the elite also dealt with actors and playwrights as patrons, as friends, and even as equals, the lure of playgoing exerted still greater power. Other factors, too, made theatergoing unusually appealing. After all, Court performances entertained only the favored few. Even with six hundred and more crowded in to see the plays at the great palace halls, thousands of gentlemen and would-be gentlemen in London could not hope to attend. Nor did the Court offer plays every day, even at the height of Stuart extravagance. The presentations at the Inns of Court and in the homes of the nobility were also restricted, both in number and in the size of their audience.

But London's public playing places provided daily dramatic fare to all with a taste for plays. At innyards, baiting rings, large open-air theaters, and smaller enclosed theaters, the professional troupes performed the same pieces seen by the courtiers and the nobility at prices calculated to fit even the slimmest purse of the most threadbare gentleman. Here a man could come "for companie, for custome, for recreation, perhaps for sleepe; or to feed [his] . . . eyes or . . . his eares."[94] As early as 1563, long before the first theaters rose in Finsbury Fields, some exclaimed against the life of the courtier who "licenciously roames in ryot, coasting the stretes w[th] wavering plumes, hangd to a long side blade, & poūced in silkes . . . haunteth plaie, feasts, bathes and banketings."[95] But it proved useless to condemn a pastime so obviously popular among the privileged classes. For better or worse, gentlemen became inveterate playgoers, like Hamlet, interested in the latest stage gossip, acquainted with even obscure performances, displayng an easy camaraderie with the players, well able to criticize acting styles or to pen a few lines for a special occasion.

[94] Joseph Hall, *Characters of Vertues and Vices* (London, 1608), p. 97.
[95] Lawrence Humphrey, *The Nobles, or of Nobilitye* (London, 1563), pp. i.i.-i.ii.

Throughout the period, scarcely a year went by without one or several extant references to the visits of gentlemen to the theaters, either alone or with friends. At first, the privileged had some choice between the adult companies and the children's troupes. The Merchant Taylors' students had ended their public performances in 1574, but at least one group of boys was performing between 1576 and 1590, with two in residence from 1577 to 1582. Some indication of their audience appeared in the prologue to Lyly's *Midas*, where the young actor spoke of "presenting our studies before Gentlemen." He also proclaimed that "At our exercises, Souldiers call for Tragedies, their obiect is bloud: Courtiers for Commedies, their subiect is loue; Countriemen for Pastoralles, Shepheards are their Saintes."[96] As his words attested, soldiers, courtiers, and men up from the country represented a fair sample of the privileged in London during these years. One country gentleman, a William Darrell, left a specific record of his attendance at a boys' theater, for his expense account included 6d. paid in 1589 to see a play at Paul's.[97] With smaller indoor, or "private," theaters and less frequent presentations, the boys could not satisfy the playgoing public to the same extent as an adult company; and when the children ceased to perform in 1590 or 1591, the older actors had the gentlemen all to themselves.

Yet even while the boys' troupes were acting, the privileged also patronized the innyards and the great public theaters with their roofed tiers of balconies surrounding the open yard. So common was public playgoing among the elite that in 1578, John Florio's English-Italian conversation book included instructions for inviting a lady to see a play at the Bull Inn. Florio even threw in a bit of moral dramatic criticism for good measure:

Where shall we goe?
To a playe at the Bull, or els to some other place.

---

[96] John Lyly, *Midas*, in *The Complete Works*, ed. R. Warwick Bond (Oxford: Clarendon Press, 1902), III, 115.

[97] Hubert Hall, *Society in the Elizabethan Age* (London: Swan, Sonnenschein, Lowrey, 1886), p. 211.

Doo Comedies like you wel?

Yea sir, on holy dayes.

They please me also wel, but the preachers wyll not
allowe them.

Wherefore, knowe you it:

They say, they are not good.

And wherfore are they vsed?

Because euery mã delites in thē.

I beleeue there is much knauery vsed at those Comedies:
what thinke you?

So beleeue I also.[98]

The following year, Gabriel Harvey, writing from Cambridge
to Edmund Spenser, then secretary to Leicester, teased his young
friend about sending the players to him for a new play: "I
suppose thou wilt go nighe hande shortelye to sende my lorde
'of Lycesters or my lorde of Warwickes,' Vawsis, or my lord
Ritches players, or sum other freshe starteupp comedanties unto
me for sum newe devised interlude, or sum maltconceivid com-
edye fitt for the Theater, or sum other paintid stage whereat
thou and thy lively copesmates in London maye lawghe ther
mouthes and bellyes full for pence or twoepence apeece."[99]
Harvey showed the easy familiarity with the various troupes,
the playhouses, and their repertoires that well-educated men
took for granted, even if their financial resources limited them
to penny and two-penny admissions.

By 1591, with the boys' companies barred from playing, the
great open-air public theaters laid exclusive claim to the privileged playgoers. Though innyards were still in use, the Theater,
the Curtain, the Rose, the Swan, and finally the first Globe
captured the principal share of the theatrical trade. These struc-
tures seemed impressive enough to be noted and visited by
foreign travelers, such as the merchant Samuel Kiechel of Ulm,
Prince Lewis of Anhalt-Cöthen, Johan DeWitt of Amsterdam

---

[98] John Florio, *First Fruites* (London, 1578), A₁.

[99] Gabriel Harvey, *Letter Book*, ed. E.J.L. Scott, Camden Society Publications,
n.s. 33 (1884): 67-68.

and Utrecht, and Thomas Platter of Basel. And the crowds that filled the great theaters on weekday afternoons unquestionably included a good many of the English privileged too. The Lord Mayor termed the theaters' wellbred patrons "such yoong gentlemen as haue small regard of credit or conscience."[100] More charitably, Henry Chettle, cautioning "the yoong people of the Cittie, either to abstaine altogether from playes, or at their comming thither to vse themselues after a more quiet order," specified that gentlemen spectators were not at fault for inciting disorders.[101]

Other records showed the presence of such respectable men as John Donne, who was "a great frequenter of Playes," and John Chamberlain, correspondent to Dudley Carleton, who went to see the new "play of humors"—"drawne alonge to yt by the common applause."[102] The Earl of Rutland, sometimes in company with others, went by boat "to the play house sondry tymes" within a single year.[103] So many young gentlemen frequented the the playhouses that when some cozeners were convicted of defrauding wellborn gulls, the Lord Treasurer "would haue those y^t make the playes to make a Comedie hereof, & to acte it w^th these names,"[104] apparently in hopes that the play would have an instructive effect upon the audience. His suggestion would have been pointless had not the gentry been attracted to comedies as well as to cozeners.

Before the end of the century, the playgoing gentleman became so familiar that he provided a favorite subject for the short

[100] Lord Mayor to Lord Burghley, 3 November 1594; *Malone Society Collections*, I, 74; Chambers, *Elizabethan Stage*, IV, 316-317.

[101] Henry Chettle, *Kind-Harts Dreame*, in *The Shakspere Allusion-Book*, ed. C. M. Ingleby, rev. John Munro (London: Oxford University Press, 1932), I, 65.

[102] Sir Richard Baker, *A Chronicle of the Kings of England* (London, 1696), p. 450; McClure, ed., *Letters of John Chamberlain*, I, 32.

[103] 1598-1599; *Rutland Manuscripts* (London: Stationery Office, 1888-1905), IV, 419-420.

[104] William Paley Baildon, ed., *Les Reportes del Cases in Camera Stellata, 1593 to 1609* (privately printed, 1894), p. 48.

satirical poems then fashionable. Sir John Davies included an excellent example in his *Epigrams*.

#### IN FUSCUM

He's like a horse, which turning round a mill,
Doth always in the self-same circle tread:
First, he doth rise at ten; and at eleuen
He goes to Gyls, where he doth eate till one;
Then sees a Play till sixe, and sups at seuen;
And after supper, straight to bed is gone;
And there till ten next day he doth remaine,
And then he dines, and sees a Comedy
And then he suppes, and goes to bed againe
Thus round he runs without variety.
    Save that sometimes he comes not to the Play,
    But falls into a whore-house by the way.[105]

#### THEATER RIVALRY

When the boys resumed their playing in 1599, the novelty of their performances, the notoriety of their plays, and the comfort of their roofed private houses for a time cut into the attendance at the public theaters. As Gilderstone expressed it in the first quarto of *Hamlet*:

Yfaith my Lord, noueltie carries it away
For the *principall publicke audience* that
Came to them, are turned to priuate playes
And to the humour of children.[106] [Italics mine]

In Jonson's *Poetaster*, an actor from the Globe complained, "this winter ha's made vs all poorer, then so many staru'd snakes: No bodie comes at vs; not a gentleman."[107] Though it has been argued that the boys attracted a new audience of aristocrats to

---

[105] Sir John Davies, *Epigrams*, in *The Complete Poems*, ed. Alexander B. Grosart (London: Chatto and Windus, 1876), II, 37-38.

[106] Shakespeare, *Hamlet* (London, 1603), $E_3$.

[107] Jonson, *Poetaster*, in *Ben Jonson*, IV, 255-256.

the theater—an audience the adults captured only when they too moved into the smaller private houses after 1609—the previous references would indicate that the children actually attracted a group already accustomed to playgoing. Men and boys, private houses and public seem to have competed for the same select audience of the privileged. Certainly the personal invective of the ensuing War of the Theaters would have been pointless unless the spectators were thoroughly acquainted with the playwrights and the social types that were so viciously satirized.

Even as the conflict raged, the gentlemen continued to attend both kinds of troupes and playhouses. In 1602, an impressment order executed against "plaie howses, Bowlinge Alleys, and Dycinge howses," to apprehend the "idle loose dissolute and suspected persons . . . nothwithstandinge they goe apparelled like gentlemen"[108] turned up an astonishing haul at the public theaters. Instead of riffraff, "they did not only presse Gentlemen, and sarvingmen, but Lawyers, Clarkes, country men that had law cawses, aye the Quens men, knightes, and as it was credibly reported one Earle."[109] Obviously a good many gentlemen preferred the public over the private playhouses on that unfortunate afternoon. Even when the visiting nobleman Duke Philip Julius of Stettin-Pomerania came to London, he bestowed his favor upon both the children's and the adults' performances.[110]

At the opposite end of the social spectrum from the visiting duke, a bizarre character named Marion Frith showed up at the theater too. Indirectly, her behavior confirmed the presence of gentlemen at the public theaters:

This day and place the said Mary appeared personally and there voluntarily confessed that she had long frequented all or most of the disorderly and licentious places in this cittie

[108] *Malone Society Collections*, II, 3: 318.

[109] Isaac H. Jeayes, ed., *Letters of Philip Gawdy* (London: Nichols, 1906), pp. 120-121.

[110] Gottfried von Bülow and Wilfred Powell, eds., "Diary of the Journey of Philip Julius, Duke of Stettin-Pomerania, through England in the Year 1602," *Transactions of the Royal Historical Society*, n.s. 6 (1892): 29.

as namely she hath usually in the habit of a man resorted to alehouses taverns tobacco shops and also to play houses there to see plaies and proses and namely being at a play about three quarters of a yeare since at ye Fortune in man's apparel and in her boots and w$^{th}$ a sword at her syde she told the company then present y$^t$ she thought many of them were of opinion that she was a man, but if any of them would come to her lodging they should finde she is a woman, and some other immodest and lascivious speaches she also used at y$^t$ time and also sat upon the stage in public viewe of all the people there present in man's apparel and played upon her lute and sange a song.[111]

What was significant about Marion Frith's testimony was not her outrageous actions but her ability to mingle with the spectators, at first undetected, while wearing clothing restricted to gentlemen—in particular, a sword. Had other gentlemen not been present at the Fortune in 1605, she could never have carried out her escapades so easily.

Evidence of another sort came from Thomas Dekker in *The Gull's Hornbook*. Under the guise of a manual of instructions, the work informed every would-be gentleman how to make a fool of himself in all the places London gallants frequented, including the playhouses. Interestingly, this piece, which missed no opportunity to make invidious distinctions between the inferior and the superior, made no distinction at all between the public and private theaters. "Whether therefore the gatherers of the publique or priuate Play-house stand to recieue the afternoones rent," the gull was advised to "aduance himselfe vp to the Throne of the Stage" where he could be seen by everyone.[112] If London's more elite audiences really preferred the boys over the adults, the *Hornbook* would probably have noted such favoritism. Other works, too, portrayed an indifferent choice between the two kinds of troupes. According to Middleton, after

[111] Francis W. X. Fincham, "Notes from the Ecclesiastical Court Records at Somerset House," *Transactions of the Royal Historical Society*, 4th ser. 4 (1921): 111-112.

[112] Dekker, *The Gvls Horne-booke*, in *Non-Dramatic Works*, II, 247.

dinner the gallant "must venture beyond sea, that is, in a choice pair of noblemen's oars, to the Bankside, where he must sit out the breaking-up of a comedy, or the first cut of a tragedy; or rather, if his humour so serve him, to call in at the Blackfriars, where he should see a nest of boys able to ravish a man."[113]

By 1608, in less than a decade, the established companies won out over their young competitors. With the Children of the Revels in and out of trouble for their indiscreet political satires and finally in disfavor with the Court itself, their manager, Henry Evans, surrendered his lease on the Blackfriars theater to Richard Burbage and the King's Men. One remaining troupe of children continued to play for another five years, and there was a brief attempt to bring boys back to the stage later in the period, but after 1608 (and possibly earlier), they ceased to be serious rivals to the men's companies.

Perhaps more important than their triumph was the movement of adult players into private theaters, first at Blackfriars in 1609, then at the Phoenix/Cockpit in 1617, and finally at Salisbury Court in 1629. Burbage had attempted such a move in 1596, a full three years before the boys resumed playing, but was blocked by the objections of powerful residents near the Blackfriars. With the return of the lease upon his property, the King's Men could offer their patrons the comfort of both a roofed building in winter and the open Globe in summer. However, other companies had to settle for the advantages of one sort of theater or the other.[114] Though the fresh air and sunshine they admitted made playgoing more pleasant in warm weather, the large public playhouses, particularly on the Bankside, could be "verie noysome for the resorte of people in the wynter tyme."[115] Thus, when John Webster's play *The White Devil* opened at the Red Bull in 1612, he blamed the weather for its

[113] Thomas Middleton, *Father Hubbard's Tale*, in *The Works*, ed. A. H. Bullen (1885-1886; reprint ed., New York: AMS Press, 1964), VIII, 77.

[114] Bentley notes a possible exception, speculating that Beeston may have used the Red Bull and the Cockpit for a time on a similar pattern (*Jacobean and Caroline Stage*, I, 225n).

[115] Walter W. Greg, ed., *Henslowe Papers* (London: A. H. Bullen, 1907), p. 49.

failure: "it was acted, in so dull a time of Winter, presented in so open and blacke a Theatre, that it wanted . . . a full and understanding Auditory."[116]

## CONTINUED PATRONAGE OF PUBLIC THEATERS

Whatever the discomforts, privileged patrons did not desert the great public playhouses even when the adult troupes moved indoors. Just as they had visited both Paul's and the Theater in the earlier era, and the Globe and Whitefriars in the middle era, so they continued to frequent the Fortune, Red Bull, and Globe, as well as Blackfriars, Phoenix, and Salisbury Court during the final era. Plays written for the public theaters referred to gentlemen in "your pennie-bench Theaters," "Gentle-folkes (that walke i' th Galleries)," a knight at the Fortune who lost his purse at "the last new play i' the *Swanne*, seuen Angels in 't," "Gentiles mix'd with Groomes," and "wits of gentry."[117] When the Globe burned in 1613, a topical poem declared,

> Out runne the Knights, out runne the Lordes,
>     And there was great adoe,
> Some lost their hatts, & some their swords;
>     Then out runne Burbidge too.[118]

John Heath ridiculed the country gentleman who came up to London in order to study the professional actors and improve his amateur performance of the fool.

> *Momus* would act the fooles part in a play,
> And 'cause he would be exquisite that way,
> Hies me to London, where no day can passe,
> But that some play-house still his presence has.

[116] John Webster, "Address to the Reader," in *The Complete Works*, ed. F. L. Lucas (London: Chatto and Windus, 1927), I, 107.

[117] Dekker, *Satiromastix* and *The Roaring Girl*, in *Dramatic Works*, I, 355, 384, and III, 89; *Pimlyco, or Runne Red-Cap* (London, 1609), C$_{[1]}$; William Fennor, *Fennors Descriptions* (London, 1616).

[118] "A Sonnett upon the Pittifull Burneing of the Globe Play House in London," in *The English Drama and Stage*, ed. William C. Hazlitt (1869; reprint ed., New York, Burt Franklin, n.d.), p. 226.

Now at the *Globe* with a iudicious eye,
Into the Vice's action doth he prie.
Next to the *Fortune*, where it is a chaunce,
But he mark's something worth his cognisance.
Then to the *Curtaine*, where, as at the rest,
He notes that action downe that likes him best.[119]

Besides such general literary references, there were any number of specific instances of the privileged at the public theaters. In 1610, Prince Lewis Frederick of Wurtemberg attended the Globe, "the usual place for acting Plays," where he saw *Othello*.[120] Sometime during his tenure in England (December 1605 to October 1608, Ambassador Giustinian of Austria spent more than twenty crowns to take the secretary of Florence and the French ambassador and his wife to see *Pericles* at the Globe.[121] It was alleged that "all the ambassadors who have come to England have gone to the plays more or less."[122] Just before his death in August of 1628, the Duke of Buckingham bestowed his presence equally upon public and private theaters. First he went to the Globe to see *Henry VIII*—"a play bespoken of purpose by himselfe."

On teusday was a play at y^e Globe of y^e downfall of y^e great Duke of Buckingham, w^runto y^e Savoian Ambassadour, y^e Duke, Earle of Hollande & oth^rs came, yet stayed only y^e disgracing not y^e beheading of y^e great Duke of Buck.

The very next day the duke saw Heywood's *Rape of Lucrece* at the Phoenix.[123] Among the less exalted but still privileged

[119] John Heath, "Epigram 39," *Two Centuries of Epigrammes* (London, 1610), E$_3$-E$_3^v$.

[120] William B. Rye, *England as Seen by Foreigners in the Days of Elizabeth and James the First* (London: J. R. Smith, 1865), p. 61.

[121] Chambers, *Elizabethan Stage*, II, 549; *C.S.P.Ven.*, XIV (1615-1617), p. 600. The Venetian records do not specify the Globe, but this was the only theater used by the King's Men at that time. They did not begin to play at Blackfriars until 1609.

[122] *C.S.P.Ven.*, XIV (1615-1617), p. 600.

[123] George Bullen, "The Duke of Buckingham and a Play of Shakespeare in 1628," *The Athenaeum* (18 October 1879), p. 497.

patrons of the Globe were such people as John Chamberlain, Simon Forman, Sir John Carleton's sister-in-law, and Sir Humphrey Mildmay, whose diary noted attendance at Globe and Blackfriars alike during the last decade of theatrical activity.[124]

During the decade of the 1620s, the Globe was host to "all the nobility still in London" when in August 1624 the politically scandalous *A Game at Chess* was presented for an unprecedented nine-day run until its suppression. According to the outraged Spanish ambassador, "There were more than 3000 persons there on the day that the audience was the smallest."[125] John Chamberlain reported the event in some detail to Sir Dudley Carleton:

> I doubt not but you have heard of our famous play of Gondomar, which hath ben followed with extraordinarie concourse, and frequented by all sorts of people, old and younge, rich and poore, masters and servants, papists and puritans, wise men, *et ct.*, churchmen and statesmen as Sir Henry Wotton, Sir Albert Morton, Sir Benjamin Ruddier, Sir Thomas Lake, and a world besides; the Lady Smith wold have gon yf she could have persuaded me to go with her. I am not so sowre nor severe but that I wold willingly have attended her, but I could not sit so long, for we must have ben there before one a clocke at farthest to find any roome.[126]

Because the Globe featured target fighting, rope dancing, juggling, and fencing displays during the winter months, the dramatists eventually capitalized on this fact for the amusement of their summer audiences. A Davenant prologue of 1635 greeted the fashionably dressed audience with these words:

A noble company! for we can spy,

---

[124] McClure, ed., *Letters of John Chamberlain*, I, 32, 544; E. K. Chambers, *William Shakespeare: A Study of Facts and Problems* (Oxford: Clarendon Press, 1930), II, 337-341; Bentley, *Jacobean and Caroline Stage*, II, 637-681.

[125] Edward M. Wilson and Olga Turner, "The Spanish Protest against 'A Game at Chesse,' " *Modern Language Review* 44 (1949): 482, 480, respectively.

[126] McClure, ed., *Letters of John Chamberlain*, II, 578.

Beside rich gaudy sirs, some that rely
More on their judgments than their clothes, and may,
With wit as well as pride, rescue our play:
And 'tis but just, though each spectator knows
This house, and season, does more promise shows,
Dancing, and buckler fights, than art or wit.[127]

Just a few years later, James Shirley echoed some of the same
ideas in "A Prologue at the Globe to his Comedy call'd the
Doubtful Heire, which should have been presented at the Blackfriers."

All that the Prologue comes for is to say,
Our author did not calculate this play
For this meridian; the Bankside, he knows
Is far more skilful at the ebbs and flows
Of water, than of wit; he did not mean
For the elevation of your poles, this scene.
No shews, no dance, and, what you most delight in,
Upon the stage, all work for cutlers barr'd;
No bawdry, nor no ballads; this goes hard;
But language clean; and, what affects you not,
Without impossibilities the plot:
No clown, no squibs, no devil in't. Oh, now,
You squirrels that want nuts, what will you do?
Pray do not crack the benches, and we may
Hereafter fit your palates with a play.
But you that can contract yourselves, and sit
As you were now in the Black-friers pit,
And will not deaf us with lewd noise and tongues,
Because we have no heart to break our lungs,
Will pardon our vast stage, and not disgrace
This play, meant for your persons, not the place.[128]

---

[127] Sir William Davenant, "Prologue," *Newes from Plymouth*, in *The Dra-matic Works*, ed. James Maidment and W. H. Logan (Edinburgh: W. Paterson, 1872-1874), IV, 109.
[128] James Shirley, "Prologue," *The Doubtful Heir*, in *The Dramatic Works*

Like the first audience to see *The Knight of the Burning Pestle*, modern interpreters have missed the "privy marke of *Ironie*"[129] about the prologue. They have taken it as the statement of a disgruntled author, whose new play was humiliatingly removed for its premiere from the aristocratic Blackfriars stage to the plebeian Globe. Actually, like other prologues of the same period, the piece stood as a standard effort to amuse the auditors with sarcastic wit, capitalizing on the chance to call them "grave understanders" and to charge them with old-fashioned tastes. Just in case the joke was not obvious enough, Shirley appealed to the regular Blackfriars crowd to behave as usual, assuring them that the play was "meant for your persons, not the place." Apparently the King's Men expected to attract their privileged customers at the Globe, even late in the period, for the theater continued to be "the *Continent of the World*, because halfe the yeere a world of *Beauties*, and braue *Spirits* resort vnto it."[130]

It might be argued that the Globe presented a special case because the prestige and ability of its company commanded a genteel following when other public theaters could not. However, members of the elite also frequented both the Fortune and the Red Bull. In 1617, the entire Venetian embassy attended a tragedy at the Fortune. According to Father Busino, who was making his first visit to an English theater, "the best treat was to see such a crowd of nobility so very well arrayed that they looked like so many princes listening as silently and soberly as possible."[131] Evidently the Venetians were not at all out of place in such a setting. On another occasion, the Spanish ambassador and his entire train visited the Fortune, "and the players (not to be overcome with courtesie) made him a banket, when the

_____

*and Poems*, ed., William Gifford and Alexander Dyce (London: J. Murray, 1833), IV, 279.

[129] Francis Beaumont, *The Knight of the Burning Pestle*, in *The Dramatic Works in the Beaumont and Fletcher Canon*, ed. Fredson Bowers (Cambridge: Cambridge University Press, 1966-1979), I, 7.

[130] Nicholas Goodman, *Hollands Leaguer*, ed. Dean Stanton Barnard, Jr. (The Hague: Mouton, 1970), p. 76.

[131] "Diaries and Despatches of the Venetian Embassy at the Court of King James I, in the Years 1617, 1618," *Quarterly Review* 102 (1857): 416.

play was don, in the garden adjoyning."[132] Two butchers were charged with "abusing certen gentlemen" at the Fortune in 1611, and a few years later, a "junior gentleman" named Nicholas Bestney was stabbed there.[133] Of course not all young gentlemen encountered abuse and danger at the Fortune. In 1611, twelve-year-old John Milton went there, presumably without incident, and the notorious Dr. Lamb, who was waylaid after leaving a Fortune performance, came to no harm in the theater.[134]

Even the much maligned Red Bull theater enjoyed a certain amount of privileged patronage, though "gentlemen," the standard term used to address the audience, did not necessarily apply to all the spectators. Nor were the gentlemen there necessarily of the highest caliber. The lover whose *"Poetry is such as he can cul, / From plays he heard at Curtaine or at Bul"* cut a sorry figure indeed.[135] He must have been first cousin to another inept gallant who planned to woo his lady "with complements drawne from the Plaies I see at the Fortune, and Red Bull, where I learne all the words I speake and vnderstand not."[136] A poem entitled "Dice, Wine, and Women, or the Unfortunate Gallant Gulled at London" satirically related the misadventures of a similarly dense young gentleman just up from Cornwall. After being tricked out of ten pounds at a bawdy house, he moved on to see a play.

> Most of my money being spent,
> > To *S. Iohns* street to the *Bull* I went,
> Where I the roaring Rimer saw,
> > And to my face was made a daw:
> And pressing forth among the folke,
> > I lost my purse, my hat and cloke.[137]

---

[132] McClure, ed., *Letters of John Chamberlain*, II, 391.

[133] J. C. Jeaffreson, ed., *Middlesex County Records* (London: Middlesex County Records Society, 1886-1892), II, 71, 88.

[134] Bentley, *Jacobean and Caroline Stage*, I, 266-268.

[135] George Wither, *Abuses Stript and Whipt* (London, 1613), p. 24.

[136] Thomas Tomkis, *Albumazar* (London, 1615), C₄ᵛ-D.

[137] "Dice, Wine and Women, or The vnfortunate Gallant gull'd at London,"

In the same vein, a Salisbury Court play, *The Careless Shepherdess*, ridiculed the skinflint country squire Thrift, who wanted admission for a groat, reluctantly parted with a shilling, and finally changed his mind altogether:

> And I will hasten to the money Box
> And take my shilling out again, for now
> I have considered that it is too much;
> I'le go to th' Bull, or Fortune, and there see
> A Play for two pense, with a Jig to boot.[138]

A chance for cheap entertainment motivated some young boys of good education and good family who got their first taste of the theater by performing on the Red Bull stage. While a student in London during the early 1620s (reportedly at Thomas Farnaby's school in St. Giles Cripplegate), Thomas Killigrew exercised an unusual means of getting free admission to the plays. "He would go to the Red-bull, and when the man cried to the boys, 'Who will go and be a divell, and he shall see the play for nothing?'—then would he go in and be a devil upon the stage, and so got to see [the] play."[139]

Yet country gulls and small boys were not the only kinds of privileged playgoers at the Red Bull. Its company enjoyed a considerable aristocratic patronage during the 1630s when the players attended a royal progress and made repeated appearances at Court. It is difficult, too, to understand why their play *The Whore New Vamped* would have brazenly satirized such topics as the new duty on wines (not a plebeian drink), aldermen, projects, and patents unless the spectators enjoyed sufficient familiarity with these matters to be amused. Despite their censure for having libelously traduced "persons of quality," the company played at Court again less than two months after the

---

in *The Pepys Ballads*, ed. Hyder Edward Rollins (Cambridge: Harvard University Press, 1929), I, 239.

[138] Thomas Goffe (?), *The Careless Shepherdess* (London, 1656), p. 8.

[139] 30 October 1662; Samuel Pepys, *The Diary of Samuel Pepys*, ed. Robert Latham and William Matthews (Berkeley: University of California Press, 1970), III, 243-244.

offending play.[140] With backing of this sort, one cannot assume the entire Red Bull audience consisted of *"Rables, Apple-wives and Chimney-boyes"* or "the meaner sort of People."[141]

## PATRONAGE OF PRIVATE THEATERS

At the private theaters, there was no question about the quality of the spectators. Despite an occasional disparaging remark about "the shop's *Foreman*" or "your sinfull sixe-penny Mechanicks,"[142] the audience consisted chiefly of the privileged. The diaries of established gentlemen like Sir Humphrey Mildmay and of Inns of Court students like John Greene and Edward Heath recorded frequent visits to Blackfriars and the Phoenix/Cockpit as a matter of course. Typical Mildmay entries were: "To a base play att the Cocke pitt" and "I wente to Westmi: dined att Whitehall & after dynner to the fox play = att bl:fryers w^th my Cozen fra. Wortley & my Brother Anth."[143] John Greene's casual line in his diary revealed that he shared his taste for plays with his fellows at Lincoln's Inn: "all the batchelors . . . were at a play, some at cockpt, some at blackfriers. The play at Cockpit was Lady of pleasure, at blackfriers the conspiracy."[144] Young Edward Heath at the Middle Temple saw some forty-nine plays in only a year and a half.[145]

Correspondence of the period also confirmed the ubiquity of

---

[140] *Calendar of State Papers, Domestic, of the Reign of Charles I* (London: Longmans, Green, Reader, and Dyer, 1858-1897), XIV (1639), pp. 529-530. Hereafter cited as *C.S.P.D.Car.I.*

[141] John Tatham, "A Prologue upon the Removing of the late Fortune Players to the Red Bull," in *The Fancies Theatre* (London, 1640), H₂ᵛ; James Wright, *Historia Histrionica: An Historical Account of the English Stage* (London, 1699), p. 5.

[142] Jonson, Commendatory verses to John Fletcher's *The Faithful Shepherdess*, in *Dramatic Works in the Beaumont and Fletcher Canon*, III, 492; "Induction" to *The Magnetic Lady*, in *Ben Jonson*, VI, 509.

[143] 20 March 1634, 27 October 1638; "The Records of Sir Humprey Mildmay," in Bentley, *Jacobean and Caroline Stage*, II, 676, 678.

[144] 8 November 1635; E. M. Symonds, "The Diary of John Greene (1635-1657)," *English Historical Review* 43 (1928): 386.

[145] Egerton MS 2983, fol. 29; as cited by Prest, *Inns of Court*, p. 155.

attendance at the private playhouses by the socially privileged. A letter to the country pleaded, "I misse you extremely, therfore I pray make haste, for *London* Streets which you and I have trod together so often, will prove tedious to me else. Amongst other things, *Black-Fryers* will entertain you with a Play *Spick and span new*, and the *Cock-Pit* with another; nor I beleeve after so long absence, will it be an unpleasing object for you to see."[146] At a more aristocratic level, Sir Dudley Carleton received this word of the Duke of Brunswicke: "The Duke of Brunswicke went hence on Newyearesday after he had taried just a weeke and performed many visits to almost all our great Lords and Ladies as the Lord of Caunterburie, the Lord Keper, and the rest, not omitting Mistris Brus nor the stage of Blacke Friers."[147] Almost lost in the scandalous talk of Lady Newport's recusancy was her visit to the Phoenix/Cockpit, reported by Garrard to the Lord Deputy of Ireland: "Here hath been an horrible Noise about the Lady *Newport's* being become a *Romish* Catholick: she went one Evening as she came from a Play in *Drury-Lane* to *Somerset-House*, where one of the Capuchins reconciled her to the *Popish* Church, of which she is now a weak Member."[148] When Christopher Beeston wanted to rehearse his new boys' troupe in 1637, he invited "some noblemen and gentlemen to see them act at his house, the Cockpit."[149]

Even if such specific accounts did not exist, the literary references would reveal the elitist character of the private theater audiences. According to Jonson, they were "Compos'd of *Gamester, Captaine, Knight, Knight's man,* / *Lady*, or *Pusill*, that weares maske, or fan, / *Velvet* or *Taffata* cap."[150] Prologues addressed themselves to gentlemen "whose angry soules were not diseasd / With law, or lending money" and epilogues to

[146] James Howell, *Epistolae Ho-Elianae* (London, 1645), Sec. 4, letter 2, Aaa$_2$.
[147] 8 January 1625; McClure, ed., *Letters of John Chamberlain*, II, 594.
[148] 9 November 1637; Knowler, ed., *Earl of Strafforde's Letters*, II, 128.
[149] *C.S.P.D.Car.I*, X (1636-1637), p. 254.
[150] Jonson, Commendatory verses to John Fletcher's *Faithful Shepherdess*, in *Dramatic Works in the Beaumont and Fletcher Canon*, III, 492.

"Ladyes," "you generous spirits of the City / That are no lesse in money then braine wity," "the Cavaliers and Gentry," and "my Countrey folkes too if here be any o'em"[151]—a fair sampling of London's privileged. James Shirley could boast that the Beaumont and Fletcher plays *"made Blackfriers an Academy, where the three howers spectacle . . . were usually of more advantage to the hopefull young Heire, then a costly, dangerous, forraigne Travell, with the assistance of a governing Mounsieur, or Signior to boot."*[152]

A quite different view of the effect of plays upon a young heir was sketched in Francis Lenton's *Young Gallant's Whirligig*. During his term at the Inns of Court,

> Your Theaters hee daily doth frequent
> (Except the intermitted time of Lent)
> Treasuring vp within his memory
> The amorous toyes of euery Comedy,
> With deepe delight. . . .

Having come into his wealth, "The Cockpit heretofore would serue his wit, / But now vpon the Fryers stage hee'll sit." No wisdom from the pen of Beaumont, Fletcher, or Shakespeare himself prevented the young gallant from wasting his entire substance:

> His silken garments, and his sattin robe
> That hath so often visited the Globe,
> And all his spangled rare perfum'd attires
> Which once so glistred in the Torchy Fryers,
> Must to the Broakers to compound his debt,
> Or else be pawned to procure him meate.[153]

---

[151] Fletcher, "Prologue" to *Love's Pilgrimage*, in ibid., II, 573; Richard Brome, *The Court Beggar*, in *The Dramatic Works* (London: John Pearson, 1873), I, 270-271.

[152] Front matter for Beaumont and Fletcher Folio of 1647, $A_3$; as cited by Bentley, *Jacobean and Caroline Stage*, VI, 4.

[153] Francis Lenton, *The Young Gallant's Whirligig* (London, 1629), pp. 7, 13, 16.

Equally memorable and equally unflattering portraits of other patrons appeared in *Notes from Blackfriars* by Henry Fitzgeffrey. The cowardly captain, boasting of his military exploits and ever sensitive to slights upon his honor and reputation, contrived to "Be counted *Valiant*, and neuer *Fight.*" The traveler, "Sir *Iland Hunt*," told of such "rarer *Rarities*" newly discovered that "younger *Brothers* sell their lands to buy / *Guyanian Plumes*: like *Icarus* to fly." The international fashion plate displayed Spanish boots, Scottish spurs, a Holland shirt, "His Haire like to your *Moor's* or *Irish* Lockes." "A *Woman* of the *masculine Gender*," perhaps a disciple of Marion Frith, made her way boldly into the gallants' row. A "plumed *Dandebrat*" basked in the ladies' favor for his skill at "skipping too and fro" in the dancing. "*Tissue slop*," the ambitious counterfeit gentleman, with neither lands nor education nor revenue, demanded a stool and cushion. The conceited "Spruse *Coxcombe*, yon Affecting *Asse*," constantly consulted his looking glass to check

How his *Band* jumpeth with his *Peccadilly*,
Whether his Band strings ballance equally:
Which way his Feather wagg's: And (to say truth)
What wordes in vtterance best become his mouth.[154]


GENERAL PATRONAGE

Yet, all things considered, these privileged patrons differed little from the privileged spectators at the public theaters. Indeed, most of the extant evidence made no distinction among the audiences of the various playhouses but simply associated the favored groups in society with playgoing in general. To cite specific cases, Sir Humphrey Mildmay usually did not bother to mention the name of the theater he attended. The Venetian ambassador Foscarini was known to have been to the playhouse at least three or four times, but the records did not specify which one.[155] George Evelyn, reporting on his courtship of a

---

[154] Henry Fitzgeffrey, *Satyres and Satyricall Epigrams: with Certaine Observations at Blacke-Fryars* (London, 1617), E[8]ᵛ-F[5].
[155] *C.S.P.Ven.*, XIV (1615-1617), pp. 593, 599.

prospective wife, said, "This day I waited on her and the rest of the ladies to a play,"[156] with no indication as to where they went or what they saw. John Chamberlain wrote that he saw the converted Catholic priest Tobie Matthew on his way to a play but mentioned no theater.[157] At least three other priests— Thomas Leke, a Mr. Thules, and a Mr. Canon—were well known as theatergoers. Leke even claimed that "most of the principal Catholicks about London doe goe to playes." Interestingly enough, when the Archpriest's assistant, John Colleton, issued a rebuke of almost ninety pages to Leke, he forbade attendance at any theater, public or private, because it was "a place of licentiousnesse, where the gallants of the kingdome flock to see, and to bee seen, and not all to good ends." Colleton approved performances at Court, the universities, the Inns of Court, and gentlemen's houses but could see no superiority in the audience that permitted the private playhouses to be exempt as well.[158]

In addition to individual cases, many literary references also connected the privileged with playgoing but not with specific playhouses. Sir Thomas Overbury's *Characters* included a Puny-Clarke who "eats Ginger-bread at a Playhouse," a country gentleman who "hath sworne to see *London* once a yeare, though all his busines be to see a play, walke a turn in *Paules*, and obserue the fashion," and an Inns of Court man who, because "he hath heard one mooting, and seen two plaies, he thinkes as basely of the *Vniversity*, as a young *Sophister* doth of the *Grammerschoole*."[159] According to one detractor of the Inns of Court gentlemen, "one of the first things they learn as

---

[156] 15 November 1639; W. G. Hiscock, *John Evelyn and his Family Circle* (London: Routledge and Kegan Paul, 1955), p. 10.

[157] McClure, ed., *Letters of John Chamberlain*, II, 137.

[158] William Harrison, "Prohibition of 9 March 1618; together with Thomas Leke's letter of protest, 25 April 1618; and the answer to it [by John Colleton] justifying the prohibition"; Folger Shakespeare Library MS V.a. 244, pp. 5, 79, 10, respectively. Hereafter cited as Harrison, Leke, Colleton correspondence.

[159] Sir Thomas Overbury, *The "Conceited Newes" of Sir Thomas Overbury and his Friends* (Gainesville, Fla.: Scholars' Facsimiles and Reprints, 1968), pp. 159, 147, 144-145, respectively.

soone as they are admitted, [is] to see Stage-playes." [160] Even
an enemy of the theater seemed to assume the actor amused
a fairly consistent audience of the privileged: "The cautions of
his judging humor . . . be a certaine number of sawsie rude
jests against the common lawyer; hansome conceits against the
fine Courtiers; delicate quirkes against the rich Cuckold cittizen;
a shadowed glaunce for good innocent Ladies and Gentlewomen;
with a nipping scoffe for some honest Justice, who hath imprisoned him; or some thriftie Trades-man, who hath allowed
him no credit." [161] In his handbook *The English Gentleman*,
Richard Braithwaite listed playgoing as a permissible *"Recreation* used by *Gentlemen*, but especially in this Citie." [162] He
did not advise the gentlemen to prefer one sort of playhouse
over another, but he did offer a caveat that indicated the popularity of theatergoing among the privileged:

> But to draw in our sailes, touching this *Recreation*: as I
> approve of the *moderate* use and recourse which our *Gentle-
> men* make to *Playes*; so I wholly condemne the daily fre-
> quenting of them: as some there be (especially in this Citie)
> who, for want of better imployment, make it their Vocation.
> And these I now speake of, be our *Ordinary* Gentlemen,
> whose day-taske is this in a word: They leave their beds to
> put on their clothes formally, repaire to an *Ordinary*, and see
> a *Play* daily. [163]

Toward the end of the period, the privileged probably grew
so numerous in London that the theaters could expect large
affluent crowds even when the law courts were not sitting and
the Court went away on a summer progress. At least that may
be inferred from Henry Glapthorne's poem, "To a Reviv'd Va-

---

[160] Prynne, "Epistle Dedicatory," *Histrio-Mastrix*, 3ᵛ.

[161] Cocke, "A common Player"; as cited by Chambers, *Elizabethan Stage*,
IV, 256.

[162] Richard Braithwaite, *The English Gentleman and The English Gentle-
woman*, 3d ed. (London, 1641), p. 103.

[163] Ibid., p. 109.

cation Play," which provided a useful look at city merchants, country gentry, and improvident gentlemen.

It is a dead Vacation: yet we see
(Which glads our souls) a wel-set Company
Adorn our Benches: We did scarce expect
So full in Audience in this long neglect
Of Court and Citie Gentry, that transfer
In Terme their Visits to our Theater.

And now we hope you've leisure in the Citie
To give the World cause to suspect you witty.
We would intreat you then put off awhile
That formall brow you wear when you beguile
Young Chapman with bad Wares; pray do not look
On us, as on the Debtors in your Book,
With a shrewd countenance; what we act to day
Was for your sakes; (some think) a pretty Play;
Nay wee ourselves almost presume it good
Because we hope it will be understood
By your capacious Brains, which know to get
Wealth, and for that cause we can't doubt your Wit;
   At least we dare not, since wee'r bound to say
   All those are witty come to see our Play.[164]

After their final exile from the stage, the actors may have been exaggerating to claim that "none use to come but the best of the Nobility and Gentry."[165] However, the claim had far more than a morsel of truth in it, and the performers directed their efforts to resume playing toward the privileged. When *A King and No King* was illegally presented at Salisbury Court in 1647, "The Sheriffes of the City of *London* with their Officers went

---

[164] Henry Glapthorne, *Plays and Poems* (London: John Pearson, 1874), II, 194-195.

[165] *The Actors Remonstrance or Complaint: for the silencing of their profession and banishment from their severall Play-houses*, in *The English Drama and Stage*, ed. William C. Hazlitt (1869; reprint ed., New York: Burt Franklin, n.d.), p. 261.

thither and found a great number of people; some young Lords, and other eminent persons."[166] To advertise another play the following year, "*Tickets were thrown into Gentlemens Coaches.*"[167] A subsequent raid was reported thus: "On Tuesday *Janu* 21 [22] 1649 bee it known unto all men, the State *Janizaries* rob'd the Play-house in *St. Johns streete*, imprisoned the Players, and listed all the Lords Ladies and Gentlewomen, who are either to serve the States or pay money, if their mightynesse please to command it for so great a contempt as breaking an Act made upon the Stage at *Westminster.*"[168] The soldiers could make it even harder on the spectators. A couple of disgruntled actors informed on an illegal performance "and so abused many of the Gentry that formerly had been their Benefactors, who were forced to pay the Souldiers 5s. a piece for their comming out, as well as for going in."[169] Many years later, the actors' miserable dependence upon their once-powerful patrons during this period was described in these terms: "Afterwards in *Oliver's* time, they used to Act privately, three or four Miles, or more, out of Town, now here, now there, sometimes in Nobelmen's Houses, in particular *Holland-house* at *Kensington*, where the Nobility and Gentry who met (but in no great Numbers) used to make up a Sum for them, each giving a broad Peice, or the like."[170] Gone for almost twenty years were the pleasures of the theater that had enlivened the idle afternoons for three successive generations of privileged Londoners.

Gone, too, was a whole style of behavior associated with the privileged playgoers, a style marked by boredom, self-indulgence, ostentation, seduction, sophistication, and caprice. No doubt many sober spectators of certifiable good character and impeccable dramatic taste graced the audiences, but their more colorful companions attracted greater attention. To the stern

---

[166] 6 October 1647, *Perfect Occurrences*; as cited by Bentley, *Jacobean and Caroline Stage*, VI, 113.

[167] 28 January to 4 February 1648, *Perfect Occurrences*, in ibid., p. 230.

[168] 22 to 29 January 1650, *Mercurius Pragmaticus*, in ibid., p. 232.

[169] 22 to 29 June 1653, *Mercurius Pragmaticus*, in ibid., p. 234.

[170] Wright, *Historia Histrionica*, p. 9.

moralist, the elite patrons all resembled the Inns of Court men against whom William Prynne made the following charges:

> That Innes of Court men were undone but for Players; that they are their chiefest guests and imployment, & the sole busines that makes them afternoons men: that this is one of the first things they learne as soone as they are admitted, to see Stage-playes, & take smoke at a Play-house, which they commonly make their Studie; where they quickly learne to follow all fashions, to drinke all Healths, to weare favours and good cloathes, to consort with ruffianly companions, to sweare the biggest oaths, to quarrell easily, fight desperately, game inordinately, to spend their patrimony ere it fall, to use gracefully some gestures of apish complement, to talke ir-religiously, to dally with a Mistresse, and hunt after harlots, to prove altogether lawlesse in steed of Lawyers, and to forget that little learning, grace and vertue which they had before.[171]

Even allowing for Prynne's violent prejudice, his sketch contained a certain amount of truth.

TRANSPORTATION TO THE PLAYHOUSE

As befitted their superior status, many privileged patrons required transportation to the playhouses. Although the theaters lay within walking distance of Westminster, the Inns of Court, and the fashionable sections of London, it was more comfortable to arrive by boat, coach, or sedan chair. At first, the boatmen had almost exclusive rights to the spectators. Serving a series of great public playhouses on the Bankside, they brought courtiers down from the royal palaces of Greenwich, Richmond, and Hampton Court, as well as from the handsome residences along the Thames. The watermen ferried students and Inns of Court men, gentlemen up from the country, and wealthy merchants across the river, avoiding the crowds and the inconvenience of the London Bridge. At the height of the theater traffic, the

---

[171] Prynne, "Epistle Dedicatory," in *Histrio-Mastrix*, 3ᵛ.

watermen claimed they transported some three or four thousand to the playhouses every afternoon. Dekker's advice to his gull concerning the status of a watery entrance showed the difficulty that the oarsmen sometimes had in collecting their fares from certain improvident gentlemen:

> If you can (either for loue or money) prouide your selfe a lodging by the water-side: for, aboue the conuenience it brings/ to shun Shoulder-clapping, and to ship away your Cockatrice betimes in the morning, it addes a kind of state vnto you, to be carried from thence to the staires of your Play-house. . . . No your Oares are your onely Sea-crabs, boord them, and take heed you neuer go twice together with one paire: often shifting is a great credit to Gentlemen; and that diuiding of your fare wil make the poore watersnaks be ready to pul you in peeces to enjoy your custome: No matter whether vpon landing, you haue money or no, you may swim in twentie of their boates ouer the riuer upon *Ticket*: mary, when siluer comes in, remember to pay trebble their fare, and it will make your Flounder-catchers to send more thankes after you, when you doe not draw, then when you doe; for they know, It will be their owne another daie.[172]

Even after the private theaters reopened in 1599, the watermen did a certain amount of business to the river stairs near Blackfriars, Whitefriars, Salisbury Court, and possibly Phoenix/ Cockpit. But increasingly the affluent preferred coach transportation. The coach claimed to be "a Benefactor to all . . . Play-houses . . . for I bring them their best customers, as they all know well enough."[173] The convergence of large numbers of coaches created such congestion that "to see their multitude, either when there is a Masque at White-Hall, a Lord-Mayors feast [or] a new play at some of the play-houses you would admire to see them, how close they stand together (like Mutton-pies in a Cookes-oven) that hardly you can thrust a pole be-

---

[172] Dekker, *Gvls Horne-booke*, in *Non-Dramatic Works*, II, 252.
[173] Henry Peacham, *Coach and Sedan* (London: Westminster Press, 1925), B$_2$.

tweene."[174] Eventually the officers and residents near Black-friars, where the coaches were "damming up the streets and lanes," petitioned the Lord Mayor to take action against "such resort of people, and such multitudes of Coaches (wherof many are Hackney Coaches, bringing people of all sorts) That some-tymes all our streets cannott containe them, But that they Clogg vpp Ludgate alsoe."[175] The Common Council banned playing at the Blackfriars, but three months later the King counter-manded the order. And so the carriages, with their affluent passengers, returned to clog the streets once more.

The Privy Council attempted to solve the problem again in 1633 with this regulation:

> Their lps remembring that there is an easie passage by water vnto that playhouse w$^{th}$out troubling the streets, and that it is much more fit and reasonable that those w$^{ch}$ goe thither should goe thither by water or else on foote rather than the necessarie businesses of all others, and the publique Com-merce should be disturbed by their pleasure, doe therefore Order: that if any pson, man or woman, of what Condicon soever repaire to the aforesayd Playhouse in Coach, so soone as they are gone out of their Coaches the Coach men shall departe thence and not retourne till the ende of the play, nor shall stay or retourn to fetch those whom they carried . . . and in ye tyme betweene their departure and returne shall either returne home or else abide in some other streets lesse frequented with passengers and so range their Coaches in those places that the way be not stopped.[176]

George Garrard reported the ineffectiveness of the order to his patron, Viscount Wentworth.

> Here hath been an Order of the Lords of the Council hung up in a Table near *Paul's* and the *Black-fryars*, to command all that Resort to the Play-House there to send away their Coaches, and to disperse Abroad in *Paul's Church-yard*,

[174] Ibid., C$_{[1]}$.
[175] *Malone Society Collections*, I, 91.
[176] Ibid., I, 4 and 5: 387-388.

*Carter-Lane*, the Conduit in *Fleet-street*, and other Places, and not to return to fetch their Company, but they must trot afoot to find their Coaches, 'twas kept very strictly for two or three Weeks, but now I think it is disorder'd again.[177]

### FAVORED SEATING

Having arrived at the playhouse, whether by coach, by boat, or on foot, the privileged patrons dropped their money in the keeper's box and selected a place from among those still available. Seating was on a first-come, first-served basis, so that "each man sate downe without respecting of persons, for he that first comes is first seated."[178] Depending upon how much he cared to spend, the playgoer could stand in the open yard of the public theater or inn, stand or sit in the tiers of roofed galleries surrounding the yard, take a place in one of the "roomes fitt and decent for gentlemen,"[179] or engage the costly Lords' room. At the private theaters, he had the choice of a seat on the benches in the pit, the tiered galleries, or the boxes.

From at least the 1590s onward, some gentlemen preferred to occupy a stool upon the stage. The custom may well have originated during that decade because of an increased demand for the best and most expensive seats. With the departure of the boys' troupes, a smaller number of companies were performing—in general, no more than three during the 1590s—but there was a growing number of gentlemen in London. The more pretentious spectators insisting on ostentatious seats began to be placed on the edges of the playing area. One such patron appeared in Sir John Davies' *Epigrams*.

### IN RUFFUM 3

Rvfus the Courtier at the theatre,
Leauing the best and most conspicuous place,

---

[177] Knowler, ed., *Earl of Strafforde's Letters*, I, 175-176.

[178] William Fennor, *Compters Common-Wealth*, in John P. Collier, *The History of English Dramatic Poetry to the Time of Shakespeare* (London: G. Bell and Sons, 1879), III, 145.

[179] Greg, ed., *Henslowe Papers*, p. 20.

Doth either to the stage himselfe transfer
Or through a grate doth shew his doubtfull face.

For that the clamorous frie of Innes of court,
Filles vp the priuate roomes of greater prise:
And such a place where all may haue resort,
He in his singularity doth despise.

Yet doth not his particular humour shunne,
The common stews and brothels of the towne,
Though all the world in troupes do thither runne,
Clean and vnclean, the gentle and the clowne:
    Then why should Rvfus n his pride abhorre
    A common seate that loues a common whore.[180]

Once established, the custom of stage sitting became firmly entrenched. Many a young gentleman would "Call for a stoole with a commanding rage," for, "Still when I come to playes, I love to sit, / That all may see me, in a publike place: / Even in the stages front."[181] The advantages, as well as the absurdities, of such prominent seating were probably best presented in *The Gull's Hornbook*. Dekker's would-be gallant was advised to prefer the stage even over the Lords' room, where he would be "smothred to death in darknesse."

By sitting on the stage, you may (with small cost) purchase the deere acquaintance of the boyes: haue a good stoole for sixpence: at any time know what particular part any of the infants present: get your match lighted, examine the play-suits lace, and perhaps win wagers vpon laying tis copper, &c. And to conclude, whether you be a foole or a Justice of peace, a Cuckold, or a Capten, a Lord Maiors sonne, or a dawcocke, a knaue or an vnder-Sheriffe, of what stamp soeuer you be, currant, or counterfet, the Stage, like time, will bring you to most perfect light, and lay you open: . . . but if the *Rabble*, with a full throat, crie, away with the foole, you were

---

[180] Sir John Davies, *Epigrammes and Elegies* (London, ca. 1590), no. 3.
[181] Henry Hutton, *Follies Anatomie* (London, 1619), A₆ᵛ; Richard Perkins, Commendatory verses to Heywood's *Apology*, A₃.

worse then a madman to tarry by it: for the Gentleman and the foole should neuer sit on the Stage together.[182]

## PERSONAL DISPLAY

The stage-sitting gallant quickly became identified with the clothes-conscious fop who, "(in the midst of his pride or riches) at a Play house . . . (before he dare enter) with the *Iacobs-Staffe* of his owne eyes and his Pages, hee takes a full suruey of himselfe, from the highest sprig in his feather, to the lowest spangle that shines in his Shoo-string."[183] Having assured himself of sufficiently impressive clothes, "His pleasure is you place him on the stage, / The better to demonstrate his array, / And how he sits attended by his page."[184] One wit even suggested that fashions changed so swiftly, "he withers his Cloathes on the Stage . . . and when the Play is done, if you marke his rising, tis with a kinde of walking Epilogue betweene the two candles, to know if his Suite may passe for currant."[185] Some idea of the details of the gallant's dress and behavior emerged from a satirical portrait of 1598:

> See you him yonder, who sits o're the stage,
> With the Tobacco-pipe now at his mouth?
> It is *Cornelius* that braue gallant youth,
> Who is new printed to this fangled age:
>> He weares a Ierkin cudgeld with gold lace,
>> A profound slop, a hat scarce pipkin high,
>> For boots, a paire of dagge cases: his face,
>> Furr'd with *Cads*-beard: his poynard on his thigh.
> He wallows in his walk his slop to grace,
> Sweares *by the Lord*, daines no salutation
> But to some iade that's sick of his owne fashion,

[182] Dekker, *Gvls Horne-booke*, in *Non-Dramatic Works*, II, 248, 249-250.
[183] *Haec-Vir: or the Womanish-Man* (London, 1620), C₂.
[184] Henry Parrot, "Epigram 55," *Laquei Ridiculosi, or Springes for Woodcocks* (London, 1613), C[6]ᵛ.
[185] Overbury, "An Improuident young Gallant," in "*Conceited Newes*," p. 176.

As *farewell sweete Captaine*, or (*boy*) *come apace*:
   Yet this Sir *Beuis*, or the fayery Knight,
   Put vp the lie because he durst not fight.[186]

The stage afforded a convenient place for display of more
than fashionable clothes. Dekker counseled his gull to "fall to
cardes" before the play and "to gul the *Ragga-muffins* that
stand aloofe gaping at you, throw the cards (hauing first torne
foure or fiue of them) round about the Stage, iust vpon the
third sound, as though you had lost: it skils not if the foure
knaues ly on their backs, and outface the Audience."[187] Lenton's
young gallant, equally foolish, "aspireth now to sit vpon the
stage / Lookes round about, then viewes his glorious selfe, /
Throws money here and there swearing hang pelfe."[188]

Quite understandably, the playwrights complained against
those who came, not to see the acting, but because they

. . . haue a longing to salute, or talke
With such a female, and from her to walke
With your discourse, to what is done, and where,
How, and by whom, in all the town; but here.
Alas! what is it to his Scene, to know
How many Coaches in *Hide-parke* did show
Last spring, what fare to day at Medleyes was,
If *Dunstan*, or the *Phoenix* best wine has?[189]

Talking during the performances was common enough for Dekker to recommend it:

. . . for by talking and laughing (like a Plough-man in a
Morris) you heap *Pelion* vpon *Ossa*, glory vpon glory. . . .
   Mary . . . my counsell is then that you turne plain Ape,
take vp a rush, and tickle the earnest eares of your fellow
gallants, to make other fooles fall a laughing: mewe at pas-
sionate speeches, blare at merrie, finde fault with the musicke,

[186] Guilpin, "Of Cornelius," in *Skialetheia*, B$_4$.
[187] Dekker, *Gvls Horne-booke*, in *Non-Dramatic Works*, II, 252, 253.
[188] Lenton, *Young Gallant's Whirligig*, p. 5.
[189] Jonson, *The Staple of News*, in *Ben Jonson*, VI, 282.

whew at the childrens Action, whistle at the songs: and aboue all, curse the sharers, that whereas the same day you had bestowed forty shillings on an embrodered Felt and Feather, (scotch-fashion) for your mistres in the Court, or your punck in the city, within two houres after, you encounter with the very same block on the stage, when the haberdasher swore to you the impression was extant but that morning.[190]

Competition like this from the audience, even if it seldom occurred, must have made for some raucous afternoons.

Other stage sitters occupied themselves somewhat more quietly in smoking. A 1599 versifier made this observation:

> It chaunc'd me gazing at the Theater,
> To spie a Lock-Tobacco-Chevalier
> Clowding the loathing ayr with foggie fume
> Of Dock-Tabacco, friendly foe to rume.[191]

Twenty years later, when Henry Hutton wrote *Folly's Anatomy*, it was much the same. "Goe take a pipe of To; the crowded stage / Must needs be graced with you and your page."[192] The pages in attendance upon the gentlemen often fetched lights for the pipes, although lights were sometimes handed from one smoker to another on the points of swords[193]—a fine way of attracting still further attention.

To relieve any discomfort occasioned by sitting for a long time upon a hard stool—and no doubt to guarantee that they continued to be noticed by the rest of the audience—the gentlemen both onstage and elsewhere in the theater rose between the acts. In *The Devil Is an Ass*, Fitzdottrell resolved to use such a ploy.

> To day I goe to the *Black-fryers Play-house*,
> Sit i' the view, salute all my acquaintance,

[190] Dekker, *Gvls Horne-booke*, in *Non-Dramatic Works*, II, 251, 254.

[191] Henry Buttes, *Dyets Dry Dinner* (London, 1599), P$_3$$^v$.

[192] Hutton, *Follie's Anatomie*, p. 17.

[193] G. L. Apperson, *The Social History of Smoking* (London: Martin Secker, 1914), p. 30.

Rise vp betweene the *Acts*, let fall my cloake,
Publish a handsome man, and a rich suite
(As that's a speciall end, why we goe thither,
All that pretend, to stand for't o' the *Stage*)
The Ladies aske who's that?[194]

Actually, Jonson had great contempt for the "hundred fastidious *impertinents*, who . . . by their confidence of rising between the Actes, in oblique lines, make *affidauit* to the whole house, of their not vnderstanding one Scene."[195] Nonetheless, the gentlemen continued "To rise betwixt the Acts, and looke about / The boxes, and then cry, God save you Madame."[196] Sometimes, however, the practice lent itself to horseplay, as it did in this vignette involving Sir Richard Cholmley. "When he was of about the age of twenty-three years, coming to London, he went to see a play at Black Friars, and coming late, was forced to take a stool, and sit on the stage, as divers others did; and, as the custom was, between every scene stood up to refresh himself. Whilst he was in that posture, a young gallant, very brave, clapped himself upon Sir Richard's stool."[197]

### VIOLENCE

Sir Richard's stolen seat did not precipitate any violence, but such was not always the case. Armed with both swords and a certain immunity from severe reprisal, the gentlemen could be quick to quarrel or to provoke a quarrel, as the stabbing and the abuse of gentlemen at the Fortune attested. At least four violent incidents also occurred in or near the Blackfriars. One concerned a certain Captain Essex and Lord Thurles of Ireland.

This Captaine attending and accompanying my Lady of Essex in a boxe in the playhouse at the blackfryers, the said lord coming upon the stage, stood before them and hindred their

[194] Jonson, *The Devil Is an Ass*, in *Ben Jonson*, VI, 178.
[195] Jonson, "Dedication to the Reader," *The New Inn*, in ibid., p. 397.
[196] Abraham Cowley, *Love's Riddle*, in *The Complete Works*, ed. Alexander B. Grosart (1881; reprint ed., New York: AMS Press, 1967), I, 47.
[197] Sir Hugh Cholmley, *Memoirs* (London, 1787), p. 18.

sight. Captain Essex told his lo:ᵖ, they had payd for their places as well as hee, and therefore intreated him not to depriue them of the benefitt of it. Wherevpon the lord stood vp yet higher and hindred more their sight. Then Capt. Essex with his hand putt him a little by. The lord then drewe his sword and ran full butt at him, though hee missed him, and might have slaine the Countesse as well as him.[198]

A second incident, involving Sir John Suckling and a Mr. Digby, was shocking enough to be mentioned in several letters written from London in November 1634. Ambrose Randolph reported to Lady Jane Bacon: "Here at home Sir John Suckling, in place of repairing his honor, hath lost his reputation for ever, and drawne himself in dainger of the law. On Tuesday last he waie layed Mʳ Digby, that had formerly strook him, and, as he came from the play, he, with many more, set upon Mʳ Digby; in which quarell Sir John Suckling had a man rune through, som say he is dead."[199] As a result of the attack, "both of them with their companyes was committed to the King's Bench," wrote Robert Leake, "but surely Sir John was bayld for I saw him this day in a coach."[200]

The very next spring a quarrel broke out in the playhouse between Will Crofts and Lord Digby, even though Crofts, in striking, was breaking bonds of £5,000.[201] A year later still another unpleasantness occurred. "A little Pique happened betwixt the Duke of Lenox and the Lord Chamberlain about a Box at a new Play in the *Black Fryars*, of which the Duke had got the Key; Which if it had come to be debated betwixt them as it was once intended, some Heat or perhaps other Inconvenience

---

[198] P.R.O. C115/8391; as cited by Herbert Berry, "The Stage and Boxes at the Blackfriars," *Studies in Philology* 63 (1966): 165.

[199] 21 November 1634; Richard Griffin Braybrooke, ed., *The Private Correspondence of Lady Jane Cornwallis, 1613-1644* (London: S. and J. Bentley, Wilson and Fley, 1842), p. 197.

[200] Robert Leake to Sir Gervas Clifton; *Historical Manuscripts Commission, Reports on MSS in Various Collections*, VIII, 408; as cited by Bentley, *Jacobean and Caroline Stage*, I, 42.

[201] Knowler, ed., *Earl of Strafforde's Letters*, I, 426.

might have happen'd. His Majesty hearing of it, sent the Earl of *Holland* to commend them both not to dispute it, but before him, so he heard it and made them Friends."[202] On the whole, such dramatic incidents seem to have been the exception rather than the rule, especially in view of the sheer numbers of performances over a sixty-six-year period. In a volatile age and in a group of particularly proud and mettlesome men, it was surprising that the privileged playgoers engaged in so little violence.

WANTON WOMEN

If the Puritans judged correctly, then vice, rather than violence, provided the chief diversion for a spectator. The moralists saw theaters as "the very markets of bawdry,"[203] where harlots sought customers, mistresses kept assignations, casual pickups abounded, and decent women were seduced. Moreover, the plays presented a veritable textbook for seduction.

> The wilines and craft of the stage is not yet so great, as it is without on the scaffoldes. For that they which are euil disposed, no sooner heare anie thing spoken that maie serue their turne, but they applie it vnto them selues. Alas, saie they to their familiar by them, Gentlewoman, is it not pittie this passioned louer should be so martyred. And if he find her inclining to foolish pittie, as commonlie such women are, then he applies the matter to himselfe, and saies that he is likewise caried awaie with the liking of her; crauing that pittie to be extended vpō him, as she seemed to showe toward the afflicted amorous stager. . . .
>
> Credite me, there can be found no stronger engine to batter the honestie as wel of wedded wiues, as the chastitie of vnmarried maides and widowes, than are the hearing of common plaies. . . . insomuch that it is a miracle, if there be foūd anie

---

[202] George Garrard to Lord Strafforde, 25 January 1636; in ibid., I, 511.
[203] Gosson, *Playes Confuted*, p. 214.

either woman, or maide, which with these spectacles of
strange lust, is not oftentimes inflamed euen vnto furie.[204]

Some women, of course, required no inflaming or seducing but
made themselves freely available for dalliance with the gentlemen. Stephen Gosson detailed the techniques involved, with
young men first surveying the prospects from the yard, then
pressing "as nere to y$^e$ fairest as they can," plying the women
with pippins and "talke vpō al occasions." The conquest com-
pleted, the young lovers "eyther bring thē home to theire
houses on small acquaintāce, or slip into tauerns whē y$^e$ plaies
are dōe. He thinketh best of his painted sheath, & taketh himselfe for a iolly fellow, y$^t$ is noted of most, to be busyest w$^{th}$
women in such places."[205] A Roman Catholic called the playhouse "a place of licentiousnesse" where "many a foul sinne
is committed, and much unhonest love begunn." After all, he
charged, "few of either sex come thither, but in theyr holy-
dayes appareil, and so set forth, so trimmed, so adorned, so
decked, so perfumed, as if they made the place a market of
wantonness."[206]

The scandalized moralists held no exclusive brief to speak out
on this subject. On the other end of the spectrum, Thomas
Nashe, like others, commended the young gentleman who
"haunts Plaies, & sharpens wits with frequenting the company
of Poets: he emboldens his blushing face by courting faire
women on the sodaine, and looks into all Estates by conuersing
with them in publike places."[207] Dekker considered the playhouse prostitute a fit subject for joking, not preaching, and
included her in his *Jests to Make You Merry*.

A Wench hauing a good face, a good body, and good clothes

[204] Munday, *Second and Third Blast*, pp. 142-143.

[205] Gosson, *Playes Confuted*, p. 215. The Ovidian paraphrase in a similar
passage in Gosson's *School of Abuse* has been noted by S. P. Zitner, "Gosson,
Ovid, and the Elizabethan Audience," *Shakespeare Quarterly* 9 (1958): 206-
208.

[206] Harrison, Leke, Colleton correspondence, pp. 79, 25, respectively.

[207] Nashe, *Pierce Penilesse*, in *Works*, I, 210.

on, but of bad conditions, sitting one day in the two-penny roome / of a play-house, & a number of yong Gentlemen about her, against all whom she maintaind talke, One that sat ouer the stage, sayd to his friend: doe you not thinke that yonder flesh will stincke anon, hauing so many flyes blowing vpon it. Oh (quoth his friend) I thinke it stinckes already, for I neuer saw so many crowes together but there was some carion not far off.[208]

Jonson took note of both the "pusil" and the "daughters of Whitefriars" at the private playhouses, and in his *Notes from Blackfriars*, Fitzgeffrey described the attempted pickup of a "Cheapside Dame" who would "holde vs dooing till the Latter Act" and then "Inuite vs Supper home."[209]

One of the most interesting accounts of a courtesan plying her trade in the theater came from Thomas Cranley. The extremely clever tactics of his "Amanda" showed how well she adapted herself to the differing tastes of her prospective customers in the audience.

The places thou dost usually frequent
Is to some playhouse in an afternoon
And for no other meaning and intent
But to get company to sup with soon;
More changeable and wavering than the moon,
> And with thy wanton looks attracting to thee
> The amorous spectators for to woo thee.

Thither thou com'st in several forms and shapes
To make thee still a stranger to the place,
And train new lovers, like young birds, to scrapes;
And by thy habit so to change thy face:
At this time plain, to'morrow all in lace:
> Now in the richest colours may be had;
> The next day all in mourning, black and sad.

---

[208] Dekker, "The 45. Iest," in *Non-Dramatic Works*, II, 292.
[209] Fitzgeffrey, *Satyres and Satyricall Epigrams*, F-F$^v$.

In a stuff waistcoat and a peticoat,
Like to a chamber-maid thou com'st to-day:
The next day after thou dost change thy note;
Then like a country wench thou com'st in grey,
And sittest like a stranger at the play:
    Tomorrow after that, thou comest then
    In the neat habit of a citizen.

The next time rushing in thy silken weeds
Embroider'd, lac'd, perfum'd, in glittering show;
So that thy look an admiration breeds,
Rich like a lady and attended so:
As brave as any countess dost thou go.
    Thus Proteus-like strange shapes thou vent'rest on
    And changest hue with the chameleon.[210]

The wanton behavior that provoked outrage from the Puritans and amusement from the writers found substantiation in several well-documented incidents at the theater. The best known of these was the experience of Father Busino, chaplain of the Venetian embassy, during his visit to the Fortune.

These theatres are frequented by a number of respectable and handsome ladies, who come freely and seat themselves among the men without the slightest hesitation. On the evening in question his Excellency and the Secretary were pleased to play me a trick by placing me amongst a bevy of young women. Scarcely was I seated ere a very elegant dame, but in a mask, came and placed herself beside me. . . . She asked me for my address both in French and English; and, on my turning a deaf ear, she determined to honour me by showing me some fine diamonds on her fingers, repeatedly taking off no fewer than three gloves, which were worn one over the other. . . . This lady's bodice was of yellow satin richly embroidered, her petticoat of gold tissue with stripes, her robe of red velvet with a raised pile, lined with yellow muslin

[210] Thomas Cranley, "Amanda," in John P. Collier, *The History of English Dramatic Poetry to the Time of Shakespeare* (London: G. Bell and Sons, 1879), III, 217-218.

with broad stripes of pure gold. She wore an apron of point lace of various patterns: her head-tire was highly perfumed, and the collar of white satin beneath the delicately-wrought ruff struck me as extremely pretty.[211]

The good chaplain of course resisted his companion's blandishments, though he paid extraordinarily close attention to every detail of her rich clothing.

More typical than Father Busino's experience, perhaps, was a certain Thomas May's lamentable effort to find "some rich lady [who] would cast her Eie upon me" at the Blackfriars. Though he sat upon the stage and stood up to salute strangers, he had no luck until after the first three acts, when "my Face withstood a fresh encounter." "Her uglinesse made me suppose that nothing could be too base for her acceptance: therefore I (following her down the Staires) resolved to discover a good-will to her, either by wanton gesture of my Body, or whispering in her Ear just as she came forth into the Street."[212]

The attitude of the playwrights, who had to compete with the distractions of flirtation, dalliance, seduction, assignation, and solicitation, came through unmistakably in this prologue to *The Obstinate Lady*.

> Troth, gentlemen, we know that now-a-days
> Some come to take up wenches at our plays;
> It is not our design to please their sense,
> We wish they may go discontented hence.
> .................................................................
> If perfum'd wantons do for eighteenpence
> Expect an angel, and alone go hence,
> We shall be glad with all our hearts, for we
> Had rather have their room than company;
> For many an honest gentleman is gone
> Away for want of place, as, look ye, yon!
> We guess some of you ladies hither come

---

[211] "Diaries . . . of the Venetian Embassy," p. 416.

[212] Thomas May, *Life of a Satyricall Puppy, Called Nim* (London, 1657), H₃ᵛ-H₅ᵛ.

To meet your servants, wh' are at dice at home;
You'll be deceiv'd, and therefore will dispraise,
And say, this is the worst of all the plays
You ever saw; but keep your censures, pray,
Until you meet them here another day.[213]


OTHER DIVERSIONS

Despite the diversions of sin and seduction, spectators did come
to the theater for other reasons. One prologue claimed, "And
many gallants hither come, we think, / To sleep, and to digest
their too much drink."[214] Instead of responding with sleepy
indifference, some gentlemen paid overclose attention to the
lines of the plays. Hoping to swell out his store of clever tidbits
for dinner conversation, many a man carried his "table-book"
into the playhouses, "To write down, what again he may repeat
/ At some great table to deserve his meat."[215] He would "hoard
vp the finest play-scraps" to feed his "leane wit . . . when the
*Arcadian* and *Euphuised* gentlewomen haue their tongues
sharpened," providing himself with an "A B C of comple-
ment."[216] The playwrights dealt harshly with any such thieves
of their wit: "if there bee any lurking amongst you in corners,
with Table-bookes, who have some hope to find fit matter to
feede his _____ mallice on, let them claspe them up, and slinke
away, or stay and be converted."[217]

Yet the playwright's strongest contempt fell not upon those
who stole his lines but upon those who scorned them:

When they haue writ a sceene in which their brains
Haue dropt there deerest sweetes, and their swoln vains

[213] Sir Aston Cokayne, *The Obstinate Lady*, in *The Dramatic Works*, ed.
James Maidment and W. H. Logan (London: H. Sotheran, 1874), p. 21.

[214] Ibid.

[215] Beaumont and Fletcher, "Prologue," *The Custom of the Country*, in
*Works*, ed. Arnold Glover and A. R. Waller (Cambridge: Cambridge University
Press, 1905-1912), I, 386.

[216] Dekker, *Gvls Horne-booke*, in *Non-Dramatic Works*, II, 254.

[217] Beaumont and Fletcher, "Prologue," *The Woman-Hater*, in *Works*, ed.
Glover and Waller, X, 71.

Emptied their Cundits of their purest spirit;
As they stand gaping to receiue their merrit,
Instead of plaudits, their chiefest blisses,
Let their desarts be crowned with mewes and hisses.
Behind each post and at the gallery corners
Sit empty guls, slight fooles and false informers.[218]

Jonson in particular resented the *"Caprichious* gallants" who "haue taken such a habit of dislike in all things, that they will approue nothing, be it neuer so conceited or elaborate, but sit disperst, making faces, and spitting, wagging their vpright eares, and cry filthy, filthy. Simply vttering their owne condition and vsing their wryed countenances in stead of a vice, to turne the good aspects of all that shall sit neere them, from what they behold."[219] He described one of these capricious gallants in detail in *Every Man out of his Humor.*

And MITIS, note me, if in all this front,
You can espy a gallant of this marke,
Who (to be thought one of the iudicious)
Sits with his armes thus wreath'd, his hat pull'd here,
Cryes meaw, and nods, then shakes his empty head,
Will shew more seueral motions in his face,
Then the new *London*, *Rome*, or *Niniueh*,
And (now and then) breakes a drie bisquet iest,
Which that it may more easily be chew'd,
He steeps in his owne laughter.[220]

Not content with noise and insult, the dissatisfied spectator sometimes rose and left altogether: "To vex the Players, and to punish their *Poet*—Keepe him in awe!"[221] Dekker advised his gull to behave in precisely this way:

Now sir, if the writer be a fellow that hath either epigrammd you, or hath had a flirt at your mistris, or hath brought either

---

[218] John Day, *The Ile of Gulls*, in *The Works*, ed. A. H. Bullen (1881; reprint ed., London: Holland Press, 1963), p. 298.

[219] Jonson, *The Case Is Altered*, in *Ben Jonson*, III, 137.

[220] *Euery Man out of his Humour*, in ibid., p. 435.

[221] *The Divell is an Asse*, in ibid., VI, 224.

your feather or your red beard, or your little legs &c. on the stage, you shall disgrace him worse then by tossing him in a blancket, or giuing him the bastinado in a Tauerne, if, in the middle of his play . . . you rise with a screud and discontented face from your stoole to be gone: no matter whether the Scenes be good or no, the better they are the worse do you distast them: and, beeing on your feet, sneake not away like a coward, but salute all your gentle acquaintance, that are spred either on the rushes, or on stooles about you, and draw what troope you can from the stage after you."[222]

PREFERENCES

Neither heavy satire nor the disgruntled Jonson's complaints should be accepted as unbiased testimony. Nevertheless, the privileged audience was undoubtedly hard to please. Sophisticated, educated, opinionated, habituated to playgoing, "each one comes / And brings a play in's head with him: . . . / If that he finds not here, he mewes at it."[223] Besides the various tastes of his audience, the playwright also had to contend with distractions from the performance. It was a difficult, if not impossible task, as Thomas Middleton openly confessed.

> How is't possible to suffice
> So many ears, so many eyes?
> Some in wit, and some in shows
> Take delight, and some in clothes.
> Some for mirth they chiefly come,
> Some for passion,—for both some;
> Some for lascivious meetings, that's their arrant;
> Some to detract, and ignorance their warrant.

[222] Dekker, *Gvls Horne-booke*, in *Non-Dramatic Works*, II, 253.
[223] Dekker, "Prologue," *Roaring Girl*, in *Dramatic Works*, III, 12. For an analysis of the tastes and expectations of the Caroline audience, see Michael Neill, " 'Wits most accomplished Senate': The Audience of the Caroline Private Theaters," *Studies in English Literature* 18 (1978): 341-360.

How is't possible to please
Opinion toss'd in such wild seas?[224]

Moreover, the dictates of fashion and taste fluctuated constantly. Jigs went out of favor and short masques came in, Queen Henrietta's company became the courtiers' darlings one year and Beeston's Boys the next, *The Faithful Shepherdess* was a miserable failure at first and later a rousing success. A French company performed with great applause at Court and then at Blackfriars was "hissed, hooted, and pippin-pelted from the stage."[225] Verse prologues and inductions enjoyed the vogue, but eventually they were "out of date, and . . . as stale as a black Velvet Cloak, and a Bay Garland."[226] For most,

Wit is become an anticke, and puts on
As many shapes of variation,
To court the times applause, as the times dare,
Change severall fashions, nothing is thought rare
Which is not new and follow'd. . . .[227]

Here and there a stubborn man would "sweare *Ieronimo*, or *Andronicus* are the best playes yet."[228] But he was the exception, ridiculed for his old-fashioned tastes, just as the early playgoers were scorned by the later ones.

For ten times more of wit, than was allow'd
Your silly ancestors in twenty year,
Y' expect should in two hours be given you here.
For they, he swears, to th' Theatre would come
Ere they had din'd to take up the best room;
Then sit on benches, not adorn'd with mats,

[224] Middleton, *No Wit, No Help Like a Woman's*, in *Works*, ed. Bullen, IV, 281.

[225] Collier, *History of English Dramatic Poetry*, I, 452-453.

[226] Beaumont, "Prologue," *Woman-Hater*, in *Works*, ed. Glover and Waller, X, 71.

[227] Beaumont and Fletcher, "Prologue," *The Noble Gentleman*, in *Dramatic Works in the Beaumont and Fletcher Canon*, III, 122.

[228] Jonson, *Bartholomew Fair*, in *Ben Jonson*, VI, 16.

And graciously did vail their high-crowned hats
To every half dress'd Player, as he still
Through th' hangings peep'd to see how th' house did fill.
Good easy judging souls, with what delight
They would expect a jig, or target fight,
A furious tale of Troy, which they ne'er thought
Was weakly written, so 'twere strongly sought;
Laught at a clinch, the shadow of a jest,
And cry a passing good one, I protest.
Such dull and humble-witted people were
Even your fore-fathers whom we govern'd here.[229]

The dramatists variously flattered, cajoled, begged, and be-
rated their fickle patrons. At the height of the War of the
Theaters, the playwrights even accused one another of organ-
izing clacques, including both the "prepar'd troope of gallants,
who for my sake shal distaste euery vnsalted line, in their fly-
blowne Comedies" and the "prepard company of gallants to
aplaud his iests and grace out his play."[230] But a play's fate was
not really determined by such artificial means of approval or
disapproval. Nor was the initial judgment necessarily just, for
sometimes the "Bacon-braines"[231] judged wrong.

A worthy story, howsoever writ
For Language, modest Mirth, Conceit or Wit,
Meets oftentimes with the sweet commendation
Of hang't, 'tis scurvy, when for approbation
A Jigg shall be clapt at, and every rhyme
Prais'd and applauded by a clamorous chime.[232]

---

[229] Davenant, "Prologue," The Unfortunate Lovers, in Dramatic Works, III, 12-13.
[230] Dekker, Satiromastix, in Dramatic Works, I, 320; Day, "Induction," The Ile of Gulls, in Works, p. 211.
[231] Thomas Randolph, "An Answer to Ben Jonson," in Poems with the Muses Looking-Glasse: and Amyntas (Oxford, 1638), p. 71.
[232] Beaumont and Fletcher, "Prologue," Fair Maid of the Inn, in Works, ed. Glover and Waller, IX, 144.

John Webster and Ben Jonson hotly defended the merits of their plays against the hostile opinion of the public, and they were right. Wealth, status, education, and power did not confer aesthetic infallibility. Worthless plays sometimes proved extraordinarily popular and excellent ones, dismal flops. Yet the privileged playgoers usually had sense enough to favor the truly great plays like *Hamlet* and *Faustus* and *Volpone* until the very end.

More important, surely, than their judgment was the fact that the privileged supported plays and players year after year. They saw performances at school, at Court, in their homes, at the Inns of Court. Though they crowded into the small private theaters, they never abandoned the great public playhouses. They acted as true patrons of the drama, though only a few consciously regarded themselves in this way: playgoing simply formed an accepted part of their lives. On a given afternoon the privileged patron did not necessarily come to the theater out of an overwhelming devotion to the drama; seeing a play just provided a good way to pass the idle part of the day. At the playhouse, a gentleman could see and be seen, pick up the latest gossip, meet his friends, stir up trouble, find himself a woman, or sleep off a heavy midday meal. If the performance turned out to be bad, hisses and insults made good sport; if it turned out to be good, so much the better. With their superior education, their claims to sophistication, their demands for pleasure, and their capricious tastes, these men and women offered a challenge to the finest playwrights of the age. Perhaps those playwrights would not now be considered the finest of any age without the continuing patronage of the privileged.

# · V ·
## Playhouses, Prices, Parasites, and Profits

Without question, London's privileged attended the playhouses. Yet, except for the sheer volume of references to these particular playgoers, the record of their attendance tells little about the extent of their patronage. Were they principally devotees of the private houses and relative strangers to the public houses? Did they crowd into the boys' performances and trickle into the adult presentations? Did they dominate the audiences at private and public houses alike or were they always in the minority? While a definitive resolution of these questions is perhaps impossible, certain aspects of the theatrical enterprise provide helpful clues in determining the degree of the companies' dependence upon their privileged patrons. The playhouse locations, their capacities and interior structure, the times of performance, the admission prices, the peripheral costs of playgoing, the number of theaters erected, the repertorial patterns, and the companies' profits all indicate, at least indirectly, how much the professional drama slanted its enterprise toward an affluent, educated, leisured clientele.

### PLAYHOUSE LOCATIONS

At first, professional companies had a somewhat limited choice of locations for their theaters. In 1574, with public playing banned inside London by the council, only the children of the royal chapels were allowed to continue performing "privately" within the City boundaries. Adult companies moved to various inns in the suburbs. Burbage followed essentially the same pattern when he built the Theater in 1576, locating it just off

Shoreditch, a principal thoroughfare, and within easy access to the city. Interestingly, both the Theater and its neighbor, the Curtain, bordered on Finsbury Fields, a large recreation area where gentlemen were already accustomed to spend their leisure in bowling and other sports. Consequently, the two playhouses were immediately accessible to any gentleman who preferred more passive recreation and also took advantage of a site already associated with elite pleasures. The Bankside theaters—the Rose, the Swan, the Globe, and the Hope—enjoyed an even more desirable location insofar as London's privileged were concerned. The Thames provided direct and easy access from the great houses along its banks, the Inns of Court, and the royal palaces. And if the pleasures of the Bankside brothels and bear gardens were a bit coarser than the athletic exercises in Finsbury Fields, they were nonetheless patronized by aristocrats as well as commoners. Thus in both of the areas where playhouses were first built, the factors of accessibility, freedom from City control, and close association with leisured pursuits seem to have been paramount in importance.

The shift of theatrical activity back across the river after 1600 brought the playhouses even nearer to their privileged followers. The private playhouses could all be reached from the Thames as well. However, the desirability of water transportation quite clearly declined in importance after 1600 as coaches and sedans became the prestigious mode of travel. Even the more far-flung sites of the Red Bull and the Fortune were close enough to visit by carriage, and both of these theaters stood near Westminster and the new suburban residences of the wealthy. Insofar as City restrictions, space requirements, property availability, and building regulations permitted, all playhouses of the period were conveniently located for the privileged in London.

PERFORMANCE TIMES

Not only the sites of the theaters but also the times of performance proved particularly advantageous for the privileged.

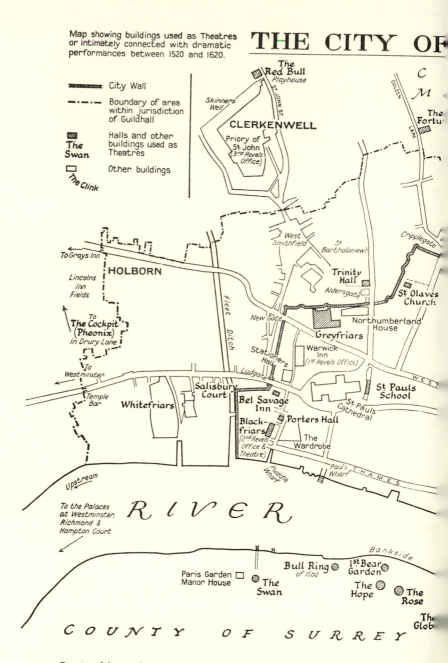

Map showing buildings used as Theatres or intimately connected with dramatic performances between 1520 and 1620.

THE CITY OF

**Legend:**
- City Wall
- Boundary of area within jurisdiction of Guildhall
- *The Swan* — Halls and other buildings used as Theatres
- *The Clink* — Other buildings

The *Red Bull* Playhouse

*C M*

*The Fortu*

Skinners Well

**CLERKENWELL**

ST JOHN ST.

Priory of St John (3rd Revels Office)

GOLDEN LANE

To Grays Inn

**HOLBORN**

Lincolns Inn Fields

West Smithfield

St Bartholomews

Cripplegate

Trinity Hall

Aldersgate

St Olaves Church

Fleet Ditch

To The Cockpit (Pheonix) in Drury Lane

New Gate

Greyfriars

Warwick Inn (1st Revels Office)

Northumberland House

To Westminster

Stationers Hall

Ludgate

WES

Temple Bar

Salisbury Court

Whitefriars

Bel Savage Inn

Black-friars (2nd Revels Office & Theatre)

Porters Hall

The Wardrobe

St Pauls School

St Pauls Cathedral

Upstream

Puddle Wharf

Paul's Wharf

THAMES

To the Palaces at Westminster, Richmond & Hampton Court

R I V E R

Bankside

Paris Garden Manor House

The Swan

Bull Ring of 1560

1st Bear Garden

The Hope

The Rose

The Glob

C O U N T Y   O F   S U R R E Y

Reprinted from Glynne Wickham, *Early English Stages, 1300 to 1660*, Vol. II, Part 1, pp. 50-51, by permission of Columbia University Press and Routledge and Kegan Paul.

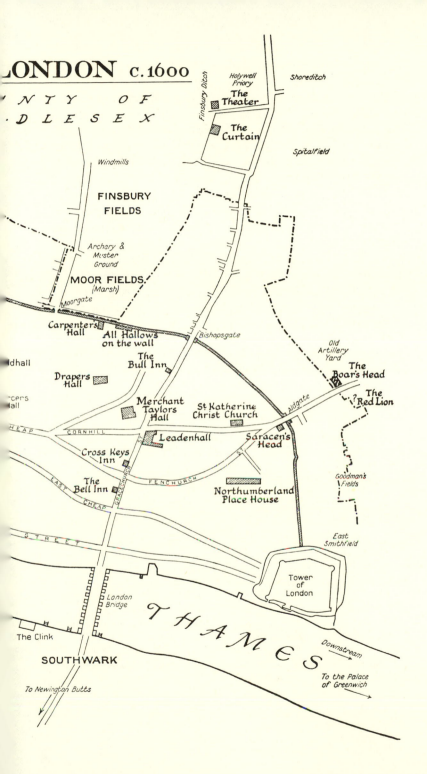

**ONDON** c.1600

*NTY OF*
*DLESEX*

Holywell Priory
Shoreditch

Finsbury Ditch

**The Theater**

**The Curtain**

Spitalfield

Windmills

**FINSBURY FIELDS**

Archery & Muster Ground

**MOOR FIELDS.**
(Marsh)

Moorgate

Carpenters Hall

Bishopsgate

All Hallows on the wall

Old Artillery Yard

**The Boar's Head**

The Bull Inn

Drapers Hall

dhall

cers all

The Red Lion

Merchant Taylors Hall

St Katherine Christ Church

Aldgate

HEAP

CORNHILL

Leadenhall

Saracen's Head

Goodman's Fields

Cross Keys Inn

The Bell Inn

EAST

FENCHURCH

GRACECHURCH

Northumberland Place House

CHEAP

STREET

East Smithfield

Tower of London

London Bridge

The Clink

**T H A M E S**

**SOUTHWARK**

Downstream

To Newington Butts

To the Palace of Greenwich

The afternoon presentations began precisely when gentlemen found themselves entirely at leisure—"the after-noone beeing the idlest time of the day; wherein men that are their owne masters (as Gentlemen of the Court, the Innes of the Courte, and the number of Captaines and Souldiers about *London*) do wholy bestow themselues vpon pleasure."[1] With dinner about noon and supper early in the evening,[2] the leisured classes had several hours with very little to do. Not that their idleness was necessarily condemned, since the freedom from manual labor constituted one distinctive mark of a gentleman. As a character in *The Careless Shepherdess* expressed it, "Courtiers, I think, have little else to do; / So to be idle, is in them a virtue."[3] Even those with legitimate business to conduct had free afternoons. Law courts sat principally in the mornings, and readings for students at the Inns of Court were held in the mornings, while their bolts and moots took place at night.[4] Though little was actually required of law students, even the most conscientious among them assumed open afternoons, as this ambitious schedule indicates.

| | |
|---|---|
| From 5 in the morning to 6. | *Ad Sacra. Begin with God by reading and prayer.* |
| From 6. to 9. | *Ad Jura. Read the law carefully and understandingly.* |
| From 9. to 11. | *Ad Arma. Carry on harmless acts of Manhood, Fencing, Dancing &.c.* |
| From 11. to 12. | *Ad Artes, Forget not Academique learning, Logick, Rhetorick.* |

[1] Thomas Nashe, *Pierce Penilesse,* in *The Complete Works,* ed. R. B. McKerrow (London: Sidgwick and Jackson, 1910), I, 212.

[2] See, e.g., G. R. Batho, ed., *The Household Papers of Henry Percy, Ninth Earl of Northumberland (1564-1632),* Camden Society Publications, 3d ser. 93 (1962): xxxvii; and William Harrison, *The Description of England,* ed. Georges Edelen (Ithaca, N. Y.: Cornell University Press, 1968), p. 144.

[3] Thomas Goffe (?), *The Careless Shepherdess* (London, 1656), p. 6.

[4] Kenneth Charlton, *Education in Renaissance England* (London: Routledge and Kegan Paul, 1965), pp. 174-175.

| | |
|---|---|
| From 12. to 2. | *Ad Victium, Eat seasonably, moderately, and allow time to digest.* |
| From 2. to 5. | *Ad Amicitias. Visit civilly your friends, and repay kindnesse in kind.* |
| From 5. to 6. | *Ad Artes, Read History, Poetry, and Romances.* |
| From 6. to 8. | *Ad Victium, Take food often, but not much, nor heavy.* |
| From 8. to 9. | *Ad Repetitionem & Sacra, Repeat your Parts and say your Prayers.* |
| From 9. to 5. | *Ad Noctem & Somnum, To Bed betimes, and rise betimes again.*[5] |

For the privileged, afternoon leisure was fixed into the pattern of life. As many like Francis Osborn testified: "It was then the fashion of those times . . . for the principall Gentry, Lords, Courtiers and men of all professions not meerely Mechanick, to meet in *Pauls Church* by eleven, and walk in the middle Ile till twelve, and after dinner from three, to six, during which time some discoursed of Businesse, others of Newes."[6]

In setting afternoon performances, therefore, the players took advantage of the free time of the thousands of privileged Londoners, entertaining them "in the best leasure of our life, that is betweene meales, the most vnfit time, either for study or bodily exercise."[7] With plays beginning at two or three o'clock,[8]

---

[5] Edward Waterhous, *Fortescutus Illustratus* (London, 1663), pp. 151-152.

[6] Francis Osborn, *Historical Memoires on the Reigns of Queen Elizabeth, and King James* (London, 1658), pp. 64-65.

[7] "An Excellent Actor," in Sir Thomas Overbury's *New and Choise Characters* . . . (London, 1615), p. 305.

[8] According to *Thomas Platter's Travels in England, 1599* (trans. Clare Williams [London: J. Cape, 1937]), plays were presented "after lunch, about two o'clock" and "daily at two o'clock in the afternoon" (p. 166). In 1611, Prince Otto of Hesse-Cassel reported that the actors played "um 3 uhr" (Karl Feyerabend, "Zu K. H. Schaible's 'Geschichte der Deutschen in England,' " *Englische Studien* 14 [1890]: 440). See also Walter W. Greg, ed., *Henslowe Papers* (London: A. H. Bullen, 1907), for the instructions to Robert Dawes "to begyn the play at the hower of three of the clock in the afternoone" (p. 124).

gentlemen could eat dinner and make their way to the theater without undue haste, though at a really popular play like *A Game at Chesse*, "we must have ben there before one a clocke at farthest to find any roome."[9] No doubt the afternoon timing reinforced the view of a play as "an Innocent Diversion for an idle Hour or two" and a playhouse as a place for "a Gentleman to spend a foolish houre or two, because you can doe nothing else."[10] The wits claimed that, without the player, "Your Innes of Court men were vndone . . . hee is their chiefe guest and imployment, and the sole busines that makes them Afternoones men."[11] The playwrights assured their audiences that "few here repent / Three hours of pretious time, or money spent."[12]

But some remained unconvinced. William Prynne thundered against "*blind Stage-haunters . . .* wasting their precious time upon them even from day to day," while another critic sourly observed that "Persons when they know not how any longer to be idle, for variety of Idlenesse goe to see Plaies."[13] With telling irony, Dekker identified Sloth as the chief benefactor to the playhouses. "The Players prayd for his [Sloth's] coming: they lost nothing by it, the coming in of tenne Embassadors was neuer so sweete to them as this our sinne was."[14] Occasionally this negative view of playgoing may have occurred to the privileged in the audience. Sir Humphrey Mildmay's diary

[9] Norman E. McClure, ed., *The Letters of John Chamberlain* (Philadelphia: American Philosophical Society, 1939), II, 578.

[10] James Wright, *Historia Histrionica: An Historical Account of the English Stage* (London, 1699), p. 5; Thomas Dekker, *The Gvls Horne-booke*, in *The Non-Dramatic Works*, ed. Alexander B. Grosart (1884; reprint ed., New York: Russell and Russell, 1963), II, 251.

[11] John Earle, "24. A Player," in *Micro-cosmographie* (London, 1628).

[12] Francis Beaumont and John Fletcher, "Epilogue," *The Loyal Subject*, in *Works*, ed. Arnold Glover and A. R. Waller (Cambridge: Cambridge University Press, 1905-1912), III, 169.

[13] William Prynne, "To the Christian Reader," *Histrio-Mastrix* (London, 1633), p. 2ᵛ; I. G., *A. Refutation of the Apology for Actors*, in Thomas Heywood, *An Apology for Actors*, ed. Richard H. Perkinson (New York: Scholars' Facsimiles and Reprints, 1941), p. 60.

[14] Dekker, *Seuen Deadly Sinnes of London*, in *Non-Dramatic Works*, II, 52-53.

contained such entries as "to a playe & loitred all the day,"
"to the Newe play att Bl:fryers w$^{th}$ my Company where I loste
the whole day," "after Noone I Loitered att a playe," and "To
a Playe & other foleryes."[15] But for the most part, Mildmay
simply recorded his frequent afternoons at the theater without
comment—an accepted pleasure for a man of his social rank.

PLAYHOUSE CAPACITIES

Though it was certainly convenient for the socially privileged
to spend their idle afternoons at the theater, it is difficult to
estimate just how many selected this particular form of entertainment. Some indirect evidence, however, comes from the
size and the price range of the various theaters. Some witnesses
specified the capacity of the largest theaters at about 3,000.
According to Johan DeWitt, the Swan, then the finest house
on the Bankside, held "tres milles homines."[16] When *A Game
at Chess* was performed, the Spanish ambassador reckoned that
at the Globe "there were 3000 people there on the day that the
audience was the smallest."[17] The Rose, too, seems to have
accommodated some 3,000 spectators.[18] In all likelihood, the
Theater and the Curtain were somewhat smaller.[19] Smaller yet
were the private playhouses, each probably holding some 500

---

[15] 8 May 1640, 15 May 1640, 24 May 1641, 21 August 1643; Gerald Eades
Bentley, *The Jacobean and Caroline Stage* (Oxford: Clarendon Press, 1941-
1968), II, 679-680.

[16] E. K. Chambers, *The Elizabethan Stage* (Oxford: Clarendon Press, 1923),
II, 362.

[17] Edward M. Wilson and Olga Turner, "The Spanish Protest against 'A Game
at Chesse,' " *Modern Language Review* 44 (1949): 480. According to the ambassador, "during these last four days more than 12,000 persons have all heard
the play" (p. 482).

[18] Walter W. Greg, ed., *Henslowe's Diary* (London: A. H. Bullen, 1904-
1908), II, 134-135n.

[19] DeWitt claimed the Swan to be larger and finer than all the other theaters
standing in 1596 (Chambers, *Elizabethan Stage*, II, 362). Computations from
Henslowe's receipts, however, indicate that the Rose was about the same size
(Greg, ed., *Henslowe's Diary*, II, 134-135n).

or so, but certainly fewer than 900.[20] In the early years of the period, therefore, a total of some 5,000 patrons could be entertained in the two playhouses at Finsbury Fields and in the smaller boys' houses.

Subsequently new theaters were built, several inns were employed, the boys quit playing, and various troupes competed against the Lord Chamberlain's and the Admiral's companies. By the decade of the 1590s, a maximum of 8,000 to 9,000 places became available on those afternoons when three different companies were all presenting performances. However, the actual capacity may well have been smaller. The return of two children's companies in 1599 to 1600, combined with the replacement of the Rose by the Fortune, would have expanded the total number of places available by perhaps 1,000. A peak was apparently reached between 1610 and 1620, when eight or nine different theaters came into use, though not all at the same time. It was during this period that Fynes Moryson claimed, "The Citty of London alone hath foure or fiue Companyes of players with their peculiar Theaters Capable of many thousands, wherein they all play euery day in the weeke but Sunday. . . as there be, in my opinion, more Playes in London then in all the partes of the worlde I haue seene."[21] The capacity finally settled down to a range of 8,000 or less to just over 10,000,

---

[20] Irwin Smith estimates the Blackfriars capacity at 516 in *Shakespeare's Blackfriars Playhouse* (New York: New York University Press, 1964), pp. 296-297; C. W. Wallace estimates 558 to 608 in *The Children of the Chapel at Blackfriars, 1597-1603* (Lincoln: Nebraska University Studies Reprint, 1908), p. 52; W. J. Lawrence sets the number at under 600 in *The Elizabethan Playhouse and Other Studies* (Stratford-upon-Avon: Shakespeare Head Press, 1913), p. 17; and Alfred Harbage, in *Shakespeare and the Rival Traditions* (New York: Macmillan, 1952), estimates "certainly less than 900 and possibly less than 700" (p. 43), setting the maximum at 955 with 3 galleries, 696 with 2 galleries. Salisbury Court was smaller than the other houses. See Bentley, *Jacobean and Caroline Stage*, VI, 92-93. The second Paul's may have held as few as 100, according to Reavley Gair, "The Presentation of Plays at Second Paul's," in *The Elizabethan Theatre VI*, ed. G. R. Hibbard (Toronto: Macmillan, 1978), p. 41.

[21] Charles Hughes, *Shakespeare's Europe . . . being unpublished chapters of Fynes Moryson's Itinerary*, 2d ed. (New York: B. Blom, 1967), p. 476.

depending on whether the King's Men were at Blackfriars or the Globe.[22]

A somewhat independent corroboration of a peak capacity of about 10,000 or so came from a scheme that never materialized. On 30 July 1620, a license was issued to three courtiers permitting them to build an amphitheater that would accommodate 12,000 spectators. It was intended "for the exercise and practize of Heroique and maiestique recreacions aswell tending to the delight and enterteynment [of] forraigne Princes and Ambassadors and strangers and the Nobility and Gentry of this Realme as for the exercise of all manner of Armes and martiall discipline" along with "maskes or other shewes or invencions, dancing, musique of all sorts . . . and maiestique playes in latin or in English"—a decidedly aristocratic bill of fare. The license requested "a prohibician to all Players within the Citty of London and the Suburbes thereof to suspend and restraine them from their playes one day in every month throughout the yeere."[23] The prohibition implied that the amphitheater intended to entertain the same audience as the theaters, so it is not surprising that its capacity of 12,000 corresponds pretty well with the estimated total capacity of the theaters in 1620.

The amphitheater proposal reappeared in 1634, with an even stronger argument of its benefit to the gentry:

The exercises in that place may quickly enable the nobler sorte of gentry and others to many excellent and lawdable seruices of their prince and Cuntrey: withdrawe many licentious, and vnlimited disposicions, from drunknes, lacivousnes, and such base or vnworthy inclinations. . . .

Latyne Scoenes also beinge presented for forraygne inter-

---

[22] I use here an estimate of 600 for the private houses—Blackfriars, Phoenix/ Cockpit, Salisbury Court—and an estimate of 3,000 for the public theaters— Globe, Red Bull, Fortune. With the Blackfriars in use, the total would have come to 7,000; with the Globe, 10,200. More sophisticated research, like that of Irwin Smith on Blackfriars, might alter the figures a few hundred in either direction, but the same general range would persist.

[23] P.R.O., P.S.C. 2/44/14; as cited in Bentley, *Jacobean and Caroline Stage*, VI, 292-293.

tainm*entes* there wilbe demonstrated the delicacy of nature
and educac*i*on of gentlemen students in the universities
whereby choise may be made of the most ingenious schollers,
and pregnant disposic*i*ons for the service, and attendancy,
peeres, or Cuntry.[24]

However, so ambitious a project, operating so infrequently,
was not financially feasible, as potential investors evidently realized.[25] Yet the very proposal of an amphitheater on this scale,
devoted entirely to elite extravaganzas, suggested both the
enormous size of the potential audience and the privileged character of that audience.

In summary, then, from 1576 onwards, London boasted room
for some 5,000 playgoers, with a gradual increase to as many
as 10,000 or so. However, on any given afternoon, that capacity
might be enlarged through the use of innyards or a combination baiting house-playhouse like the Hope or an old theater
hired temporarily. That London could not support a permanent
increase beyond the customary capacity may have been demonstrated by the financial reverses of the adult companies when
two boys' troupes suddenly appeared in 1599 to draw away
several hundred of their patrons—"No bodie comes at vs; not
a gentleman."[26] Moreover, the unstable conditions during the
years immediately following, when companies formed and reformed and so many different playhouses came into use, may
well have represented an expansion beyond the limits of the
playgoing public in London, since the final decades of the period
witnessed a retrenchment in the total number of theaters despite
the continued growth of the city's population.

The usual capacity of the playing places corresponds rather
well with both the London population as a whole and with the

[24] P.R.O., S.P. 16/281/94; as cited in ibid., pp. 302-303.
[25] A large theater in Fleet Street, "forty yards square at the most," which
was projected in 1639, was never realized either, perhaps, as Bentley suggests,
because of the "deadly threat of a large playhouse with courtly patronage and
novel entertainment" (ibid., pp. 305, 307).
[26] Ben Jonson, *Poetaster*, in *Ben Jonson*, ed. C. H. Herford and Percy Simpson
(Oxford: Clarendon Press, 1925-1952), IV, 256.

privileged segment of that population. As already indicated, the city grew from approximately 150,000 in 1576 to approximately 350,000 in 1642, while the numbers of the privileged probably increased from about 27,000 to 52,500 or so. Quite clearly, the privileged patrons could have filled every seat in every house. But so could the rest of London's vast population. A correspondence in capacity with the size of a particular group is a useful but hardly conclusive bit of evidence, despite the corroboration of the amphitheater scheme. Similarly, the maximum number of places does not tell how many of those places were filled nor how many were intended to be filled by the more affluent playgoers. For this information, other sources are more helpful.

PLACES AND PRICES

A number of useful clues inhere in the structure of the playhouses and in the scale of admission prices. It has long been assumed that the private theaters catered rather exclusively to the elite. At first, the boys, who occupied the smaller theaters, were officially part of the royal chapels, with a primary duty to entertain the Court. Then, too, the houses where they "rehearsed" before the public closely resembled the shape and size of the great halls in the royal palaces. These royal halls ranged from a maximum of 120' x 53' in the first Jacobean Banquet House at Whitehall to a minimum of 71' x 29' in the Great Chamber of Hampton Court.[27] By comparison, the first Black-

[27] The dimensions of the other palace halls are as follows:

| | |
|---|---|
| *Hampton Court* | |
| Hall | 115' x 40' |
| Great Chamber | 71' x 29' |
| *Windsor* | |
| Hall | 100'(?) x 33' |
| Great Chamber | 80' x 33' |
| *Whitehall* | |
| Hall | 100' x 40' |
| Elizabethan Banquet House | 110' x 50' |
| 1st Jacobean Banquet House | 120' x 53' |

friars hall used for plays measured 66' x 46', while the larger
upper chamber used in the seventeenth century measured 100'
x 44'. The Whitefriars' proportions were approximately 85' x
35', and Salisbury Court, 40' x 40'.[28] Thus the comparatively
small indoor playhouse, illuminated by candlelight, had close
and immediate affinities with the great halls of royalty and the
nobility, where exclusively aristocratic audiences watched special performances.

Of even more importance, perhaps, was the fact that the
private theaters charged higher admission prices than the public
theaters. At Pauls in 1589, "two pence is the price for the going
into a newe playe."[29] A Lyly pamphlet of the same year, urging
a satiric performance, said, "If it be shewed at Paules, it will
cost you foure pence: at the Theater two pence,"[30] though instances of even higher prices are on record during this early
period. As already stated, William Darrell paid 6d. in 1589 to
see a play at Paul's.[31] With the reopening of private houses after
1599, prices seem to have begun at 6d. and ranged upward.

| | |
|---|---|
| 2nd Jacobean Banquet House | 110' x 55' |
| Masking House | 112' x 57' |
| *Denmark House* | |
| House for Mask | 76' x 36' |
| *Eltham* | |
| Hall | 100' x 36' |
| *Richmond* | |
| Hall | 100' x 40' |

See Glynne Wickham, *Early English Stages, 1300 to 1660* (New York: Columbia
University Press, 1972), II, 2: 155; Chambers, *Elizabethan Stage*, I, 15. For
variations in stage sizes, see *Malone Society Collections* (Oxford: Oxford
University Press, 1907-1975), X, xx.

[28] Wickham, *Early English Stages*, II, 2: 128, 132, 123, respectively; Bentley,
*Jacobean and Caroline Stage*, VI, 6, 92. For correspondences in shape between
the halls in other great houses and theaters, see Richard Hosley, "Three Renaissance Indoor Playhouses," *English Literary Renaissance* 3 (1973): 166-182.

[29] William Percy, *The Cuck-queanes and Cuckolds Errants*; as cited by Chambers, *Elizabethan Stage*, II, 556.

[30] John Lyly, *Pappe with an Hatchet*, in *The Complete Works*, ed. R. Warwick
Bond (Oxford: Clarendon Press, 1902), III, 408.

[31] Hubert Hall, *Society in the Elizabethan Age* (London: Swan, Sonnenschien,
Lowrey, 1886), p. 211.

Prince Otto of Hesse-Cassel claimed that "it costs half a shilling to enter, but for the other places at least half a crown."[32] A shilling was a common charge, but some paid eighteenpence, two shillings, or even more.[33] Except for an occasional "sinful six-penny Mechanick,"[34] these prices probably barred most plebeian playgoers from the private houses.

At the great public playhouses, prices also spanned a considerable range, although the initial admission, at least in the early years, was only a penny—half the initial cost at the private houses at that time. However, the penny bought only standing room in the open area around the stage, where the playgoer was exposed to sun, wind, rain, sleet, or snow for two or three hours. To stand or sit in one of the three roofed galleries, a man paid more, as the traveler Thomas Platter and other witnesses observed: "There are different galleries and places . . . where the seating is better and more comfortable and therefore more expensive. For whoever cares to stand below only pays one English penny, but if he wishes to sit he enters by another door, and pays another penny, while if he desires to sit in the most comfortable seats which are cushioned, where he not only sees

[32] William B. Rye, *England as Seen by Foreigners in the Days of Elizabeth and James the First* (London: J. R. Smith, 1865), p. 143. The original reads, "hier kostet der eingang einen halben schilling nur, da an andern arten wohl eine halbe kron" (Feyerabend, "Zu K. H. Schaible's 'Geschichte den Deutsche in England,' " p. 440).

[33] See, e.g., Beaumont and Fletcher, "Prologue," *The Captain*: "Twelve pence goes farther this way than in drink"; and *The Mad Lover*: "Remember ye're all venturers; and in this Play / How many twelve-pences ye have 'stow'd this day"; in *Works*, ed. Glover and Waller, V, 318; III, 75, respectively. In Goffe's *Careless Shepherdess*, the "Prelude" specifies a shilling as the lowest price of admission (p. 1). Damplay, in Jonson's *Magnetic Lady*, says, "I see no reason, if I come here, and give my eighteene pence, or two shillings for my Seat, but I should take it out in censure, on the *Stage*" (*Ben Jonson*, VI, 545). Francis Lenton's *Young Gallant's Whirligig* (London, 1629) laments that "this expensive foole / Should pay an angell for a paltry stoole" (p. 13). And Fletcher's *Wit Without Money* refers to "the Half-crown boxes, Where you might sit and muster all the Beauties," *Works*, ed. Glover and Waller, II, 149.

[34] Jonson, "Induction," *The Magnetic Lady*, in *Ben Jonson*, VI, 509. See also Thomas Middleton's "Induction" to *Michaelmas Term*, with its reference to "sixpenny fees all the year long," in *The Works*, ed. A. H. Bullen (1885; reprint ed., New York: AMS Press, 1964), I, 218.

everything well, but can also be seen, then he pays yet another English penny at another door."[35] William Lambarde reported a similar scale of admissions: "one pennie at the gate, another at the entrie of the Scaffolde, and the thirde for a quiet standing."[36] Besides the standings in the pit and the seats or standings in the galleries, there were also "the priuate roomes of greater prise"[37] (in particular the Lords' room) and, by the 1590s, the more expensive stools on the stage. In addition, the admission to the public playhouses was doubled for new plays.[38] Thus, at least up to the end of the sixteenth century, the contrast between the prices at the public and private theaters was not especially pronounced.

Moreover, it would be a mistake to assume that low prices meant a low clientele. Many a man of unquestioned privilege had very little ready money. Masters at the Merchant Taylors' School received but £10 per year, and lesser courtiers or retainers of noblemen fared little better.[39] Wellborn apprentices, students at the Inns of Court on strict allowances, and the like would have been glad enough to sit in the twopenny gallery or even to stand in the yard. As a youth, Edmund Spenser and his

[35] Platter, *Travels in England*, p. 167. See Chambers, *Elizabethan Stage*, II, 365, for other examples.

[36] William Lambarde, *A Perambulation of Kent* (London: Baldwin, Cradock, and Joy, 1826), p. 233.

[37] John Davies, Epigram 3, "In Ruffum," *Epigrammes and Elegies* (London, ca. 1590).

[38] Writing of Jonson's *Volpone*, Jasper Mayne said: "When the Fox had ten times acted been / Each day was first, but that 'twas cheaper seen"; and Marmion's *Fine Companion* makes this comparison: "A new play and a gentleman in a new suit claim the same privilege,—at their first presentment their estimation is double" (John P. Collier, *The History of English Dramatic Poetry to the Time of Shakespeare* [London: G. Bell and Sons, 1879], III, 148, 214). See also K. D. Hassler, ed., *Die Riesen des Samuel Kiechel* (Stuttgart: Literarischer Verein, 1866), p. 29. Kiechel visited London in 1585.

[39] F.W.M. Draper, *Four Centuries of Merchant Taylors' School, 1561-1961* (London: Oxford University Press, 1962), p. 10; Charlton, *Education in Renaissance England*, p. 124; Harrison, *Description of England*, p. 28; A. Monroe Stowe, *English Grammar Schools in the Reign of Queen Elizabeth* (New York: Columbia University Teachers College, 1908), pp. 180-183; Chambers, *Elizabethan Stage*, I, 93-94.

"lively copesmates" saw the comedians for "pence and twopence apiece."[40] And of course during the 1590s, when the private houses were closed, the privileged playgoers came exclusively to the public theaters, paying whatever prices suited their pleasure and their pocketbooks, from a penny or two on up.

With the reappearance of the boys' troupes, charging higher prices, the public playhouses seem to have begun charging higher prices too. Though there were still plenty of references to the twopenny places right up to the end of the period,[41] all mention of penny admissions eventually ceased. The upper price limits also increased, at least to a schilling. "I say, any man that hath wit, may censure (if he sit in the twelve-penny roome.)"[42] Sixpenny rooms were noted by both Beaumont and Middleton.[43] On special occasions the prices were identical to those at the private houses, as when Ben Jonson premiered *Bartholomew Fair* for the opening of the new Hope theater. His prologue solemnly charged the spectators to criticize according to the money they had paid:

[40] Gabriel Harvey, *Letter Book*, ed. E.J.L. Scott, Camden Society Publications, n.s. 33 (1884): 68.

[41] See, e.g., Jonson's *Euery Man out of his Humour*, in *Ben Jonson*, III, 439; Edward Blount's "Epistle Dedicatory" to Tommaso Garzoni's *The Hospitall of Incurable Fooles* (London, 1600); Dekker's *News from Hell, Iests to Make You Merrie, The Gvls Horne-booke,* and *The Rauens Almanacke*, in *Non-Dramatic Works*, II, 96, 292, 247, and IV, 184, respectively; *Vox Graculi,* or *Iacke Dawes Prognostication* (London, 1623), p. 21; and the "Prologue" to Beaumont and Fletcher's *The Woman-Hater*, in *The Dramatic Works in the Beaumont and Fletcher Canon*, ed. Fredson Bowers (Cambridge: Cambridge University Press, 1966-1979), I, 157.

[42] John Marston, "Induction," *The Malcontent*, in *Plays*, ed. H. Harvey Wood (London: Oliver and Boyd, 1934), I, 142. Shakespeare's "Prologue" to *Henry VIII* speaks of those who "see away their shilling / Richly in two short hours" (*The Complete Works*, ed. Alfred Harbage [Baltimore: Penguin Books, 1969], p. 784); and Overbury's "The Proud Man" testifies: "if he haue but twelue pence in his purse he will giue it for the best roome in a play house," in *The "Conceited Newes" of Sir Thomas Overbury and his Friends* [Gainsville, Fla.: Scholars' Facsimiles and Reprints, 1968], p. 270).

[43] E.J.L. Scott, "Beaumont's Grammar Lecture," *The Athenaeum* (27 January 1894), p. 115; Middleton, *Works*, ed. Bullen, VIII, 41; *The Actor's Remonstrance*, in *The English Drama and Stage*, ed. William C. Hazlitt (1869; reprint ed., New York: Burt Franklin, n.d.), p. 265.

It shall bee lawfull for any man to iudge his six pen'orth, his twelue pen'orth, so to his eighteene pence, 2. shillings, halfe a crowne, to the value of his place: Prouided alwaies his place get not aboue his wit. And if he pay for halfe a dozen, hee may censure for them too. . . . mary, if he drop but sixe pence at the doore, and will censure a crownes worth, it is thought there is no conscience, or iustice in that.[44]

Though such fees may not have been standard, they do indicate that admissions could be as steep at public houses as at private houses. Sir Humphrey Mildmay paid exactly the same price— a shilling—whether he went to Blackfriars or the Globe.[45]

Not all the privileged were so generous, of course; a good many preferred the lesser tariffs. Even so distinguished a patron as Edward Alleyn paid only twopence to get into the Red Bull in October of 1617, though he came to the playhouse by coach.[46] Commoners may have dominated the very cheapest places in the pit, but the privileged held sway in the lower-priced galleries. There a patron could "come, and sit in the two-pennie galleries amongst the Gentlemen, and see their Knaueries and their pastimes."[47] There he could "crack Nuts with the Scholars in peny Rooms."[48] As a scornful groundling put it, "Tut, giue me the penny, giue me the peny, I care not for the Gentlemen I, let me haue a good ground."[49] And satirists who feared they had too deeply insulted their more elite patrons cried out, "I recant, beare witnes all you Gentle-folkes (that walke i'the Gal-

---

[44] "Induction," *Bartholomew Fair*, in *Ben Jonson*, V, 15.

[45] Bentley, *Jacobean and Caroline Stage*, II, 674-680. With minor variations, this also seems to have been the price he paid when he took along guests. The last entry recorded (16 November 1643) is for a "Playe of Warre . . . where was a Disaster," which cost Mildmay only 6d., perhaps because performances were by then illegal.

[46] William Young, *The History of Dulwich College* (Edinburgh: Morrison and Gibb, 1889), II, 51: "Oct. 1, 1617. I came to London in y$^e$ coach & went to y$^e$ red bull. 0 0 2."

[47] Dekker, *Seuen Deadly Sins*, in *Non-Dramatic Works*, II, 53.

[48] Fletcher, *Wit Without Money*, in *Works*, ed. Glover and Waller, II, 194.

[49] *The Case is Altered*, in *Ben Jonson*, III, 108.

leries) I recant the opinions which I helde of Courtiers, Ladies, and Cittizens."[50]

## GALLERY VERSUS PIT

Well might the playwrights beware of offending the gentlefolk in the galleries, for the higher-priced galleries held the majority of the audience in the public theaters. Whether square or round, the basic structure was the same—an open space accommodating

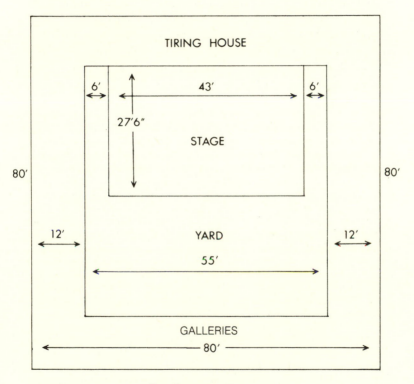

THE FORTUNE THEATRE

---

[50] Dekker, *Satiromastix*, in *The Dramatic Works*, ed. Fredson Bowers (Cambridge: Cambridge University Press, 1953-1961), I, 385.

the stage and standees, surrounded by tiers of galleries. The Fortune contract even provided the exact dimensions for that particular playhouse, so that the proportion of space allotted to the higher priced places is fairly easy to determine.[51]

On the first floor, part or all of the area behind the stage was used as a tiring house, but even so the gallery space on three sides amounted to at least 2,280 square feet, while the standing room amounted to 1,842 square feet. In the two upper galleries, where there was a ten-inch overhang at each level, the entire circumference of the house would have yielded some 3,258 square feet on the second floor, and 3,276 on the third floor, or a total of 8,814 square feet or more available in the galleries. At a minimum, with none of the space on the tiring house wall allotted to the audience, the galleries still contained about 6,900

[51] Greg, ed., *Henslowe Papers*, pp. 4-7. I use the Fortune contract in estimating the proportion of gallery places to yard places because it is the only certain set of dimensions we have. Conjectures about the round or octagonal theaters, most notably the Globe, vary from the Adams-Smith hypothesis of an 84' diameter to the Hosley-Orrell hypothesis of a 101' diameter. Together with Hodges, who has recently shifted from a conjecture of 92' to the 101' figure, most theorists suggest 12' galleries, with an overhang of 10 inches in each of the upper stories, as in the Fortune contract. If the Globe actually were as large as 100' in diameter, the galleries might well have been even deeper and the stage larger, as John Orrell theorizes in "Peter Street at the Fortune and the Globe," *Shakespeare Survey* 33 (1980): 151. However, even assuming the maximum space in the yard, the amount of gallery space is still disproportionate, as in the Fortune. With due allowance for the stage and with a subtraction of some 25 percent to account for the tiring house, the area comes to approximately 3,000 square feet in the yard versus 7,500 in the galleries for a 100' diameter and 1,700 square feet in the pit, with about 6,500 in the galleries for an 84' diameter. The same ratio shows up in Adams-Smith estimations of spectator capacity, for they allow only 600 standees in the yard out of a total of 2,028 in the theater (p. 64). For fuller details on the size of the Globe, see Irwin Smith, *Shakespeare's Globe Playhouse* (New York: Charles Scribner's Sons, 1956); C. Walter Hodges, *Shakespeare's Second Globe: The Missing Monument* (London: Oxford University Press, 1973); Richard Hosley, "The Playhouses," in *The Revels History of Drama in English*, ed. Clifford Leech and T. W. Craik (London: Methuen, 1975), III, 141-196. See also papers by Hosley, Hodges, and Orrell in a volume on the second Globe forthcoming from Wayne State University.

square feet. Even allowing for stairs, passageways, partitions, and seats, this is a staggeringly favorable allotment of space to gallery places over yard places.

How many people the galleries held is debatable, since some stood and some sat. By the most conservative estimate, in a large theater like the Swan or the Fortune, the gallery capacity certainly exceeded 1,500 and probably exceeded 2,000.[52] When filled to a peak capacity of 3,000 or so, between 2,000 and 2,200 would have packed into the galleries, while in the yard, "Within one square a thousand heads are laid."[53] Without going into complicated and questionable calculations of space per person, it seems safe to say that the galleries in the public theaters could accommodate at least twice as many playgoers as the pit.

The logic behind this kind of playhouse structure is fairly obvious. If there were sufficient numbers of potential customers to pay higher prices to sit or stand in the galleries,[54] then the

[52] I follow here Harbage's allotment of 2.25 square feet of space to each groundling. I question, however, his figure of 7,156.65 square feet of gallery space holding 1,526 people. Not only does his footage fail to conform to the dimensions of the Fortune (and unfortunately he gives no clue as to how he arrived at this figure) but he assumes a wholly seated audience in the galleries, despite the wealth of references to people standing there too. Furthermore, as he admits, he makes a very generous allowance of space for each seated patron. His estimate of a 2,344 person capacity for the Fortune diverges considerably from the 3,000 figure reported by contemporaries for this and similar theaters (Alfred Harbage, *Shakespeare's Audience* [New York: Columbia University Press, 1941], p. 23). By his calculations, the Rose, Henslowe's earlier theater, turns out to have had a larger capacity than the later and far grander Fortune—2,495 as compared with 2,344 (p. 30). Despite the deficiencies of his analysis, Harbage still comes out with a preponderance of gallery places over pit places by a margin of two to one. For further objections to Harbage's computations, see Hosley, "The Playhouses," p. 142n.

[53] Dekker, *Roaring Girl*, in *Dramatic Works*, III, 17.

[54] Carpenters' bills from the Office of Works at the Court call for the "making of Scaffoldes for the noble men and women to stande on" (Greenwich, 1585-1586), for "Settinge up degrees Brackettes boordes & other necessaries for the plaies in the greate chamber & halpaces [platforms] for the people to stande on there" (Richmond, 1590-1591), and for "makinge degrees for the Ladies of honor and people to stande on" (Hampton Court, 1592-1593); as cited by Leslie Hotson, *Shakespeare's Wooden O* (London: Rupert Hart-Davis, 1959), p. 289.

theater entrepreneurs made more money by filling the gallery than by filling the yard. It took only simple arithmetic for investors to realize that a couple of people in good places in the gallery could bring more income than half a dozen standing in front of the stage, while a gentleman who commanded a stool on the stage or a place in the Lords' room might surpass a score of groundlings in profit to the company. Thus, it is not surprising to find the following advice concerning the rebuilding of the north galleries at the Boar's Head in 1600: "yf they were myne . . . I would pull downe that long gallery & bringe yt forwarder into y$^e$ yarde . . . foure foote or thereab. . . . then would there be roome for three or foure seates more in a gallery and for many mo people, yet never the lesse roome in the yarde." When the Boar's Head was remodeled, the stage was moved forward and the galleries enlarged at the expense of the space and sightlines in the yard.[55]

Nor is it surprising to find that it was most common for a portion of gallery receipts, not yard receipts, to go to investors. That shrewd businessman Henslowe took half the gallery profits as his share at the Rose, and the company agreed to pay his heirs a quarter of the takings "out of & for the whole galleryes of the playehowse comonly called the hope."[56] At the Swan in 1597, Francis Langley provided the company with clothes and in return received a "moytie of th gains for the seuerall standinges in the galleries of the said howse," while Oliver Woodliffe, the owner of a gallery at the Boar's Head, had taken "half the profits" from "the said weste galleryes over the said Stage" as his rent. From 1602 to 1603, the gatherings in these galleries brought in a substantial £10 to £12 a week.[57]

[55] P. R. O., Samuel V. Woodliff; as cited by Hotson, in ibid., pp. 287-288; and Herbert Berry, "The Playhouse in the Boar's Head Inn, Whitechapel," in *The Elizabethan Theatre*, ed. David Galloway (Toronto: Archon Books, 1970), p. 71. For a discussion of the remodeling and its effects on the yard, see Berry, "The Boar's Head Again," in *The Elizabethan Theatre III*, ed. David Galloway (Toronto: Macmillan, 1973), pp. 54-55.

[56] Greg, ed., *Henslowe's Diary*, II, 134n; Bentley, *Jacobean and Caroline Stage*, VI, 208.

[57] Chambers, *Elizabethan Stage*, I, 368n; Woodliff v. Browne et Jurdaine,

Evidently the galleries offered a more secure profit not just because they accommodated patrons who paid more but because they were not subject to the vagaries of the weather. Stow's *Annals* were filled with reports of frosts, snows, storms, wind, hail, rain, and cold that might well have emptied the unprotected pit. Meteorologists have called the years from 1540 to 1680 the "Little Ice Age."[58] On 4 February 1579, for instance, there was deep snow, two feet or more: "it snowed till the eight day, and freezed till the 10. Then followed a thaw with continuall raine a long time after, which caused such high flouds, that the marshes and low grounds being drowned for the time, the water rose so high in Westminster hall, that after the fall thereof, some fishes were founde there to remaine."[59] No wonder that when Gosson published his *Playes Confuted* in 1582, he complained, "Commedies are neither chargable to yᵉ beholders purse, nor painful to his body; partly, because he may sit out of the raine to viewe the same, when many other pastimes are hindred by wether."[60] One of the least remarkable predictions

---

uncalendered Proceedings of the Court of Requests; as cited by Hotson, *Shakespeare's Wooden O*, pp. 264, 268; and Berry, "Playhouse in the Boar's Head," pp. 50-51. For an account of the dispute over the gallery receipts at the Boar's Head, see C. J. Sisson, *The Boar's Head Theatre* (London: Routledge and Kegan Paul, 1972), p. 68. To see how higher-priced places compared with lower-priced ones in total box office takes in a theater with a similar structure and similar scales, see John Lough, *Paris Theatre Audiences in the Seventeenth and Eighteenth Centuries* (London: Oxford University Press, 1957), pp. 108-111.

[58] Y. S. Brenner, "The Inflation of Prices in England, 1551-1650," *Economic History Review*, 2d ser. 15 (1962-1963): 281. For more technical discussions of the "Little Ice Age," see Emmanuel LeRoy Ladurie, *Times of Feast, Times of Famine: A History of Climate Since the Year 1000* (Garden City, N.Y.: Doubleday, 1971), pp. 129-226; and H. H. Lamb, *Climate Past, Present and Future* (London: Methuen, 1977), II, 452-453, 461ff.

[59] John Stow, *Annales, or a General Chronicle of England*, continued and augmented . . . by Edmund Howes, Gent. (London, 1631), p. 685; see also pp. 689, 760, 767, 768, 788, 790, 792, 891, 1,023, and 1,034 for other instances of bad weather.

[60] Stephen Gosson, *Playes Confuted in Fiue Actions*, in *The English Drama and Stage*, ed. William C. Hazlitt (1869; reprint ed., New York: Burt Franklin, n.d.), p. 202.

made for the month of April in *Vox Graculi* was the assurance that "if at this time, about the houres of foure and fiue, it waxe cloudy, and then raine downeright, they shall sit dryer in the Galleries, then those who are the vnderstanding men in the yard."[61] Apparently, even the weather conspired to assure that the playhouses had to depend upon the gallery patrons rather than the groundlings to stay in business.

The structure of the public playhouses reflected this hard economic fact. The yard was there, to be filled whenever possible with low-paying standees or perhaps with the overflow from the galleries at sellout performances. But the galleries far surpassed the yard in both potential revenue and in absolute size. It was the gallery upon which the players truly depended for their livelihood. Yet dependence upon the galleries meant dependence upon those prepared to pay double and triple the initial charge or even more. To a large extent, it must have meant dependence upon London's privileged, as indicated by the repeated references to gentlemen, scholars, and gentlefolk in the galleries.

ATTENDANCE FIGURES

Thus far, the discussion has centered upon the potential capacity of the theaters rather than upon actual attendance. It is unreasonable to assume that all the theaters were ever filled to capacity on any given day, with the possible exception of holidays. Thomas Platter reported of the acting troupes that "those which play best obtain most spectators,"[62] a statement pointing towards a shared, limited, and fluctuating audience. For proof that attendance varied and that packed houses were not the rule, one has only to look at Henslowe's receipts from the galleries of the Rose from July 1594 to June 1597. They ranged from a low of 3s. to a high of £7 6s. 6d., reaching the upper limits on holidays and at the premieres of new plays. The top amount recorded, £7 6s. 6d., no doubt represented a full house, but the average amount recorded was only £3 2s. 5d. or so.[63] On an ordinary

---

[61] *Vox Graculi*, p. 61.

[62] Platter, *Travels in England*, p. 167.

[63] Greg, ed., *Henslowe's Diary*, I, 13-25, 27-28, 30, 42, 49-54; for extrapo-

day, then, the big theaters could expect to pull in about half their house capacity, at least in the galleries.

During the period covered by Henslowe's *Diary*, there were two, and subsequently three, theaters on the Bankside—the Swan (1595) and the Globe (1599), each with a capacity of some 3,000, and his own Rose, with an unknown but possibly smaller capacity. In 1600, Henslowe left the Bankside for the magnificent new Fortune. Eventually the Hope was built on the south bank of the Thames in 1613, but it featured plays irregularly, catering more to animal baiting.[64] For a brief time, however, from 1598 to 1600, the Bankside could accommodate 8,000 or more playgoers. With gallery places outnumbering pit places by a margin of at least two to one, upwards of 5,500 occupied the galleries on holidays and just under 3,000 on most other afternoons. These were the palmy, profitable days recalled by the watermen when they brought suit in 1613 to force the players back across the Thames: "the players have all (except the Kings men) left their usual residency on the Bankside, and do play in Middlesex far remote from the Thames, so that every day in the week they do draw unto them three or four thousand people, that were used to spend their monies by water."[65] Since both the Red Bull (1605) and the Fortune (1600) were by then in Middlesex, it was only a slight exaggeration to claim that these theaters had drawn away 3,000 or 4,000 patrons from the Bankside each day. Three thousand would seem to be a standard draw for two big playhouses on an ordinary day, with 2,000 of those patrons occupying places in the gallery.

How, then, do the estimates of actual attendance—rough and scanty as they are—compare with the population of London as a whole and with the number of privileged persons living there? In the beginning, with only the Theater and the Curtain plus

lations from the figures, see Harbage, *Shakespeare's Audience*, pp. 28-30, 174-177.

[64] Chambers, *Elizabethan Stage*, II, 470; Bentley, *Jacobean and Caroline Stage*, VI, 206-214.

[65] John Taylor, *The True Cause of the Water-men's Suit concerning Players*, in *The Old Book Collector's Miscellany*, ed. Charles Hindley (London: Reeves and Turner, 1872), II, no. 15, pp. 6-7.

various inns and a private theater or two serving as irregular playing places, performances could have drawn no more than 5,000 or so, even at peak capacity. An average attendance, assuming plays by two adult companies and possibly a boys' troupe, would have been fewer than 3,000. By the 1590s, with the Rose (1587), the Swan (1595), and the Globe (1599), that regular attendance would have swelled to some 3,000 or 4,000. After 1609, with the King's Men in the Blackfriars in winter and the Globe in summer, and the Red Bull and the Fortune out in Middlesex, attendance would have been just in excess of 4,000, increasing to about 4,500 with the addition of the Phoenix/Cockpit (1617) and Salisbury Court (1629). Out of London's total population (150,000 to 350,000), regular theater attendance ranged between 1⅓ and 2 percent. Out of London's privileged residents (27,000 to 52,500), a mere 5 percent could have taken a majority of the places on an average day and 20 percent could have filled the houses to capacity. It would be a mistake to conclude that the privileged were the sole supporters of the playhouses, but to establish even the possibility that the acting companies relied primarily upon their patronage, it is necessary to show a reasonable relationship between the capacity of the theaters, the customary attendance, and the number of potential spectators among the privileged. Such a reasonable relationship would seem to exist when only 5 to 10 percent of the privileged in London could have comprised more than half the number in the audiences at any time during the period, regardless of whether the theaters were operating at average or at peak capacity.

A few other factors concerning attendance seem to point to the privileged spectators as the chief patrons of the playhouses. One is the high level of attendance during the term times, when the gentry and their representatives were up from the country in larger numbers than usual.[66] Another is the high

[66] James Shirley's "Prologue at the Black-Friars" protested a slim term crowd with:

> Does this look like a Term? I cannot tell;
> Our poet thinks the whole town is not well,

level of attendance at new plays, despite their doubled admissions.[67] Evidently a large group of theatergoers considered novelty more important than money. Then, too, according to Henslowe's practice, plays were frequently changed, so that a new play would be presented, then offered again at intervals of a week or so, until receipts fell too low for it to be profitable.[68] Though good plays, like *Faustus* or *Hamlet*, were never dropped entirely from the repertoire but continued to draw audiences year after year, most plays had outlived their profitability with a dozen showings. This practice suggests that anyone who wanted to be *au courant* had to see a new play when it first came out—and pay the higher rates. The practice also indicates an audience limited in size and quickly sated with all but the best plays, if everyone in London who cared to see a particular offering could do so in only a dozen performances. Moreover, the sheer number of new plays given each year (Henslowe averaged one a fortnight at the Rose)[69] shows how many patrons were willing to pay the doubled rates and how quickly the potential audience was exhausted.

Except for the first performances, many in the playhouses would have been repeaters, for it was common practice to go

---

Has took some physic lately, and, for fear
Of catching cold, dares not salute the air.
*The Doubtful Heir*, in *The Dramatic Works and Poems*, ed. William Gifford and Alexander Dyce (London: J. Murray, 1833), IV, 279.

[67] Henslowe's receipts always show a rise at new plays (Harbage, *Shakespeare's Audience*, p. 28). See also *Vox Graculi*: "About this time, new Playes will be in more request, then old: and if company come currant to the *Bull* and *Curtaine*, there will be more money gathered in one after-noone, then will be giuen to *Kings-land* Spittle in a whole moneth" (pp. 60-61); and Dekker's *News from Hell*, which refers to "a crowding (as if it had been a new play)" (*Non-Dramatic Works*, II, 118).

[68] Harbage, *Shakespeare's Audience*, p. 43. Long consecutive runs are not mentioned until the 1630s. Even then, the run was usually less than ten days in length (Bentley, *Jacobean and Caroline Stage*, I, 13n, 278).

[69] See, e.g., Greg, ed., *Henslowe's Diary*, pp. 17-18, 25, 30, 42. See also Bentley, *Jacobean and Caroline Stage*, I, 101-108, for license record of new plays for the King's Men.

to the theater every day. Both Shakespeare's First Folio and Jonson's *Bartholomew Fair* refer to those who "arraign Playes dailie," and it was said of the Inns of Court man, "Your Theaters hee daily doth frequent."[70] Years after the theaters closed, gentlemen recalled the actors and claimed to have "hum'd them off a hundred times."[71] Spectators were explicitly urged to come often to plays, not just once.

> Tis not the hands, or smiles, or common way
> Of approbation to a well lik'd Play,
> ........................................................................
> Not in your praise, but often seeing it.[72]

This meant, of course, that a regular patron or anyone who especially liked a particular play might see the same production over and over again each time the company offered it. Eventually, some plays got so wellworn that "euery punck and her squire (like the Interpreter and his poppet) can rand [them] out by heart they are so stale, and therefore so stincking."[73]

By the 1590s, the gentleman whose life was filled with little but playgoing had become a fit subject for satire.

> *Luscus*, what's play'd to day? Fayth now I know
> I set thy lips abroach, from whence doth flow
> Naught but pure *Iuliet* and *Romeo*.
> Say, who acts best? *Drusus* or *Roscio*?
> Now I haue him, that nere of ought did speake
> But when of playes or Plaiers he did treate—
> H'ath made a common-place booke out of playes,
> And speakes in print, at least what ere he sayes
> Is warranted by Curtaine *plaudities*,

[70] Lenton, *Young Gallant's Whirligig*, p. 7.

[71] John Tatham (?), *Knavery in All Trades: Or, The Coffee-House* (London, 1664), $D_4^v$.

[72] Beaumont and Fletcher, "Epilogue," *The Elder Brother*, in *Works*, ed. Glover and Waller, II, 59. See also the "Prologue" to Jonson's *The Devil Is an Ass*: "And when six times you ha' seen't / If this *Play* doe not like, the Diuell is in't" (*Ben Jonson*, VI, 163).

[73] Dekker, *Iests to Make You Merrie*, in *Non-Dramatic Works*, II, 353.

If ere you heard him courting *Lesbias* eyes;
Say (Courteous Sir), speakes he not mouingly
From out some new pathetique Tragedie?
He writes, he railes, he iests, he courts, what not,
And all from out his huge long scraped stock
Of well penn'd players.[74]

What may be overlooked among all the references to frequent attendance is the fact that it required means and leisure as well as a taste for plays. Logically, then, habitués of the theater, whether Luscus in the foregoing satire or Sir Humphrey Mildmay in real life, had to come from the ranks of the privileged. They alone had both money and idle afternoons on a continuing basis.

### TRANSPORTATION COSTS

In addition to the cost of admission—a perpetually repeated cost for the regulars—there were other expenses associated with playgoing. Before paying the tariff to the gatherers at the theater doors, a good many patrons had already paid out money for transportation. As already indicated, the watermen claimed the daily loss of "three or four thousand people, that were used to spend their monies by water"[75] when two companies moved away from the Bankside. Evidently, thousands of spectators each day could afford the threepenny fare[76] across the Thames in addition to the fees exacted at the playhouses. According to the watermen's suit, "there went such great concourse of people by water that the small number of watermen remaining at home were not able to carry them, by reason of the court, the terms, the players, and other employments, so that we were enforced and encouraged . . . to take and entertain men and boys."[77]

[74] Marston, *The Scourge of Villany*, ed. G. B. Harrison (London: Bodley Head, 1925), pp. 107-108.

[75] Taylor, *True Cause of the Water-men's Suit*, II, 6-7.

[76] For examples of boat costs, see *Rutland Manuscripts* (London: Sationery Office, 1888-1905), IV, 419-420.

[77] Taylor, *True Cause of the Water-men's Suit*, II, 6.

Their petition attested not only to the large crowds at the theater but also to the kinds of people accustomed to hiring boats, in particular those connected with the Court and the terms. Such people, of course, were among London's privileged.

They had to be. While the 4d. Edward Alleyn paid out in boathire in 1617 or the 6d. Sir Humphrey Mildmay paid in 1634 seem small enough, those sums represented an entire day's wages for unskilled workmen during the period.[78] To add the cost of playhouse admission to the cost of transportation lifted playgoing to the level of a minor luxury, especially if enjoyed often. Yet thousands indulged in such luxury every afternoon. So dependent was the waterman upon the affluent spectators that "The Play-houses only keep him sober; and as it doth many other Gallants, make him an afternoones man."[79] When deserted by the theatergoers, the watermen's income fell "by the one half of their living."[80] Not that the privileged cared. They left the questionable delight of a trip across the Thames, especially unpleasant in winter, to patronize the houses on the more fashionable side of the river. And those who declined to arrive on foot and hired a coach or sedan paid even more than they had when traveling by water. Sir Humphrey Mildmay paid out a shilling "To a Coachman that day" on 3 February 1634.[81] Apparently the expense of transportation, whatever it was, offered no hindrance to many spectators.

FOOD AND DRINK

Among the smaller tolls on the playgoer's purse were the refreshments sold during the performances. As Thomas Platter described the practice, "And during the performance food and drink are carried round the audience, so that for what one cares to pay one may also have refreshment."[82] Another traveler,

[78] See Chapter VI, pp. 228-236, and Appendix A, pp. 277-280.
[79] Overbury, "Conceited Newes," p. 192.
[80] Taylor, True Cause of the Water-men's Suit, II, 6.
[81] Bentley, Jacobean and Caroline Stage, II, 675.
[82] Platter, Travels in England, p. 167. The German original reads, "Vnndt

Paul Hentzner, specified that the food and drink included various seasonal fruits, such as apples, pears, and nuts, as well as wine and ale.[83] Youths pressed pippins upon pliant women, while some in the crowd complained of being "made *Adder*-deafe with *Pippin*-crye."[84] Actors objected to the noise of cracking nuts during the performance.[85] On occasion, however, they had to suffer worse than the noise of nuts cracking, fearing "We may be pelted off for ought we know, / With apples, egges, or stones from thence belowe."[86] If the performance displeased the audience, "Oranges, Apples, Nuts, flew about most liberally."[87]

The cost of the apples and nuts was probably modest enough, but oranges ranked as a luxury because they were imported.[88] The ale, the beer, and especially the wine were expensive too. Some ale and beer could be had for less than 1d. a quart, but the price was often closer to 2d. or 3d.[89] The costs of claret and

---

tragt man in wehrender Comedy zu essen vndt zu trinken vnder den Leüten herumb, mag einer vmb sein gelt sich also auch erlaben" (Chambers, *Elizabethan Stage*, II, 364).

[83] Paul Hentzner, *A Journey into England*, trans. R. Bentley, ed. Horace Walpole (Reading: T. E. Williams, 1807), p. 23.

[84] Gosson, *Playes Confuted*, p. 215; Henry Fitzgeffrey, *Satyres and Satyricall Epigrams: with Certaine Obseruations at Blacke-Fryars* (London, 1617), E[7]v.

[85] Dekker's *Satiromastix* refers to a spectator with "his Squirrell by his side cracking nuttes" (*Dramatic Works*, I, 355). See also W. J. Lawrence's article in *Those Nut-Cracking Elizabethans* (London: Argonaut Press, 1935), pp. 1-9.

[86] Robert Tailor, "Prologue," *The Hogge Hath Lost his Pearle* (Oxford: Malone Society Reprints, 1967), A₃ᵛ.

[87] Edmund Gayton, *Pleasant Notes upon Don Quixote* (London, 1654), p. 271.

[88] At wholesale, apples cost anywhere from 1s. 4d. to 2s. 4d. per hundred, while walnuts cost 8d. per hundred or 4s. 4d. per bushel. Pears sold variously for 1½d. each, 20 for 10d., and 100 for 8s. and 10s. In 1599, a dozen oranges cost a shilling, a penny apiece, at wholesale. See James E. Thorold Rogers, *A History of Agriculture and Prices in England* (Oxford: Clarendon Press, 1887), V and VI, 322-323, 464. It may be fair to suggest that the price of food was well above wholesale in the playhouses.

[89] According to 1584 injunction, "Aleconners' Complaint," in John Stow, *A Survey of London*, ed. Charles Lethbridge Kingsford (Oxford: Clarendon Press,

sack doubled between the 1580s and the 1640s, so that customers would have paid from 4d. to 8d. for a quart of claret and from 7d. to 16d. for a quart of sack, perhaps more inside the theater.[90] Yet there were obviously enough playgoers with sufficient money left over after paying admission to make the sale of food and drink profitable. Both the first and the second Globe had a taphouse.[91] Henslowe granted exclusive rights to a man named Cholmley to sell food and drink on the premises of the Rose, providing him with a small house nearby "to keepe victualinge in."[92] He also included both a taphouse and a garden in the grounds of the Fortune.[93] Complaints about "Tiplinge howses to Neighbour"[94] playhouses also indicated theatergoers with enough money to buy drinks before or after the plays.

Far more expensive than just drinking was the practice of dining at a tavern or ordinary before and/or after the performances. Young men incurred censure because they would "slip into tauerns whē yᵉ plaies are dõe" in company with women.[95] The tavernkeepers, however, were delighted to have the business, especially in view of the prices of meals at ordinaries. The threepenny ordinary suited only "your London Vsurer, your stale Batchilor, and your thrifty Atturney" in 1609.[96] According

---

1908), I, lxiv-lxv. See also Jonson's *Bartholomew Fair*, in *Ben Jonson*, VI, 43, 45; and J. U. Nef, "Prices and Industrial Capitalism in France and England, 1540-1640," in *Essays in Economic History*, ed. E. M. Carus-Wilson (London: Edward Arnold, 1954), I, 120. By 1619, James had to issue a proclamation decreeing that the price of beer should not exceed 1d. for 2 quarts. See James F. Larkin and Paul L. Hughes, eds., *Stuart Royal Proclamations* (Oxford: Clarendon Press, 1973), I, 412.

[90] Prices for claret ranged from a low of 1s. 4d. to a high of 2s. 8d.; for sack they increased from 2s. 5½d. to 4s. 9½d. (Rogers, *History of Agriculture and Prices*, V and VI, 470-472).

[91] Chambers, *Elizabethan Stage*, II, 421, 434; *Malone Society Collections*, II, 2: 366; Bentley, *Jacobean and Caroline Stage*, VI, 185-186.

[92] 10 January 1587; Greg, ed., *Henslowe Papers*, p. 3.

[93] Ibid., p. 28.

[94] *Malone Society Collections*, IV, 60; Bentley, *Jacobean and Caroline Stage*, VI, 80.

[95] Gosson, *Playes Confuted*, p. 215.

[96] Dekker, *Gvls Horne-booke*, in *Non-Dramatic Works*, II, 244-245.

to Fynes Moryson, a meal at a common table in an inn cost 6d., but gentlemen customarily spent two shillings or more per person.[97] As early as 1592, eighteenpenny establishments catered to "Caualiers and braue courtiers."[98] In 1634, in the fashionable Spring Garden, "there was kept . . . an ordinary of six shillings a meal (when the King's proclamation allows but two elsewhere)," where gentlemen indulged in "continual bibbing and drinking of wine all day long under the trees, two or three quarrels every week."[99] Sir Humphrey Mildmay recorded a payment of 8s. 6d. on 15 February 1641 for "dynner & soe to the playe & supper w[th] D[r] Doriela & late home to bed."[100] How much of his expense went for food was not clear, but quite obviously an afternoon that included both dinner and a play was costly. Those who indulged in such pleasures needed plenty of money.

## TOBACCO AND BOOKS

Yet another costly aristocratic pleasure repeatedly associated with the theater was smoking. Both Platter and Hentzner noted the use of tobacco in the playhouses, as did Prynne.[101] The smoker—"He that dares take tobacco on the stage"[102]—became the object of scorn and ridicule, but at the same time smoking became the mark of a fashionable man. In *Every Man Out of*

[97] Fynes Moryson, *An Itinerary* (London, 1617), Pt. 3, p. 61.

[98] Thomas Nashe, *Pierce Penilesse*, in *Works*, I, 170.

[99] George Garrard to Lord Wentworth, as quoted by F. J. Fisher, "The Development of London as a Centre of Conspicuous Consumption in the Sixteenth and Seventeenth Centuries," in *Essays in Economic History*, ed. E. M. Carus-Wilson (London: Edward Arnold, 1962), II, 205.

[100] Bentley, *Jacobean and Caroline Stage*, IV, 679.

[101] Platter, *Travels in England*, pp. 170-171; Hentzner, *Journey into England*, p. 23. See also Jonson's "Induction," *Cynthia's Revels*, in *Ben Jonson*, IV, 39; *Actors Remonstrance*, pp. 264-265; Tatham (?), *Knavery*, E₁; and Beaumont, *Knight of the Burning Pestle*, in *Dramatic Works in the Beaumont and Fletcher Canon*, I, 21. There are dozens of other references.

[102] Sir John Davies, Epigram 28, "In Sillam," in *The Complete Poems*, ed. Alexander B. Grosart (London: Chatto and Windus, 1876), II, 28.

*his Humor*, for instance, Fastidious Briske talked "as if he had
. . . ta'ne tabacco with them, ouer the stage, i' the lords roome,"
while Shift promised to teach the art to the clownish would-be
gentleman Sogliardo so that he could "take it plausibly in any
. . . theatre."[103] No doubt Sogliardo longed to be like the gallant
at the theater who was said to "wanton Italianly; / Go Frenchly:
Duchly drink: breath Indianly."[104]

To "breath Indianly" cost a good deal of money. When the
Blackfriars playgoer commanded, "A pipe heere (Sirra) no *So-
phisticate*. / (Villain) the *best*: what ere you *prize* it at,"[105] he
could expect considerable expense. Ursula the pig-woman might
charge only 3d. for a pipeload of tobacco doctored with coltsfoot,
but a "pipe of rich smoake" commonly cost twice that sum.[106]
A man could brag of smoking "the best in Europe, 'tcost mee
ten Crownes an ounce, by this vapor."[107] The tax alone ranged
from a modest 2d. per pound under Elizabeth to an outrageous
7s. 8d. per pound at one point in James's reign, though it finally
settled at a rate of 18d.[108] Tobacco that sold for 3s. per pound
under Elizabeth rose to 18s. a pound for the best quality and
10s. for the inferior sort. Sir Henry Oglander's diary, for in-

[103] *Ben Jonson*, III, 475, 513.

[104] Henry Buttes, *Dyets Dry Dinner* (London, 1599), P₄.

[105] Fitzgeffrey, *Satyres and Satyricall Epigrams*, F₃ᵛ. See also Jonson's *Bartholomew Fair*: "Ha'you none of your pretty impudent boyes, now; to bring
stooles, fill Tabacco, fetch Ale, and beg money, as they haue at other houses?"
(*Ben Jonson*, VI, 119).

[106] Jonson, *Bartholomew Fair*, in *Ben Jonson*, VI, 26. See also Dekker's *Roaring Girl*, in *Dramatic Works*, II, 26; and *Everie Woman in Her Humor* (London,
1609), F₄, where the inventory of a gentleman's pocket included a half-ounce
of tobacco worth 6d.

[107] John Day, *Law Tricks*, in *The Works*, ed. A. H. Bullen (1881; reprint ed.,
London: Holland Press, 1963), p. 133.

[108] Neville J. Williams, "England's Tobacco Trade in the Reign of Charles I,"
*The Virginia Magazine* 65 (1957): 404-405. For James's efforts to control the
profiteering on tobacco, as well as its proliferation, see Larkin and Hughes, eds.,
*Stuart Royal Proclamations*, I, 481-483, 600. James, of course, was bitterly
opposed to the weed, claiming, "the Gentry of this land beare witnesse, some
of them bestowing three, some foure hundred pounds a yeare vpon this precious
stinke" (*A Covnterblaste to Tobacco* [London, 1604], C₄ᵛ).

stance, recorded that he spent "For eight ounces of tobacco, five shillings."[109] Predictably, the use of "that costlye Gentleman-like Smoak"[110] was chiefly associated with the wealthy and the socially privileged. A Chapman play called it "the gentleman's saint and the soldier's idol."[111] Essex, together "with those Noblemen and Gentlemen on foot beside him, took tobacco" at the Azores expedition, as did the peers at the Essex trial in 1601.[112] Lord Herbert of Cherbury, Sir Robert Cecil, and Sir Walter Raleigh are but a few of the age's more famous smokers. Thus, when the weed's "gentleman-like smell"[113] arose in the theater, it forcefully suggested the presence of men wealthy enough to enjoy the luxury of smoking as well as the price of admission to the play.

In addition to food, drink, and tobacco, the audience also had an opportunity to buy books. Some authors, like Henry Parrot, scorned to have their works "at Play-houses 'mongst Pippins solde."[114] But others, like William Fennor, were not so scrupulous. He frankly admitted in his address *"To the Gentlemen Readers,"* "Worthy gentlemen, of what degree soeuer, I suppose this Pamphlet will hap into your hands, before a play begin, with the importunate clamour, of *Buy a new Booke*, by some

[109] The diary for 1626 is cited by W. A. Penn, *The Soverane Herbe* (London: Grant Richards, 1901), p. 68.

[110] Dekker, *Lanthorne and Candle-Light*, in *Non-Dramatic Works*, III, 290. Only one contemporary reference suggests that tobacco was used extensively by ordinary people, and here hyperbole is apparently being employed. In the midst of a debate in Commons that took place on 16 April 1621, Sir Grey Palmes claimed that tobacco "is now so common that he hath seen ploughmen take it as they are at plough." See G. L. Apperson, *The Social History of Smoking* (London: Martin Secker, 1914), p. 34.

[111] See Apperson, *Social History of Smoking*, p. 55, which also quotes Bishop Hall's satire on the man of fashion who "Quaffs a whole tunnel of tobacco smoke" (p. 26). Dekker's *Old Fortunatus* claimed that among gallants "Tobacco choakes" care (*Dramatic Works*, I, 125).

[112] Testimony of Sir Francis Vere, the French ambassador, cited by Apperson, *Social History of Smoking*, pp. 35-36.

[113] Davies, Epigram 36, "Of Tobacco," in *Complete Poems*, ed. Grosart, II, 35.

[114] Henry Parrot, *The Mastive* (London, 1615), $A_4^v$.

needy companion." He confessed that since "I haue beene ear-
nestly intreated by noble personages (who haue had priuate
copies for their owne vse) to print it for publike delight, at
length I consented, & since I am won, haue amongst you gallants, let it speed as it will."[115] The sale of books to "gallants,"
and "gentlemen readers" presumed not only literacy but a certain degree of affluence in the audience, for books were not
cheap. There were penny broadsides and twopenny pamphlets,
to be sure, but even a small quarto cost from sixpence to two
shillings.[116] "For a booke & the play of pastorell," Sir Humphrey
Mildmay paid two shillings.[117]

The brisk publication of playbooks throughout the period
further indicated an educated, well-to-do audience eager to read
as well as to see the plays, despite the expense. Inns of Court
men like William Freke, who bought a copy of *Othello* in 1624,
perhaps considered such purchases merely "good to keepe you
in an afternoone from dice, at home in your chambers," as
Dekker said.[118] Nonetheless, the outlay of money for published
plays and for books at the playhouse could only have been made
by the literate, who could read them, the affluent, who could
afford them, and the leisured, who had time to enjoy them.

PROSTITUTES

Prostitutes unquestionably provided the most notorious way to
spend money at the theater. If the Puritans and the City officials
are to be believed, the theaters were regularly filled with harlots
and whoremongers making bargains.[119] Stephen Gosson spoke
as an eyewitness: "Mine eyes throughly behold the manner of

[115] William Fennor, front matter, *Fennors Descriptions* (London, 1616).

[116] Marjorie Plant, *The English Book Trade* (London: Allen and Unwin, 1939),
pp. 220, 241.

[117] 6 February 1634; Bentley, *Jacobean and Caroline Stage*, II, 675.

[118] Wilfrid R. Prest, *The Inns of Court under Elizabeth I and the Early Stuarts,
1590-1640* (London: Longmans, 1972), p. 161; Dekker, *Roaring Girl*, in *Dramatic Works*, III, 11. The play also refers specifically to the readers as "Tearm-
ers" (p. 11).

[119] For a comprehensive analysis of this activity, see Ann Jennalie Cook,

Theaters, when I wrote plays my selfe & found them to be the very markets of bawdry, where choise w^thout shame hath bene as free, as it is for your money in the royall exchaung, to take a short stocke, or a longe, a falling bad, or a french ruffe."[120] The players themselves admitted their houses were "the receptacles of Harlots, the exchanges where they meet and make their bargaines with their franck chapmen of the Country and City" and that "men of our quality" had been involved in "the inveigling in young Gentlemen, Merchants Factors, and Prentizes to spend their patrimonies and Masters estates upon us and our Harlots in Tavernes."[121] The playhouses were certainly not brothels, but prostitution was persistently connected with the theaters. "Adulterers, Whore-masters, Whores, &c. are the greatest Patriots, applauders, frequenters, upholders of these lascivious Stage-playes; . . . since such creatures . . . *spread their nets, where they are alwayes sure for to catch their prey,* which they seldome misse at Stage-playes . . . the common rode from the Play-house, being either with an adulteresse to a Taverne; or with a Whore to a bawdy-house."[122] Though critics like Stephen Gosson and William Prynne exaggerated the licentiousness of the playgoers, punks unquestionably made the theaters a favorite haunt.

Morality aside, the prostitutes would scarcely have frequented the playhouses unless they could expect to find rich customers there. After all, the woman not only tied up her entire afternoon at the play but she also had to pay admission. The fee she charged her client had to cover her investment in time and money as well as services rendered. According to the record, her expenses could be substantial. Punks sat in the twopenny rooms, in the sixpenny rooms, and in boxes.[123] At the private houses, "perfum'd wantons do for eighteenpence / Ex-

---

" Bargaines of Incontinencie': Bawdy Behavior at the Playhouses," *Shakespeare Studies* 10 (1977): 271-290.

[120] Gosson, *Playes Confuted*, pp. 214-215.

[121] *Actors Remonstrance*, pp. 260, 262.

[122] Prynne, *Histrio-Mastrix*, pp. 389-390.

[123] Thomas Middleton, *A Mad World, My Masters*, ed. Standish Henning

pect an angel."[124] Coaches were used by "*Dol Turn-up*, and *Peg Burn-it*, your silken wenches of *Hackney*, to carry them to the *Red-Bull*, and other Play-houses, to get trading."[125] Some of the courtesans wore masks and jewels, satins and velvets and silks—all extremely costly.[126] Even a common whore looked for a dinner after the play. "Euery Vauter in one blind Tauerne or other is Tenant at will, to which shee tolleth resorte, and playes the stale to vtter their victualls, and to helpe them emptie their mustie cakes. There is she so intreated with wordes and receiued with curtesie, that euery back roome in the house is at her commaundement."[127] "Six-penny whordome" may have been a minimum charge for a prostitute's favors, but "a most insatiate drabber" could be hyperbolically accused of giving "a hundred pound a leap."[128] Something decidedly less than a hundred pounds but decidedly more than sixpence had to be allowed for the expenses of most "light-taylde huswives"[129] who frequented the theaters. For them, a profitable trade depended on men with plenty of money to spend. Had they not found such men at London's playhouses, they would not have come.

---

(London: Edward Arnold, 1965), p. 91; Dekker, *Non-Dramatic Works*, II, 96, 292; III, 269; *Actors Remonstrance*, p. 265; Fitzgeffrey, *Satyres and Satyricall Epigrams*, F$^v$.

[124] Sir Aston Cokayne, *The Obstinate Lady*, in *The Dramatic Works*, ed. James Maidment and W. H. Logan (London: H. Sotheran, 1874), p. 21.

[125] Henry Peacham, *Coach and Sedan* (London: Westminster Press, 1925), C$_1$.

[126] John Lane, *Tom Tell-Troths Message and his Pens Complaint*, ed. F. J. Furnivall, New Shakspere Society Publications, ser. 6, no. 2 (London: N. Trubner, 1876), p. 133; "Diaries and Despatches of the Venetian Embassy at the Court of King James I, in the Years 1617, 1618," *Quarterly Review* 102 (1857): 416; Collier, *History of English Dramatic Poetry*, III, 217-218.

[127] Stephen Gosson, *The Schoole of Abuse*, ed. Edward Arber, English Reprints, no. 3 (London: A. Murray and Son, 1869), p. 36. Other examples appear in Dekker, *Lanthorne and Candle-Light*, in *Non-Dramatic Works*, III, 269-270; and Fitzgeffrey, *Satyres and Satyricall Epigrams*, F$^v$.

[128] Nashe, *Christ's Tears* and *Pierce Penilesse*, in *Works*, II, 148, and I, 217; Philip Massinger, *The City Madam*, in *Plays*, ed. W. Gifford (1813; reprint ed., New York: AMS Press, 1966), IV, 79.

[129] Lane, *Tom Tell-Troths Message*, p. 133.

PICKPOCKETS

Though a whore or courtesan may have been costly, she at least gave a gentleman pleasure for his money. Others in the play-house took his money and gave nothing in return. Thieves and theaters kept a mutually profitable company. Even though the pickpocket, like the prostitute, had to pay admission, the purses inside were apparently worth the expense of both time and money. As Dekker pointed out, the cutpurse haunted the assemblies of the privileged—Paul's, Westminster, Chancery Lane in term time, London Bridge, suits at the Star Chamber, the Lord Mayor's oath taking, and alehouses—all of which cost him nothing. But there were also "(places of more benefit) publick, & by your leaue priuat play houses."[130] Greene agreed, saying, "their chief walks is Paul's, Westminster, the Exchange, plays, beargarden, running at tilt, the Lord Mayor's day, and festival meetings, frays, shootings, or great fairs."[131] Not content with the public pit, thieves sought the twopenny galleries and six-penny rooms. One play made reference to "a nip, I tooke him once i'the twopenny gallery at the *Fortune*."[132] And Middleton's *Black Book* of 1604 said, "I give and bequeath to you, Benedick Bottomless, most deep cutpurse, all the benefit of . . . the sixpenny rooms in play-houses, to cut, dive, or nim."[133]

Some idea of their takings showed in the records of arrest. One William Hawkins, a barber by trade, stole a purse and £1 6s. 6d. at the Curtain in 1600, while Alexander Fulsis relieved Alexander Sweet's pocket of a purse containing £3 at the Red Bull in 1614.[134] That most topical of plays, *The Roaring Girl*, identified a gentleman by saying, "Heart, there's a Knight to

---

[130] Dekker, *Iests to Make You Merrie*, in *Non-Dramatic Works*, II, 326.

[131] Robert Greene, *Second and Last Part of Conycatching*, in Arthur V. Judges, ed., *The Elizabethan Underworld* (London: G. Routledge and Sons, 1930), p. 162. See also Dekker's *The Belman of London* and *Lanthorne and Candle-Light*, in *Non-Dramatic Works*, II, 157-158, 212.

[132] Dekker, *Roaring Girl*, in *Dramatic Works*, III, 89.

[133] Middleton, *Black Book*, in *Works*, ed. Bullen, VIII, 41.

[134] 11 March 1600 and 3 March 1614; J. C. Jeaffreson, ed., *Middlesex County Records* (London: Middlesex County Records Society, 1886-1892), I, 259, and II, 86.

whom I'me bound for many fauors, lost his purse at the last new play i'the *Swanne*, seuen Angels in't."[135] The knight got off lightly compared to the Almain who lost three hundred crowns at a performance of *Every Man in his Humor* in 1598.[136] Occasionally, instead of cutting purses, thieves brought stolen goods to peddle to the wealthy theatergoers. About 1594, a diamond stolen from the loot of a Spanish carrack was bought from a sailor by some London goldsmiths. They met him "at a play in the theatre at Shoreditch" and later viewed the gem in Finsbury Fields.[137]

Considering the potential rewards, thieves willingly paid admission and risked arrest to get at the fat purses of the theatergoers. If caught in the act, they risked a rough immediate punishment as well. Will Kemp recalled "a noted Cut-purse, such a one as we tye to a poast on our stage, for all people to wonder at, when at a play they are taken pilfring."[138] Yet the cutpurse was scarcely daunted. "Know at a new play, he is alwaies about the playhouse dore, watches out of which side you draw your purse, & then gessing whether the lyning be worth the ventring."[139] Once inside the theater, "here and there (whilst with obsequious eares, / Throng'd heapes do listen) a cut purse thrusts and leeres / With haukes eyes for his prey."[140] Sometimes a team worked together. Greene told of an expert thief, his female confederate, and a young apprentice in the trade who stood at the theater among "a company of seemly

---

[135] Dekker, *Roaring Girl*, in *Dramatic Works*, III, 89.

[136] Chambers, *Elizabethan Stage*, II, 197.

[137] *Cecil Papers*, VII, 504; as cited by Chambers, *Elizabethan Stage*, I, 264. According to John Stow, "These Goldsmiths have commonly, besides Plate, dealt in Jewels and precious Stones," a fact that made these merchants likely prospects for the sailor. See *A Survey of the Cities of London and Westminster and the Borough of Southwark*, Corrected, Improved, and very much Enlarged . . . by John Strype (London: W. Imrys, J. Richardson et al., 1754-1755), II, 271.

[138] William Kemp, *Kemps Nine Daies Wonder: Performed in a Daunce from London to Norwich* (London: Bodley Head, 1923), p. 6.

[139] Dekker, *Iests to Make You Merrie*, in *Non-Dramatic Works*, II, 327.

[140] Dekker, *Roaring Girl*, in *Dramatic Works*, III, 17.

men." The thief cut the purse and then passed it to his ac-
complice.[141] No doubt by the end of the play the gang were all
amply compensated for their outlay of time, money, and talent.
If the playhouses had not attracted the affluent, they never
would have attracted the thieves: the "company of seemly men"
accounted for the company of cutpurses.

DIVERSION OF MONEY

Other Londoners also cast greedy eyes upon the bulging purses
of the playgoers. According to the complaint of the preachers,
the playhouses soaked up money that should have been given
to the destitute. *"The poore are spoiled of that almes, that
succour, and reliefe which should refresh their bowels, and
make glad their hearts."*[142] And according to the London Council, the playhouses also hindered trade by drawing away customers from deserving businessmen.[143] Two wits made swift
reply to this particular charge. Thomas Nashe said, "As for the
hindrance of Trades and Traders of the Citie by them, that is
an Article foysted in by the Vintners, Alewiues, and Victuallers,
who surmise, if there were no Playes, they should haue all the
companie that resort to them, lye bowzing and beere-bathing
in their houses euery after-noone."[144] Henry Chettle agreed
with Nashe, suggesting that the "Bowling-allyes in Bedlam
and other places that were wont in the afternoones to be left
empty" ought to "ioine with the Dicing houses to make suit."
He went on at some length about the plight of the retailers
whose shops lay far away from the theaters:

> Is it not a greate shame that the houses of retaylers neare
> the Townes end, should be by their continuance impouer-
> ished: Alas good hearts, they pay great rentes; and pittie it

[141] Greene, *Thirde and Last Part of Conycatching*, p. 195.

[142] Prynne, *Histrio-Mastrix*, p. 45.

[143] Lord Mayor to Archbishop Whitgift, 25 February 1592; *Malone Society
Collections*, I, 68; Chambers, *Elizabethan Stage*, IV, 307.

[144] Nashe, *Pierce Penilesse*, in *Works*, I, 214.

is but they be prouided for. While Playes are vsed, halfe the day is by most youthes that haue libertie spent vpon them, or at least the greatest company drawne to the places where they frequent. If they were supprest, the flocke of yoong people would bee equally parted. But now the greatest trade is brought into one street.

In a final burst of sarcasm, Chettle lamented over the loss in trade suffered by the houses of ill repute, "for in euery house where the venerian virgins are resident, hospitalitie is quite exiled. . . . And therefore seeing they live so hardly, its pitie Players should hinder their takings a peny."[145] Beneath this set of charges and countercharges lay one indisputable fact: each afternoon London boasted a substantial number of men with money and leisure to bestow upon shopping, "gameing, following of harlots, drinking, or seeing a Playe."[146] The howls of the merchants, as expressed in the petition to the Privy Council, strongly suggested that the players drew more than their share of these well-heeled customers.

PROFITS

In fact, the playhouses enjoyed a remarkable success at attracting patrons in sufficient numbers and with sufficient affluence to ensure handsome profits to some of the shareholders and to support huge outlays of capital for handsome buildings. It must never be forgotten that the dramatic companies were formed not just to entertain but to make money. Shareholders invested capital in the expectation of a profit over and above the expense of paying for doorkeepers, actors, musicians, playwrights, costumes, properties, and playhouses. Amazingly enough, despite the peripheral costs of transportation, food and drink, tobacco, perhaps the purchase of a book or pamphlet, the favors of a

[145] Henry Chettle, *Kind-Harts Dreame*, in *The Shakspere Allusion-Book*, ed. C. M. Ingleby, rev. John Munro (London: Oxford University Press, 1932), I, 63-64.

[146] Nashe, *Pierce Penilesse*, in *Works*, I, 212.

pliant woman, dinner at a tavern, or the loss of a stolen purse, the playgoers' admission fees financed a flourishing theatrical business for sixty-six years. As early as 1578, it was charged that "the gaine that is reaped of eighte ordinarie places in the Citie whiche I knowe, by playing but once a weeke (whereas many times they play twice, and sometimes thrice) it amounteth to 2000 pounds by the yeare."[147] "Pounds and hundreds can be well ynough afforded, in following these least pleasures," raged the Puritans, though "euery dore hath a payment, & euery Gallerie maketh a yearely stipend."[148]

And they were right. As early as 1578, the Theater paid its housekeepers a handsome 8s. and 10s. respectively each week.[149] The total day's take in 1585 was estimated at £10 to £12, "especially when they act anything new, which has not been given before, and double prices are charged."[150] Henslowe pulled in anywhere from 3s. to £7 6s. 6d. from his half of the gallery receipts at the Rose,[151] an amount far in excess of wages for even the most skilled workman and far better than the stipends paid many courtiers and gentlemen retainers. At the Blackfriars, Henry Evans got about 30s. a week just "for the vse of the stooles standing vppon the Stage at Blackfryers," and when his boys fell upon hard times, it cost £20 a year to buy them out in 1609.[152] The yield from a marginal house like Salisbury Court could never compare with the income of the prestigious

[147] John Stockwood, *A Sermon Preached at Paules Crosse* (London, 1578), p. 137.

[148] John Feilde, *A Godly Exhortation, by Occasion of the Late Iudgement of God, Shewed at Parris-Garden, the Thirteenth Day of Ianuarie* (London, 1583), B₆.

[149] Chambers, *Elizabethan Stage*, II, 388. For an account of the substantial costs involved in running the Boar's Head, see Sisson, *Boar's Head Theatre*, pp. 72ff.

[150] Hassler, ed., *Die Riesen des Samuel Kiechel*, p. 29.

[151] Harbage, *Shakespeare's Audience*, p. 28, as derived from *Henslowe's Diary*; see previous note 63.

[152] A 1609 Chancery suit cited in Bentley, *Jacobean and Caroline Stage*, VI, 7. Henry Evans apparently managed to get a share of the playhouse in addition to a separate payment when he surrendered the lease to the King's Men. See Smith, *Shakespeare's Blackfriars Playhouse*, pp. 246-247, 523, 537, 539, 558.

King's Men at the Blackfriars (£17 11s. to the housekeepers for six performances at Salisbury Court in 1631 versus £13 for a single performance at Blackfriars in the same year).[153] But it was sufficient to support a series of troupes there for over a decade. With a really popular play, of course, the receipts could be enormous. Richard Brome, though doubtless exaggerating, charged that Salisbury Court made £1,000 from his *Sparagus Garden*.[154] The notorious *Game at Chess* was variously estimated to have made from £100 to more than £160 per day during its nine-day run.[155] There was enough for everyone. "Our very doore-keepers" managed "to scratch their heads where they itch not, and drop shillings and halfe crowne-pieces in at their collars."[156]

There was also enough profit to finance the construction of magnificent theaters—seventeen in less than sixty years.[157] According to Stow's *Annals*, "Before the space of threescore yeares agon-said I neither knew heard nor read of any such Theaters, set Stages, or Play-houses as haue beene purposely built."[158] Some thought, "It is an evident token of a wicked time when players wax so rich that they can build such houses."[159] For at a time when land and building costs were rapidly escalating in the city, the dramatic entrepreneurs nonetheless found it lucrative to invest thousands of pounds in new buildings. The Theater was valued at £666, and the second Globe

---

[153] Bentley, *Jacobean and Caroline Stage*, VI, 93.

[154] Ibid., p. 102.

[155] Sir Francis Nethersole to Dudley Carleton, 14 August 1624; *Calendar of State Papers, Domestic, of the Reigns of Edward VI, Mary, Elizabeth, and James* (Great Britain: Public Record Office, 1852-1872), XI (1623-1625), p. 327; Middleton, *Works*, ed. Alexander Dyce (London: Edward Lumley, 1840), I, xxxv.

[156] *Actors Remonstrance*, p. 263.

[157] Theater, Curtain, Rose, Swan, Boar's Head, first Globe, second Globe, Hope, first Fortune, second Fortune, Red Bull, first Blackfriars, second Blackfriars, Whitefriars, Phoenix/Cockpit, Salisbury Court, Paul's.

[158] Stow, *Annales* (1631), p. 1,004.

[159] Harrison, *Description of England*, p. 186n.

cost £1,400 to construct.[160] Maintenance took its toll too, for Henslowe laid out some £108 in late 1592 and more money in 1595 for repairs on the Rose.[161] Still, the admissions provided handsome returns on the sharers' investments.

Much has been made of the supposed shift of wealthy patronage from the public to the private playhouses, especially after the King's Men took over the Blackfriars in 1609. Yet the company never gave up the Globe, and when the house burned to the ground in 1613, it was not abandoned but immediately—and expensively—rebuilt. A new combination theater-baiting ring, the Hope, went up in 1614. And in 1621, "a fayre strong new built Play-house, near Gouldinglane called the Fortune, by negligence of a candle, was cleane burnt to the ground, but shortly after, rebuilt farre fairer."[162] What can be concluded from all this costly building and rebuilding except that the profits from London audiences could support large capital investments and that the profits flowed from both public and private playhouses to the very end of the period? All the playhouses attracted audiences large enough and rich enough to maintain "sumptuous Theatre houses, a continuall monument of Londons prodigalitie and folly."[163]

EXTENT OF PRIVILEGED PATRONAGE

Considering some of the superb plays performed in the theaters, the charge of folly was perhaps unjustified. But the charge of

[160] Chambers, *Elizabethan Stage*, II, 391; Bentley, *Jacobean and Caroline Stage*, VI, 182. The Globe's cost compares with the £1,320 it took to build the first Fortune (Chambers, *Elizabethan Stage*, II, 436), and the £1,000 to build the second (Greg, ed., *Henslowe Papers*, p. 29). It cost £200 to £300 just to build the new galleries at the Boar's Head (Sisson, *Boar's Head Theatre*, pp. 43-44).

[161] Greg, ed., *Henslowe's Diary*, II, 47, 54.

[162] Edmund Howes, continuation of Stow's *Annales* of 1631, I₃ᵛ. See also McClure, ed., *Letters of John Chamberlain*, II, 415.

[163] T[homas] W[hite], *A Sermon Preached at Paules Crosse on Sunday the thirde of November 1577 in the time of the Plague* (London, 1578), p. 47.

prodigality had some substance. True, playgoing did not rank with dicing, lavish clothing, or plate as an expenditure. But, it did cost money. The minimum penny admission applied only to the groundlings in the yard and then only at the beginning of the period. Everyone else doubled or tripled or multiplied that sum many times over each time he came to the playhouse. With double rates for new plays and ever-rising admissions during the course of the period, just getting into the theater took a toll on the purse. And repeated playgoing meant a steady rather than an occasional drain on that purse. And what of the peripheral costs of playgoing? To buy pippins or oranges, to crack nuts, to quaff ale or wine, to purchase a pamphlet, to call for tobacco—all these made an afternoon at the theater much more expensive, albeit more pleasurable. To come by boat, as thousands did in the 1590s, or by hired coach or sedan later in the period might involve greater expense than the play itself. The price of a woman, the cost of a dinner, or the loss of a purse could drive playgoing up to the level of a luxury. Of the many thousands who thronged London, the privileged seem by far the most likely candidates for regular patrons of the theaters. Even the humblest gentleman retainer or the student with the slenderest stipend could afford a couple of pennies, while the grand gallants could pay "an angell for a paltry stoole"[164] and command the best the house afforded, whether wine or pipe or courtesan. And the privileged could enjoy such pleasures repeatedly. With their afternoons idle and the playhouses nearby, with their intellects challenged by poetry and their spirits by spectacle, London's gentlemen inevitably gravitated toward the plays.

Nor did it seem to matter much where the plays were presented. The public playhouses, with their vast galleries and private rooms, seem quite as deliberately structured for the comfort of the higher-paying patron as the smaller private houses. In addition, the same plays were often presented in

[164] Lenton, *Young Gallant's Whirligig*, p. 13.

both settings. Dekker's *Satiromastix* was acted "publikely" by the Lord Chamberlain's men and "priuately" by Paul's boys.[165] Other plays like *The Malcontent* and *Bussy D'Ambois* transferred with ease from children's to adult troupes. Furthermore, during the War of the Theaters, the close interconnections among such works as *Eastward Ho, Westward Ho*, and *Northward Ho* quite clearly point toward a shared audience that could understand the continuing line of jokes and parody.[166] For thirty years, Heywood's *Rape of Lucrece* moved back and forth among adult companies at both the Phoenix and the Red Bull and then went to Beeston's Boys at the Phoenix/Cockpit in 1639.[167] With the same stock of plays and actors, Queen Anne's company moved from the Red Bull to the Phoenix in 1617, while Prince Charles's company moved from the Hope to the Red Bull in 1617 and from there to the Phoenix in 1619.[168] The King's Men entertained the public at both the Blackfriars and the Globe, premiered new plays at both theaters, and offered the same repertoire at both theaters. Even the productions for the aristocrats at Court were the same plays that the acting troupes performed in public. At the theaters, however, the courtiers could see the plays as often as they pleased, joined by that host of lesser gentlemen and would-be gallants, upstart merchants'

[165] Dekker, *Satiromastix*, in *Dramatic Works*, I, 299.

[166] Clifford Leech makes this argument in "Three Times *Ho* and a Brace of Widows: Some Plays for the Private Theatre," in *The Elizabethan Theatre III*, ed. David Galloway (Toronto: Macmillan, 1973), pp. 15-17. Brian Gibbons also points out that the masterpieces of City Comedy appeared not at the coterie theaters, with which they have been too narrowly associated, but at the public theaters. See *Jacobean City Comedy* (Cambridge, Mass.: Harvard University Press, 1968), p. 28. Although her basic argument places different audiences at different theaters, Muriel Bradbrook also admits the ties between private and public houses in *The Living Monument: Shakespeare and the Theatre of his Time* (Cambridge: Cambridge University Press, 1976); see pp. 8, 30, 119, e.g. The most powerful argument for interchangeability of drama among private, public, and Court audiences is made by J. A. Lavin, "Shakespeare and the Second Blackfriars," in *Elizabethan Theatre III*, ed. Galloway, pp. 66-81.

[167] Bentley, *Jacobean and Caroline Stage*, I, 174.

[168] Ibid., VI, 220.

sons and fashionable ladies who could only dream of attending a glittering performance before royalty or nobility. Some have claimed that the more elite spectators patronized the private theaters almost exclusively. Yet the interchangeability of plays for Court and for the public, together with the presentation of the same plays at both public and private playhouses and the movement of troupes from one kind of theater to another, makes the theory of exclusive patronage unlikely. Instead, the privileged theatergoers seem to have attended plays no matter where they were performed.

Penny patrons alone could never have made Henslowe or the Burbages rich. Profitable theatrical enterprises had to lure the privileged—moneyed, leisured, educated, sophisticated. The proof of the companies' success lay in the astounding dramatic activity between 1576 and 1642, when a procession of magnificent buildings and a steady flow of acting troupes were all maintained despite plague closures, political opposition, and the capricious whim of fashion. Whose pockets save the privileged were fat enough to pay the price of admission, support the many parasites sucking a living from the theatergoers, and guarantee large profits to the major companies? Even a bitter Puritan catalogue of the playgoers listed only the privileged and their parasites:

> But to particularize some amongst all. The prophane gallant to feed his pleasure; the Citty dames to laugh at their owne shames: the Country Clowne to tell wonders when hee comes home of the vanities he hath seene, the baudes to intice, the whores and courtezans to set themselues to sale, the cutpurse to steale, the pickpocket to filch, the knaue to be instructed in more cosoning trickes, youth to learne amorous conceits, some for one wicked purpose, some for another: none to any good intent, but all fruitlesly to mispend their time.[169]

Employing wit rather than invective, Dekker perhaps put it best: "Your Gallant, your Courtier, and your Capten had wont

[169] I. G., *Refutation of the Apology for Actors*, p. 50.

to be the soundest paymaisters, and I thinke are still the surest chapmen: and these, by meanes that their heades are well stockt, deale vpō this comical freight by the grosse.''[170] Those "sound paymaisters," the privileged, supported the actors, who in turn stocked their heads with "comical freight by the grosse." The arrangement proved mutually profitable and pleasurable for more than six decades.

[170] Dekker, *Gvls Horne-booke*, in *Non-Dramatic Works*, II, 246-247.

# · VI ·

## Plebeian Playgoers

As frankly commercial enter-
prises, the theaters opened their doors to anyone with the price
of admission. Except for the performances at Court and at private gatherings, the privileged could not lay exclusive claim to
any presentation, for money in any hand bought admission to
a playhouse. Thus, according to Thomas Dekker, "the place is
so free in entertainment, allowing a stoole as well to the Farmers
sonne as to your Templer: that your Stinkard has the selfe-
same libertie to be there in his Tobacco-Fumes, which your
sweet Courtier hath: and that your Car-man and Tinker claime
as strong a voice in their suffrage, and sit to giue iudgment on
the plaies life and death, as well as the prowdest *Momus* among
the tribe of *Critick*."[1] Though it is doubtful that a mere farmer's
son could afford a stool onstage or a stinkard the cost of tobacco,
behind the satiric hyperbole of *The Gull's Hornbook* lay an
indisputable fact: the privileged shared the playhouses with
plebeians. An adequate understanding of the gentleman's role
in the audience therefore requires an understanding of the commoner's role in that same audience.

Without question, commoners came to the plays. Their presence was well documented in sermons, government records,
plays, and other literature of the period. Puritans denounced
playgoing on the part of ordinary subjects, "the common people
which resorte to Theaters being but ã assemblie of Tailers, Tinkers, Cordwayners, Saylers, olde Men, yong Men, Women,
Boyes, Girles, and such like."[2] Another voice cried, "Now the

---

[1] Thomas Dekker, *The Gvls Horne-booke*, in *The Non-Dramatic Works*, ed.
Alexander B. Grosart (1884; reprint ed., New York: Russell and Russell, 1963),
II, 247.
[2] Stephen Gosson, *Playes Confuted in Fiue Actions*, in *The English Drama*

common haunters are for the most part, the leaudest persons in the land, apt for pilferie, periurie, forgerie, or any rogories, the very scum, rascallitie, and baggage of the people, thieues, cut-purses, shifters, cousoners; briefly, an vncleane generation and spaune of vipers."[3] According to the government, plays lured servants, apprentices, and workmen from their tasks and also provided havens for pickpockets, whores, and rioters. Playwrights complained of the "Greasie-apron *Audience*," "the *Foeces*, or grounds of your people, that sit in the oblique caves and wedges of your house, your sinfull six-penny Mechanicks," and the "noyse / of *Rables, Apple-wives* and Chimneyboyes."[4] Here and there a neutral voice merely said that "all the Roomes / Did swarme with Gentiles mix'd with Groomes," or, more colorfully,

When ended is the play, the dance, and song,
A thousand townesmen, gentlemen, and whores,
Porters and serving-men together throng.[5]

Of primary concern is not simply the presence of common citizens but the extent of their patronage compared with that of the privileged playgoers. Did the circumstances of the commoners' lives foster theatergoing? Did they attend the plays often or seldom? Did they come to both public and private playhouses? Did they ever dominate the theater audiences?

---

*and Stage*, ed. William C. Hazlitt (1869; reprint ed., New York: Burt Franklin, n.d.), p. 184.

[3] Henry Crosse, *Vertues Common-wealth: Or the High-way to Honour*, in *Occasional Issues*, ed. Alexander B. Grosart (Manchester: C. E. Simms, 1878), VII, 183.

[4] Dekker, *If This Be not a Good Play*, in *The Dramatic Works*, ed. Fredson Bowers (Cambridge: Cambridge University Press, 1953-1961), III, 121; Ben Jonson, "Induction," *The Magnetic Lady*, in *Ben Jonson*, ed. C. H. Herford and Percy Simpson (Oxford: Clarendon Press, 1925-1952), VI, 509; John Tatham, *The Fancies Theatre* (London, 1640), $H_2^v$-$H_3$.

[5] *Pimlyco, or Runne Red-Cap* (London, 1609), $C_{[1]}$; Sir John Davies, Epigram 17, "In Cosmun," in *The Complete Poems*, ed. Alexander B. Grosart (London: Chatto and Windus, 1876), II, 18.

These are the questions that must be explored before a balanced assessment of either the privileged or the plebeian playgoers can emerge.

According to the contemporary accounts, two radically different kinds of commoners came to the theaters. On the one hand were the respectable (if irresponsible) people—servants, apprentices, workers, and other citizens of various sorts. On the other hand were the destitute and the disreputable—beggars, vagabonds, masterless men, whores, panders, thieves, cozeners, rioters, and troublemakers of every kind. Depending upon his bias, each witness testified differently about the proportion of the respectable to the disreputable. For William Prynne, *"what else are the residue* (at least the Maior part) *of our assiduous Play-haunters, but Adulterers, Adulteresses, Whoremasters, Whores, Bawdes, Panders, Ruffians, Roarers, Drunkards, Prodigals, Cheaters, idle, infamous, base, profane, and godlesse persons."*[6] For one more dispassionate, the plebeian playgoers seemed merely "Citizens, and the meaner sort of People."[7] In order to preserve some sort of perspective amid the invective, one should first analyze these two groups of commoners—the citizens and the meaner sort—separately and then analyze the testimony regarding their presence in the playhouse audiences.

## APPRENTICES

Of the respectable plebeians, apprentices were perhaps most frequently mentioned, especially in the official complaints that plays lured the apprentices from their work. With several thousand such young men in London,[8] no doubt some did slip away

---

[6] William Prynne, *Histrio-Mastrix* (London, 1633), p. 145.

[7] James Wright, *Historia Histrionica: An Historical Account of the English Stage* (London, 1699), p. 5.

[8] According to Peter Laslett, "the actual number of apprentices formally so called, seems to have been very much exaggerated by historians, and by contemporaries too." See *The World We Have Lost* (London: Methuen, 1965), p. 241n.

to the theater in the afternoons, but such behavior required considerable ingenuity. To begin with, the apprentice stood under the total authority of his master, who in turn assumed total responsibility for his charge's behavior. By order of the Common Council, no one could permit his apprentice "to go at his large Liberty and Pleasure."⁹ The attitude toward any master lenient enough to allow an apprentice to attend plays received trenchant, if harsh, expression by Stephen Gosson: "if Diogenes were nowe aliue, . . . hee would wyshe rather to bee a Londoners hounde then his apprentice, bicause hee rateth his dogge, for wallowing in carrion; but rebukes not his seruaunt for resorting to playes, that are rank poyson."¹⁰ In the face of this kind of criticism, the guilds enacted measures requiring masters to prohibit their apprentices, servants, and journeymen from going to see plays.¹¹ Granted, some apprentices proved clever enough or rebellious enough to defy their masters. When threatened with punishment, one young man declared to the goldsmiths that he would "leap out of the window and break his neck rather than abide it."¹² Yet strict supervision and discipline were made easier by a limitation of the number of apprentices to each household, with only one, two, or at most three or four apprentices being allowed to any individual guildsman.¹³ Even with so few to supervise, total control could not

⁹ John Stow, *A Survey of the Cities of London and Westminster and the Borough of Southwark*, Corrected, Improved and very much Enlarged . . . by John Strype (London, W. Imrys, J. Richardson et al., 1754-1755), II, 431. See Chapter II, note 41.

¹⁰ Stephen Gosson, *The Ephemerides of Phialo and a Short Apologie of the Schoole of Abuse* (London, 1579), p. 88.

¹¹ *Malone Society Collections* (Oxford: Oxford University Press, 1907-1975), II, 3:313.

¹² Sir Walter Sherburne Prideaux, *Memorials of the Goldsmiths' Company* (London: Eyre and Spottiswoode, 1896), I, 109.

¹³ O. Jocelyn Dunlop and Richard D. Denman, *English Apprenticeship and Child Labour* (New York: Macmillan, 1912), p. 45. The number of apprentices allotted to each master depended upon his rank in the company, with the larger numbers going only to the handful of master members at the top. The ordinary guildsman had only one or two apprentices, some guildsmen none at all.

be imposed upon adolescent youths of fourteen to twenty-four,[14] but the number of apprentices in their distinctive blue caps[15] to be found at the theater on a workday afternoon would have been severely limited by most masters. Few, if any, like the Grocer in *The Knight of the Burning Pestle*, were so lenient or so generous as to treat wife and apprentice to a play, except on a rare holiday.

Besides the disciplinary restrictions, a lack of money prevented apprentices from attending the theater in any great numbers. Some would "break in at playes . . . for three a groat, and crack Nuts with the Scholars in peny Rooms again, and fight for Apples,"[16] but they could count themselves lucky to have so much as a groat. Many young people in the society, including apprentices, never had money of their own.[17] According to the law, "if any Freeman or Freewoman of this City give any Wages to his or her Apprentice, or suffer the said Apprentices to take any Part of their own Getting or Gains," the master was permanently disfranchised.[18] For his trouble in training, feeding, and clothing an apprentice, a master expected to be paid a fee at the boy's enrollment—legally only 2s. 6d.

---

[14] By law, apprenticeship was a mandatory seven years, though some groups such as the goldsmiths required an even longer term of service. No one was freed before the age of twenty-four: "no maner of persone . . . shalbe by any maner of wayes or meanes made free of the saide Cytie . . . vntyll suche tyme as he and they shall seurallie atteyne and come to the Age of xxiiii[tie] yeres fullye Complete." See Edward Arber, *A Transcript of the Registers of the Company of Stationers of London, 1554-1640* (London: privately printed, 1875), I, xli. See also Stow, *Survey*, II, 431, and the Statute of Artificers, 5 Eliz. cap. 4.

[15] Stow, *Survey*, II, 432-433, gives the full regulations for clothing required of apprentices.

[16] John Fletcher, *Wit Without Money*, in *Works*, ed. Arnold Glover and A. R. Waller (Cambridge: Cambridge University Press, 1905-1912), II, 194.

[17] Laslett, *World We Have Lost*, p. 105.

[18] Stow, *Survey*, II, 431. See also Mildred Campbell, *The English Yeoman under Elizabeth and the Early Stuarts* (New Haven: Yale University Press, 1942), p. 214; Dunlop and Denman, *English Apprenticeship*, p. 55; and George Unwin, "Commerce and Coinage in Shakespeare's England," in *Studies in Economic History* (London: Macmillan, 1927), p. 308.

but often much more.[19] A guildsman certainly did not expect to hand out pennies to his charges for frivolities like the theater or for any other purpose. With no wages, no share of the income from his trade, and no pocket money from his master, an apprentice had to rely on wit, windfall, or personal wealth to get in to see a play. Of course, a few succeeded, but on most days, the number was surely limited.

One kind of apprentice stood apart from his fellows. Unlike the forcibly apprenticed children of vagrants and paupers,[20] or even the sons of ordinary craftsmen and small farmers, these young men actually belonged to the privileged ranks of society. Either they came to London as younger sons of good families to enter a profitable trade or else they came as heirs to the lucrative crafts they learned—oftentimes by means of patrimony, without serving any real apprenticeship.[21] This tiny minority among the blue caps had the means and the background to behave much like the privileged anywhere else in London. In 1582, in an attempt to curb their excesses, the Common Council issued an order against apprentices who "did affect to go in costly Apparel, and wear Weapons, and frequent Schools of Dancing, Fencing and Music."[22] These few apprentices, ac-

---

[19] Dunlop and Denman, *English Apprenticeship*, p. 59; Stow, *Annales, or a General Chronicle of England*, continued and augmented . . . by Edmund Howes, Gent. (London, 1631), p. 1,040, and Stow, *Survey*, II, 432; Alan Simpson, *The Wealth of the Gentry, 1540-1660* (Chicago: University of Chicago Press, 1961), p. 116.

[20] These were the provisions of the Poor Law of 1597, 39 Eliz. cap. 4.

[21] Prideaux, *Memorials of the Goldsmiths' Company*, pp. xv-xvi, 94; Dunlop and Denman, *English Apprenticeship*, pp. 86-90. Ivy Pinchbeck and Margaret Hewitt, *Children in English Society* (London: Routledge and Kegan Paul, 1969), I, 226-227; Steven R. Smith, "The London Apprentices as Seventeenth-Century Adolescents," *Past and Present* 61 (November 1973): 150. Frank Freeman Foster points out that favored apprentices were promoted to such an extent that Burghley complained in 1591 because they were allowed to become members of the Turkey Company before they could even provide stock or engage in trade. See *The Politics of Stability: A Portrait of the Rulers in Elizabethan England* (London: Royal Historical Society, 1977), pp. 94-95.

[22] Stow, *Survey*, II, 432-433.

tually not plebeians at all, would seem likely candidates for playgoers. At least one such playgoer, a feltmaker's apprentice named John Gill, enacted a gentleman's role when he went so far as to demand a duel to avenge his honor. After being wounded by the actor Richard Baxter at the Red Bull, Gill sent the following note:

> Mr. Blackster So it is that vppon Monday last . . . uppon your stage intendinge noe hurte to any one, . . . I was greeuously wounded in my head as may appear. . . . And therefore in kindnes I desire you to giue mee satisfaccion seeing I was wounded by your owne hand. . . . If you refuse then looke to your selfe and avoyde the daunger which shall this day ensue upon your Company and House For . . . I am a Feltmakers prentice and have made it knowne to at the least one hundred and fortye . . . who are all here present readie to take revenge vppon you vnles willingly you will give present satisfaction. . . . And as you have a care for your owne safeties, so let me have Answere forthwith.[23]

Here the skillful approximation of sophisticated language and behavior, plus the fact that Gill was apparently sitting on the stage when the accident occurred, should serve as a caution against assuming that all apprentices in the audience were necessarily plebeian rather than privileged.

ADULT WORKERS

Far outnumbering the apprentices were London's craftsmen, common laborers, and servants. Like the apprentices and all other groups in society, they represented a broad range of income, skill, and importance. At the upper end of the spectrum ranked the great merchants, the masters of the companies, the aldermen, the wealthy, the titled. Men of business by occu-

---

[23] 6 March 1622; J. C. Jeaffreson, ed., *Middlesex County Records* (London: Middlesex County Records Society, 1886-1892), II, 175-176; Gerald Eades Bentley, *The Jacobean and Caroline Stage* (Oxford: Clarendon Press, 1941-1968), I, 166-167.

pation, by life style, these were men of privilege, whose presence at the theater seemed as welcome and natural as any courtier's.

> You are our daily and most constant Guests,
> Whom neither Countrey bus'nesse nor the Gests
> Can ravish from the Citie; tis your care
> To keepe your Shope, 'lesse when to take the Ayr
> You walke abroad, as you have done to day,
> To bring your Wives and Daughters to a Play.
> How fond are those men then that think it fit
> T' arraigne the Citie defect of Wit?
> When we do know, you love both wit and sport,
> Especially when you've vocation for 't.[24]

Just below the eminent merchants stood the prosperous but unpretentious shopkeepers and artisans—butchers, tailors, plasterers, skinners, pewterers, and the like. Comprising the principal body of London's guilds, they hired journeymen, trained apprentices, kept servants to run their households, paid taxes, and supplied the goods and services demanded by the city and the world. Journeymen ranked considerably lower on the scale. Though skilled in his art or craft, a journeyman lacked the money to set up his own shop or to be admitted to the higher echelons of his company. While not bound to any one master, the journeyman nonetheless had to depend upon the wages paid him by a master to support himself and, if married, his family. His day's payment included either food and drink or extra money for such sustenance, but it did not include clothing, shelter, or other necessities.

A host of workers remained outside the guild system altogether. They included aliens from the Continent and the rest of the world practicing skilled and unskilled trades in competition with the English companies. They also included

---

[24] Henry Glapthorne, "To a Reviv'd Vacation Play," in *Plays and Poems* (London: John Pearson, 1874), II, 194. For less literary analyses of London's wealthy merchants, see Foster, *Politics of Stability;* and R. G. Lang, "Social Origins and Social Aspirations of Jacobean Merchants," *Economic History Review*, 2d ser. 27 (1974): 28-47.

"strangers"—the Englishmen pouring in from other areas, often driven by famine or crop failure, to seek whatever common labor the city offered. And of course they included the army of servants performing the menial domestic duties in every household. Together with a few more exotic types, principally soldiers and sailors, these were the respectable London commoners. At least some of them found their way into the playhouses, but certain circumstances make it doubtful that they came regularly or in large numbers, except possibly on holidays.

WORKING HOURS

The chief restriction against playgoing on the part of ordinary folk was the length of the working day. For all but the master, hours of labor and leisure, including the times allotted for meals and rest, were set by law:

> And be it further enacted by the authority aforesaid, That all artificers and labourers being hired for wages by the day or week shall, betwixt the midst of the months of March and September, be and continue at their work, at or before five of the clock in the morning, and continue at work, and not depart, until between seven and eight of the clock at night (except it be in the time of breakfast, dinner or drinking, the which times at most shall not exceed two and a half in a day, that is to say, at every drinking one half-hour, for his dinner, one hour, and for his sleep, when he is allowed to sleep, the which is from the midst of May, to the midst of August, half an hour at the most, and at every breakfast one half-hour). And all the said artificers and labourers, between the midst of September, and the midst of March, shall be and continue at their work from the spring of the day in the morning, until the night of the same day, except it be in time afore appointed to breakfast and dinner.[25]

A penny was to be deducted from the wages for every hour of

[25] Statute of Artificers, 5 Eliz. cap. 4.

work missed, and judges were required to prosecute workers who "do not continue from Five of the Clock in the Morning till Seven at Night in the Summer, and from Seven till five in Winter."[26] The workday could be even longer. According to a London regulation, "No Hammer-man, as a Smith, a Pewterer, a Founder, and all Artificers making great Sound, shall not work after the Hour of Nine in the Night, nor afore the Hour of Four in the Morning, under Pain of three Shillings four Pence."[27] Presumably, those at quieter labor could work indefinitely.

With hours like these six days a week, most laborers would have found it difficult, if not impossible, to attend the theater, even if some managed to circumvent the law. The players performed just when workers were expected to be at their tasks. Counting the time it took to walk to and from the playhouse (and a laborer had to walk unless he had money for a boat or a carriage), an afternoon at the theater meant the loss of a half-day's pay, not to mention the risk of a fine and possible dismissal. Of course the shopkeeper or master artisan was free to take in a play since he was not working for wages, but his absence would have left his business unsupervised.

Not surprisingly, the records showed few specific instances of such masters at the theater, except in a comedy like *The Knight of the Burning Pestle*. Even there, the supreme joke may have been the presence of a grocer and his wife at a play. Certainly their behavior—climbing up onto the stage from the yard, demanding a different play with an impossible plot starring their apprentice Ralph—showed a gross unfamiliarity with the theater. The inexperience of common folk as playgoers was sufficiently accepted to perpetuate the joke about a butcher who leaped onto the stage to rescue Hector from the attacking Myrmidons, thinking the actor was really about to be killed. "He strooke moreover such an especiall acquaintance with *Hector*, that for a long time *Hector* could not obtaine leave of him to be kill'd, that the Play might go on; and the cudgelled *Mir-*

---

[26] *The Harleian Miscellany* (London, 1744), II, 13.
[27] Stow, *Survey*, II, 410.

*mydons* durst not enter againe, till *Hector,* having prevailed upon his unexpected second, return'd him over the Stage againe into the yard from whence he came."[28]

Perhaps household servants might have slipped away from their daily tasks to take in a play. Lady Bacon felt that her son Anthony should not have settled in Bishopsgate "on account of its neighbourhood to the Bull-inn, where plays and interludes were continually acted, and would, she imagined, corrupt his servants."[29] (She expressed no similar fears for her son's possible corruption.) But for the most part, servants, like other workers, had to confine their pleasure to free hours. Thus Henry Crosse particularly objected to night plays because they "entice seruants out of their maisters houses."[30] He did not charge that performances during the day offered such enticement.

Far more common as spectators than servants, butchers, grocers, or journeymen were the soldiers and sailors about London. Unlike others in the lower working orders, they enjoyed free time during the day. Though regiments were only irregularly summoned and then disbanded, depending on the danger at hand, discharged soldiers hung around London in sufficient numbers to cause frequent complaint. Sailors, who were always paid off at the end of a voyage, had little to do before signing on again but seek amusement or trouble. A playhouse seemed a likely place for both.

Most other respectable commoners had no idle afternoons to attend the theater except on holidays or Sundays. After the ban on Sunday playing in 1586, only such days as Shrove Tuesday or Midsummer's Day, when the Lord Mayor was elected, remained available for ordinary workers to indulge in playgoing alongside subjects with more leisure. Interestingly enough, new plays were never performed on holidays, at least not in Hens-

---

[28] Edmund Gayton, *Pleasant Notes upon Don Quixote* (London, 1654), p. 3.

[29] Thomas Birch, *Memoirs of the Reign of Queen Elizabeth, from the Year 1581 till her Death* (London, 1754), I, 173.

[30] Crosse, *Vertues Common-wealth,* p. 111.

lowe's theater. It seems strange that Henslowe would pass up
the chance to pack his house with holiday crowds at double the
usual admission prices—unless, perhaps, he was appealing to
an inexperienced audience who did not care what they saw, so
long as the price was not prohibitive. This possibility receives
considerable support from an account of holiday behavior on
the part of commoners at a playhouse.

if it be on Holy dayes, when Saylers, Water-men, Shoomakers, Butchers and Apprentices are at leisure, then it is
good policy to amaze those violent spirits, with some tearing
Tragaedy . . . the spectators frequently mounting the stage,
and making a more bloody Catastrophe amongst themselves,
then the Players did. I have known upon one of these *Fes-
tivals*, but especially at *Shrove-tide*, where the Players have
been appointed, notwithstanding their bils to the contrary,
to act what the major part of the company had a mind to:
sometimes *Tamerlane*, sometimes *Jugurth*, sometimes the
Jew of *Malta*, and sometimes parts of all these, and at last,
none of the three taking, they were forc'd to undresse and
put off their Tragick habits, and conclude the day with the
merry milk-maides. And unlesse this were done, and the
popular humour satisfied, as sometimes it so fortun'd, that
the Players were refractory; the Benches, the tiles, the laths,
the stones, Oranges, Apples, Nuts, flew about most liberally,
and as there were Mechanicks of all professions, who fell
every one to his owne trade, and dissolved a house in an
instant, and made a ruine of a stately Fabrick. It was not then
the most mimicall nor fighting man, *Fowler*, nor *Andrew
Cane* could pacifie; Prologues nor Epilogues would prevaile;
the Devill and the fool were quite out of favour. Nothing but
noise and tumult fils the house, untill a cogg take 'um, and
then to the Bawdy houses, and reforme them; and instantly
to the Banks side, where the poor Beares must conclude the
riot, and fight twenty dogs at a time beside the Butchers,
which sometimes fell into the service; this perform'd, and

the Horse and Jack-an-Apes for a jigge, they had sport enough
that day for nothing.[31]

Unmistakably the picture here was one of "Saylers, Water-men,
Shoomakers, Butchers and Apprentices" briefly released from
the usual restraints of dawn-to-dusk labor and far more interested in violence than in any subtleties of performance. The
costly ruin of the playhouse—hardly the work of customers
who enjoyed coming over and over again—would seem to have
been sheer vandalism wreaked by those who wanted "sport
enough that day for nothing."

WAGES AND PRICES

The reference to free entertainment was anything but casual.
Besides the restrictive hours of work, the second major drawback
to playgoing for plebeians was the cost. Wages were so low and
prices so high that even a penny could seldom be spared for a
luxury like the theater. Pay scales in London were set forth in
royal proclamations, determined by the year, the week, or the
day, either with meat and drink or without. (See Appendix A.)
They ranged from a high of £10 per year earned by brewers
down to a low of £3 earned by girdlers, horners, gray tawers,
and barbers. Such wages, however, represented the maximum,
paid to "the best and most skillful workmen, journeymen, or
hired servants."[32] Common laborers got no more than the sta-
tutory 5d. per day with meat and drink, 9d. without. In practice,
they often received much less because the supply of hungry,
unskilled workers moving off the land and into London far

---

[31] Gayton, *Pleasant Notes upon Don Quixote*, pp. 271-272.

[32] See Appendix A. The same wage scale was proclaimed over and over again
during Elizabeth's reign. See, e.g., Paul L. Hughes and James F. Larkin, eds.,
*Tudor Royal Proclamations* (New Haven: Yale University Press, 1969), II, 401-
403, 422-423; III, 22-25, 40-42, 59. See also Campbell, *English Yeoman*, p.
213, for wages paid to farm labor. The scale is confirmed by the carpenters'
wages paid for building stages and stands at Court in 1572 to 1573, though
higher rates were paid under Charles I. See *Malone Society Collections*, X, 6,
39, 45, 52, 54.

outstripped the demand. Thus a hireling who belonged to no company worked for whatever he could get. In addition, the thousands of artisans in the suburbs, some English and some foreign, were unregulated by either the City or its guilds.[33] Many, without shop or license, hawked their wares on the streets and from door to door. In view of the persistent complaints against unfair competition from such people, it would seem that they worked for substandard wages and sold at substandard prices.[34] Even from prosperous families, household servants could expect only minimal rewards for their services— a "bare forty shillings a yeere (seruingmens wages)."[35] For example, when the will of the barrister Ralph Rokeby was executed by William Lambarde in 1600, the servants received only two or three pounds "for a y$^r$ wages and rewarde."[36] John Stow quite correctly observed that "The priuate riches of London resteth chiefly in the handes of the Marchantes and Retaylers, for Artificers haue not much to spare, and Labourers haue neede that it were giuen vnto them."[37]

The income figures for London's vast army of workers reveal only half the story, however. On the surface, it might appear that almost anyone could afford to spend a penny for two or three hours of amusement at the playhouse. Yet in view of the cost of basic necessities—food, shelter, clothing, and fuel—it

[33] Dunlop and Denman, *English Apprenticeship*, pp. 94-97.

[34] Stow, *Survey*, II, 511-514; "A brief Discoverie of the great perpesture of newe Buyldinges neere to the Cittie . . . ," Lansdowne MS 160, fol. 90, *Archaeologia* 23 (1831): 121; Anthony Richard Wagner, *English Genealogy* (Oxford: Clarendon Press, 1960), p. 261.

[35] Dekker, *Worke for Armourers*, in *Non-Dramatic Works*, IV, 130.

[36] J. Payne Collier, ed., *The Egerton Papers*, Camden Society Publications, vol. 12 (1840), p. 310. See also Simpson, *Wealth of the Gentry*, p. 125; G. R. Batho, ed., *The Household Papers of Henry Percy, Ninth Earl of Northumberland (1564-1632)*, Camden Society Publications, 3d ser. 93 (1962): 149ff. (note wages of ordinary servants); Campbell, *English Yeoman*, Appendix 3 (servants' wages ranged from £5 yearly for a bailiff, without apparel, to 13s. 4d. for "A woman servant of the second-best sort").

[37] John Stow, *A Survey of London*, ed. Charles Lethbridge Kingsford (Oxford: Clarendon Press, 1908), II, 209. Hereafter cited as Stow, *Survey*, ed. Kingsford, to avoid confusion with the 1754-1755 edition cited elsewhere.

seems doubtful that even so little as a penny could often be spared from most pockets. The increase of base admission prices from 1d. to 2d. barely reflected the rate of inflation, for prices of basic goods more than doubled. Unfortunately, wages remained fixed by law. Indeed, over the course of seven centuries, real purchasing power never sank so low as it did between 1576 and 1642. The year 1599, when the Globe was new, the Fortune in the planning, and the boys' companies set to return, saw the absolute nadir of the economy for the wage earner.[38] (See Appendix B.)

The plight of the London worker became particularly pitiable in these times. Unable to grow food himself and totally dependent upon modest earnings, he had to pay exorbitant prices in competition for the smaller quantities of food brought in from the outlying shires during years of bad harvests. Despite attempts to fix prices and to commandeer the grain reserves hoarded by the guilds, food costs rose inexorably.[39] A combi-

---

[38] For a full picture, see all three of the articles by E. H. Phelps Brown and Sheila W. Hopkins: "Seven Centuries of Building Wages," "The Price of Consumables, Compared with Builders' Wage Rates," and "Wage Rates and Prices: Evidence for Population Pressure in the Sixteenth Century," *Economica* 22 (1955): 195-206; 23 (1956): 291-314; 24 (1957): 289-299. J. U. Nef assumes that "the demand for grates, window panes, cloth, bedding, tobacco and crude ware" implied an improved prosperity "among the common people." See "Prices and Industrial Capitalism in France and England, 1540-1640," in *Essays in Economic History*, ed. E. M. Carus-Wilson (London: Edward Arnold, 1954), I, 133-134. However, the yeomen in the countryside and the modestly prosperous craftsmen and retailers in the cities, rather than the salaried worker, seem to have been the commoners who enjoyed these comforts. See B. E. Supple, *Commercial Crisis and Change in England, 1600-1642* (Cambridge: Cambridge University Press, 1959), p. 23; and Y. S. Brenner, "The Inflation of Prices in Early Sixteenth Century England," *Economic History Review*, 2d ser. 14 (1961-1962): 228, and "The Inflation of Prices in England, 1551-1650," *Economic History Review*, 2d ser. 15 (1962-1963): 281-282.

[39] Bread was the principal object of price stabilization. The Assize of Bread fixed the weight of a 1d. loaf at 22 ounces, while the Privy Council fixed certain sizes of loaves at each price level—farthing, halfpenny, and penny. To protect established bakers, itinerants had to make their penny loaves 3 ounces heavier. Fines were levied for infringement. See Neville J. Williams, ed., *Tradesmen in Early-Stuart Wiltshire, A Miscellany*, Wiltshire Archaeological and Natural

nation of bad weather and crop failures made the years 1594 to 1597 especially devastating. Stow reported in 1595, "In this time of dearth and scarcity of victuals at London, an hens egg was sold for a penny, or three egges for two pence at the most, a pound of sweet butter for 7 pence, and so the like of fish or flesh, exceeding measure in price."[40] William Harrison told much the same story: "of late years . . . such a price of corn continueth in each town and market . . . that the artificer and poor laboring man is not able to reach unto it but is driven to content himself with horse corn, I mean, beans, peason, oats, tares, and lentils. . . . If the world last awhile after this rate, wheat and rye will be no grain for poor men to feed on."[41] As early as 1574, with the worst yet to come, it was observed that "All this dearth notwithstanding (thankes be giuen to God) there was no want of any thing to him that wanted not money."[42]

---

History Society, Records Branch, vol. 15 (1959), p. x. See also the mobilization order of 1588 (Hughes and Larkin, eds., *Tudor Royal Proclamations*, III, 20-22) for examples of official allowances for other foods supplied to the army. As a consequence of the rising costs of food, the suppliers grew richer at the expense of consumers. For the prosperity of the landed yeoman compared with the salaried Londoner, see Brenner, "Inflation of Prices in Sixteenth Century England," p. 236; Campbell, *English Yeoman*, pp. 184-193; Sidney Pollard and David W. Crossley, *The Wealth of Britain, 1085-1966* (New York: Schocken Books, 1969), pp. 84-85; and L. A. Clarkson, *The Pre-Industrial Economy in England, 1500-1750* (London: B. T. Batsford, 1971), pp. 216, 225-226.

[40] Stow, *Annales* (1631), p. 770. Compare egg prices with the ceiling set in the mobilization order of 1599—seven eggs for 2d. (Davis P. Harding, "Shakespeare the Elizabethan," in *Shakespeare: Of an Age and for All Time*, ed. Charles Tyler Prouty [Hamden, Conn.: Shoe String Press, 1954], p. 17). See also eggs priced at 2d. for seven, 1d. for three in the earlier mobilization order of 1588 (Hughes and Larkin, eds., *Tudor Royal Proclamations*, III, 21). For a broader analysis, see W. G. Hoskins, "Harvest Fluctuations and English History, 1480-1619," *Agricultural History Review* 12 (1964): 44; and Andrew P. Appleby, *Famine in Tudor and Stuart England* (Stanford, Calif.: Stanford University Press, 1978), esp. pp. 106-107, 138-145.

[41] William Harrison, *The Description of England*, ed. Georges Edelen (Ithaca, N. Y.: Cornell University Press, 1968), p. 133.

[42] Stow, *Annales* (1631), p. 678.

For laborers working at or below the fixed rates, the want of money was precisely the problem, especially if they had families. Their basic diet consisted of bread, cheese, butter, some eggs, poultry, game, a few seasonal vegetables, meat on rare occasions, milk, ale, and beer. Official rates set 1d. for a loaf of bread, 1½d. for a pound of cheese, 1d. for three eggs, 3d. for a pound of butter, 6d. to 8d. for a couple of chickens or rabbits, with meats far more expensive, and a quart of ale or beer ½d.[43] However, with the possible exception of bread, prices far exceeded official rates in hard times. Not only did eggs reach 1d. apiece, as Stow reported, but cheese sold for as much as 4d. a pound and butter 5d. a pound, while chickens fetched 1s. each and rabbits 8d. apiece. Under the Stuarts, prices on some items climbed even higher than they had been during the worst years of the 1590s.[44]

Such food costs simply devastated the earnings of most workmen. By the year, the best craftsman commanded only £10, which averaged less than 7d. a day to clothe and shelter himself and his family and to feed all but himself as well. The most poorly paid, at £3 6s. 8d. a year, took home less than 3d. a day. Skilled workers could hire out by the day at rates ranging from 5d. to 9d., including meat and drink, but under these conditions the work was short-term, seasonal, or temporary, leaving many days with no employment or income. According to the differential between wages with meat and drink and those without, it cost from 4d. to 6d. each day to feed an able-bodied man. Similarly, out of a daily allowance of 8d., the Queen's soldiers were expected to pay a total of 6d. for dinner and supper. Military regulations specified meals of "good wheaten bread and drink, beef, mutton or veal boiled, and pig, beef, mutton, veal, or lamb roasted, or otherwise upon the fishdays, to have good wheaten bread and good drink, salt fish or ling, eggs, butter, peas or beans buttered, and so having competent and

[43] Hughes and Larkin, eds., *Tudor Royal Proclamations*, III, 21.

[44] See James E. Thorold Rogers, *A History of Agriculture and Prices in England* (Oxford: Clarendon Press, 1887), V and VI, 347-351, for meat prices, and pp. 372-375, for prices of dairy products and poultry.

sufficient thereof for the sustenation of their bodies."[45] Sixpence simply would not purchase this kind of meal twice each day.

Nor would the meager pennies London's artisans, craftsmen, and laborers carried home purchase such fare for their wives and children, for in addition to food, wages had to be stretched to provide clothing, fuel, and shelter. No kinder prices prevailed for these necessities. Shoes could cost more than a shilling, a boy's shirt 1s. 8d., a man's shirt 3s. 2½d., a frieze jerkins 4s. 1½d. Even a dozen lengths of ordinary sheeting or shirting cost a shilling apiece. The price of fuel climbed steadily during the period, with a hundred faggots priced anywhere from 6s. 6d. to 39s. 6d., a load of firewood from 7s. 2d. to 33s., and a mere sack of charcoal from 11d. to 1s. 10d. A dozen pounds of candles inched up from 3s. 1¾d. to 5s. 6d.,[46] despite the fact that the City council forbade certain kinds of soapmaking because "it would so waste in short Time the Tallow of the Realm, that the Poor would have no Candles, but must pay 6d. or 7d. yea and more, for a Pound of Candles."[47]

Rents were so exorbitant that the poorer artisans lived underneath stalls in holes that were termed "injurious both to the Beauty and Wholsomeness of the City."[48] They crowded into hovels, with little more than a straw mattress on the floor and perhaps a few sticks of furniture if they were better off. Officials tried to deal with the problem, but it exceeded their control: "Thes sorte of covetous Buylders exacte greate renttes, and daiely doe increase them, in so muche that a poore handie-craftsman is not able by his paynefull laboure to paye the rentte of a smale Tenement and feed his ffamilie."[49] In short, though the merchants, the builders, and the food suppliers profited, the

---

[45] Hughes and Larkin, eds., *Tudor Royal Proclamations*, III, 21. Hunnis asked more than 6d. a day to feed each of the children in his troupe. See E. K. Chambers, *The Elizabethan Stage* (Oxford: Clarendon Press, 1923), II, 37-38.

[46] Rogers, *History of Agriculture and Prices*, V and VI, 733, 734, 561, 398-401, respectively.

[47] Stow, *Survey*, II, 327.

[48] Ibid., p. 541.

[49] "A brief Discoverie," p. 124.

laboring groups fought a hopeless battle, pitting their fixed wages against the spiraling cost of all basic necessities.[50] James finally replaced the old wage schedules that had prevailed since 1563 because they "have not been rated and proportioned according to the plenty, scarcity, necessity, and respect of the time."[51] But earnings never rose to meet the level of costs.

AN ORDINARY HOUSEHOLD

A somewhat clearer view of the situation appears by analyzing the expenses in a single London household. In 1619 or 1620, the bakers submitted a petition asking for an increase in the 6s. they were allowed as overhead for baking each quarter of wheat. Attached to their request was the following outline of expenses, one of the few surviving documents for an ordinary household.

A Computation of a Baker's perticuler charges ariseing uppon the bakeing of Ten quarters of wheat by weeke in London.

|  | £. | s. | d. |
|---|---|---|---|
| Imprimis for howsrent after the rate of 30*l.* per ann. is by the weeke ............... | 0 | 11 | 6 |
| For 4 Journeymens wages att 2*s.* 6*d.* a peece per weeke ................................... | 0 | 10 | 0 |
| For meate and drinck for them and for two apprentices at 4*s.* a peece per weeke ............................................... | 1 | 4 | 0 |
| For Yeist ............................................... | 0 | 10 | 0 |
| For Woodde ......................................... | 0 | 12 | 0 |

[50] For further elaboration, see Pollard and Crossley, *Wealth of Britain*, esp. pp. 116-117, 124; Clarkson, *Pre-Industrial Economy*, pp. 225-226, 234; and D. C. Coleman, "Labour in the English Economy of the Seventeenth Century," *Economic History Review*, 2d ser. 8 (1955-1956): 288. "The overwhelming bulk of the income of ordinary persons was spent on necessities of life and on a very small range of conventional consumer goods" (Coleman, p. 288).

[51] 1 James I cap. 6.

|                                                                                                      | £ | s. | d. |
|------------------------------------------------------------------------------------------------------|---|----|----|
| For Salt                                                                                             | 0 | 1  | 0  |
| For Boulters                                                                                         | 0 | 1  | 0  |
| For Garner Rent                                                                                      | 0 | 2  | 0  |
| For wheat bought att the waterside the porters and fillers have 2*d.* ob per quarter                 | 0 | 2  | 0  |
| For sacks                                                                                            | 0 | 1  | 0  |
| For Wages for two maidservants                                                                       | 0 | 1  | 8  |
| For their dyett                                                                                      | 0 | 8  | 0  |
| For a dyett for a mans self and his wife                                                             | 0 | 10 | 0  |
| A commonlie man hath not lesse than three or foure children, which cannot be lesse then fourepence a day for their dyett | 0 | 7  | 0  |
| And for their apparell and teaching at Schole at 12*d.* a peece                                      | 0 | 3  | 0  |
| For Seacoles for fireing by the weeke after 4 Chauldron per yeare                                    | 0 | 1  | 4  |
| For Basketts after 13*s.* per ann. is                                                                | 0 | 0  | 3  |
| For Water weeklie                                                                                    | 0 | 0  | 8  |
| Item the Miller hath for his Toll out of everie quarter for grinding half a bushell, which is in tenn quarters 5 bushells, after 24*s.* the quarter | 0 | 15 | 0  |
| Item for apparell for a man's selfe, his Wife, and two apprentices after 20*l.* per ann. is per weeke | 0 | 7  | 8  |
| Item for duties in his parishe to the Parson, the Skavengers, for the Poore for watching and wardeing at the least weeklie | 0 | 1  | 0  |
| Summa totalis is per weeke                                                                           | £6 | 10 | 2  |

Besides all duties to the Kinges Ma[tie], charges in the Cittie and in the Warde, charges in his Companie, charges of reparacons of his howse, charges for howshould stuff dailie brought into the howse and amended. Also losses by stale bread, ill debtors, bad servants, and other like hindrances.

Item there is a penny in everie shilling given away for vantage.

Item many Bakers do scarce bake ten quarters a weeke, and yf anie man do bake more his charge is accordinglie the greater.

And so it plainlie appeareth that a quarter of Wheat cannott be baked with 6s. allowance for charges.[52]

Several things are noteworthy about this document. First, there was a large number of dependents or employees supported by the master of the household—four journeymen, two apprentices, two maidservants, a wife, and three or four children. Second, no money of any kind, beyond food and clothing, was allotted to the wife, the children, or the apprentices. Third, even this late in the period, after James had revised the rates upward, extremely low wages were paid: 5d. a day for each journeyman and less than 2d. a day for each maidservant. Finally, there was the high cost of all basic necessities. The food allowance ranged from 4d. a day for the children to 7d. a day for the employees and almost 9d. a day for the master and his wife. Rent came to £30 a year, clothing (including that for the children) to more than £20 a year. Fuel, especially the wood, was very expensive. For the journeymen and servants, the financial burden of providing everything but food for themselves out of their meager earnings was clearly enormous in view of such costs. Even the master felt the economic pinch. The thrust of the petition, after all, was to show that bakers could not meet their reasonable expenses, much less show a profit, if they were allowed only 6s. in charges for every quarter of wheat. From a household like this, few if any could have afforded a visit to the theater, even if they had leisure to go.

---

[52] *Analytical Index, to the Series of Records Known as the Remembrancia, 1579-1664* (London: E. J. Francis, 1878), pp. 386-387. Hereafter cited as *Remembrancia,* I.

### THE POOR

Yet the baker's household surely ranked as prosperous and comfortable compared to many others in London. At least its members enjoyed food, clothing, and honest work. Thousands could not claim such blessings and were accordingly classed among the disreputable. In theory, the deserving poor were different from the undeserving poor. According to Harrison, "the poor by impotency and the poor by casualty . . . are the true poor indeed . . . for whom the Word doth bind us to make some daily provision." By contrast, the "thriftless poor, as the rioter that hath consumed all, the vagabond that will abide nowhere but runneth up and down from place to place (as it were seeking work and finding none), and finally, the rogue and strumpet" merited only the "sharp execution and whip of justice."[53] In reality, little distinction was made between the true poor and the thriftless poor, particularly as they crowded into London, hopelessly compounding both their own misery and the officials' problems in dealing with them. From the government's point of view,

> many People of bad and lewd Condition daily resort, from the most Parts of this Realm, to the said City, Suburbs, and Places adjoining, procuring themselves small Habitations, namely, one Chamber-Room for a poor Foreigner and his Family, in a small Cottage, with some other as Poor as himself, in the City, Suburbs, or Places adjacent, to the great Increase and Pestering of this City with poor People; many of them proving Shifters, living by cozening, stealing, and imbezzling of Men's Goods, as Opportunity may serve them, removing from Place to Place accordingly; many Times running away, forsaking their Wives and Children, leaving them to the Charge of the said City, and the Hospitals of the same.[54]

The causes of the massive poverty lay in both the economic

---

[53] Harrison, *Description of England*, pp. 180, 181.
[54] Stow, *Survey*, II, 516.

system and the social structure. As prices rose inexorably, so that a penny bought a third less than it had a century earlier, more and more people slipped downward financially, rendering themselves and their families increasingly vulnerable to chronic malnutrition, disease, and outright starvation during the worst of times.[55] If the breadwinner died, fell ill, or could not find work, his family had to rely upon charity, begging, or crime to survive. Despite bequests from the affluent, the resources of charity dwindled continually, particularly after the dissolution of the monasteries.[56] Furthermore, a series of disastrous harvests devastated the livelihood of marginal farmers and agricultural hirelings, leaving them no choice but to starve or seek sustenance elsewhere.[57] The collapsing feudal system simply exacerbated the crisis by weakening the obligation of the great lord to care for his petty dependents, by separating increasing numbers of men from the land, and by enlarging the number of men wholly dependent upon salaried employment. In des-

[55] For an excellent analysis of the syndrome of population pressure, food shortage, rat starvation and consequent succumbing to endemic plague, flight of fleas to human hosts, plague, high marriage rate, high birth rate, and another population pressure, see W. C. Howson, "Plague, Poverty and Population in Parts of North-West England, 1580-1720," *Transactions of the Historic Society of Lancashire and Cheshire* 112 (1960): 29-55. On the appalling consequences of famine, see Laslett, *World We Have Lost*, pp. 112-116. See also Clarkson, *Pre-Industrial Economy*, pp. 234-236.

[56] The most extensive study of charity is W. K. Jordan's *Philanthropy in England, 1480-1660* (New York: Russell Sage Foundation, 1959), though his central thesis that bourgeois-mercantile wealth replaced landed-gentry-aristocratic wealth as the primary source of charity has come under attack. See, e.g., William G. Bittle and R. Todd Lane, "Inflation and Philanthropy in England: A Re-Assessment of W. K. Jordan's Data," *Economic History Review*, 2d ser. 29 (1976): 203-210, as well as the articles by J. F. Hadwin, D. C. Coleman, J. D. Gould, and Bittle and Lane in *Economic History Review*, 2d ser. 31 (1978): 105-128.

[57] See Campbell, *English Yeoman*, e.g., pp. 215-216; J. F. Pound, *Poverty and Vagrancy in Tudor England* (Harlow: Longmans, 1971); A. L. Beier, "Vagrants and the Social Order in Elizabethan England," *Past and Present* 64 (August 1974): 3-29, together with a response and defense in *Past and Present* 71 (May 1976): 126-134.

peration, Parliament finally enacted the great Poor Law of 1597, a masterful instrument designed to cope with the threatening chaos of poverty. The legitimate poor were remanded to their local parishes for succor, children forcibly apprenticed or otherwise set to work, vagrants and masterless men severely punished and either imprisoned or forced to work.[58]

Unfortunately, England's social and economic crisis was too great to respond at once to such measures, sensible as they seemed to their framers. Years passed before the Poor Law began to take significant effect. In the meantime, the destitute and dispossessed swarmed into the warrens of London and its suburbs, spawning rebellion, crime, beggary, plague, starvation, and misery. By 1594, the problem had grown so severe that the Lord Mayor asked the Privy Council to command the justices of Surrey and Sussex either to banish suburban beggars from London or to bar them from crossing the bridge. Though the Mayor may have been exaggerating, he set their numbers at twelve thousand.[59] Besides beggars in the suburbs, there were all the wretched poor throughout the City itself. In addition, there were residents of almshouses and hospitals, whores and thieves and other criminals, plus the discharged soldiers complained of everywhere. In short, an army of social outcasts jammed themselves into London.

City officials deplored the fact that "there are such great Multitudes of People brought to inhabite in small Roomes, whereof a great Part are seene very poore, yea, such as must liue of Begging or by worse Means, and they are heaped vp together, and in a Sort smothered with many Families of Children and Seruantes in one House or small Tenement."[60] The

---

[58] Enforcement of similar provisions, vividly described in Harrison, *Description of England*, p. 185, included such penalties as whipping, branding, or service to a responsible citizen for a year.

[59] *Analytical Indexes to Volumes II and VIII of the Series of Records Known as the Remembrancia* (London: Pardon and Son, 1870), II, 74; hereafter cited as *Remembrancia*, II; Frank Aydelotte, *Elizabethan Rogues and Vagabonds* (Oxford: Clarendon Press, 1913), p. 74.

[60] Stow, *Survey*, II, 539.

influx of the poor and the ensuing social problems, they charged, occurred because

> the multitude of newly erected tenements in Westminster, the Strand, Covent Garden, Holborn, St. Giles's, Wapping, Ratcliff, Limehouse, Southwark, and other places . . . had brought great numbers of people from other parts, especially of the poorer sort, and was a great cause of beggars and other loose persons swarming about the City, who were harboured in those out places. That by these multitudes of new erections the prices of victuals were greatly enhanced, and the greater part of the soil was conveyed with the sewers in and about the City, and so fell into the Thames.[61]

Laws against overcrowding by tenement owners proved useless: "Sir Henry Mountague, Recorder of London, . . . informed, that these Causes being infinite, this Court two years ago appointed a Commission, and by it they found three hundred faulty in this, and in four large houses they found now 8,000 inhabitants, & the last great plague 800 out of one of them died of the pest; and if it be not reformed the people cannot have food, nor can they be governed."[62]

No accurate count of the destitute was possible, though they certainly comprised more than 10 percent of the city's population and may well have reached 20 or even 30 percent.[63] Here,

---

[61] *Remembrancia*, I, 49.

[62] William Paley Baildon, ed., *Les Reportes del Cases in Camera Stellata, 1593 to 1609* (privately printed, 1894), p. 329. See also Hughes and Larkin, eds., *Tudor Royal Proclamations*, II, 466-468, and III, 245-248; James F. Larkin and Paul L. Hughes, eds., *Stuart Royal Proclamations* (Oxford: Clarendon Press, 1973), I, 47, 111, 267, 269, 398, 597; Stow, *Survey*, II, 541-542. "A brief Discoverie" complains of the

> poore and vagrante people, as there is not any sufficiente meanes of releife for the aged, impotente, and distressed inhabitantes, w$^{ch}$ is not only dangerous to his Ma$^{ties}$ Chamber the Cittie of London, but also to his Highnes royall person, to admitte such multitudes of people to continue nere the Cittie, of such lewde and evell disposiĉon, and in such confusion, w$^{th}$out any manner of controlement as now they doe (p. 126).

[63] Coleman estimates, with corroboration from other analysts, that one-half

surely, was a massive body of Londoners, with few exceptions, barred from the theater by poverty. Granted, Henry Crosse sermonized about the lure of the playhouse upon the poor, claiming, "Nay many poore pincht, needie creatures, that liue of almes, and that haue scarce neither cloath to their backe, nor foode for the belley, yet will make hard shift but they will see a Play, let wife & children begge, languish in penurie, and all they can rappe and rend, is little inough to lay vpon such vanitie."[64] If Crosse was relating the truth, however, and not merely indulging in moralistic hyperbole, his testimony was seldom supported by other witnesses.

### THE DISREPUTABLE

By contrast with the deserving poor, disreputable subjects who chose crime over privation often had both money and motive for playgoing. As indicated in the preceding chapter, whores, pimps, bawds, thieves, and the like made playhouses a standard haunt. Any catalogue of commoners in the audience had to include those reprobates, the undeserving poor. However, cutpurses, courtesans, and cozeners did not patronize the theater because they felt an overwhelming desire to see the plays but went there because they found profit among the other playgoers. The presence of such social parasites pointed toward an audience with plenty of money to be stolen or to be squandered on pleasure. A theater principally filled with struggling craftsmen and starving beggars would hardly have tempted thieves and prostitutes to ply their trades within. After all, on the open streets, they could rob or seduce common citizens without paying for the privilege.

---

to one-fourth of England's entire population lived in poverty by the Stuart period ("Labour in the English Economy," pp. 283-284). Using the authority of Gregory King, Wagner claims that half the population were poor by 1595 (*English Genealogy*, p. 176), though he and Coleman include both the working poor and the nonworking or occasionally working poor.

[64] Crosse, *Vertues Common-wealth*, Q$^v$.

Some roisterers, not seeking victims but merely looking for trouble, simply broke into the theater when they lacked the price of admission.

> To a play they will hazard to go, though with never a rag of money: where after the *second Act*, when the *Doore* is weakly guarded, they will make *forcible entrie*; a knock with a Cudgell is the worst; whereat though they grumble, they rest pacified upon their admittance. Forthwith, by violent assault and assent they aspire to the two-pennie roome; where being furnished with Tinder, Match, and a portion of decayed *Barmoodas*, they smoake it most terribly, applaude a prophane jeast unmeasurably, and in the end grow distastefully rude to all the Companie. At the Conclusion of all, they single out their *dainty Doxes*, to cloze up a fruitless day with a sinnefull evening.[65]

Even in this instance, however, the gatecrashers parodied privileged behavior—commandeering a room, smoking bogus tobacco, applauding noisily, exchanging insults, and strolling off with a harlot.

CLERICS' COMPLAINTS

In view of the harsh economic realities of the period, the references to playgoing commoners, whether respectable or not, need to be examined with particular care. If, except for parasites, few outside the ranks of the privileged had money or leisure, opportunity or inclination to attend the theaters, then why was their presence reported? For the most part, the chroniclers had fairly obvious motives. The preachers, for example, bitterly resented the superior attraction of Sunday plays over Sunday sermons. "Wyll not a fylthye playe, wyth the blast of a Trum-

---

[65] Richard Brathwaite, *Whimzies: or a New Cast of Characters* (London, 1631), pp. 134-135.

pette, sooner call thyther a thousande, than an houres tolling of a Bell, bring to the Sermon a hundred?"[66] One lamented,

> I am of that opinion, that the Lord is neuer so il serued as on the holie-daies. For then hel breakes loose. Then wee permit our youth to haue their swinge; and when they are out of the sight of their maisters, such gouernment haue they of themselues, that what by il companie they meete withal, & il examples they learne at plaies, I feare me, I feare me their harts are more alienated in two houres from virtue, than againe maie wel be amended in a whole yeare.[67]

The clear intent of such complaints was to convince the government officials that Sunday performances should be banned. Only on Sundays were most young people and working people free to come to the theaters, and only on Sundays did the theaters directly compete with the pulpits. The charge that the plays corrupted the morals of the common people and exposed the youth to dissolute company served as a powerful argument for their Sabbath suppression.

Yet even in their ardor to control Sunday sin, the clerics seldom suggested that theaters were entirely filled with commoners. Out of all the Puritan diatribes, the only specific reference to vulgar patrons came from Gosson, who called "the common people which resorte to Theaters . . . but ā assemblie of Tailers, Tinkers, Cordwayners, Saylers, olde Men, yong Men, Women, Boyes, Girles, and such like."[68] But in the context of his argument, Gosson was claiming that rude and foolish commoners in an audience were unfit to judge the faults or rebuke the manners presented on the stage; he certainly did not rule out the presence of more discerning and judiciously educated

---

[66] John Stockwood, *A Sermon Preached at Paules Cross* (London, 1578), pp. 23-24.

[67] [Anthony Munday], *A Second and Third Blast of Retrait from Plaies and Theaters*, in *The English Drama and Stage*, ed. W. C. Hazlitt (1869; reprint ed., New York: Burt Franklin, n.d.), pp. 134-135.

[68] Gosson, *Playes Confuted*, p. 184.

men, men who were not of "the common people." Besides, he
directed his appeal to cleanse the Augean stable of the theater
at Sir Francis Walsingham, as the only "Hercules in the Court,
whom the roare of the enimy cā neuer daunt," and followed
it with an epistle "To the Rightworshipful Gentlemen and students, of both Vniversities, and the Innes of Court."[69] Apparently Gosson knew whom he had to convince if plays were to
be reformed.

No doubt the affluent shared the playhouses on Sunday with
a sizable number of ordinary folk, but the audiences do not
seem to have been entirely plebeian. Significantly, once plays
were proscribed on Sunday, the number of sermons against
their wicked effects upon the general populace declined notably.
After 1586, Puritan diatribes like *Histrio-Mastrix* directed
themselves at more aristocratic playgoers, such as the Inns of
Court men. Moralizers still resented the fact that "More haue
recourse to Playing houses, then to Praying houses."[70] But commoners who continued to be mentioned were principally thieves,
bawds, and whores—a group, as already noted, attracted by the
money in the patrons' pockets rather than by the plays themselves. Moreover, the Puritans' association of playgoing with
"ydlenes, vnthriftynes, whordom, wantonnes, drunkennes, and
what not" also pointed to their awareness of the theater as one
of several pursuits requiring money and leisure: "poundes and
hundreds can be well ynough afforded, in following these least
pleasures."[71]

CITY FATHERS' COMPLAINTS

Though the ministers eased their complaints against plebeian
playgoers, officials of the City of London refused to be silent.
They were concerned not with promoting larger audiences for

[69] Ibid., pp. 161, 162.
[70] I. H., *This World's Folly*; as cited by Chambers, *Elizabethan Stage*, IV,
254.
[71] Philip Stubbes, *The Anatomie of Abuses* (London, 1583), p. x; John Feilde,

sermons on Sundays and holy days but with preserving order every day of the week. Moreover, they faced two enclaves of power as rivals to the ancient authority of the City: the Privy Council and the burgeoning suburban counties. With the playhouses located in the immunity of the suburbs and the troupes protected by their courtier patrons, the dramatic enterprises provided a natural target for the London Council. A stream of petitions urging action against the theaters flowed to Court. In all of them, the audience was characterized in low terms. After all, if the council could brand the playhouses as haunts for criminals, snares for working folk, centers of rebellion, and nests of disease, then the City ban on playing could prevail throughout the metropolitan area. Only the Court would remain immune. This is not to suggest that political pique played the chief role in the council's complaints. Some of their objections no doubt had substance. But to accept at face value the London fathers' derogatory description of the audience is to miss their fairly obvious bias.

The documents that moved from City to Court dealt chiefly with closing the theaters in plague time and at Lent and with complaints of disorder. The communication between the Lord Mayor and the Lord Chancellor on 12 April 1580 mentioned "assembles of Cittizens and their families" and the "great corruption of youthe with vnchast and wicked matters, occasion of muche incontinence, practises of many ffrayes, querrells, and other disorders and inconueniences bisid that the assemble of terme and parliament being at hand."[72] It is hard to see how the plays could have brought danger to those in town for the term or for Parliament unless people with legal or legislative business attended the plays. And as for the frays, quarrels, and disorders, they were not restricted to the lower social orders. The men arrested for fighting with the players the very next

---

*A Godly Exhortation, by Occasion of the Late Iudgement of God, Shewed at Parris-Garden, the Thirteenth Day of Ianuarie* (London, 1583), B$_4$$^v$-B$_5$.

[72] *Malone Society Collections*, I, 46; Chambers, *Elizabethan Stage*, IV, 279.

year were "a dysordered companye of gentlemen of the Innes of Courte."[73] The youths and citizens mentioned by the Lord Mayor could have been anybody.

As the period progressed and the complaints were consistently ignored by the Privy Council, the catalogue of vulgar, troublesome playgoers and their offenses grew longer and longer, with each new phrase achieving a permanent place in the developing litany. "Seruantes and children" who should not "be absent from their parentes and masters attendance and presence" on late holiday evenings were added in 1582, followed shortly by "many poore people" and "the basist sort of people."[74] By 1592, the theater attracted "prentizes and seruants withdrawen from their woorks," as well as "great numbers of light & lewd disposed persons, as harlotts, cutpurses, cuseners, pilferers, & such lyke."[75] When "all maisterlesse men who lyve idelie in the Cyttye without any lawfull calling" received mention in orders sent down from the Privy Council to the mayor and aldermen, the City officials immediately began to include them in the audience, as "vagrant persons & maisterles men that hang about the Citie."[76] In 1595, the language referred to "the refuse sort of evill disposed & vngodly people," along with "vagabond persons that haunt the high waies to meet together & to recreate themselfes."[77]

By 1597, the catalogue was complete. In a final grand salvo, the Lord Mayor and the alderman repeated the entire list:

Amonge other inconveniences it is not the least that they

[73] 11 July 1581; Chambers, *Elizabethan Stage*, IV, 282.

[74] Lord Mayor to Privy Council, 13 April 1582; *Orders . . . for Releefe of the Poore*, ? Autumn 1582; Lord Mayor to Sir Francis Walsingham, 3 May 1583; *Malone Society Collections*, I, 54, 63; Chambers, *Elizabethan Stage*, IV, 288, 291, 294.

[75] Lord Mayor to Archbishop Whitgift, 25 February 1592; *Malone Society Collections*, I, 68; Chambers, *Elizabethan Stage*, IV, 307.

[76] Ca. July-October 1594; Lord Mayor to Lord Burghley, 3 November 1594; *Malone Society Collections*, I, 206, 211, 74, respectively; Chambers, *Elizabethan Stage*, IV, 315-316, 317.

[77] Lord Mayor to Privy Council, 13 September 1595; *Malone Society Collections*, I, 76; Chambers, *Elizabethan Stage*, IV, 318.

give opportunity to the refuze sort of euill disposed & vngodly
people, that are within and abowte this Cytie, to assemble
themselves & to make their matches for all their lewd &
vngodly practices; being as heartofore wee haue fownd by
th'examination of divers apprentices & other seruantes whoe
have confessed vnto vs that the said Staige playes were the
very places of theire Randevous appoynted by them to meete
with such otheir as wear to ioigne with them in theire designes
& mutinus attemptes, beeinge allso the ordinarye places for
maisterles men to come together & to recreate themselves.
. . .

    1. They are a speaciall cause of currupting their Youth.
. . . Whearby such as frequent them, beinge of the base &
refuze sort of people or such young gentlemen as haue small
regard of credit or conscience, drawe the same into imitacion
and not the avoidinge the like vices which they represent.

    2. They are the ordinary places for vagrant persons, Mais-
terles men, thieves, horse stealers, whoremongers, Coozeners,
Conycatchers, contrivers of treason, and other idele and daungerous persons to meet together & to make theire matches
to the great displeasure of Almightie God & the hurt & an-
noyance of her Maiesties people, which cannot be prevented
nor discovered by the Gouernours of the Citie for that they
are owt of the Citiees iurisdiction.

    3. They maintaine idlenes in such persons as haue no vo-
cation & draw apprentices and other seruantes from theire
ordinary workes and all sortes of people from the resort vnto
sermons and other Christian exercises, to the great hinderence
of traides & prophanation of religion established by her
highnes within this Realm.

    4. In the time of sicknes it is fownd by experience, that
many hauing sores and yet not hart sicke take occasion hearby
to walk abroad & to recreat themselves by heareinge a play.
Whearby others are infected, and them selves also many
things miscarry.[78]

[78] Lord Mayor and aldermen to Privy Council, 13 September 1595; *Malone
Society Collections*, I, 78; Chambers, *Elizabethan Stage*, IV, 321-322.

After this massive complaint, the Privy Council issued an order to have the playhouses pulled down. However, the order coincided with the scandalous *Isle of Dogs*, for which Pembroke's Men were arrested and punished, and thus may be attributed as much to the general air of outrage as to the validity of the City's lengthy objections. In any case, the order was never carried out, and performances resumed again before the three-month restraint against playing had expired. A compromise, restricting the companies to two and playing to twice a week, was worked out that fall—though not observed.[79]

The flow of complaints continued intermittently after 1597 but stopped almost entirely with the accession of James. With the companies firmly under royal, rather than just noble, protection, the City officials fell silent, save for the usual Lenten and plague restrictions or support of an occasional petition from titled citizens.[80] Even when direct jurisdiction over the royal enclaves of Blackfriars and Whitefriars was granted to the City of London in 1608, the mayor and aldermen did not shut down any private playhouse located there. After the deposition of Charles I, however, they moved immediately against their old enemy, the theater, and closed the playhouses for eighteen years.

What is to be made of the council's image of the playgoers? First, their testimony was severely biased. In order to get any cooperation from the powerful aristocrats of the Privy Council

[79] Privy Council Minutes, 19 February 1598, 22 June 1600, 31 December 1601, 31 March 1602; John Roche Dasent, ed., *Acts of the Privy Council, 1542-1604* (London: Stationery Office, 1890-1964), XXVIII, 327; XXX, 395, 411; XXXII, 466, 488; Chambers, *Elizabethan Stage*, IV, 325, 329-335. For the best analysis of the 1597 order, see Glynne Wickham, "The Privy Council Order of 1597 for the Destruction of All London's Theatres," in *The Elizabethan Theatre*, ed. David Galloway (Toronto: Archon Books, 1970), pp. 21-44. It may be of some significance too that both London and the Privy Council were desperately trying to cope with the effects of the continuing dearth. See Appleby, *Famine*, pp. 138-145.

[80] Walter de Gray Birch, *The Historical Charters and Constitutional Documents of the City of London* (London: Whiting, 1887), pp. 144-145.

(themselves the patrons of the companies), the London officials had to make complaints as harsh as possible. Second, their descriptions of the audience were flatly contradicted by other contemporary data. While whores, thieves, apprentices, rogues, and the idle poor were sometimes present at the plays, so were other sorts of people, as the preceding analysis has indicated—and as even the council occasionally admitted. Third, the London governors were quick to seize upon any unfavorable event and turn it to their own purposes. One fray or riot on the record became translated into constant disorder. A spate of conycatching pamphlets or a statute against vagrant and masterless men provided a new category for the composition of the audience. Fourth, the real point here was the ineffectiveness of the complaints. Had there truly been huge daily assemblies of the destitute, the criminal, the traitorous, the plague-ridden, and the vagrant, such gatherings would have been promptly suppressed. The Privy Council's inaction was a good indication that such persons never constituted more than a fraction of the audience and that the wellborn councilors knew it.

### DISORDERS AND DISTURBANCES

A number of incidents that never took place in theater audiences were used at the time to denounce the playgoers or have been used since that time to identify the playgoers. The famous collapse of Paris Garden on a Sunday in 1583 was one such incident. All the casualties were ordinary citizens: a fellmonger, a baker, several servants, a waterbearer's daughter. The same people present at a baiting ring on Sunday would not necessarily have been present at a playhouse on a working day. Nonetheless, ministers seized upon the occasion to deliver harsh attacks against the theaters. "For surely it is to be feared, besides the distruction bothe of bodye and soule, that many are brought vnto, by frequenting the *Theater*, the *Curtin* and such like, if one day those places wyl likewise be cast downe by God himselfe, & with thē a huge heape of such contempners & prophane persons vtterly killed & spoyled in their bodies."[81]

Another much exploited incident occurred in 1584, the year after the Paris Garden collapse. It began one Monday afternoon, not in the audience at all but "very nere the Theatre or Curten at the tyme of the Playes." A young gentleman kicked a sleeping apprentice, insults were exchanged, and finally a pitched battle between apprentices and gentlemen broke out. Neither the original conflict nor the various "mutines and assembles" of the apprentices the following day occurred at the playhouses. As for the climax on Wednesday, the record bears careful examination:

> Vpon Weddensdaye one Browne, a serving man in a blew coat, a shifting fellowe having a perrelous witt of his owne, entending a spoile if he cold have browght it to passe, did at Theatre doore querell with certen poore boyes, handicraft prentises, and strook some of theym, and lastlie he with his sword wondend and maymed one of the boyes vpon the left hand; where vpon there assembled nere a ml. people.[82]

Browne may have been a servingman of some privilege, since he carried a sword. No one specified whether Browne, the apprentices, or the "ml. people" were inside or outside the playhouse, or whether it was time for a performance, though such a rapid congregation of a crowd would make this supposition likely. In any case, none of the commoners involved in the disturbance could definitely be placed in the audience, and most of them were clearly outside the theater. Yet afterwards the City officials exaggerated and interpreted the incident to charge the playhouses with fomenting disorder. Writing a few years later, Henry Chettle probably came nearer the truth:

> And lette . . . the yoong people of the Cittie, either abstaine . . . altogether from playes, or at their comming thither to

[81] Feilde, *Godly Exhortation*, C[5]ᵛ.

[82] William Fleetwood to Lord Burghley, 18 June 1584; *Malone Society Collections*, I, 163; Chambers, *Elizabethan Stage*, IV, 297.

vse themselues after a more quiet order. . . . The beginners are neither gentlemen, nor citizens, nor any of both their seruants, but some lewd mates that long for innouation; & when they see aduantage that either Seruingmen or Apprentises are most in number, they will be of either side, though indeed they are of no side, but men beside all honestie, willing to make boote of cloakes, hats, purses, or what euer they can lay holde on in a hurley burley. These are the common causes of discord in publike places.[83]

Ambiguity also surrounded another disorder involving common citizens in June of 1592. When a feltmaker's servant was imprisoned upon a false charge, his fellow workers decided to take action: "For rescuing of whome the sayd companies assembled themselves by occasion & pretence of their meeting at a play, which bysides the breach of the Sabboth day giveth opportunitie of committing these & such lyke disorders."[84] Three things seem noteworthy about this statement. First, it was Sunday, when no work had to be performed; second, there was no way to tell whether the feltmakers actually attended the play or simply joined the crowd near the theater; third, the lowborn rioters did not assemble because they wanted to see a dramatic performance. Whatever the situation, no disorder erupted until eight o'clock that night, long after the play, when the Lord Mayor himself and one of the sheriffs were called to Southwark to disperse "great multitudes of people assembled togither."[85] The Privy Council sensibly responded by shutting down all public entertainments throughout the London area until after the midsummer holiday as a precaution against a repeat of the disturbances.[86] Their action would indicate that

---

[83] Henry Chettle, *Kind-Harts Dreame*, in *The Shakspere Allusion-Book*, ed. C. M. Ingleby, rev. John Munro (London; Oxford University Press, 1932), I, 65.

[84] Lord Mayor to Lord Burghley, 12 June 1592; *Malone Society Collections*, I, 70, 187; Chambers, *Elizabethan Stage*, IV, 310.

[85] Ibid.

[86] Privy Council Minute, 23 June 1592; Dasent, ed., *Acts of the Privy Council*, XXII, 549; Chambers, *Elizabethan Stage*, IV, 310-311.

large numbers of apprentices and other workers could not gather at the playhouses for any purpose except when they were at liberty on Sundays and holidays.

Further substantiation for such a conclusion derived from the reign of James I, when the apprentices "or rather the unruly people of the suburbs"[87] rioted on Shrove Tuesday in 1617. Among the various accounts of the disorders, one in the State Papers provided the greatest detail concerning the damage to the Cockpit:

> The Prentizes on Shrove Tewsday last, to the nomber of 3. or 4000 comitted extreame insolencies; part of this nomber, taking their course for Wapping, did there pull downe to the grownd 4 houses, spoiled all the goods there-in, defaced many others, & a Justice of the Peace coming to appease them, while he was reading a Proclamacion, had his head broken with a brick batt. Th' other part, making for Drury Lane, where lately a newe playhouse is erected, they besett the house round, broke in, wounded divers of the players, broke open their trunckes, & what apparrell, bookes, or other things they found, they burnt & cutt in peeces; & not content herewith, gott on the top of the house, & untiled it, & had not the Justices of Peace & Shrerife levied an aide, & hindred their purpose, they would have laid that house likewise even with the ground. In this skyrmishe one prentise was slaine, being shott throughe the head with a pistoll, & many other of their fellowes were sore hurt, & such of them as are taken his Majestie hath commaunded shal be executed for example sake.[88]

John Chamberlain reported that three were shot and several others hurt by the besieged actors.[89] Along with the unfortunate

[87] John Chamberlain to Sir Dudley Carleton, 8 March 1617; Norman E. McClure, ed., *The Letters of John Chamberlain* (Philadelphia: American Philosophical Society, 1939), II, 59.

[88] Halliwell-Phillipps's transcription of a letter from State Papers in the Public Records Office, dated "8th Marche, 1616" by Edward Sherburne; Bentley, *Jacobean and Caroline Stage*, VI, 54.

[89] 8 March 1617; Thomas Birch, *The Court and Times of James The First* (London: H. Colburn, 1849), I, 464; Bentley, *Jacobean and Caroline Stage*, I,

Cockpit, the holiday mob also attacked "many victualing houses, and . . . all other houses which they suspected to bee bawdie houses,"[90] including that of the famous Madam Leake. Subsequently, the notorious affair was satirized in the Inner Temple's Christmas revels.

> Stand forth *Shrouetuesday*, one 'a the silenc'st Bricke-
>     Layers,
> Tis in your charge to pull downe Bawdyhouses,
> To set your Tribe aworke, cause spoyle in *Shorditch*,
> And made a Dangerous Leake there, deface Turnbul,
> And tickle Codpiece Rowe, ruine the Cockpit, the
> Poore Players ne're thriued in't, a my Cõscience some
> Queane pist vpon the first Bricke.[91]

Most assuredly the poor players never thrived from rowdies like the Shrove Tuesday crew. The following year the apprentices purportedly sent out a call to meet at the Fortune, not to enjoy a play, but "to rase and pull downe" the Fortune, the Red Bull, and the Phoenix[92]—hardly the acts of dedicated theatergoers. Rather than regular patrons they behaved like outcasts, raging against expensive pleasures denied to them. Nonetheless, the playhouses were still branded as the fomenters of tumult among the masses, at least by the London council. Following the plague closures in 1625, the council recommended that the theaters remain closed: "But wee are of opinion that yf may bee given to contynue plaies, it wilbe a meanes to drawe together a great concourse of people, and that of the meaner and lewder sorte, who there make matches and appointe theire meeting places, and so consequently to indanger the renvinge & dis-

---

161-162. See also Privy Council to Lord Mayor, 4 March 1617; *Malone Society Collections*, I, 374; Bentley, *Jacobean and Caroline Stage*, I, 161.

[90] Stow, *Annales* (1631), p. 1,026. Stow describes the culprits as "many disordered persons of sundry kindes, amongst whom were very many young boyes, and lads."

[91] Thomas Middleton, *Inner-Temple Masque, or Masque of Heroes* (London, 1619), $B_3{}^v$.

[92] Privy Council to Lieutenants of Middlesex, 12 February 1618; *Malone Society Collections*, I, iv-v, 377; Bentley, *Jacobean and Caroline Stage*, I, 163.

persinge of the sicknes, w^ch (blessed bee god) is nowe in a manner totally abated w^thin this Citty."[93] Their attitude and argument had changed very little in twenty years.

Two events in 1626 received attention. The first, occurring on 16 May, was characterized as a "daungerous and great ryott" but was considerably less than that. Apparently some sailors got into a fight at the Fortune and managed to assault both a constable, Francis Foster, and a resident at the playhouse named Thomas Faulkner. One of the sailors, Thomas Alderson, "joyninge with the rest of the Riotters in beatinge and assaultinge of Thomas Faulkener . . . and beinge charged in the Kinges name to yeelde and keepe the peace hee saide hee cared not for the Kinge, for the Kinge paide them noe wages and . . . further sayinge hee would bringe the whole Navy thither, to pull downe the playehouse." Arrests promptly followed, as did rescue attempts. A fellow sailor named Richard Margrave was picked up "for publishinge certaine discoveries of an intended assemblie at the Beare Garden, for revenge of an injurye done to a saylor." Two days later, on 18 May, one Patrick Gray again disturbed the Fortune by "callinge to his fellow-saylors to knocke them all downe that were present." Another seaman threatened that if "the saylers were not putt in a stronger then the New Prison, they would all be fetched out before the next morowe." Finally, a seafarer named William Collison climaxed the afternoon's events by "assaultinge and strikinge of Edward Heather the Headboroughe."[94] Here was the familiar pattern of idle commoners, a real or imagined grievance, a fight, arrests, rescue attempts, and violence against the playhouse. Even though the sailors at the Fortune that first day may have come merely for amusement on an empty afternoon, their friends who attended two days later had not come to enjoy a play. It should also be pointed out again that sailors on shore constituted one of the few groups of ordinary citizens who had both money and free afternoons.

[93] B. M. Egerton MS 2623, fol. 30; as cited by Bentley, *Jacobean and Caroline Stage*, II, 656.

[94] Jeaffreson, ed., *Middlesex County Records*, III, 161-163; Bentley, *Jacobean and Caroline Stage*, VI, 160-161.

Sailors, apprentices, and other commoners took part in the events surrounding the death of Dr. Lamb, following his visit to the Fortune on 13 June 1626. However, only Lambe, the charlatan conjurer and a hated associate of Buckingham, was actually present at the performance.

> On Friday evening, June 13, Dr. Lamb having been at a playhouse, as he was coming thence, some boys and such like began to quarrel with and affront him, calling him the *duke's devil*, and in such sort, that he hired some sailors and others that he gathered to guard him home. He came in at Moorgate, and the people following him. He supped at a cook's shop, where the people watched him, whilst his guard defended him from their violence. Thence he goes to the Windmill Tavern, in Lothbury, the tumult still increasing. At length, as he came thence, the people set upon him. He flies to another house, where they threw stones, and threatened to pull down the house, unless Lamb were delivered to them. The master of the house, a lawyer, fearing what might ensue, wisely sends for four constables to guard him out of his house. But the rage of the people so much increased (no man can tell why or what cause) that in the midst of these auxiliaries they struck him down to the ground, giving him divers blows and wounds, and quite beat out one of his eyes. Thus being left half dead, and in such a case, that he never spoke after he was carried to the Compter, in the Poultry (no other house being willing to receive him) where the next morning he ended a wretched life.[95]

Amid the sensationalism of the murder, it was easy to associate the entire mob with the theater. In actual fact, only the victim—

[95] Joseph Mead to Sir Martin Stuteville, 21 June 1626; Thomas Birch, *The Court and Times of Charles the First* (London: H. Colburn, 1848), I, 364-365. For other accounts of the murder, see Sir Francis Nethersole to Queen of Bohemia, 19 June 1626, in *Calendar of State Papers, Domestic, of the Reign of Charles I* (London: Longmans, Green, Reader, and Dyer, 1858-1897), III (1628-1629), p. 169; *A Brief Description of the notorious Life of Iohn Lambe* . . . (Amsterdam, 1628), C$_3$$^v$; "The Tragedy of Doctor *Lambe*," in *A Pepysian Garland*, ed. Hyder Edward Rollins (Cambridge: Cambridge University Press, 1922), pp. 278-282; Bentley, *Jacobean and Caroline Stage*, I, 267-268.

a man enjoying privilege, if not popularity—had spent his afternoon at the Fortune. The others stood outside on the streets, taking their violent pleasure for free.

The congregation of unruly riffraff on the streets surrounding the theaters may have been rather common by the time Dr. Lamb was killed. Residents near the theaters went so far as to complain about the ruffians who showed up after the performances. A petition of 1631 claimed that "many disorderly people towards night gathered thither, under pretence of attending and waiting for those at the playes."[96] Though the petition advanced a wide range of strong arguments for closing the playhouses, it placed the troublemakers outside the theater, not inside.

All the disturbances associated with the theater should be viewed in the context of other similar incidents of the period, for they were not isolated occurrences. A so-called "Insurrection" of apprentices against the Dutch and French in 1586 resulted in the arrest of several plasterers, all under the age of twenty-one.[97] In 1593, more than two thousand apprentices revolted against the foreigners in London, and in 1595 a smaller but similar revolt burst out against the same group in Southwark.[98] When several poor tradesmen rioted against strangers (anyone from a parish outside London) in June of 1595, some of their "Fellow-Apprentices and Servants gathered in a Body, and attempted to break open the *Compter*" to free "some young Rioters" under arrest. Twenty more were arrested for their trouble.[99] Because of the continuing bad harvests, the year 1595 was particularly difficult. Stow reported the June disturbance in some detail. "Some prentices and other young people about the City of London, being pinched of their victuals, more then

[96] John P. Collier, *The History of English Dramatic Poetry to the Time of Shakespeare* (London: G. Bell and Sons, 1879), I, 456; Bentley, *Jacobean and Caroline Stage*, VI, 24.

[97] Stow, *Survey*, II, 405.

[98] Joan Evans, "Huguenot Goldsmiths in England and Ireland," *Huguenot Society Proceedings* 14 (1929-1933): 499. Such hostilities had been occurring at least since the May Day riot against the Flemish in 1517 (p. 496).

[99] Stow, *Survey*, II, 407.

they had been accustomed, tooke from the market people in Southwarke, butter for their money, paying for the same but three pence the pound, whereas the owners would haue had 5. pence." The youths were whipped, set in the pillory, and imprisoned. Two days later, "The 29. of June, being Sunday in the afternoone, a number of vnruly youths on the Tower hill" threw stones at the warders and created such disorder that the Lord Mayor himself appeared to clear the hill and the Queen sent armed men into the streets. Five of the youths arrested on Tower Hill were executed on 24 July 1595.[100] Less severe measures sometimes quelled trouble. On 24 September 1590, for example, the Queen imposed a 9:00 P.M. curfew for six days on all apprentices, journeymen, and their families because of "a very great outrage lately committed by some apprentices and others being masterless men and vagrant persons in and about the suburbs of the city of London, in assaulting of the house of Lincolns Inn, and the breaking and spoiling of divers chambers in the said house."[101]

Several common features applied to all these disturbances, including those connected with the theater. First, the people involved were either young or unemployed—rebellious perhaps as a release to high spirits, resentment, or idleness. Thomas Nashe declared that the City masters "heartily wishe they might bee troubled with none of their youth nor their prentises; for some of them (I meane the ruder handicrafts seruants) neuer come abroad, but they are in danger of vndoing."[102] His charge was not entirely unjustified. Second, while the depredations may have caused considerable property loss, the rioters themselves seldom spent money for the risky excitement of making trouble. Disturbances generally occurred on the streets, where a crowd could assemble and a swift escape was possible. Third, much of the action, especially any counterattack or rescue effort, took place on a Sunday or a holiday, the only times when large

---

[100] Stow, *Annales* (1631), pp. 769-770.

[101] Hughes and Larkin, eds., *Tudor Royal Proclamations*, III, 60.

[102] Thomas Nashe, *Pierce Penilesse*, in *The Complete Works*, ed. R. B. McKerrow (London: Sidgwick and Jackson, 1910), II, 214.

numbers of commoners had liberty. The Venetian ambassador noted that "The little devils are the apprentices, alias shopboys, who, on two days of the year, which prove fatal to them, Shrove Tuesday and the first of May, are so riotous and outrageous, that in a body, three or four thousand strong, they go committing excesses in every direction, killing human beings and demolishing houses."[103] Shrove Tuesday or May Day behavior, however, could not be an everyday event. Finally, the fury of the rioters was apparently directed at targets of resentment: foreigners, food sellers, officers of the law, attorneys, swindlers, bawdy houses, and theaters. The rebels lashed out at strangers who undercut the guild system, at farmers who charged exorbitant prices in hard times, at warders who imprisoned their fellows, at seats of privilege like the Inns of Court, at centers of costly pleasures like the brothels. Had the theaters truly been prime sources of entertainment for the masses, as some have suggested, then the attack on Shrove Tuesday would appear pointless. Why destroy a favored haunt? More likely, the vandals were assaulting theaters, bawdy houses, and taverns as pleasures too costly for a poor man or a mere apprentice to enjoy. All things considered, the riots seem to augur against the likelihood that the "baser sort" came to the playhouses regularly or in large numbers.

### VIOLENCE IN THE AUDIENCE

Other kinds of disturbances, however, did attest to the presence of at least a few plebeians in the audience. The recognizances taken before the magistrates of Middlesex contained a sprinkling of charges for disorderly conduct at the Red Bull and Fortune, which were both located in that county. For example, in May of 1610, a yeoman named William Tedcastle, and four feltmakers—John Fryne, Edward Brian, Edward Purfett, and Thomas Williams—were called to answer for a "notable outrage att the Playhowse called the Redd Bull." The next year, 1611,

---

[103] "Diaries and Despatches of the Venetian Embassy at the Court of King James I, in the Years 1617, 1618," *Quarterly Review* 102 (1857): 413-414.

two butchers, Ralph Brewyn and John Lynsey, were charged "for abusinge certen gentlemen at the playhouse called The Fortune." A more serious incident occurred in 1614, when a yeoman, Richard Bradley, "assaulted Nicholas Bestney junior gentleman, and with a knife gave him two grievous wounds, by stabbing him with the said weapon in the first place on the right breast, and then in the left part of his belly, of which two wounds the said Nicholas languished and still remains in danger of death."[104] In both the latter two instances, gentlemen, the unlucky victims, were obviously present alongside the yeoman and craftsmen.

An act of common violence may have caused the death of "George Wilson kild at ye play house in salesburie court." Since his name did not bear the gentlemanly prefix of "Mr.," Wilson was perhaps an ordinary citizen. One Thomas Jacob was arrested "for committing a greate disorder in the Red Bull playhouse and for assaultinge and beating divers persons there" in 1638. And in that same year, a silkweaver named Thomas Pinnocke had to answer "for menacing and threatening to pull down the Redbull playhouse and strikinge divers people with a great cudgell as he went along the streets,"[105] though again it was not clear that the angry weaver actually attended the Red Bull.

When added together, the number of disturbances involving plebeian theatergoers was remarkably small for a span of almost seven decades. If the playhouses filled up each day with common citizens ever ready to break out in violence, as the City fathers claimed, then the civil records should have reflected that fact. Instead, the records noted an occasional ruffian who broke up the performance with noise and fists, sometimes to the peril of the gentlemen spectators.

PLAYWRIGHTS' COMPLAINTS

The City council and the exaggerated notoriety of violent incidents were not the only sources perpetuating the idea of base

[104] Jeaffreson, ed., *Middlesex County Records*, II, 64-65, 71, 88.
[105] Burial Register, St. Bride's Church, Guildhall MS 6538; as cited by

stinkards as spectators. The playwrights themselves often referred to their audiences in low terms. They variously scorned "the Rout," "the thick-brayn'd Audience," and "Peny Stinkards."[106] However, the playwrights rather consistently degraded their detractors and elevated their supporters. William Fennor expressed the attitude typical of a poet whose creation was hissed from the stage.

> Yet to the multitude it nothing shewed;
> They screwed their scurvy iawes and look't awry,
> Like hissing snakes adiudging it to die:
> When wits of gentry did applaud the same,
> With Siluer shouts of high lowd sounding fame:
> Whil'st vnderstanding grounded men contemn'd it,
> And wanting wit (like fooles to iudge) condemn'd it.
> Clapping, or hissing, is the only meane
> That tries and searches out a well writ Sceane.
> So is it thought by *Ignoramus* crew,
> But that good wits acknowledge's vntrue;
> The stinckards oft will hisse without a cause,
> And for a baudy ieast will giue applause.
> Let one but aske the reason why they roare
> They'l answere, cause the rest did so before.
> But leauing these who for their iust reward,
> Shall gape, and gaze, amongst the fooles in th'yard.[107]

The bitterness Fennor described was rivaled, if not surpassed, by that of Dekker, who regularly reviled "The Stinkards speaking all things, yet no man vnderstanding any thing."[108] He sneered at "*Tearme* times, when the *Two-peny Clients,* and

---

Bentley, *Jacobean and Caroline Stage,* VI, 99; Jeaffreson, ed. *Middlesex County Records,* III, 168.

[106] Sir Aston Cokayne's "Praeludium" for Richard Brome's *Five New Plays,* in *The Dramatic Works of Richard Brome* (London: John Pearson, 1873), I, A$_2$; Michael Drayton, "The Sacrifice to Apollo," in *The Works of Michael Drayton,* ed. J. William Hebel (Oxford: Shakespeare Head Press, 1961), II, 358; Dekker, *Work for Armourers,* in *Non-Dramatic Works,* IV, 96.

[107] William Fennor, *Fennors Descriptions* (London, 1616), B$_2$$^v$.

[108] Dekker, *Strange Horserace,* in *Non-Dramatic Works,* III, 340.

*Peny Stinkards* swarme together to heere the *Stagerites*,"[109] even though the kinds of Englishmen attracted to London during the law terms would scarcely have been "Peny Stinkards" and might not have been mere "Two-peny Clients" either. But some distortion could perhaps be expected from a man who titled a play *If This Be not a Good Play, the Devil's in It* and opened it with the following prologue:

> But tis with *Poets* now, as tis with Nations,
> Th'il fauouredst *Vices*, are the brauest *Fashions*.
> A Play whose *Rudenes, Indians* would abhorre,
> Ift fill a house with Fishwiues, *Rare, They All Roare*.
> It is not Praise is sought for (Now) but *Pence*,
> Tho dropd, from Greasie-apron *Audience*.
> Clapd may he bee with *Thunder*, that plucks *Bayes*,
> With such *Foule Hands*, and with *Squint-Eyes* does gaze
> On *Pallas Shield*. . . .
> . . . . . . . . . . . . . . . . . . . . . . . . . . . . . . . . . . . . . . . . . . . . . . .
> . . . Giue me *That Man*,
> Who . . .
> . . . . . . . . . . . . . . . . . . . . . . . . . . . . . . . . . . . . . . . . . . . . . . .
> Can draw with *Adamantine Pen*, (euen creatures
> Forg'de out of th'*Hammer*,) on tiptoe, to *Reach-vp*,
> And (from *Rare silence*) clap their *Brawny hands*,
> T'*Applaud*, what their *charmd* soule scarce vnderstands.[110]

According to Dekker, it was contemptible to aim for any audience but the highest in intellect and aesthetic sensibility. Greasy aprons should not be basely courted but should be charmed in spite of their ignorance.

Dekker was not the only playwright who charged brawny auditors with a lack of brains. Shakespeare remarked upon "the groundlings, who for the most part are capable of nothing but inexplicable dumb shows and noise."[111] Jonson, too, lashed out at "the rude barbarous crue, a people that haue no braines, and

---

[109] Dekker, *Work for Armourers*, in ibid., IV, 96.

[110] Dekker, *If This Be not a Good Play*, in *Dramatic Works*, III, 121-122.

[111] William Shakespeare, *Hamlet* (III, ii), in *The Complete Works*, ed. Alfred Harbage (Baltimore: Penguin Books, 1969), p. 952.

yet grounded iudgements, these will hisse any thing that mounts aboue their grounded capacities."[112] Of course, to his critics, Jonson's lack of popularity looked rather different. Instead of blaming it on a low, ignorant audience, they suggested he had aimed too high in trying to please the Blackfriars with fare like *The Magnetic Lady*, when the play was really suitable only for "prentizes and apell-wyfes":

Is this your loade-stone, Ben, that must attract
Applause and laughter att each scaene and acte?
Is this the childe of your bed-ridden witt,
An none but the Blacke-friers foster ytt?
If to the Fortune you had sent your ladye
Mongst prentizes and apell-wyfes, ytt may bee
Your rosie foole might haue some sport haue gott,
With his strang habitt and indiffinett nott:
But when as silkes and plush, and all the witts
Are calde to see, and censure as befitts,
And yff your follye take not, they, perchance,
Must here them selfes stilde, gentle ignorance.
Foh! how ytt stinckes! what generall offence
Giues thy prophanes, and grosse impudence![113]

By contrast, the friends of a playwright like John Fletcher consoled him for the failure of *The Faithful Shepherdess*, telling him that only the ignorant commoners disliked it.

This play was never liked, unlesse by few
That brought their judgements with um, for of late
First the infection, then the common prate
Of common people, have such customes got
Either to silence plaies, or like them not.[114]

---

[112] Jonson, *The Case Is Altered*, in *Ben Jonson*, III, 137.

[113] Alexander Gill's verses on *The Magnetic Lady*, in Anthony Wood, *Athenae Oxoniensis* (Hildesheim: Georg Olms, 1969), II, 598.

[114] Sir Walter Aston, "Commendatory Verses," in *The Dramatic Works in the Beaumont and Fletcher Canon*, ed. Fredson Bowers (Cambridge: Cambridge University Press, 1966-1979), III, 493.

Thomas Carew similarly assured William Davenant that "men great and good / Haue by the Rabble beene misunderstood."[115] Thus the plebeian playgoer became identified with the ignorant playgoer, and the ignorant playgoer, with anyone who applauded an enemy's work or hissed one's own or a friend's work. Such aggrieved pride, while understandable, hardly constituted indisputable evidence for an audience of commoners.

In the same vein, writers sometimes accused the actors of catering to London's lowest. Dekker said they would "basely prostitute themselues to the pleasures of euery two-penny drunken *Plebian*," and were "glad to play three houres for two pence to the basest stinkard in Londō."[116] He thought it contemptible that "their houses smoakt euery after noone with Stinkards who were so glewed together in crowdes with the Steames of strong breath, that when they came foorth, their faces lookt as if they had beene per boyld."[117] Gainsford filled in a few more details of the vain actor's courtship of the mob: "Player is much out of countenance, if fooles doe not laugh at them, boyes clappe their hands, pesants ope their throates, and the rude raskal rabble cry excellent, excellent."[118] No doubt there were stinkards, fools, boys, and peasants in the theater, but the patent resentment of writers such as these should caution anyone against assuming the entire audience was no more than a "rude raskal rabble."

Nor can the testimony of rival troupes and theaters be accepted uncritically. During the War of the Theaters, the boys charged that a refined spectator would be "pasted against the

---

[115] Sir William Davenant, *The Just Italian* (London, 1630), A$_{[4]}$. See also Beaumont and Fletcher, "Prologue" to *The Coxcombe*, in *Works*, ed. Arnold Glover and A. R. Waller (Cambridge: Cambridge University Press, 1905-1912), VIII, 309; John Webster, "To the Reader," *The White Devil*, in *The Complete Works*, ed. F. L. Lucas (London: Chatto and Windus, 1927), I, 107-108.

[116] Dekker, *Dead Terme* and *Rauens Almanacke*, in *Non-Dramatic Works*, IV, 55, 194, respectively.

[117] Dekker, *Seuen Deadly Sinnes*, in ibid., II, 53.

[118] T. G[ainsford], *The Rich Cabinet Furnished with Varietie of Descriptions*, in *The English Drama and Stage*, ed. William C. Hazlitt (1869; reprint ed., New York: Burt Franklin, n.d.), p. 230.

barmy jacket of a Beer-brewer" at the public playhouses. Their own spectators, of course, were "this choise selected influence."[119] Davenant, smarting from the slim crowds he drew in 1630 at the Blackfriars, had supporters who scored the ignorant masses that preferred less refined offerings at the Red Bull and the Cockpit.

> . . . they'l still slight
> All that exceeds Red Bull, and Cockpit flight.
> These are the men in crowded heapes that throng
> To that adulterate stage, where not a tong
> Of th'untun'd Kennell, can a line repeat
> Of serious sense: but like lips, meet like meat;
> Whilst the true brood of Actors, that alone
> Keepe naturall vnstrayn'd Action in her throne
> Behold their Benches bare, though they rehearse
> The tearser *Beaumonts* or great *Iohnsons* verse.[120]

When the company at the Fortune was forced to leave that playhouse and begin playing at the Red Bull in 1640, they promptly peopled their former home with apple-wives and chimney-boys who demanded more room for the rabble.

> Who would rely on Fortune, when *shee's* knowne
> An *enemie* to Merit, and hath shewne
> Such an example here? Wee that have pay'd
> Her tribute to our losse, each night defray'd
> The charge of her attendance, now growne poore,
> (Through her expences) thrusts us out of doore.
> . . . . . . . . . . . . . . . . . . . . . . . . . . . . . . . . . . . . . . . . . . . . . . . . . . . . . . . .
> Those that now sojourne with *her*, bring a noyse
> Of *Rables*, *Apple-wives* and Chimney-boyes,

---

[119] John Marston, *Jack Drum's Entertainment*, in *Plays*, ed. H. Harvey Wood (London: Oliver and Boyd, 1934), III, 234. In Paris too distinctions were made among various groups at the theater, but they were largely invented distinctions, meant to flatter the aristocratic audience. See John Lough, *Paris Theatre Audiences in the Seventeenth and Eighteenth Centuries* (London: Oxford University Press, 1957), pp.117-125.

[120] Thomas Carew, "Commendatory Verses" to Davenant's *The Just Italian*,

Whose shrill confused Ecchoes loud doe cry,
Enlarge your *Commons*, Wee hate *Privacie*.
........................................................................
Here Gentlemen, our Anchor's fixt; And wee
(Disdaining Fortunes mutability)
Expect your kinde acceptance; then wee'l sing
(Protected by your smiles our ever-spring;)
As pleasant as if wee had still possest
Our lawful Portion out of Fortunes brest:
Onely wee would request you to forbeare
Your wonted custome, banding *Tyle* or Peare,
Against our *curtaines*, to allure *us* forth.
I pray take notice *these* are of more Worth,
Pure Naples silk not *Worstead*.[121]

Ironically, though the Red Bull spectators were courteously addressed as "Gentlemen," they were also cautioned against their "wonted custome" of flinging bricks and fruit at the curtain—a strong hint that not all the ruffians had followed Prince Charles's company to the Fortune.

Questions of taste and popularity frequently expressed themselves as a division of the audience into the vulgar and the discriminating, with the vulgar identified as those who paid less. In the private theater, where the pit held the choicest seats, the gallery patrons supposedly preferred sensation to sense.

 . . . if he had been wise
He should have wove in one, two *Comedies*;
The first for th' Gallery, in which the Throne
To their amazement should descend alone,
The rosin-lightning flash, and Monster spire
Squibs, and words hotter then his fire.
   Th' other for the Gentlemen oth' Pit,
Like to themselves, all Spirit, Fancy, Wit. . . .[122]

---

[121] Tatham, "A Prologue spoken upon removing of the late Fortune Players to the Bull," *Fancies Theatre*, $H_2$<sup>v</sup>-$H_3$.

[122] Richard Lovelace, "Prologue" to *The Scholars*, in *The Poems of Richard Lovelace*, ed. C. H. Wilkinson (Oxford: Clarendon Press, 1925), II, 60.

But in the public theater, the players carefully classified the groundlings as the sensation seekers. In this prologue to a Red Bull play, for example, those in the yard could scarce understand the lines, but the gentlemen were promised good words for their money.

We hope, for your owne good, you in the Yard
Will lend your Eares, attentiuely to heare
Things that shall flow so smoothly to your ear;
That you returning home, t'your Friends shall say,
How ere you vnderstand't, 'Tis a fine Play:
For we haue in't a Conjurer, a Deuill,
And a Clowne too; but I feare the euill,
In which perhaps vnwisely we may faile,
Of wanting Squibs and Crackers at their taile,
But howsoeuer, Gentlemen I sweare,
You shall haue Good Words for your Money here;
Stuffe that will last, we hope, and dy'd in graine:
And as yee lik't, pray know the House againe.[123]

It was true enough that the public theaters offered a larger number of places at the cheaper prices and thus probably attracted more commoners than the private theaters. But the idea that the Red Bull and the Fortune "were mostly frequented by Citizens and the meaner sort of People"[124] is open to question. What seems more likely is that a difference in the quality of the plays and the status of the players was equated with a difference in the quality and status of the audience. Gentlemen were known to frequent the public playhouses and even to enjoy bad plays and good fights. Yet, at the time, critics eagerly attributed the popularity of "lowd Clamors" and the occurrence

---

[123] I. C., "Prologue," *The Two Merry Milke-maids* (London, 1620).

[124] Wright, *Historia Histrionica* , p. 5. This description of the two theaters appeared more than fifty years after the playhouses shut down. Then, too, the economic realities of the day made it extremely unlikely that "the meaner sort" could have afforded the more expensive and more numerous gallery places upon which the companies had to rely for a profit.

of "dayly Tumults" to the low degree of the spectators. The passage of time had its effect too. In 1653, after a decade of closed playhouses, it was easy to remember the public houses as "Our *Theaters* of lower note" and to hope that someday they "shall scorne the rustick Prose / of a *Jack-pudding*, and will please the Rout / With wit enough to beare their Credit out."[125] By 1671, the Restoration critics, deploring the current success of "the most irregular, and illiterate, obscene and insipid Plays crowded with audiences" looked back thirty years to a supposedly similar situation for consolation: "but we may remember that the Red Bull writers, with their Drums, Trumpets, Battels, and Hero's had this success formerly, and perhaps have been able to number as many Audiences as our Theatres, (I will not presume to make the comparison otherwise)."[126] In 1699, after fifty years, the notion of a vulgar public theater and an aristocratic private theater had become legend, with the Red Bull and the Fortune "mostly frequented by Citizens and the meaner sort of People."[127]

In point of fact, the strictly contemporary references to audiences and theaters divided along class lines were relatively few, and they were strongly outnumbered by the references that made absolutely no mention of rank or status, as others have long since pointed out.[128] Even so severe a critic as Gosson conceded, "Indeede I must confesse there comes to Playes of all sortes, old and young; it is hard to say that all offend."[129] The playgoers were termed "the multitude" or "ten thousand spectators," the "full-stufft audience," "many spectators," "Throng'd heapes," "numerous and mighty Auditories," or

---

[125] Sir Aston Cokayne, in *The Dramatic Works*, ed. James Maidment and W. H. Logan (London: H. Sotheran, 1874), p. 21. Because he was writing a commendatory verse for Richard Brome's *Five New Plays* (1653), he may have been influenced by the fact that Brome wrote exclusively for the private theaters.

[126] Edward Howard, *The Six Days Adventure* (London, 1671), A$_4^v$-a.

[127] Wright, *Historia Histrionica*, p. 5.

[128] Alfred Harbage, *Shakespeare's Audience* (New York: Columbia University Press, 1941), p. 19.

[129] Stephen Gosson, *The Schoole of Abuse*, ed. Edward Arber, English Reprints, no. 3 (London: A. Murray and Son, 1869), p. 60.

simply a "concurse of people."[130] While these descriptions implied large audiences, they did not necessarily refer to common audiences.

Still other references implied disorderly but not necessarily baseborn playgoers. An early writer described a crowd headed for the theater as a "concourse of unruly people," while no less a poet than Spenser spoke of "womens cries, and shouts of boyes / Such as the troubled Theaters oftimes annoyes."[131] As early as 1574, the Merchant Taylors were much offended by "the tumultuous disordered persones" at their scholars' plays, and Shakespeare characterized a band of forty young club-swingers as "the Hope o' the Strand," adding "These are the youths that thunder at a playhouse, and fight for bitten apples: that no audience but the tribulation of Tower Hill, or the limbs of Limehouse, their dear brothers, are able to endure."[132] Though such comments reinforced the reputation of a noisy, volatile audience, they did not identify plebeians as the only troublemakers. The privileged could be rowdy too.

### OTHER ATTRACTIONS

Certain attractions other than the theater may have catered principally to commoners. The baiting houses, for example, pulled in large numbers from the lower social ranks. When the Duke of Newcastle advised Charles II about public entertain-

[130] Henry Peacham, "Epigram 94," *Thalia's Banquet* (London, 1620); Nashe, *Pierce Penilesse*, in *Works*, I, 212; Marston, *What You Will*, in *Plays*, II, 266; 27 August 1619, *Calendar of State Papers, Domestic, of the Reigns of Edward VI, Mary, Elizabeth, and James* (Great Britain: Public Record Office, 1856-1872), X (1619-1623), p. 71; Dekker, *Roaring Girl*, in *Dramatic Works*, III, 17; Thomas Heywood, "To the Reader," *The Iron Age*, in *The Dramatic Works*, ed. R. H. Shepherd (1874; reprint ed., New York: Russell and Russell, 1964), III, 264; Bentley, *Jacobean and Caroline Stage*, II, 659.

[131] *Tarlton's News out of Purgatory* (London, 1590), p. 1; Edmund Spenser, *Faerie Queene*, 4.3.37.

[132] Charles M. Clode, *The Early History of the Guild of Merchant Taylors* (London: Harrison and Sons, 1888-1889), I, 234; Shakespeare, *Henry VIII* (V. iv), in *Complete Works*, p. 816.

ment in the model of his father's reign, he stated, "First for London Paris Garden will holde good for the meaner people."[133] Those killed at Paris Garden in 1583 were all "meaner people." And certainly the plebeian preference for bears was openly stated by Jonson, who contemptuously rebuked an ignorant audience thus: "You are fitter *Spectators* for the *Beares*, then us, or the Puppets. This is a popular ignorance indeed, somewhat better appareld in you, then the People: but a hard-handed, and stiffe ignorance, worthy a Trewel, or a Hammer-man."[134] Gentlemen enjoyed a bloody baiting too, but evidently in smaller numbers. The contract for the Hope in 1613 specified only "Two Boxes in the lowermost storie fitt and decent for gentlemen to sit in."[135] And a later description of that house contained one of the few contemporary references to a mixed society: "the other was a building of excellent *Hope*, and though *wild beasts* and *Gladiators*, did most possesse it, yet the Gallants that come to beholde those combats, though they were of a mixt Society, yet were many Noble worthies amongst them."[136]

Wild beasts did not provide the sole alternative to plays for ordinary subjects. London was filled with amusements, some free, like the Lord Mayor's pageant,[137] and some requiring the outlay of a coin or two.

> To see a strange out-landish Fowle,
> A quaint Baboon, an Ape, an Owle,
> A dancing Beare, a Gyants bone,

[133] Sandford A. Strong, *A Catalogue of Letters*; as cited by Bentley, *Jacobean and Caroline Stage*, VI, 122.

[134] Jonson, *Magnetic Lady*, in *Ben Jonson*, VI, 546.

[135] Walter W. Greg, ed., *Henslowe Papers* (London: A. H. Bullen, 1907), p. 20.

[136] Nicholas Goodman, *Holland's Leaguer*, ed. Dean Stanton Barnard, Jr. (The Hague: Mouton, 1970), $F_2^v$. For the most comprehensive analysis of the baiting rings in relation to the theaters, see Oscar Lee Brownstein, "Stake and Stage: The Baiting Ring and the Public Playhouse in Elizabethan England," Ph.D. diss., State University of Iowa, 1963.

[137] The most thorough treatment of the pageants is David Bergeron's *English Civic Pageantry, 1558-1642* (Columbia: University of South Carolina Press, 1971).

A foolish Ingin moue alone,
A Morris-dance, a Puppit play,
Mad *Tom* to sing a roundelay,
A Woman dancing on a Rope;
Bull-baiting also at the *Hope;*
A Rimers Iests, a Iuglers cheats,
A Tumbler shewing cunning feats,
Or Players acting on the Stage,
There goes the bounty of our Age
 But vnto any pious motion,
 There's little coine, and lesse deuotion.[138]

John Feilde complained about a whole host of pleasures alluring decent folk into decadence upon Sundays and holidays: "Both in Sommer and Winter, they can finde occasions, to bereaue themselues of spiritual comforts, eyther to runne out into the countrie with their bagges and bottels, or els beeing at home to follow wicked exercises. Euery dore hath his stake, and the streetes are ful of blazers of iniquitie. There is gadding to al kind of gaming, and there is no Tauerne or Alehouse, if the drinke be strong, that lacketh any company."[139]

His concern about the alehouses was shared by other people. About 1581, a remonstrance was presented to the Lord Mayor asking him to reduce the number of licensed wine sellers because they "kept the most disorderly houses."

> The Reducing these licensed Men would be great Cause, as he urged, of avoiding Whoredom, Dancing, Dicing, and Banqueting of Apprentices, serving Men, and such-like, daily used in Taverns, with the better Observation of Days prescribed to be fasted on. . . . And that the Order for decent Apparel might be observed and used, and the Over-heightening of the Prices of any Commodities, whereby Men became Bankrupts, should be remedied.[140]

---

[138] Henry Farley, *St. Pavles-Chvrch her Bill for the Parliament* (London, 1621), E₄-E₄ᵛ. See also Richard D. Altick, *The Shows of London, 1600-1862* (Cambridge, Mass.: Belknap Press, 1978).

[139] Feilde, *Godly Exhortation*, B₍₅₎-B₍₅₎ᵛ.  [140] Stow, *Survey*, II, 284.

Significantly, the vices mentioned all required money. Hence both the complaints against violations of the statutes on apparel and the "Banqueting of Apprentices, serving Men, and such-like" pointed toward that small group of well-heeled young men who could afford the pleasures of the privileged. For the masses, however, even the pleasures of drink proved costly. According to Stow, "quaffing . . . is mightily encreased, though greatlie qualified among the poorer sort, not of any holy abstinencie, but of meere necessitie, Ale and Beere being small, and Wines in price aboue their reach."[141]

Along with wine, playgoing too was much above the reach of the poorer sort. London's theaters, whether public or private, opened their doors to anyone with the price of admission. During sixty-six years, all sorts came in—lords and ladies, profligates and prostitutes, burghers and beggars, admirals and apprentices. Yet the playhouses neither fostered democracy nor presented a social microcosm. On weekday afternoons, with most decent, ordinary folk hard at work, only the idle, the criminal, or the irresponsible could join the privileged at a play. Admission prices presented a tremendous barrier, for "euery dore hath a payment."[142] Common people worked desperately hard for a few meager pennies and had little to spare for luxuries like the theater, although to gain entrée to wealthy prospects, a courtesan or cutpurse might invest in a visit to the theater. A discharged soldier or a sailor ashore might try what spectacle the playhouse could provide, but other ordinary citizens rarely had such leisure, except on a Sunday or a holiday, when they could easily turn a performance into a brawl. Those who spoke of vulgar playgoers usually had special reasons for downgrading the spectators: preachers with shrunken congregations, hostile City officials, disgruntled playwrights, rival companies. The actors gladly played to any receptive, paying audience. But the social and economic realities of Renaissance London decreed an audience more privileged than plebeian.

---

[141] Stow, *Survey*, ed. Kingsford, I, 83.
[142] Feilde, *Godly Exhortation*, B[6].

# · VII ·
## *Epilogue*

London's large and lively priv-
ileged set ruled the playgoing world quite as firmly as they
ruled the political world, the mercantile world, and the rest of
the cultural world. Their own ranks were tremendously varied,
reaching from bright but impoverished students, younger sons
of gentry families set to a trade, and minor retainers in noble
households all the way up to lords, ambassadors, merchant
princes, and royalty itself. Though the clever, the ambitious,
and the newly rich enormously expanded the ranks of the privileged under Elizabeth and James, they still stood firmly apart
from the mass of society. Most people ate, dressed, worked, and
lived as best they could. The fortunate wrote music and poetry.
They made the laws. They ruled the government and the
church. They monopolized education. They led armies. They
claimed estates and controlled companies. They elevated dining
and dress and decor to an art. And they were avid playgoers,
men and women alike.

By focusing upon the privileged playgoer and comparing him
with the plebeian spectators, the preceding chapters have
attempted to clarify the indistinct picture of all playgoers.
Among the privileged, plays were accepted and enjoyed as a
matter of course. Both patrons and friends of the actors, privileged ladies and gentlemen enjoyed plays at Court, at private
gatherings, and in all the theaters throughout the period. Moreover, the numbers of gentlemen and would-be gentlemen in the
society at large, together with their disproportionate congregation in London, would have made it possible for them to
dominate the audiences of the huge public theaters as well as
the small private playhouses. The fact that their style of living
actively fostered the pursuit of pleasure each afternoon made

their dominance not only possible but probable. While not all privileged families possessed great wealth, they were virtually the only group with enough money to pay repeatedly for admission regardless of the price scale, to finance sumptuous buildings and handsome profits for the acting companies, and to afford all the extra charges associated with playgoing—boat or carriage hire, food, drink, tobacco, books, harlots, and stolen purses. With their penchant for display and their pretension to superior judgment, privileged folk may not have been an easy audience to satisfy, but their insatiable interest in plays certainly made them the actors' most consistent audience.

Though excluded from the performances at Court and the seats of the nobility, the rest of London's populace could share the playhouses with their social betters. Few, however, had both the leisure and money playgoing demanded. The long working day always included the afternoons when plays were given. Earnings were not merely small but actually shrinking, buying less as each year passed. Thousands upon thousands endured the starkest poverty, with a spare penny far more likely to buy a loaf of bread than to purchase a place in the pit. On most weekday afternoons, theaters might draw a handful of idle workers, some truant apprentices, a few soldiers or seamen, and a fair number of thieves and strumpets seeking prospects. But the companies could expect large crowds of lesser citizens only on Sundays and holidays, when the commoners sometimes wrecked the playhouse instead of applauding the play. However appreciative of Shakespeare or Jonson or Marlowe, the masses simply did not follow a pattern of existence that fostered playgoing, except on rare occasions.

The conclusion that the privileged represented the most consistent patrons of the drama, no matter where or when it was performed, marks only a starting point and not a final destination. Knowing who came to the theaters, how they behaved, or what the rest of their life was like does not explain the plays nor mark the audiences as either superior or inferior. It simply extends the possibilities for understanding the remarkable drama of that place and time. It means, for example, that the complex philosophical, theological, or aesthetic ideas embedded in a Shakespearean play are not merely an unconscious reflection of the accepted thought of the day. Nor are they the unjustified inventions of modern critics. More likely, they typify the effort of a superb dramatist to engage the minds as well as the emotions of an intelligent audience. With a crowd of habitués, many of whom were sophisticated and accomplished, a play had to offer real substance if it were to survive more than a brief showing. Shakespeare's multileveled works, unfolding new complexities at each viewing, were deservedly satisfying and popular throughout the period.

In a similar way, the modes of behavior by dramatic characters from various social levels can be understood better by knowing what sort of audience observed such behavior and how closely the actions onstage resembled their own existence. Reality did not look the same to the beggar and the baron. Here is no covert suggestion that the audiences wrote the plays—far from it. But the playwrights did know who the principal playgoers were likely to be. Within the limits of their materials and their talents, dramatists wrote with an eye to the abilities and liabilities of their spectators. Thus by identifying the makeup of the audience more exactly, the critic can interpret the playwrights' work more accurately.

Dispelling old ideas opens fresh possibilities. Some will be reluctant to part with the notions of a mixed or vulgar audience at the public theaters and an aristocratic audience reigning at Court and in the private theaters. The myth offers too convenient an explanation for certain aspects of theater history. But if it can be established that, with minor variations, the audiences at all kinds of dramatic performances came largely from the privileged few, then new explanations for differences among various kinds of plays can be sought. The specialized requirements of a children's troupe, as compared with an adult troupe, for example, surely bear upon the nature of the private theater repertoire. The ability of the King's Men to attract the most talented actors, playwrights, and managers must have been a factor in their triumph at public and private house alike. The simple fact that status is no guarantee of good taste may have much to do with the success of loud, vulgar, or obscene plays and the failure of superb ones. And the weather, after all, may have moved the Burbages indoors to the Blackfriars in winter and outdoors to the Globe in summer. Many other matters, major and minor, lie open to reexamination.

Yet it would be wrong to claim too much for the foregoing analysis; it is enough if it revises previous misconceptions for scholars and if it provides an enlightening account of the theater's staunchest patrons for interested readers. The final questions concerning those far distant audiences may never be answered. Yet they continue to tantalize across the gulf of four centuries—not merely because the London theatergoers were privileged by virtue of their rank, wealth, education, or birth but because they were privileged to see the birth of the commercial theater and to enjoy plays by the astonishing group of dramatists that included William Shakespeare. They were indeed privileged playgoers.

# London Wages

[Westminster, 23 July 1589, 31 Elizabeth I]

To the best and most skillful workmen, journeymen, and hired servants of any of the companies hereunder named:

Clothworkers by the year with meat and drink £5
Fullers by the year with meat and drink £5
Shearmen by the year with meat and drink £5
Dyers by the year with meat and drink £6 13s. 4d.
Tailors hosier by the year with meat and drink £4
Drapers being hosiers by the year with meat and drink £4
Shoemakers by the year with meat and drink £4
Pewterers by the year with meat and drink £3 6s. 8d.
Whitebakers by the year with meat and drink £4 13s. 4d.
Brewers by the year with meat and drink £10
The underbrewer by the year with meat and drink £6
The foredrayman by the year with meat and drink £6
The miller by the year with meat and drink £6
The other drayman by the year with meat and drink £3 6s. 8d.
The tunman by the year with meat and drink £3 6s. 8d.
Alebrewers by the day with meat and drink 8d.
Saddlers by the year with meat and drink £4
Turners by the year with meat and drink £4 6s. 8d.
Cutlers by the year with meat and drink £4 6s. 8d.
Blacksmiths by the year with meat and drink £6
Curriers by the year with meat and drink £6
Bowyers by the year with meat and drink £4
Fletchers by the year with meat and drink £4
Brownbakers by the year with meat and drink £3 6s. 8d.
Farriers by the year with meat and drink £4
Glovers by the year with meat and drink £3 6s. 8d.
Cappers by the year with meat and drink £4 13s. 4d.
Hatmakers and feltmakers by the year with meat and drink
    £4 13s. 4d.
Butchers by the year with meat and drink £6
Cooks by the year with meat and drink £6

To the workmen, journeymen, or hired servants of any the companies hereunder named:

Goldsmiths by the year with meat and drink £8, by the week 3s. 4d., by the day 7d.; without meat and drink by the week 6s., by the day 12d.

Skinners by the year with meat and drink £4, by the week 3s. 4d., by the day 8d.; without meat and drink by the week 5s., by the day 13d.

Painter stainers by the year with meat and drink £4, by the week 4s., by the day 9d.; without meat and drink by the year £8, by the week 6s. 8d., by the day 13d.

Girdlers by the year with meat and drink £3, by the week 16d., by the day 4d.; without meat and drink by the week 5s. 6d., by the day 10d.

Coopers by the year with meat and drink £4 6s. 8d., by the week 3s. 4d., by the day 8d.; without meat and drink by the year £8 13s. 4d., by the week 6s. 8d., by the day 13d.

Broderers by the year with meat and drink £5, by the week 4s. 6d., by the day 8d.; without meat and drink by the week 6s. 8d., by the day 13d.

Plumbers by the year with meat and drink £3 6s. 8d., by the week 3s. 4d., by the day 8d.; without meat and drink by the week 6s., by the day 13d.

Waxchandlers by the year with meat and drink £4, by the week 2s., by the day 6d.; without meat and drink by the week 4s. 6d., by the day 11d.

Armorers by the year with meat and drink £3 6s. 8d., by the week 3s. 4d., by the day 8d.; without meat and drink by the week 6s., by the day 13d.

Woolwinders by the year with meat and drink £3 6s. 8d., by the week 3s. 4d., by the day 8d.; without meat and drink by the week 6s., by the day 13d.; his apprentice having served three years with meat and drink by the week 3s. 4d., by the day 8d.; without meat and drink by the week 5s., by the day 10d.

Tilers with meat and drink by the week 4s. 6d., by the day 9d.; without meat and drink by the week 6s. 6d., by the day 13d.; his apprentice with meat and drink by the week 3s. 4d., by the day 7d.; without meat and drink by the week 6s., by the day 11d.

Masons with meat and drink by the week 3s. 4d., by the day 11d.; without meat and drink by the week 5s., by the day 13d.

Joiners by the year with meat and drink £5, by the week 4s. 6d., by the week 7s., by the day 14d.; his servant by the year with meat and drink £4, by the week 2s., by the day 4d.; without meat and drink by the week 4s., by the day 10d.

Plasterers with meat and drink by the day 9d., without meat and drink by the day 14d.

Linen weavers by the year with meat and drink £4, by the day 6d.; without meat and drink by the day 10d.

Horners by the year with meat and drink £3, by the week 20d.

Glaziers with meat and drink by the day 9d., without meat and drink by the day 13d.

Pavers with meat and drink by the day 9d., without meat and drink by the day 13d.

Longbow stringmakers by the year with meat and drink £4, by the day 8d.; without meat and drink by the day 12d.

Founders by the year with meat and drink £5, by the day 12d.; without meat and drink 16d.

Lorimers with meat and drink by the year £4 6s. 8d., by the week 20d.

Barbers by the year with meat and drink £3, by the week 20d.

Carmen by the week with meat and drink 2s. 6d.

Watermen by the year with meat and drink 40s., by the week 12d., by the day 4d.; without meat and drink by the week 3s., by the day 7d.

Porters with meat and drink by the day 8d.; without meat and drink by the day 12d.

Carpenters with meat and drink by the week 4s. 6d., by the day 9d.; without meat and drink by the week 6s. 2d., by the day 13d.; his apprentice that hath served three years with meat and drink by the week 3s. 4d., by the day 7d.; without meat and drink by the week 5s., by the day 11d.

Sawyers with meat and drink by the week 4s., by the day 8d.; without meat and drink by the week 6s., by the day 12d.; to him that saweth the 100 [board feet] with meat and drink by the day 20d.

Common laborers with meat and drink by the day 5d.; without meat and drink by the day 9d.

---

*Source*: Paul L. Hughes and James F. Larkin, eds., *Tudor Royal Proclamations*, Vol. III (New Haven: Yale University Press, 1969), pp. 39-41. The original document is in the Public Record Office, London.

# Wage and Price Fluctuations, 1264-1954

CHANGES IN PRICE OF A COMPOSITE UNIT OF CONSUMABLES
IN SOUTHERN ENGLAND, 1264-1954

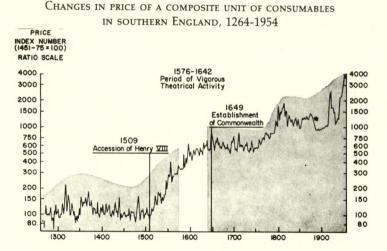

CHANGES IN THE PURCHASING POWER OF THE WAGE RATE OF A
BUILDING CRAFTSMAN EXPRESSED IN A COMPOSITE UNIT OF
CONSUMABLES IN SOUTHERN ENGLAND, 1264-1954

"REAL WAGE"
INDEX NUMBER
(1451-75 = 100)
RATIO SCALE

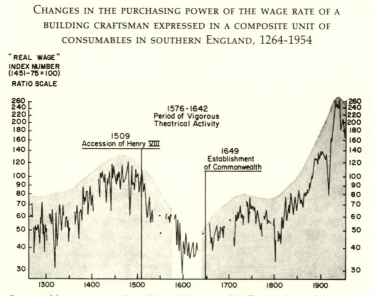

Reprinted by permission from Mary I. Oates and William J. Baumol, "On the
Economics of the Theater in Renaissance London," *The Swedish Journal of
Economics* 74 (1972):150. The original charts appeared in E. H. Phelps Brown
and Sheila W. Hopkins, "The Price of Consumables, Compared with Builders'
Wage Rates," *Economica* 23 (1956):302, and are also used by permission.

# Bibliography

MODERN SOURCES

Akrigg, G. P. V. *Jacobean Pageant, or The Court of King James I.* New York: Atheneum, 1967.

Allison, K. J. "An Elizabethan Village 'Census.' " *Bulletin of the Institute of Historical Research* 36 (1963): 91-103.

Altick, Richard D. *The Shows of London, 1600-1862.* Cambridge, Mass.: Belknap Press, 1978.

Apperson, G. L. *The Social History of Smoking.* London: Martin Secker, 1914.

Appleby, Andrew P. *Famine in Tudor and Stuart England.* Stanford, Calif.: Stanford University Press, 1978.

Armstrong, William A. "The Audience of the Elizabethan Private Theatres." *Review of English Studies* 10 (1959): 234-249.

—————. *The Elizabethan Private Theatres: Facts and Problems.* London: Society for Theatre Research, 1958.

Arnott, James Fullerton, and Robinson, John William. *English Theatrical Literature, 1559-1900: A Bibliography.* London: Society for Theatre Research, 1970.

Ashley, Maurice. *England in the Seventeenth Century.* 3d ed. Baltimore: Penguin Books, 1952.

Ashmore, A. "Household Inventories of the Lancashire Gentry, 1550-1700." *Transactions of the Historic Society of Lancashire and Cheshire* 110 (1958): 59-105.

Aubrey, John. *Brief Lives.* Edited by Oliver Lawson Dick. Ann Arbor: University of Michigan Press, 1957.

Aydelotte, Frank. *Elizabethan Rogues and Vagabonds.* Oxford: Clarendon Press, 1913.

Aylmer, Gerald Edward. *The King's Servants: The Civil Service of Charles I, 1625-1642.* London: Routledge and Kegan Paul, 1961.

Barnett, Richard C. *Place, Profit, and Power: A Study of the Servants of William Cecil, Elizabethan Statesman.* The James Sprunt Studies in History and Political Science, vol. 51. Chapel Hill: University of North Carolina Press, 1969.

Barroll, J. Leeds. "The Social and Literary Context." In *The Revels History of Drama in English*, edited by Clifford Leech and T. W. Craik. Vol. III: 1576-1613. London: Methuen, 1975.

Baskervill, C. R. "The Custom of Sitting on the Elizabethan Stage." *Modern Philology* 8 (1911): 581-589.

Beckerman, Bernard. *Shakespeare at the Globe, 1599-1609*. New York: Macmillan, 1962.

Beier, A. L. "Vagrants and the Social Order in Elizabethan England." *Past and Present* 64 (August 1974): 3-29.

Bennett, H. S. *Shakespeare's Audience*. Annual Shakespeare Lecture, 26 April 1944.

———. "Shakespeare's Stage and Audience." *Neophilologus* 33 (1949): 40-51.

Bentley, Gerald Eades. *The Jacobean and Caroline Stage*. 7 vols. Oxford: Clarendon Press, 1941-1968.

———. *The Profession of the Dramatist in Shakespeare's Time, 1590-1642*. Princeton: Princeton University Press, 1971.

———. *Shakespeare and His Theatre*. Lincoln: University of Nebraska Press, 1964.

Bergeron, David. *English Civic Pageantry, 1558-1642*. Columbia: University of South Carolina Press, 1971.

Berry, Elizabeth K. *Henry Ferrers, an Early Warwickshire Antiquary*. Dugdale Society Occasional Papers, no. 16 (1965).

Berry, Herbert. "The Boar's Head Again." In *The Elizabethan Theatre III*, edited by David Galloway. Toronto: Macmillan, 1973.

———. "The Playhouse in the Boar's Head Inn, Whitechapel." In *The Elizabethan Theatre*, edited by David Galloway. Toronto: Archon Books, 1970.

———. "The Stage and Boxes at the Blackfriars." *Studies in Philology* 63 (1966): 163-186.

Binns, J. W. "Women or Transvestites on the Elizabethan Stage?: An Oxford Controversy." *Sixteenth Century Journal* 5 (1974): 95-120.

Birch, Thomas. *The Court and Times of Charles the First*. 2 vols. London: H. Colburn, 1848.

———. *The Court and Times of James the First*. 2 vols. London: H. Colburn, 1849.

———. *Memoirs of the Reign of Queen Elizabeth, from the Year 1581 till her Death*. 2 vols. London, 1754.

Bittle, William G., and Lane, R. Todd. "Inflation and Philanthropy in

England: A Re-Assessment of W. K. Jordon's Data." *Economic History Review*, 2d ser. 29 (1976): 203-210.

Bradbrook, M. C. *The Living Monument: Shakespeare and the Theatre of his Time*. Cambridge: Cambridge University Press, 1976.

————. *The Rise of the Common Player*. London: Chatto and Windus, 1962.

————. "Shakespeare and the Multiple Theatres of Jacobean London." In *The Elizabethan Theatre VI*, edited by G. R. Hibbard. Toronto: Macmillan, 1978.

————. "Shakespeare and the Structure of Tudor Society." *Review of National Literatures* 3 (1972): 90-105.

————. *Shakespeare: The Poet in His World*. New York: Columbia University Press, 1978.

Bradley, A. C. "Shakespeare's Theatre and Audience." In *Oxford Lectures on Poetry*. London: Macmillan, 1909.

Bradley, E. T. *The Life of Lady Arabella Stuart*. 2 vols. London: Richard Bentley and Son, 1889.

Brenner, Y. S. "The Inflation of Prices in Early Sixteenth Century England." *Economic History Review*, 2d ser. 14 (1961-1962): 225-239.

————. "The Inflation of Prices in England, 1551-1650." *Economic History Review*, 2d ser. 15 (1962-1963): 266-284.

Bridges, Robert. "The Influence of the Audience on Shakespeare's Drama." In *Collected Essays*. Vol. I. London: Oxford University Press, 1927.

Brown, E. H. Phelps, and Hopkins, Sheila W. "The Price of Consumables, Compared with Builders' Wage Rates." *Economica* 23 (1956): 291-314.

————. "Seven Centuries of Building Wages." *Economica* 22 (1955): 195-206.

————. "Wage Rates and Prices: Evidence for Population Pressure in the Sixteenth Century." *Economica* 24 (1957): 289-299.

Brownstein, Oscar Lee. "Stake and Stage: The Baiting Ring and the Public Playhouse in Elizabethan England." Ph.D. diss., State University of Iowa, 1963.

Bullen, George. "The Duke of Buckingham and a Play of Shakespeare in 1628." *The Athenaeum* (18 October 1879), p. 497.

Burney, Charles. *A General History of Music from the Earliest Ages to the Present Period*. Edited by Frank Mercer. 4 vols. London, 1782-1789.

Byrne, Muriel St. Clare. "Shakespeare's Audience." In *A Series of Papers on Shakespeare and the Theatre*. London: Oxford University Press, 1927.

Campbell, Mildred. *The English Yeoman under Elizabeth and the Early Stuarts*. New Haven: Yale University Press, 1942.

Chambers, E. K. *The Elizabethan Stage*. 4 vols. Oxford: Clarendon Press, 1923.

————. *William Shakespeare: A Study of Facts and Problems*. 2 vols. Oxford: Clarendon Press, 1930.

Charlton, Kenneth. *Education in Renaissance England*. London: Routledge and Kegan Paul, 1965.

Cheyney, Edward Potts. *A History of England from the Defeat of the Armada to the Death of Elizabeth*. 2 vols. New York: Longmans, Green, 1914-1926.

Christianson, Paul. "The Causes of the English Revolution: A Reappraisal." *Journal of British Studies* 15 (1976): 40-75.

Clark, Peter, and Slack, Paul. *Crisis and Order in English Towns, 1500-1700*. London: Routledge and Kegan Paul, 1972.

Clarkson, L. A. *The Pre-Industrial Economy in England, 1500-1750*. London: B. T. Batsford, 1971.

Cliffe, J. T. *The Yorkshire Gentry, From the Reformation to the Civil War*. London: Athlone Press, 1969.

Clode, Charles M. *The Early History of the Guild of Merchant Taylors*. 2 vols. London: Harrison and Sons, 1888-1889.

Coleman, D. C. "Labour in the English Economy of the Seventeenth Century." *Economic History Review*, 2d ser. 8 (1955-1956): 281-295.

Collier, John P. *The History of English Dramatic Poetry to the Time of Shakespeare*. 3 vols. London: G. Bell and Sons, 1879.

Collins, Arthur. *The Peerage of England*. 8 vols. London, 1779.

Cook, Ann Jennalie. "The Audience of Shakespeare's Plays: A Reconsideration." *Shakespeare Studies* 7 (1974): 283-305.

————. " 'Bargaines of Incontinencie': Bawdy Behavior at the Playhouses." *Shakespeare Studies* 10 (1977): 271-290.

————. "The London Theater Audience, 1576-1642." Ph.D. diss., Vanderbilt University, 1972.

Cornwall, Julian. "English Population in the Early Sixteenth Century." *Economic History Review*, 2d ser. 23 (1970): 32-44.

Cressy, David. "Describing the Social Order of Elizabethan and Stuart England." *Literature and History* 3 (1976): 29-44.

————. "Educational Opportunity in Tudor and Stuart England." *History of Education Quarterly* 16 (1976): 301-320.

Curtis, Mark H. "The Alienated Intellectuals of Early Stuart England." *Past and Present* 23 (November 1962): 25-43.

————. *Oxford and Cambridge in Transition.* Oxford: Clarendon Press, 1959.

Darby, H. C. "The Age of the Improver: 1600-1800." In *A New Historical Geography of England,* edited by H. C. Darby. Cambridge: Cambridge University Press, 1973.

DeMolen, Richard L. "Richard Mulcaster: An Elizabethan Servant." *Shakespeare Studies* 8 (1975): 29-82.

Draper, F.W.M. *Four Centuries of Merchant Taylors' School, 1561-1961.* London: Oxford University Press, 1962.

Dunlop, O. Jocelyn, and Denman, Richard D. *English Apprenticeship and Child Labour.* New York: Macmillan, 1912.

Eagle, Roderick L. " 'Shakespeare's Second Globe.' " Letter to the editor. *Times Literary Supplement,* 25 January 1974, p. 81.

Emery, F. V. "England *circa* 1600." In *A New Historical Geography of England,* edited by H. C. Darby. Cambridge: Cambridge University Press, 1973.

Evans, Joan. "Huguenot Goldsmiths in England and Ireland." *Huguenot Society Proceedings* 14 (1929-1933): 496-554.

Farr, M. W. *The Fetherstons of Packwood in the Seventeenth Century.* Dugdale Society Occasional Papers, no. 18 (1968).

Feyerabend, Karl. "Zu K. H. Schaible's 'Geschichte den Deutsche in England.' " *Englische Studien* 14 (1890): 437-452.

Finch, M. E. *The Wealth of Five Northamptonshire Families, 1540-1640.* Publications of the Northamptonshire Record Society, vol. 19 (1954-1955).

Fincham, Francis W. X. "Notes from the Ecclesiastical Court Records at Somerset House." *Transactions of the Royal Historical Society,* 4th ser. 4 (1921): 103-139.

Finkelpearl, Philip. *John Marston of the Middle Temple: An Elizabethan Dramatist in His Social Setting.* Cambridge, Mass.: Harvard University Press, 1969.

Fisher, F. J. "The Development of London as a Centre of Conspicuous Consumption in the Sixteenth and Seventeenth Centuries." In *Essays in Economic History,* edited by E. M. Carus-Wilson. Vol. II. London: Edward Arnold, 1962.

Foster, Frank Freeman. *The Politics of Stability: A Portrait of the Rulers in Elizabethan London.* London: Royal Historical Society, 1977.

Gair, Reavley. "The Presentation of Plays at Second Paul's." In *The Elizabethan Theatre VI*, edited by G. R. Hibbard. Toronto: Macmillan, 1978.

Gibbons, Brian. *Jacobean City Comedy.* Cambridge, Mass.: Harvard University Press, 1968.

Glass, D. V. "Socio-Economic Status and Occupations in the City of London at the End of the Seventeenth Century." In *Studies in London History*, edited by A.E.J. Hollaender and William Kellaway. London: Hodder and Stoughton, 1969.

"The Globe Mark Two." Review of C. Walter Hodges' *Shakespeare's Second Globe. Times Literary Supplement*, 4 January 1974, p. 14.

Grassby, Richard. "The Personal Wealth of the Business Community in Seventeenth-Century England." *Economic History Review*, 2d ser. 23 (1970): 220-234.

Gurr, Andrew. *The Shakespearean Stage, 1574-1642.* Cambridge: Cambridge University Press, 1970.

Hall, Hubert. *Society in the Elizabethan Age.* London: Swan, Sonnenschein, Lowrey, 1886.

Harbage, Alfred. *Annals of English Drama, 975-1700.* Revised by S. Schoenbaum. Philadelphia: University of Pennsylvania Press, 1964.

———. *As They Liked It.* New York: Macmillan, 1947.

———. *Shakespeare and the Rival Traditions.* New York: Macmillan, 1952.

———. *Shakespeare's Audience.* New York: Columbia University Press, 1941.

Harding, Davis P. "Shakespeare the Elizabethan." In *Shakespeare: Of an Age and for All Time*, edited by Charles Tyler Prouty. Hamden, Conn.: Shoe String Press, 1954.

Havran, Martin J. *Caroline Courtier: The Life of Lord Cottington.* Columbia: University of South Carolina Press, 1973.

Hexter, Jack H. *Reappraisals in History.* London: Longmans, 1961.

Hieatt, Charles W. " 'Shakespeare's Second Globe.' " Letter to the editor. *Times Literary Supplement*, 1 March 1974, p. 369.

Hiscock, W. G. *John Evelyn and His Family Circle.* London: Routledge and Kegan Paul, 1955.

Hodges, C. Walter. *Shakespeare's Second Globe: The Missing Monument*. London: Oxford University Press, 1973.

Hollingsworth, T. H. *Historical Demography*. Ithaca, N.Y.: Cornell University Press, 1969.

Holmes, Martin. *Shakespeare's Public: The Touchstone of His Genius*. London: John Murray, 1960.

Holzknecht, Karl J. *The Backgrounds of Shakespeare's Plays*. New York: American Book Company, 1950.

Hoskins, W. G. "Harvest Fluctuations and English History, 1480-1619." *Agricultural History Review* 12 (1964): 28-46.

Hosley, Richard. "Elizabethan Theatres and Audiences." *Renaissance Drama Supplement* 10 (1967): 9-15.

————. "The Playhouses." In *The Revels History of Drama in English*, edited by Clifford Leech and T. W. Craik. Vol. III: 1576-1613. London: Methuen, 1975.

————. "Three Renaissance English Indoor Playhouses." *English Literary Renaissance* 3 (1973): 166-182.

Hotson, Leslie. *Shakespeare's Wooden O*. London: Rupert Hart-Davis, 1959.

Howson, W. C. "Plague, Poverty and Population in Parts of North-West England, 1580-1720." *Transactions of the Historic Society of Lancashire and Cheshire* 112 (1960): 29-55.

Ingram, William. *A London Life in the Brazen Age*. Cambridge, Mass.: Harvard University Press, 1978.

John, Lisle C. "Roland Whyte, Elizabethan Letter-Writer." *Studies in the Renaissance* 8 (1961): 217-235.

Jones, Marion. "The Court and the Dramatists." *Elizabethan Theatre*. Stratford-upon-Avon Studies, no. 9. New York: St. Martin's Press, 1967.

Jordon, W. K. *The Charities of London, 1480-1660*. London: Allen and Unwin, 1960.

————. *Philanthropy in England, 1480-1660*. New York: Russell Sage Foundation, 1959.

Kearney, Hugh. *Scholars and Gentlemen: Universities and Society in Pre-Industrial Britain, 1500-1700*. London: Faber and Faber, 1970.

Kelso, Ruth. *Doctrine for the Lady of the Renaissance*. 1956. Reprint. Urbana: University of Illinois Press, 1978.

Kelso, Ruth. *The Doctrine of the English Gentleman in the Sixteenth Century.* University of Illinois Studies in Language and Literature, no. 14 (1929).

Ladurie, Emmanuel LeRoy. *Times of Feast, Times of Famine: A History of Climate Since the Year 1000.* Garden City, N.Y.: Doubleday, 1971.

Lamb, H. H. *Climate: Past, Present and Future.* 2 vols. London: Methuen, 1977.

Lang, R. G. "Social Origins and Social Aspirations of Jacobean Merchants." *Economic History Review,* 2d ser. 27 (1974): 28-79.

Laslett, Peter. *The World We Have Lost.* London: Methuen, 1965.

Lavin, J. A. "Shakespeare and the Second Blackfriars." In *The Elizabethan Theatre III,* edited by David Galloway. Toronto: Macmillan, 1973.

Lawrence, W. J. *The Elizabethan Playhouse and Other Studies.* Stratford-upon-Avon: Shakespeare Head Press, 1913.

———. *Those Nut-Cracking Elizabethans.* London: Argonaut Press, 1935.

Lee, Sidney. "Shakespeare and the Elizabethan Playgoer." In *Furnivall's English Miscellany.* Oxford: Clarendon Press, 1901.

Leech, Clifford. "The Caroline Audience." *Modern Language Review* 36 (1941): 304-319.

———. "Three Times *Ho* and a Brace of Widows: Some Plays for the Private Theatre." In *The Elizabethan Theatre III,* edited by David Galloway. Toronto: Macmillan, 1973.

Levin, Harry. "Dramatic Auspices: The Playwright and His Audience." In *Shakespeare and the Revolution of the Times.* New York: Oxford University Press, 1976.

Levin, Richard. " 'Shakespeare's Second Globe.' " Letter to the editor. *Times Literary Supplement,* 25 January 1974, p. 81.

Lewis, B. Roland. "Shakspere's Audience as Viewed by Doctor Harbage." *Shakespeare Association Bulletin* 17 (1942): 150-155.

Lough, John. *Paris Theatre Audiences in the Seventeenth and Eighteenth Centuries.* London: Oxford University Press, 1957.

MacCaffrey, Wallace T. "Place and Patronage in Elizabethan Politics." In *Elizabethan Government and Society,* edited by S. T. Bindoff, Joel Hurstfield, C. H. Williams. London: Athlone Press, 1961.

McConica, James. "Scholars and Commoners in Renaissance Oxford." In *The University in Society,* edited by Lawrence Stone. Vol. I. Princeton: Princeton University Press, 1974.

Mason, Alexandra. "The Social Status of Theatrical People." *Shakespeare Quarterly* 18 (1967): 429-430.

Matthews, Brander. *Shakspere as a Playwright*. New York: Charles Scribner's Sons, 1916.

Nef, J. U. "Prices and Industrial Capitalism in France and England, 1540-1640." In *Essays in Economic History*, edited by E. M. Carus-Wilson. Vol. I. London: Edward Arnold, 1954.

Neill, Michael. " 'Wits most accomplished Senate': The Audience of the Caroline Private Theaters." *Studies in English Literature* 18 (1978): 341-360.

Nicolas, Sir Nicholas Harris. *Memoirs of the Life and Times of Sir Christopher Hatton*. London: Richard Bentley, 1847.

Orrell, John. "Peter Street at the Fortune and the Globe." *Shakespeare Survey* 33 (1980): 139-151.

Pearl, Valerie. *London and the Outbreak of the Puritan Revolution: City Government and National Politics, 1625-43*. London: Oxford University Press, 1961.

Penn, W. A. *The Soverane Herbe*. London: Grant Richards, 1901.

Pinchbeck, Ivy, and Hewitt, Margaret. *Children in English Society*. Vol. I. London: Routledge and Kegan Paul, 1969.

Plant, Marjorie. *The English Book Trade*. London: Allen and Unwin, 1939.

Pollard, Sidney, and Crossley, David W. *The Wealth of Britain, 1085-1966*. New York: Schocken Books, 1969.

Pound, J. F. *Poverty and Vagrancy in Tudor England*. Harlow: Longmans, 1971.

Prest, Wilfrid R. *The Inns of Court under Elizabeth I and the Early Stuarts, 1590-1640*. London: Longmans, 1972.

Prior, Moody E. "The Elizabethan Audience and the Plays of Shakespeare." *Modern Philology* 49 (1951): 101-123.

Rabb, Theodore K. "Investment in English Overseas Enterprise, 1575-1630." *Economic History Review*, 2d ser. 19 (1966): 70-81.

Ramsey, Peter. *Tudor Economic Problems*. London: V. Gollancz, 1963.

Raumer, Friedrich Ludwig Georg von. *History of the Sixteenth and Seventeenth Centuries, Illustrated by Original Documents*. 2 vols. London: J. Murray, 1835.

Read, Conyers, ed. *William Lambarde and Local Government*. Ithaca, N.Y.: Cornell University Press, 1962.

Reddaway, T. F. "London and the Court." *Shakespeare Survey* 17 (1964): 3-12.

Rogers, James E. Thorold. *A History of Agriculture and Prices in England.* Vols. V and VI: 1583-1702. Oxford: Clarendon Press, 1887.

Rosenberg, Eleanor. *Leicester: Patron of Letters.* New York: Columbia University Press, 1955.

Rowse, A. L. *The England of Elizabeth.* London: Macmillan, 1950.

Russell, Josiah Cox. *British Medieval Population.* Albuquerque: University of New Mexico Press, 1948.

Scott, E.J.L. "Beaumont's Grammar Lecture." *The Athenaeum*, 13 (1894): 115.

————. "The Elizabethan Stage." *The Athenaeum* 1 (1882): 103.

Simpson, Alan. *The Wealth of the Gentry, 1540-1660.* East Anglian Studies. Chicago: University of Chicago Press, 1961.

Sisson, C. J. *The Boar's Head Theatre.* London: Routledge and Kegan Paul, 1972.

Smith, Irwin. *Shakespeare's Blackfriars Playhouse.* New York: New York University Press, 1964.

————. *Shakespeare's Globe Playhouse.* New York: Charles Scribner's Sons, 1956.

Smith, Steven R. "The London Apprentices as Seventeenth-Century Adolescents." *Past and Present* 61 (November 1973): 149-161.

Sprague, Arthur Colby. *Shakespeare and the Audience.* 1935. Reprint. New York: Russell and Russell, n.d.

Stone, Lawrence. "The Anatomy of the Elizabethan Aristocracy." *Economic History Review* 18 (1948): 1-53.

————. *The Crisis of the Aristocracy.* Oxford: Clarendon Press, 1965.

————. "The Educational Revolution in England, 1560-1640." *Past and Present* 28 (July 1964): 41-80.

————. "The Elizabethan Aristocracy—A Restatement." *Economic History Review*, 2d ser. 4 (1951-1952): 302-321.

————. "Elizabethan Overseas Trade." *Economic History Review*, 2d ser. 2 (1949-1950): 30-58.

————. *An Elizabethan: Sir Horatio Palavicino.* Oxford: Clarendon Press, 1956.

————. *The Family, Sex and Marriage in England, 1500-1800.* New York: Harper and Row, 1977.

————. "Marriage among the English Nobility in the Sixteenth and Seventeenth Centuries." *Comparative Studies in Society and History* 3 (1960-1961): 182-206.

————. "Social Mobility in England, 1500-1700." *Past and Present* 33 (April 1966): 16-55.

————, ed. *The University in Society*. Vol. I: Oxford and Cambridge. Princeton: Princeton University Press, 1974.

Stowe, A. Monroe. *English Grammar Schools in the Reign of Queen Elizabeth*. New York: Columbia University Teachers College, 1908.

Strong, Roy. *Splendor at Court: Renaissance Spectacle and the Theater of Power*. London: Weidenfeld and Nicolson, 1973.

Styles, Philip. *Sir Simon Archer, 1581-1662*. Dugdale Society Occasional Papers, no. 6 (1946).

Supple, B. E. *Commercial Crisis and Change in England, 1600-1642*. Cambridge: Cambridge University Press, 1959.

Tawney, R. H. "The Rise of the Gentry, 1558-1640," and "Postscript—July, 1954." In *Essays in Economic History*, edited by E. M. Carus-Wilson. Vol. I. London: Edward Arnold, 1954.

Thirsk, Joan. *Economic Policy and Projects: The Development of a Consumer Society in Early Modern England*. Oxford: Clarendon Press, 1978.

————. "The European Debate on Customs of Inheritance, 1500-1700." In *Family and Inheritance*, edited by Jack Goody et al. Cambridge: Cambridge University Press, 1976.

Thompson, F.M.L. "The Social Distribution of Landed Property in England since the Sixteenth Century." *Economic History Review*, 2d ser. 19 (1966): 505-517.

Thrupp, Sylvia Lettice. *The Merchant Class of Medieval London (1300-1500)*. Chicago: University of Chicago Press, 1948.

Trevor-Roper, H. R. "The Elizabethan Aristocracy: An Anatomy Anatomized." *Economic History Review*, 2d ser. 3 (1950-1951): 279-298.

————. *The Gentry, 1540-1640. Economic History Review*, supplement 1 (1953).

Tucker, G.S.L. "English Pre-Industrial Population Trends." *Economic History Review*, 2d ser. 16 (1963): 205-218.

Turberville, A. S. *A History of Welbeck Abbey and its Owners*. Vol. I: 1539-1755. London: Faber and Faber, 1938.

Unwin, George. "Commerce and Coinage in Shakespeare's England." In *Studies in Economic History*. London: Macmillan, 1927.

Wagner, Anthony Richard. *English Genealogy*. Oxford: Clarendon Press, 1960.

Wallace, C. W. *The Children of the Chapel at Blackfriars, 1597-1603*. Lincoln: Nebraska University Studies Reprint, 1908.

Weimann, Robert. *Shakespeare and the Popular Tradition in the Theater*. Edited by Robert Schwartz. Baltimore: Johns Hopkins University Press, 1978.

Wheatley, Henry B., and Cunningham, Peter. *London Past and Present*. 3 vols. London: John Murray, 1891.

Whitaker, T. D. *The Life and Original Correspondence of Sir George Radcliffe*. London: J. Nichols and Son, 1810.

White, Arthur. *Palaces of the People*. London: Rapp and Whiting, 1968.

Wickham, Glynne. *Early English Stages, 1300 to 1660*. Vol. II, Parts 1 and 2. New York: Columbia University Press, 1963, 1972, respectively.

———. "The Privy Council Order of 1597 for the Destruction of all London's Theatres." In *The Elizabethan Theatre*, edited by David Galloway. Toronto: Archon Books, 1970.

Williams, Neville J. "England's Tobacco Trade in the Reign of Charles I." *The Virginia Magazine* 65 (1957): 404-449.

———, ed. *Tradesmen in Early-Stuart Wiltshire, A Miscellany*. Wiltshire Archaeological and Natural History Society, Records Branch, vol. 15 (1959).

Wilson, Charles. *England's Apprenticeship, 1603-1763*. London: Longmans, 1965.

Wilson, Edward M., and Turner, Olga. "The Spanish Protest against 'A Game at Chesse.' " *Modern Language Review* 44 (1949): 476-482.

Wolff, Max J. "Shakespeare und Sein Publikum." *Shakespeare Jahrbuch* 71 (1935): 94-106.

Wright, Louis B. *Middle-Class Culture in Elizabethan England*. Chapel Hill: University of North Carolina Press, 1935.

Young, Robert Fitzgibbon. *Comenius in England*. Oxford: Oxford University Press, 1932.

Young, William. *The History of Dulwich College*. 2 vols. Edinburgh: Morrison and Gibb, 1889.

Zitner, S. P. "Gosson, Ovid, and the Elizabethan Audience." *Shakespeare Quarterly* 9 (1958): 206-208.

CONTEMPORARY SOURCES

*The Actors Remonstrance or Complaint: for the silencing of their profession and banishment from their severall Play-houses.* In *The English Drama and Stage,* edited by William C. Hazlitt. 1869. Reprint. New York: Burt Franklin, n.d.

Adams, Joseph Quincy, ed. *The Dramatic Records of Sir Henry Herbert, Master of the Revels, 1623-1673.* New Haven: Yale University Press, 1917.

*Analytical Index, to the Series of Records Known as the Remembrancia, 1579-1664.* London: E. J. Francis, 1878.

*Analytical Indexes to Volumes II and VIII of the Series of Records Known as the Remembrancia.* London: Pardon and Son, 1870.

Arber, Edward. *A Transcript of the Registers of the Company of Stationers of London, 1554-1640.* Vol. I. London: privately printed, 1875.

Baildon, William Paley, ed. *Les Reportes del Cases in Camera Stellata, 1593 to 1609.* Privately printed, 1894.

Baker, Sir Richard. *A Chronicle of the Kings of England.* London, 1696.

Batho, G. R., ed. *The Household Papers of Henry Percy, Ninth Earl of Northumberland (1564-1632).* Camden Society Publications, 3d ser. 93 (1962).

Beaumont, Francis, and Fletcher, John. *The Dramatic Works in the Beaumont and Fletcher Canon.* Edited by Fredson Bowers. 4 vols. Cambridge: Cambridge University Press, 1966-1979.

———. *Works.* Edited by Arnold Glover and A. R. Waller. 10 vols. Cambridge: Cambridge University Press, 1905-1912.

———. *The Works of Beaumont and Fletcher.* Edited by Alexander Dyce. 11 vols. London: E. Moxon, 1843-1846.

Birch, Walter de Gray. *The Historical Charters and Constitutional Documents of the City of London.* London: Whiting, 1887.

Bird, William. *The Magazine of Honour, or a Treatise of the Severall Degrees of the Nobility of this Kingdom.* Enlarged by Sir John Doderidge. London, 1642.

*The Black Books.* Records of the Honorable Society of Lincoln's Inn. Vols. I and II. London: Lincoln's Inn, 1897-1898.

Bohun, Edmund. *The Character of Queen Elizabeth.* London, 1693.

Bolton, Edmund. *The Cities Aduocate.* London, 1629.

Botero, Giovanni. *The Reason of State,* translated by P. J. and D. P. Waley, and *A Treatise Concerning the Causes of the Magnificencie and Greatness of Cities,* translated by Robert Peterson. New Haven: Yale University Press, 1956.

Brathwaite, Richard. *The English Gentleman and The English Gentlewoman.* 3d ed. London, 1641.

————. *Whimizies: or a New Cast of Characters.* London, 1631.

Braybrooke, Richard Griffin, ed. *The Private Correspondence of Lady Jane Cornwallis, 1613-1644.* London: S. and J. Bentley, Wilson and Fley, 1842.

Breton, Nicholas. *The Court and the Country.* In *Inedited Tracts,* edited by William Carew Hazlitt. London: Roxburghe Library, 1868.

*A Brief Description of the Notorious Life of John Lambe.* . . . Amsterdam, 1628.

"A brief Discoverie of the great purpesture of newe Buyldinges neere to the Cittie . . . ," Lansdowne MS 160, fol. 90. *Archaeologia* 23 (1831): 120-129.

Brome, Richard. *The Dramatic Works of Richard Brome.* 3 vols. London: John Pearson, 1873.

Buck, Sir George. "The Third Universitie of England." In John Stow, *Annales, or a General Chronicle of England,* continued and augmented . . . by Edmund Howes. London, 1631.

Burnett, Gilbert. *The Life and Death of Sir Matthew Hale.* London, 1682.

Buttes, Henry. *Dyets Dry Dinner.* London, 1599.

C., I. *The Two Merry Milke-Maids.* London, 1620.

*Calendar of State Papers, Domestic, of the Reign of Charles I.* 23 vols. London: Longmans, Green, Reader, and Dyer, 1858-1897.

*Calendar of State Papers, Domestic, of the Reigns of Edward VI, Mary, Elizabeth, and James.* 12 vols. Great Britain: Public Record Office, 1856-1872.

*Calendar of State Papers, Venice.* 38 vols. Great Britain: Public Record Office, 1864-1947.

*Calendar of Wills Proved and Enrolled in the Court of Husting, London, 1258-1688,* edited by Reginald R. Sharpe. Part II: 1358-1688. London: Corporation of the City of London, 1890.

Chettle, Henry. *Kind-Harts Dreame.* In *The Shakspere Allusion-Book,* edited by C. M. Ingleby, revised by John Munro. 2 vols. London: Oxford University Press, 1932.

Cholmley, Sir Hugh. *Memoirs*. London, 1787.

Churchyard, Thomas. *A Generall Rehearsall of Warres*. London, 1579.

Cokayne, Sir Aston. *The Dramatic Works*. Edited by James Maidment and W. H. Logan. London: H. Sotheran, 1874.

Collier, J. Payne, ed. *The Egerton Papers*. Camden Society Publications, vol. 12 (1840).

Collins, Arthur, ed. *Letters and Memorials of State*. 2 vols. London, 1746.

Coryat, Thomas. *Coryat's Crudities*. 2 vols. Glasgow: James Mac-Lehose and Sons, 1905.

Cowley, Abraham. *The Complete Works*. Edited by Alexander B. Grosart. 2 vols. 1881. Reprint. New York: AMS Press, 1967.

Crosse, Henry. *Vertues Common-wealth: Or the High-way to Honour*. In *Occasional Issues*, edited by Alexander B. Grosart. Vol. VII. Manchester: C. E. Simms, 1878.

Crotch, W.J.B. *The Prologues and Epilogues of William Caxton*. Early English Text Society, no. 176 (1928).

Culpepper, Sir Thomas. *A Tract against Usurie*. London, 1621.

Daniel, Samuel. *The Complete Works in Verse and Prose*. Edited by Alexander B. Grosart. 5 vols. London: Hazell, Watson, and Viney, 1885-1896.

Dasent, John Roche, ed. *Acts of the Privy Council, 1542-1604*. 32 vols. London: Stationery Office, 1890-1964.

Davenant, Sir William. *The Dramatic Works*. Edited by James Maidment and W. H. Logan. 5 vols. Edinburgh: W. Paterson, 1872-1874.

————. *The Just Italian*. London, 1630.

Davies, Sir John. *The Complete Poems*. Edited by Alexander B. Grosart. 2 vols. London: Chatto and Windus, 1876.

————. *Epigrammes and Elegies*. London, ca. 1590.

————. *The Poems*. Edited by Robert Krueger. Oxford: Clarendon Press, 1975.

Day, John. *The Works*. Edited by A. H. Bullen, with an introduction by Robin Jeffs. 1881. Reprint. London: Holland Press, 1963.

Dekker, Thomas. *The Dramatic Works*. Edited by Fredson Bowers. 4 vols. Cambridge: Cambridge University Press, 1953-1961.

————. *The Non-Dramatic Works*. Edited by Alexander B. Grosart. 5 vols. 1884. Reprint. New York: Russell and Russell, 1963.

De l'Isle and Dudley, Algernon Sidney. *Report on the Manuscripts of Lord de l'Isle and Dudley.* 6 vols. Great Britain: Historical Manuscripts Commission, 1925-1966.

Dewar, Mary, ed. *A Discourse of the Commonweal of this Realm of England.* Attributed to Thomas Smith. Charlottesville: University Press of Virginia, 1969.

D'Ewes, Sir Simonds. *The Autobiography and Correspondence.* Edited by James O. Halliwell. 2 vols. London: Richard Bentley, 1845.

"Diaries and Despatches of the Venetian Embassy at the Court of King James I, in the Years 1617, 1618." *Quarterly Review* 102 (1857): 398-438.

"Dice, Wine and Women, or The vnfortunate Gallant gull'd at London." In *The Pepys Ballads,* edited by Hyder Edward Rollins. Vol. I. Cambridge, Mass.: Harvard University Press, 1929.

Drayton, Michael. *The Works of Michael Drayton.* Edited by J. William Hebel. 5 vols. Oxford: Shakespeare Head Press, 1961.

Earle, John. *Micro-cosmographie.* London, 1628.

*Everie Woman in her Humor.* London, 1609.

Farley, Henry. *St. Pavles-Chvrch her Bill for the Parliament.* London, 1621.

Feilde, John. *A Godly Exhortation, by Occasion of the Late Iudgement of God, Shewed at Parris-Garden, the Thirteenth Day of Ianuarie.* London, 1583.

Fennor, William. *Compters Common-wealth.* In John P. Collier, *The History of English Dramatic Poetry to the Time of Shakespeare.* Vol. III. London: G. Bell and Sons, 1879.

―――. *Fennors Descriptions.* London, 1616.

Ferne, John. *The Blazon of Gentrie.* London, 1586.

Feuillerat, Albert. *Documents Relating to the Office of the Revels.* Louvain: A. Uystpruyst, 1908.

Fitzgeffrey, Henry. *Satyres and Satyricall Epigrams: with Certaine Obseruations at Blacke-Fryars.* London, 1617.

Fletcher, Reginald J., ed. *The Pension Book of Gray's Inn.* 2 vols. London: Chiswick Press, 1891.

Florio, John. *First Fruites.* London, 1578.

Fuller, Thomas. *The Holy State and The Profane State.* Edited by Maximilian Graff Walten. 2 vols. New York: Columbia University Press, 1938.

Furnivall, F. J., ed. *Quene Elizabethes Achademy, A Booke of Precedence, etc.* Early English Text Society, extra ser., no. 8 (1869).

G., I. *A Refutation of the Apology for Actors.* In Thomas Heywood, *An Apology for Actors,* edited by Richard H. Perkinson. New York: Scholars' Facsimiles and Reprints, 1941.

G[ainsford], T. *The Rich Cabinet Furnished with Varietie of Descriptions.* London, 1616.

Garzoni, Tommaso. *The Hospitall of Incurable Fooles.* London, 1600.

Gascoigne, George. *The Steele Glas.* London, 1576.

Gayton, Edmund. *Pleasant Notes upon Don Quixote.* London, 1654.

*Gesta Grayorum.* London: Malone Society, 1914.

Glapthorne, Henry. *Plays and Poems.* London: John Pearson, 1874.

[Goffe, Thomas?] *The Careless Shepherdess.* London, 1656.

Goodman, Nicholas. *Hollands Leaguer.* Edited by Dean Stanton Barnard, Jr. The Hague: Mouton, 1970.

Gosson, Stephen. *The Ephemerides of Phialo and a Short Apologie of the Schoole of Abuse.* London, 1579.

———. *Playes Confuted in Fiue Actions.* In *The English Drama and Stage,* edited by William C. Hazlitt. 1869. Reprint. New York: Burt Franklin, n.d.

———. *The Schoole of Abuse.* Edited by Edward Arber. English Reprints, no. 3. London: A. Murray and Son, 1869.

Greene, Robert. *Groats-worth of Witte.* Edited by G. B. Harrison. New York: Barnes and Noble, 1966.

———. *The Repentance of Robert Greene.* Edited by G. B. Harrison. London: Bodley Head Quartos, 1923.

———. *Second and Last Part of Conycatching.* In *The Elizabethan Underworld,* edited by Arthur V. Judges. London: G. Routledge and Sons, 1930.

Greg, Walter W., ed. *Henslowe Papers.* London: A. H. Bullen, 1907.

———. *Henslowe's Diary.* 2 vols. London: A. H. Bullen, 1904-1908.

Guilpin, Edward. *Skialetheia.* London, 1598.

*Haec-Vir: or The Womanish-Man.* London, 1620.

Hall, Joseph. *Characters of Vertues and Vices.* London, 1608.

———. *Virgidemiarum.* London, 1597.

Harington, John. "A Treatise on Playe." In *Nugae Antiquae.* 2 vols. London: J. Wright, 1804.

*The Harleian Miscellany.* 8 vols. London, 1744-1746.

Harrison, William. *The Description of England.* Edited by Georges Edelen. Ithaca, N.Y.: Cornell University Press, 1968.

Harrison, William. "Prohibition of 9 March 1618; together with Thomas Leke's letter of protest, 25 April 1618; and the answer to it justifying the prohibition." MS V.a. 244 in Folger Shakespeare Library, Washington, D. C.

Harvey, Gabriel. *Letter Book.* Edited by E.J.L. Scott. Camden Society Publications, n.s. 33 (1884).

Hassler, K. D., ed. *Die Riesen des Samuel Kiechel.* Stuttgart: Literarischer Verein, 1866.

Havinden, M. A., ed. *Household and Farm Inventories in Oxfordshire, 1550-1590.* London: Stationery Office, 1965.

Heath, John. *Two Centuries of Epigrammes.* London, 1610.

Hentzner, Paul. *A Journey into England.* Translated by R. Bentley, edited by Horace Walpole. Reading: T. E. Williams, 1807.

Heywood, Thomas. *"An Apology for Actors" (1612) with "A Refutation of the Apology for Actors" (1615).* Edited by Richard H. Perkinson. New York: Scholars' Facsimiles and Reprints, 1941.

————. *The Dramatic Works.* Edited by R. H. Shepherd. 6 vols. 1874. Reprint. New York: Russell and Russell, 1964.

Howard, Edward. *The Six Days Adventure.* London, 1671.

Howell, James. *Epistolae Ho-Elianae.* London, 1645.

Hughes, Charles. *Shakespeare's Europe . . . being unpublished chapters of Fynes Moryson's Itinerary.* 2d ed. New York: B. Blom, 1967.

Hughes, Paul L., and Larkin, James F., eds. *Tudor Royal Proclamations.* Vols. II and III. New Haven: Yale University Press, 1969.

Humphrey, Lawrence. *The Nobles, or of Nobilitye.* London, 1563.

Hutton, Henry. *Follie's Anatomie.* London, 1619.

Inderwick, F. A., ed. *A Calendar of the Inner Temple Records.* 3 vols. London: H. Sotheran, 1896-1904.

*The Institucion of A Gentleman.* London, 1568.

"Instructions Touching Salesbery Cort Playhouse." *Shakspere Society Papers* 4: 99-100. London: Shakspere Society, 1849.

James I. *A Covnterblaste to Tobacco.* London, 1604.

Jeaffreson, J. C., ed. *Middlesex County Records.* 4 vols. London: Middlesex County Records Society, 1886-1892.

Jeayes, Isaac H., ed. *Letters of Philip Gawdy.* London: Nichols, 1906.

Jonson, Ben. *Ben Jonson.* Edited by C. H. Herford and Percy Simpson. 11 vols. Oxford: Clarendon Press, 1925-1952.

————. *Discoveries, 1641,* and *Conversations with William Drummond of Hawthornden, 1619.* Edited by G. B. Harrison. 1923. Reprint. New York: Barnes and Noble, 1966.

"The Journal of Sir Roger Wilbraham." *Camden Miscellany*, 3d ser. 4 (1902): v-xxi, 1-139.

Kemp, William. *Kemps Nine Daies Wonder: Performed in a Daunce from London to Norwich.* London: Bodley Head, 1923.

Knowler, William, ed. *The Earl of Strafforde's Letters and Dispatches.* 2 vols. London, 1739.

Lambarde, William. *A Perambulation of Kent.* London: Baldwin, Cradock, and Joy, 1826.

*Lancashire and Cheshire Wills and Inventories.* Chetham Society, Remains, Historical and Literary, vols. 33, 51, 54 (1857-1861).

Lane, John. *Tom Tell-Troths Message and his Pens Complaint.* Edited by F. J. Furnivall. New Shakspere Society Publications, ser. 6, no. 2, pp. 107-135. London: N. Trubner, 1876.

La Perrière, Guillaume de. *The Mirrour of Policie.* London, 1598.

Larkin, James F., and Hughes, Paul L., eds. *Stuart Royal Proclamations.* Vol. I. Oxford: Clarendon Press, 1973.

Lenton, Francis. *The Young Gallant's Whirligig.* London, 1629.

Lovelace, Richard. *The Poems of Richard Lovelace.* Edited by C. H. Wilkinson. 2 vols. Oxford: Clarendon Press, 1925.

Lyly, John. *The Complete Works.* Edited by R. Warwick Bond. 3 vols. Oxford: Clarendon Press, 1902.

McClure, Norman E., ed. *The Letters of John Chamberlain.* 2 vols. Philadelphia: American Philosophical Society, 1939.

*Malone Society Collections.* 10 vols. Oxford: Oxford University Press, 1907-1975.

Manningham, John. *Diary.* Edited by John Bruce. Camden Society Publications, vol. 99 (1868).

Marston, John. *Plays.* Edited by H. Harvey Wood. 3 vols. London: Oliver and Boyd, 1934.

————. *The Scourge of Villainy.* Edited by G. B. Harrison. London: Bodley Head, 1925.

Martin, Charles Trice, ed. *Minutes of Parliament of the Middle Temple.* 2 vols. London: Butterworth, 1904.

Massinger, Philip. *Plays.* Edited by W. Gifford. 4 vols. 1813. Reprint. New York: AMS Press, 1966.

May, Thomas. *The Life of a Satyrical Puppy, Called Nim.* London, 1657.

Middleton, Thomas. *The Inner-Temple Masque, or Masque of Heroes.* London, 1619.

————. *A Mad World, My Masters.* Edited by Standish Henning. London: Edward Arnold, 1965.

Middleton, Thomas. *The Works.* Edited by A. H. Bullen. 8 vols. 1885-1886. Reprint. New York: AMS Press, 1964.

———. *Works.* Edited by Alexander Dyce. London: Edward Lumley, 1840.

Moryson, Fynes. *An Itinerary.* London, 1617.

Mulcaster, Richard. *Positions.* London, 1581.

[Munday, Anthony]. *A Second and Third Blast of Retrait from Plaies and Theaters.* In *The English Drama and Stage,* edited by W. C. Hazlitt. 1869. Reprint. New York: Burt Franklin, n.d.

Nashe, Thomas. *The Complete Works.* Edited by R. B. McKerrow. 5 vols. London: Sidgwick and Jackson, 1910.

Northbrooke, John. *A Treatise wherein Dicing, Dauncing, Vaine playes, or Enterluds, with other idle pastimes, commonly used on the Sabboth day are reproued.* . . . Edited by John P. Collier. London: Shakespeare Society, 1843.

Northumberland, Henry Percy, Ninth Earl of. *Advice to his Son.* Edited by G. B. Harrison. London: Ernest Benn, 1930.

Osborn, Francis. *Historical Memoires on the Reigns of Queen Elizabeth and King James.* London, 1658.

Overbury, Sir Thomas. *The "Conceited Newes" of Sir Thomas Overbury and his Friends.* Gainesville, Fla.: Scholars' Facsimiles and Reprints, 1968.

———. *New and Choise Characters.* . . . London, 1615.

Parrot, Henry. *Laquei Ridiculosi, or Springes for Woodcocks.* London, 1613.

———. *The Mastive.* London, 1615.

Peacham, Henry. *Coach and Sedan.* London: Westminster Press, 1925.

———. *The Compleat Gentleman.* Edited by G. S. Gordon. Oxford: Clarendon Press, 1906.

———. *Thalia's Banquet.* London, 1620.

———. *Worth of a Penny.* In *An English Garner,* edited by Edward Arber. Vol. VI. Westminster: A. Constable, 1903.

Pepys, Samuel. *The Diary of Samuel Pepys.* Edited by Robert Latham and William Matthews. 9 vols. Berkeley: University of California Press, 1970.

*Pimlyco, or Runne Red-Cap.* London, 1609.

Platter, Thomas. *Thomas Platter's Travels in England, 1599.* Translated by Clare Williams. London: J. Cape, 1937.

Prideaux, Sir Walter Sherburne. *Memorials of the Goldsmiths' Company.* Vol. I. London: Eyre and Spottiswoode, 1896.

Prynne, William. *Histrio-Mastrix*. London, 1633.

Radcliffe, Aegremont, trans. *Politique Discourses*. London, 1578.

Randolph, Thomas. *Poems with The Muses Looking-Glasse: and Amyntas*. Oxford, 1638.

Rich, Barnaby. *Roome for A Gentleman*. London, 1609.

Rowlands, Samuel. *The Letting of Humour's Blood in the Head-Vein*. London, 1600.

Rudyerd, Sir Benjamin. *Memoirs*. Edited by James Alexander Manning. London: T. and W. Boone, 1841.

Rushworth, John. *Historical Collections*. 2 vols. London, 1721.

*Rutland Manuscripts*. 4 vols. London: Stationery Office, 1888-1905.

Rye, William B. *England as Seen by Foreigners in the Days of Elizabeth and James the First*. London: J. R. Smith, 1865.

Shakespeare, William. *The Complete Works*. Edited by Alfred Harbage. Baltimore: Penguin Books, 1969.

————. *The Famous Historie of Troylus and Cresseid*. London, 1609.

————. *Hamlet*. London, 1603.

Shirley, James. *The Dramatic Works and Poems*. Edited by William Gifford and Alexander Dyce. 6 vols. London: J. Murray, 1833.

Smith, Sir Thomas. *The Commonwealth of England*. London, 1635.

Smyth, John. *The Berkeley Manuscripts*. Vol. II. Gloucester: Printed by John Bellows for the Subscribers, 1883.

Sneyd, Charlotte Augusta, ed. and trans. *A Relation, or rather A True Account, of the Island of England. . . .* Camden Society Publications, vol. 37 (1847).

Stockwood, John. *A Sermon Preached at Paules Crosse*. London, 1578.

Stow, John. *The Annales of England*. London, 1592.

————. *The Annales of England*. London, 1601.

————. *The Annales of England*. London, 1605.

————. *Annales, or a Generall Chronicle of England*, continued and augmented . . . by Edmund Howes, Gent. London, 1631.

————. *The Annales, or Generall Chronicle of England*, continued and augmented . . . by Edmund Howes, gentleman. London, 1615.

————. *A Survey of London* (1603). Edited by Charles Lethbridge Kingsford. 3 vols. Oxford: Clarendon Press, 1908.

————. *The Survey of London*, . . . continued, corrected and much enlarged . . . by A[nthony] M[unday]. London, 1618.

————. *The Survey of London*, . . . finished by the study and labour of A[nthony] M[unday], H[umphrey] D[ysen], and others. London, 1633.

Stow, John. *A Survey of the Cities of London and Westminster and the Borough of Southwark*, Corrected, Improved, and very much Enlarged . . . by John Strype. 2 vols. London: W. Imrys, J. Richardson et al., 1754-1755.

————. *A Survey of the Cities of London and Westminster*, Corrected, Improved, and very much Enlarged . . . by John Strype. . . . 2 vols. London, 1720.

Stubbes, Philip. *The Anatomie of Abuses*. London, 1583.

Symonds, E. M. "The Diary of John Greene (1635-1657)." *English Historical Review* 43 (1928): 385-394.

Tailor, Robert. *The Hogge Hath Lost his Pearl*. Oxford: Malone Society Reprints, 1967.

*Tarlton's News out of Purgatory*. London, 1590.

Tatham, John. *The Fancies Theatre*. London, 1640.

[Tatham, John?]. *Knavery in All Trades: Or, The Coffee-House*. London, 1664.

Taylor, John. *The True Cause of the Water-men's Suit concerning Players*. In *The Old Book Collector's Miscellany*, edited by Charles Hindley. Vol. II, no. 15. London: Reeves and Turner, 1872.

Tomkis, Thomas. *Albumazar*. London, 1615.

*The Visitation of London in the Year 1568*. Edited by Joseph Jackson Howard and George John Armytage. Harleian Society Publications, vol. 1 (1869).

*The Visitation of London, 1633, 1634, and 1635*. Edited by Joseph Jackson Howard and Joseph Lemuel Chester. Harleian Society Publications, vols. 15 (1880) and 17 (1883).

Von Bülow, Gottfried, and Powell, Wilfred, eds. "Diary of the Journey of Philip Julius, Duke of Stettin-Pomerania, through England in the Year 1602." *Transactions of the Royal Historical Society*, n.s. 6 (1892): 1-67.

*Vox Graculi, or Iacke Dawes Prognostication*. London, 1623.

Waterhous, Edward. *Fortescutus Illustratus*. London, 1663.

Webster, John. *The Complete Works*. Edited by F. L. Lucas. 4 vols. London: Chatto and Windus, 1927.

Whetstone, George. *The English Myrror*. London, 1586.

W[hite], T[homas]. *A Sermon Preached at Paules Crosse on Sunday the thirde of November 1577 in the time of the Plague*. London, 1578.

Whitelock, Bulstrode. *Memorials of the English Affairs*. 4 vols. Oxford: Oxford University Press, 1853.

Wilson, Sir Thomas. "The State of England (1600)." Edited by F. J. Fisher. In *Camden Miscellany*, 3d ser. 52 (1936): i-vii, 1-47.

Winwood, Sir Ralph. *Memorials of Affairs of State in the Reigns of Q. Elizabeth and K. James I.* Edited by Edmund T. Sawyer. 3 vols. London, 1725.

Wither, George. *Abuses Stript and Whipt.* London, 1613.

Wood, Anthony. *Athenae Oxoniensis.* Hildesheim: Georg Olms, 1969.

Wright, James. *Historia Histrionica: An Historical Account of the English Stage.* London, 1699.

Wright, Thomas, and Halliwell, James O. *Reliquae Antiquae.* 2 vols. London: William Pickering, 1843.

Wybarne, Joseph. *The New Age of Old Names.* London, 1609.

# Index

*Library of Congress Cataloging in Publication Data*

Cook, Ann Jennalie, 1934-
  The privileged playgoers of Shakespeare's London,
1576-1642.

  Bibliography: p.
  Includes index.
  1.  Theater audiences—England—London—History—16th
century.    2.  Theater audiences—England—London—History—17th century.    3.  English drama—Early modern
and Elizabethan, 1500-1600—History and criticism.
  4.  English drama—17th century—History and criticism.
  5.  London (England)—History—16th century.    6.  London
(England)—History—17th century.    I.  Title.
PN2596.L6C6      792'.09421'2      80-8542
ISBN 0-691-06454-7                AACR2